Improving Student Learning

Using Research to Improve Student Learning

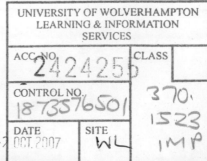
Editor Graham Gibbs

Published by
THE OXFORD CENTRE FOR STAFF DEVELOPMENT
Oxford Brookes University
Gipsy Lane
Headington
Oxford
OX3 OBP

1996

Improving Student Learning –
Using Research to Improve Student Learning

ISBN 1 873576 50 1

British Library Cataloguing-in-Publication Data.
A catalogue record for this book is available from the British Library.

Designed and Typeset in Palatino by Ann Trew

Printed in Great Britain by
Oxonian Rewley Press Ltd
Oxford

Printed on paper produced from sustainable forests.

Preface

These proceedings from the third International Improving Student Learning Symposium which took place at Exeter University, UK, in September 1995, illustrate perfectly the mission of these annual events. The papers are concerned with learning, rather than with teaching, and are informed by research and theory, rather than just empirical evaluation of practice much less simple description of practice. They also demonstrate the value of a truly international approach in a number of ways.

First, Ferenc Marton addressed the Symposium for the first time. Marton's phenomenographic work in Sweden has provided the conceptual and methodological background for a good proportion of the papers at the first three Symposia. It formed the central theoretical framework for the CNAA 'Improving the Quality of Student Learning' project in the late 80's which was partly responsible for the growth of interest in and use of the concepts of 'deep' and 'surface' approaches to learning which have inspired so much action research in the UK. The first two Symposia gave a platform for the related work of Biggs and Ramsden in Australia and Knapper in Canada. At this Symposium we went back to our roots.

Second, we had a strong American presence. In the USA there has been a reaction against theory-free student feedback on teaching and a huge upsurge in various forms of small scale research undertaken by faculty in order to understand and improve their students' learning, most commonly focussing on the quality of student learning outcomes - the same focus as much of the Swedish phenomenographic work, albeit within a different methodological tradition. Pat Cross gave an overview of the 'Classroom Assessment' movement in the USA, and illustrated its use, and Tom Angelo from the AAHE ran packed workshops on classroom assessment techniques. Marcia Mentkowski from Alverno College showed how far it is possible to go in using research into student learning as an integral part of institutional change processes.

Third, we had the largest overseas contingent yet, with the University most represented by participants being not the host University, Exeter, but the University of Lund in Sweden! Papers from Fiji, New Zealand and Australia as well as North America and Europe revealed the breadth of interest in the 'improving student learning' movement.

As before the emphasis has been on practitioners researching their practice rather than on either researchers describing their research or on practitioners describing their practice. As before the work by 'full-time' researchers has provided research tools for practitioners to use, designs of studies for practitioners to follow, findings to replicate and concepts to apply. But it is the use of research by practitioners which best characterises these proceedings. Their studies are perhaps less extensive and sophisticated than those of the professional educational research community, but they are embedded in contexts in which they practice, and directly inform decisions they take to improve practice. This is the future of using research to improve student learning.

Twenty or so reports of work in progress, seminars and workshops from the Symposium are not included in these proceedings but may appear in the form of full papers on completed work in proceedings from subsequent symposia - another heartening trend revealing the growth of a stable and maturing research community.

Finally these papers show a growing awareness of other work being undertaken in the same field, especially in other countries, building on previous and related work, concepts and methodology and on previous 'improving student learning' symposia. References are more international in flavour and themes and parallels are becoming easier to discern. These proceedings present a picture of a vibrant and valuable research movement.

Graham Gibbs

Contents

Part IV   Using research to improve assessment

Part V   Using theory to understand student learning

Part VI   Using research to improve small-group teaching

Part VII   Researching students' conceptions of learning

Part VIII   Course validation and student learning

Part IX   Improving students' reflection on their skills

Part X   Improving students' problem-solving and
numeracy

Part XI   Improving students' learning skills

1 Improving teaching and learning through classroom assessment and classroom research

K. Patricia Cross
David Pierpont Gardner Professor of Higher Education
University of California, Berkeley

It is a special privilege for me to join with colleagues at this conference in thinking about what we can do, in our various roles as educators, to restore learning to its proper place as the first priority for institutions of higher education. To date, it seems that educators everywhere have been subjected to a barrage of advice from legislators, the public, the media, and a wide variety of experts within our own ranks about what we can do to improve student learning. Ironically, the people most likely to be actually able to do something about the quality of learning in higher education — namely teachers and students — have been strangely quiet.

This chapter is directed mainly to discussion about what teachers and students can do about improving the learning that is taking place in their own classrooms. One of the functions they can perform better than anyone else is monitoring learning as it is taking place day-by-day. I call this monitoring function **classroom assessment**. Its purpose is to inform teachers how effectively they are teaching and students how effectively they are learning.

Teaching is in an essentially primitive state of development today. We are not standing on the shoulders of giants in advancing knowledge and improving practice with each new generation of teachers. Teaching is one of the few professions that lacks a 'wisdom of practice' (Shulman, 1987). Most professions — at least the most esteemed professions — build on the knowledge of previous generations. Architects leave behind buildings; law has its cases; medicine has internships and 'rounds'; engineering has bridges and roads. All of this accumulated 'wisdom of practice' can be preserved and studied by future generations. We learn something when bridges and buildings collapse in an earthquake, and we build them better the next time around. But the wisdom of practice in teaching ends with the career of the individual teacher. Classroom teaching today is a very personal and private profession. It is learned in private, and for the most part it is practised in private, without much input from any external source.

I have been interested in classroom assessment and classroom research as self-study techniques that honour the autonomy of college professors while engaging them in some conversations and curiosity about the effectiveness of their teaching.

I am going to organize my observations around the three 'critical conditions for excellence' identified by a group of distinguished researchers in higher education in the United States who wrote an influential educational reform report entitled, *Involvement in Learning* (Study Group on the Conditions of Excellence in American Higher Education, 1984). They advised that research over the past several decades indicates that if colleges are to pursue excellence in undergraduate education three conditions are critically important: colleges must (1) hold high expectations for student performance, (2) encourage active student involvement in learning, and (3) provide useful assessment and feedback.

Since the primary purpose of classroom assessment is to provide useful feedback to both teacher and students, let us start with that 'critical condition for excellence'. One of the basic principles of learning is that learners need feedback. They need to know what they are trying to accomplish, and then they need to know how close they are coming to the goal. Imagine, if you will, that you are trying to learn archery in a darkened room where both the target and feedback on hitting it are invisible to you. You are provided with the best and most sophisticated equipment that money can buy; you have one-on-one coaching from an expert teacher who is demonstrating effectively how to hold the bow, get the right tension in the string and place the arrow, plus you have access to study materials on the dynamics of flight and the arc of the trajectory. Despite all this help on the input side, it's pretty clear that you are not going to improve your performance until you get some feedback on whether you are hitting the target.

We don't pay a lot of attention right now to giving students feedback on their progress as learners. Almost all students get grades that tell them how they have done relative to their classmates. That sort of information is not useful feedback on their progress as learners, nor does it do anything to help them develop the skills they need for self-assessment as lifelong learners. The current direction of institutional assessment does not address these learning issues either. The situation now in most institutional assessment programmes is akin to turning on the lights in the target practice room after the students have left, and reporting on the total number of hits to whoever is paying for the archery lessons. But it is students, after all, who make the hits; and the score is not going to improve for the institution until it improves for individual learners.

Turning on the lights after practice — which we are beginning to do with some of the educational outcomes assessments — is probably better than leaving us in the dark on what the archers are doing. When the lights go on, the institution at least gets feedback on how well students did. The problem is that there isn't any useful information about what caused good or poor performance since the lights were off during practice. We might carry this analogy further to point out that if research showed that even a dim light in the room improved scores dramatically, then the message is clear. Institutions should turn on the lights during practice so students as well as institutions can see what they are doing.

One way to turn on the lights is to engage teachers and students directly and personally in assessment. People who are serious about learning are intensely interested in feedback. Dick Light writes that one of the major findings from the Harvard Assessments is that assessment of their learning is extremely important to students. 'Undergraduates are very clear about which of their courses they respect most, where they learn most, and why . . . The big point', he says, '— it comes up over and over as crucial — is the importance of quick and detailed feedback' (Light, 1990, p. 31). We know that, I think, but as classes get bigger and more impersonal, it is increasingly difficult to give good and useful feedback. That is where classroom assessment may be helpful to students as well as to teachers.

For nearly a decade now my colleague, Tom Angelo, and I have been working on developing some simple **classroom assessment techniques** (CATs) that can be used by any college teacher of any subject to get immediate feedback on how well students are learning what the teacher is trying to teach (Angelo and Cross, 1993). This is a form of assessment in which teachers and students work together to monitor learning while it is in process in the classroom. In classroom assessment, students and teachers are colleagues with a common goal and an exceptional opportunity to observe one another in action.

Let me start with a quick summary and a few concrete examples of some classroom assessment techniques (CATs). Classroom assessment's most famous CAT is the **minute paper**. It works like this: Shortly before the end of a class period, the instructor asks students to write brief answers to two questions: (1) What is the most important thing that you learned in class today? and (2) What is the main, unanswered question you leave class with today?

The minute paper requires all students in the class to reflect on what they have learned, to synthesize and articulate 'the big picture', to express themselves in writing, and to think actively about what they did not understand, and what they would like further information about. If students are told that the minute paper is going to be requested at the end of a given class session, they may ask themselves along the way what they are learning, and they tend to be more involved and more active in sorting out the major message. Thus, even if the instructor failed to learn something important about students' responses to the teaching of that class session, the minute paper would still be worthwhile as a pedagogical technique.

But teachers do learn a great deal from the minute papers. Dick Light comments in his report that 'This extraordinarily simple idea is catching on throughout Harvard. Some experienced professors comment that it is the best example of high payoff for a tiny investment they have ever seen' (Light, 1990, p. 36).

The second critically important 'condition for excellence' in undergraduate education is active involvement in learning. We hear a lot today about the necessity for active involvement on the part of learners. But active involvement is not a new idea. Charles Gragg, the inspired teacher at the Harvard Business School 50 years ago, put it eloquently when he wrote these words:

> *No one can learn in any basic sense from another except by subjecting what that other has to offer to a process of creative thinking; that is unless the learner is actively and imaginatively receptive, he will emerge from the experience with nothing more than a catalog of facts and other people's notions.*
> *(Gragg, 1940)*

Classroom assessment involves both teachers and students in learning. To illustrate, one of the case studies in our *Handbook on Classroom Assessment* (Angelo and Cross, 1993) describes the experience of a writing teacher who modified the minute paper to get some idea of what students were learning from the small-group work sessions that she used to engage students in critiquing one another's papers. She asked students to answer these two questions when they had finished their group-work session: (1) What specific suggestions did members of your group offer to you that are likely to help you improve your draft essay? and (2) What suggestions did you offer to others that are likely to help them improve their draft essays?

The good news is that she found that most students mentioned things they had learned from others that they thought would improve their papers. The bad news is that only three out of 24 students could think of something they had offered that might have been helpful to the other students in their group! What became clear to this teacher was that, for all our talk about the advantages of collaborative learning, students don't automatically know how to reap the benefits of cooperative learning. Just having to write out the benefits of the group sessions is a gentle reminder of the two-sided obligation of collaborative learning.

CATs can be used to involve students in monitoring their own learning. One of the major conclusions from the research on cognition over the past 20 years is that students who monitor their own learning are more effective learners than those who do not. Good learners are aware of themselves as learners; they are able to watch themselves in the process of learning, and therefore able to direct and control their use of learning strategies.

Classroom teachers can help students become active, self-regulated learners through a variety of rather simple classroom assessment techniques. For example, a CAT labelled 'Punctuated Lectures' calls for stopping the class occasionally to ask students to reflect on what they were doing during the lecture and how their behavior, while listening, helped or hindered their understanding. They are then asked to write down any insights about their own learning that they have gained and give feedback to the teacher in brief anonymous notes.

The major advantage of the punctuated lecture is pedagogical; it teaches students to become aware of how they are using their learning time. Secondarily, it informs teachers about distractions in the environment. A similar assessment technique called 'Productive Study-Time Logs' assesses the effective use of study time. It asks students to keep brief records of how much time they spend studying for a particular class, when they study, and how productively they study.

While these simple classroom assessment techniques appear rather far afield from what we usually think of as assessment, they emphasize the potential power of using assessment to promote learning. Involving students in assessing and monitoring their own learning is a do-able and constructive approach to making students members of the team in improving learning.

Finally, the third condition for excellence identified by the authors of *Involvement in Learning* is holding high expectations for student performance. What teachers expect of students often determines what students expect of themselves.

Holding high expectations for students, by its very nature, has to be geared to the performance of individuals. It is not a normative or competitive matter. A teacher cannot constructively hold high expectations for a student by hoping that the student will do better than someone else. Rather the expectation must be based on the premise that individuals will improve their own performance. Classroom assessments are, by definition, non-competitive, non-graded, and usually anonymous. Students are engaged in trying to become more aware of their own learning, and CATs help students to assess themselves.

It is also true, of course, that in using classroom assessment, teachers are setting an example of holding high expectations for their own performance as teachers. As a matter of fact, one of the advantages of classroom assessment that is mentioned most frequently by teachers is the bonding that is formed between students and teacher when teachers are demonstrating their own interest in using assessment for self-improvement.

Now let me conclude with a brief introduction to the difference between classroom assessment and classroom research. Classroom assessment is a way of taking the temperature of a classroom; it tells what is, not necessarily what should be. Classroom assessment answers the 'what' questions of teaching and learning. *What* did students find interesting or memorable? *What* did they learn from that day's lesson? *What* did they fail to understand or *what* did they have further questions about? Classroom research, on the other hand, attempts to answer the 'why' and 'how' questions. *Why* did students respond as they did? *Why* did they confuse two concepts that you worked especially hard to distinguish? *How* do students learn to contrast two different points of view? Classroom research helps us to understand the processes of teaching and learning well enough to improve them —

perhaps just by very small steps taken by a lot of teachers and students in individual classrooms.

Indeed, one of the more encouraging research findings on the improvement of classroom instruction involved a meta-analysis of 22 research studies investigating the power of feedback via student ratings to improve instruction (Cohen, 1980). The researcher reported that teachers who received mid-term feedback from students raised their student ratings from the 50th to the 65th percentile by the end of the semester — but to the 74th percentile if the student feedback was augmented by consultation about the ratings with a teaching improvement specialist .

It would be hard to think of any national or institutional policy that would bring about that amount of change is so brief a period of time. Granted, the improvement was in students' *perceptions* of instruction, but the extensive amount of research that has been done on student ratings is quite positive (Cross, 1988). Students are one very good source of information on the quality of teaching and learning in individual classrooms.

The point is that if students are made active members of the team for improving learning, we stand to see very substantial improvement in immediate learning, and even more substantial results in lifelong learning as students become the masters of their fate with respect to learning.

One way to involve students in learning more about their own learning is through classroom research in which they become investigators as well as subjects. Often the information collected in classroom assessment raises questions calling for classroom research. Data collected via the simple CAT of the minute paper, for example, might raise any of these questions: are the topics mentioned as important more likely to come from the end than from the beginning of the class period, that is, is recency the major factor — or does attention lag as we reach the end of the standard 50 minutes? Does repetition of major themes throughout the class period enhance students grasp of the big picture? What happens if the minute paper is held over and administered at the beginning of the next class, i.e. what are students most likely to remember from one class period to the next? Are poor students especially likely to fail to differentiate important from peripheral information? If so, are there ways to label the big ideas? These are questions that occur to teachers who have trained themselves to be careful and systematic observers of students in the act of learning. And all teachers can learn to raise interesting questions about the teaching and learning that goes on in their own classrooms every day.

Some of you may be familiar with the questions raised by Mina Shaughnessy about how students learn to write. Perhaps no book ever written on teaching and learning has had as much influence in the United States as Mina Shaughnessy's *Errors and Expectations*, written in 1977. Her book grew out of a careful and systematic analysis of students' writing errors. I would call the methods used in her book 'classroom research'. Shaughnessy was, by profession and by disposition, a teacher. She had no training as a researcher, and certainly would not have viewed herself as such. Her abiding interest was in understanding why the open-admissions students who flooded the gates of New York's City University when they swung wide in the 1970s wrote so badly that their writing essays 'stunned the teachers who read them' (Shaughnessy, 1977, p. 3). Shaughnessy's task as Director of City University's Instructional Resource Center was to help teachers understand how these students interpreted the alien writing tasks that faced them. Because at the time, there were no guides, textbooks, or research studies to turn to, Shaughnessy embarked upon her own study in a very pragmatic way. She describes her research methods as follows:

I have drawn from three resources: my students and the explanations they have given me, directly and indirectly, of their difficulties with written English; my colleagues, who have shared their insights with me over the years in many different settings, both formal and informal; and my own experience as someone who writes and therefore understands the pressures and peculiarities of that behavior.

From these resources, I have reached the persuasion that underlies this book — namely, that BW (Basic Writing) students write the way they do, not because they are slow or non-verbal, indifferent to or incapable of academic excellence, but because they are beginners and must, like all beginners, learn by making mistakes. These they make aplenty and for such a variety of reasons that the inexperienced teacher is almost certain to see nothing but a chaos of error when he first encounters their papers. Yet a closer look will reveal very little that is random or 'illogical' in what they have written. And the keys to their development as writers often lie hidden in the very features of their writing that English teachers have been trained to brush aside with a marginal code letter or a scribbled injunction to 'Proofread!' Such strategies ram at the doors of their incompetence while the keys that would open them lie in view. (p. 5)

One cannot help observing that Shaughnessy's beautiful and lucid writing style sets her apart from most educational researchers. But beyond that, her work is likely to be read and heeded by writing teachers who perceive that she knows intimately the problems they face in teaching remedial writing. The point I want to make is that her research involves methods that are available to any classroom teacher — sensitive observation, careful listening, a sincere desire to understand, and experience (her own as well as that of her colleagues) in teaching remedial writing. Those research methods, honed to excellence by Shaughnessy, have proved very powerful in influencing the teaching of remedial writing. Since the theme of this symposium is 'Using Research to Improve Student Learning', I want to suggest that just as we need some change in teaching practices, we also need some change in our research methodologies.

Most traditional educational researchers assume that there is an underlying order to the world, and that through the rational and objective methods of science, they can discover how this world of ours is put together. Questions are now being raised about the application of this sort of science to the vagaries of human behavior. Donald Schön of MIT observes that in the hard sciences, the problems to be solved are usually clearly identified. Not so in the world of professional practice: 'problems do not present themselves to the practitioner as givens', he writes. 'They must be constructed from the materials of problematic situations which are puzzling, troubling and uncertain' (Schön, 1983, p. 40).

Schön contends that there is a choice to be made between the 'rigor' of science and the 'relevance' of practice in the social sciences. In professional practice, he writes,

there is a high, hard ground where practitioners can make effective use of research-based theory and technique, and there is a swampy lowland where situations are confusing 'messes' incapable of technical solution. The difficulty is that the problems of the high ground, however great their technical interest, are often relatively unimportant to clients or to the larger society, while in the swamp are the problems of greatest human concern. Shall the practitioner stay on the high, hard ground where he can practice rigorously, as he understands rigor, but where he is constrained to deal with problems of relatively little social importance? Or shall he descend to the swamp where he can engage the most important and challenging problems if he is willing to forsake technical rigor? [. . .]

There are those who chose the swampy lowlands. They deliberately involve themselves in messy but crucially important problems and, when asked to describe their methods of inquiry, they speak of experience, trail and error, intuition, and muddling through. (p. 42—3)

In classroom research the relevance of the questions is more important than the rigor of the investigation. The questions that traditional researchers can address are often constrained by their methods. Classroom researchers start with the questions they really want answered and frequently have to devise or invent the best methods they can to investigate them. Thus, classroom research requires intimate knowledge of the classroom, the subject matter, and the students; its methods must be devised by the sensitive observation and intellectual curiosity of classroom teachers.

Classroom research is not for everyone; although anyone can do it. Classroom research will appeal most to teachers who are intensely interested in teaching and who are intellectually curious about learning and interested in observing their students in the process of learning. Many teachers are not content to be adequate teachers. They have a drive to be outstanding — not usually for extrinsic rewards such as promotion and recognition, but more often for intrinsic rewards such as the joy of helping students learn and the satisfaction of scratching the itch that represents the desire to learn all they can about their students and their struggles and triumphs with learning.

Classroom assessment, however, is for everyone, and in my opinion, every teacher should do it. If higher education is to become truly engaged in improving undergraduate learning, then faculty and students must be directly and intimately involved in the process. Classroom assessment and classroom research are ways to involve teachers and students in teaching and learning that is directly relevant to them — that taking place in their own classrooms, departments, and colleges.

References

Angelo, T. A. and Cross, K. P. (1993) *Classroom Assessment Techniques: A Handbook for College Teachers*, 2nd edn. San Francisco: Jossey-Bass.

Cohen, P.A. (1980) Effectiveness of student-rating feedback for improving college instruction: a meta-analysis of findings. *Research in Higher Education* 13(4).

Cross, K. P. (1988) *Feedback in the Classroom: Making Assessment Matter*. Washington, D.C.: American Association for Higher Education.

Gragg, C. I. (1940) Teachers also must learn. *Harvard Educational Review* 10, 30—47.

Light, R. J. (1990) *The Harvard Assessment Seminars*. Cambridge, MA: Harvard University.

Schön, D. A. (1983) *The Reflective Practitioner*. New York: Basic Books.

Shaughnessy, M. P. (1977) *Errors and Expectations*. New York: Oxford University Press.

Shulman, L. S. (1987) Knowledge and teaching: foundations of the new reform. *Harvard Educational Review* 57, February, 1—22.

Study Group on the Conditions of Excellence in American Higher Education (1984) *Involvement in Learning: Realizing the Potential of American Higher Education*. Washington, DC.: National Institute of Education.

2   Experiencing learning and learning to experience

Ference Marton
University of Gotenburg

Differing approaches to learning can be seen as differing ways of experiencing learning in particular situations and in relation to particular objects of learning.

A way of experiencing something is considered to be an internal relation between the subject (the experiencer) and the object (the experienced). The whole of a person's experience of the world is her awareness. A way of experiencing something reflects the structure of someone's awareness: certain aspects of that which is experienced are discerned and present simultaneously in focal awareness. Discernment and simultaneity are thus the critical features of variation among qualitatively different ways of experiencing a certain phenomenon. Adopting a deep approach to reading a text implies, for instance, that meaning is discerned from text and both are seen simultaneously, one (meaning) being figure and the other (text) being ground. In the case of surface approach meaning may not be discerned from text, or it may be discerned but seen as ground while the text is seen as figure. For a third approach identified in studies with Chinese learners, the discernment of meaning and text, both being seen as figure, is characteristic.

More generally, having an aspect of something as the object of focal awareness corresponds to an open dimension of variation. Focusing the 'manyness' of a set of objects, for instance, means that we are trying to find out how many objects there are. The actual value is then implicitly seen against the background of other possible (but not actual) values. Focusing on what is the case implies focusing on what is not the case (see, for example, focusing on personal characteristics such as gender, age, education, etc.).

Having several aspects of something or of someone as objects of focal awareness simultaneously means thus experiencing potential variation in those aspects simultaneously. We may refer to this as the architecture of variation.

The situations in which we encounter the phenomenon we experience we discern from greater wholes, from more or less personally meaningful contexts. A phenomenon as it appears in a situation — or in several situations — has a particular relevance structure.

We learn to experience the world and this is the most fundamental form of learning. By characterizing it in terms of the architecture variation and in terms of relevance structure we arrive at a pedagogically sufficient description. We can in principle find out for each object of learning what it takes to develop the capability of experiencing it in a particular way.

Reference

Marton, F. and Booth, S. (forthcoming) Learning and Awareness. Manuscript, accepted for publication. For details contact Agneta sterlund (email: Agneta.Osterlund@ped.gu.se).

3 Reflecting on our practice: research to understand and improve student learning across the curriculum[1]

Marcia Mentkowski[2]
Professor of Psychology
Director, Office of Research and Evaluation
Alverno College, Milwaukee, Wisconsin

Introduction

I am honoured that you have asked me to think through this topic with you: research to understand and improve student learning across the curriculum. My thesis is that our ability as educators to move toward this ideal lies in taking responsibility for student learning, by the teaching staff and their institutions, and ultimately, by the students themselves.

At this point in the conference, K. Patricia Cross has discussed classroom research and assessment and why we should research teaching-for-learning. Ferenc Marton has described what learning is, and what the benefits are for student learning. I take up the task of exploring some of the challenges that arise when we bring research and assessment from the classroom level to the curriculum, programme or institutional level. Extending our work in this way can help with two new issues: (1) continually improving and transforming our institutions so they can better support student learning, and (2) dealing with the crisis of public confidence in the preparation and performance of college graduates. Those in the societies we serve are questioning educators' ability to judge the level and quality of student achievement. Considering programme research and assessment to improve student learning can play an important role in resolving these issues.

Considering other levels of practice than the classroom, the lecture hall or the seminar is a much larger leap than appears on the surface. I map the terrain as a series of questions that take responsibility for understanding and improving student learning. I then use this map as a guide — a kind of conceptual framework — for considering some of the issues that have

---

[1] The author acknowledges the contributions of the Office of Research and Evaluation. Members are: Marcia Mentkowski, PhD, Professor of Psychology and Director; Glen Rogers, PhD, Senior Research Associate; William Rickards, PhD, Senior Research Associate; Tamar Ben-Ur, M Ed, Senior Research Analyst; Lynne Kleinman, PhD, Senior Research Analyst; Judith Reisetter Hart, MS, Senior Research Analyst; Karen Adair, MS, Research Analyst; Kathleen Schwan Minik, MA, Research Analyst; Beverly Weeden, MA, Office Coordinator; Lynn Chabot-Long, Secretary III/Word Processor.

[2] Handouts for this talk are available from the author: Mapping Elicia's Journey ... From Entry to Five Years and The Proof is in the Performance. Author's address: Alverno College, 3401 South 39th Street, PO Box 343922, Milwaukee, WI 53234-3922; phone 414-382-6265; FAX 414-382-6354; E-mail

been the most challenging for me in my twenty years of experience working with colleagues at Alverno College, and with those at other institutions and associations.

There are two parts to my map. First, I briefly take up educational values and assumptions that ground research and assessment. I ask:

- Why should I research and assess?
- What should I research and assess?
- What is good assessment?
- What is good judgment?
- What is good evidence?

I illustrate my map, not with my own journey, but rather, with parts of 'Elicia's' journey through college and five years into her profession. This case was prepared with a teaching staff's perspective in mind. I also illustrate my map with a document prepared for others outside my institution who support education: *The Proof is in the Performance*.

Along the way, I ask that we stand aside from any educational approach to challenge its value for each student, for ourselves as educators, and for those across society who are looking to us for better education and who are trusting us to provide it. I ask:

- Does teaching lead to learning?
- Does assessment lead to learning?
- Does this kind of learning last?

To reflect on practice actively, I pose these questions within an overarching one that is the special purview of conference participants. It deals with the critical connections between understanding student learning and improving it.

How do emerging insights about student learning lead to improvement?

I take up the challenge to map this landscape with some trepidation. What is still to be learned looms large on the horizon. It is tempting to paint the possibilities in ideal terms with tiresome enthusiasm, much like Thomas Doughty did in painting his eighteenth-century fanciful landscapes. Those of you who have seen Tom Stoppard's play, *Arcadia*, recognize the romantic period. So, I will begin with a dose of reality.

As we use research and assessment to improve student learning, we are caught between a familiar and unfamiliar landscape. I grew up on the Great Plains. When I first visited the rain forest, I felt overwhelmed. I thought I could not take photographs, because it was raining. My host said, 'Marcia, that is why they call it the rain forest. Take your picture!' The photograph was hazy, and if I had to use it as a map, I would be immediately lost. In the beginnings of moving from the classroom level to the programme and institutional level, an enthusiastic but naïve explorer in the rain forest, without a map, is a good metaphor.

The need for a map arises because policy-makers continue to want to know:

Are students achieving complex, multidimensional learning outcomes?
- are these outcomes needed now and later?
- what standards are they being compared to?

- is this achievement to the level we/they/others expect?
- and is this as a result of curriculum, the programme of study?

In the US, these questions increase pressures on students, faculty, departments, institutions, disciplines, professions, accrediting agencies, and state and national departments of education. Each level of practice is expected to demonstrate that students are learning and performing in ways that enable them to contribute to work and civic life. Admittedly, expectations for assessment are enormously complex. Assessment is expected to serve each student's learning, to help teaching staff ensure teaching-for-learning, to stimulate college-wide discourse about the improvement of education, and to guide public policy on how and where education should be fixed and funded.

Making the move from the classroom to the department and institutional level is not easy. Indeed, when scholars in action research, such as Holly (1991), Nixon (1987) and Zeichner (1987, 1992), take a critical perspective, they often argue that classroom research and assessment can be helpful in individual classes without necessarily advancing broader curriculum and institutional development. Yet, if our new understanding of learning and our professional values do not make the move with us, we can easily create a bureaucratic nightmare or an erosion of the very values that sustain us. Research suggests that when groups work together, the results are better than what one individual can do alone. But are results really better? Too many of us have experienced programmes and institutions that do not work as well as we expect. Using research and assessment to improve programmes and transform institutions can easily become another well-meaning exercise in futility, as we confront old ways of thinking and decreased resources.

Educators experienced in the last ten years of school and undergraduate reform in the US argue that one cannot fundamentally change education by tinkering with parts of the system. Fixing each element separately does not result in the fundamental changes that new learning principles suggest. The system needs changing. How then can the variety and richness of research and assessment efforts be pulled together to have a coherent influence? I have learned that understanding student learning is a necessary, but not sufficient condition for improvement. I believe that 'knowing better' implies individual and collective responsibility for 'doing better'. What are the challenges? Bringing research or assessment from the classroom to the curriculum, programme, or institutional level means:

- incorporating learning principles, practices, professional values;
- linking learning goals, processes, outcomes;
- building a community of learning and judgment;
- using multidisciplinary methods for generating evidence; and
- creating public dialogue for linking understanding to improvement.

If we make this move, from classroom to curriculum, I have learned that it means incorporating new learning principles and practices, not just new research and assessment models. I think it is essential to build on the professional values that guide responsible teaching and learning. We also have to consider how to link learning goals, processes, and outcomes, a difficult task if staff have not made programme or institutional goals public and explicit even to themselves. Building on a community of learning, we need a community of judgment that is respected, just as we respect the autonomy and professional judgment of the individual staff member. I have learned that when we move across a college curriculum, for example, we need to use methods from multiple disciplines. Ultimately, if we are to link new insights to improvement and gain funding support, we need to create opportunities for dialogue and discourse. In my experience, these are formidable challenges.

Taking responsibility for student learning: why should I research and assess?

These challenges take us to the first questions on our assessment map: the why and what of assessment (Mentkowski, 1994, in press).

> *Assessment that is connected with teaching and learning should improve learning, enhance teaching, and focus on student performance.* In the US, most assessment practitioners note that widespread interest in assessment of student learning outcomes began in 1985 as a press for accountability from outside the academy rapidly developed to make improvement of programmes primary. Nevertheless, the programme or institution remained the primary unit of analysis and a critical connecting element was too often missing: a focus on student learning as the heart of assessment and student performance as the unit of analysis. Newer directions now lie in linking assessment to learning models, first, and to measurement models, second. Common learning and assessment principles have emerged from practice despite the diversity across settings and levels of practice ... These new ideas can become a common language and a substantive foundation for discourse. If they are powerful enough, they may capture interest across colleges, accreditation groups, and state and national policy-making agencies.
>
> *Assessment that is integral to teaching and learning contributes to coherence in a particular context and within and across levels of practice: student, course, curriculum, department and institution.* If so, involvement in broader policy issues is most effective and unifying for all when it flows from a central concern for students and their learning. In my experience, assessment that is truly connected to learning as the ultimate goal — no matter who does the learning (faculty, student, administrator, or state policy-maker) — requires investment from persons from diverse disciplines and positions across levels of practice. Such an ideal goal should not deny the difficult experiences we have all had trying to bridge communication gaps and diverse perspectives about the purposes and means of assessment. That road is long and hard, but it can lead us to integrated assessment systems, provided we acknowledge the role of all interests in the various decisions about assessment ... *The more we are unified around improving student learning, the better we can overcome disciplinary barriers, cross contexts, and unite levels of assessment practice (pp. 1—2).*

I now move to a range of examples of collaborative judgment about what is good education, what is good learning, and what is good assessment. Each example illustrates collaborative work. Examples are from an 11-member consortium of institutions across the educational spectrum, a learned society in psychology, a professional association of educators in higher education, and one institution's interdisciplinary and interprofessional faculty. Each of these groups has created public dialogue around their judgments.

What is striking is that all six of these groups across levels of practice focus on student learning. In fact, Ted Marchese argued recently that academics have captured the meaning of assessment away from policy-makers — even though I do not think it feels that way to most of the teaching faculty in US higher education.

This example is from the Consortium for the Improvement of Teaching, Learning and Assessment (1992), made up of 11 institutions from high school, through community college, through college, through university, through professional school, who worked together at Alverno.

- Student learning is a primary purpose of an educational institution.
- Education goes beyond knowing to being able to do what one knows.
- Learning must be active and collaborative.
- Assessment is integral to learning.
- A coherent curriculum calls for faculty investment in a community of learning and judgment.
- Responsibility for education involves assessing student outcomes, documenting inputs, and relating student performance over time to the curriculum.

In June 1991, the steering committee for the American Psychological Association (APA) National Conference to Enhance the Quality of Undergraduate Education in Psychology, prepared Principles for Quality Undergraduate Psychology Programs (McGovern, 1993). The first principle is: *Quality undergraduate programs set clear and high expectations for their students, promote their active learning, and give students systematic assessment and feedback on their progress.* A 1991 APA Wingspread conference directed to similar issues in K-12 ultimately resulted in a set of learner-centred psychological principles for learner-centred assessment developed by APA and McRel (McCombs and Lambert, in press). The first principle is: *The fundamental purpose of any educational assessment of students should be to promote meaningful learning.*

In 1992, the American Association for Higher Education assessment council — made up of persons from a range of levels of practice — developed the AAHE *Principles of Good Practice for Assessing Student Learning* (Astin, *et al.*, 1992). They include: *Assessment is most effective when it reflects an understanding of learning as multidimensional, integrated, and revealed in performance over time.* A similar example emerged from a 1994 AAHE discussion by interdisciplinary assessment practitioners from the classroom to the state level. They gave this advice to the AERA, APA and NCME Joint Committee that is revising the standards for educational and psychological testing: *Assessment is justified because it facilitates learning by the student, the department, and by the institution.* And, from a consensus across the Alverno faculty, comes this assumption: *Assessment is integral to learning* (Alverno College Faculty, 1992, 1994, note 1). These assumptions deal with the question, why should I research and assess? Now we turn to the question of what to research and assess.

What should I research and assess?

From all reports, we should assess what students have been taught and what they have practised, of course. Our ultimate purpose is to create better linkages among learning goals, processes and outcomes. Teaching is for learning. This purpose has profound implications for practice. For example, at Alverno in the early 1970s Alverno faculty asked: how do we want our students to turn out? What is an educated person? What kind of abilities and capacities, knowledge, skills and values do students need to master during college? Will these abilities transfer after college? Will students continue learning? Will they be able to contribute in novel roles, in work and civic life, that we cannot even imagine now?

What evolved at my own institution is this assumption: *education goes beyond knowing to being able to do what one knows*. But that meant that faculty had to observe and judge complex performance. Learning outcomes, such as critical thinking in action, are complex. For example, critical thinking has many dimensions and comes in many different forms. Thinking is different in psychology than it is in history. Thinking like a therapist is different from thinking like a health care administrator. Thinking is not a unitary skill but a set of complex, integrated ones that overlap and influence each other, and are gradually integrated in performance over time. A single assessment strategy, such as the often-used college essay or lab project, will not be adequate in itself to assess this kind of thinking performance.

Further, preparing our students for work and graduate or professional school means considering what alumnae may face in work and civic roles. Therefore, Alverno faculty designed student assessment based on this assumption: *what to assess must be carefully identified in relation to what contemporary life requires*. What kind of thinking is needed in doing a study and writing it up for a TV documentary, making a therapeutic diagnosis, creating a treatment plan, hiring personnel for starting up a small business, making public policy in health care or education? What kind of thinking will be needed in those complex tasks 15 years from now?

Now we have come full circle. We join our own goals with that of the graduate who wants to get and keep meaningful work and have a meaningful life. We are not so far from public policy-makers who expect competent performance and civic contribution, and who ask us to demonstrate that students are achieving complex, multi-dimensional learning outcomes.

So let us turn to mapping 'Elicia's' journey (not her real name). She majored in nursing with psychology as her support area. Obviously, faculty must assess in various modes, make multiple judgments, and use different sources of evidence, especially if they are assessing complex abilities. What is performance? What makes performances open? sustained? dynamic? interactive? observable over time? Some performances in Elicia's case are:

- essay;
- speech, inbasket, group discussion;
- research project in the lab;
- thinking patterns in the discipline;
- diagnosis and care plan in an uncharted area;
- interpersonal decision-making in a health care context

The complete case, *Mapping Elicia's Journey ... From Entry to Five Years After College*, is a portrait of one student's performance during college and five years beyond. Analysis of Elicia's performance across the years was generated from multiple sources, including judgments by faculty, external assessors from the Milwaukee business and professional community, and researchers. The case was prepared by the Alverno College Office of Research and Evaluation (1995). The case illustrates making multiple judgments, based on multiple kinds of evidence, by multiple persons, including Elicia herself. Each judgment and data source is a lens that casts its own kind of light across the examples that form the performance portrait. Two of those data sources are included here: both examples are from the end of Elicia's journey. Example one, 'Graduate as Performer in Work and Civic Life' is from a behavioral event interview five years after graduation, as she is engaged in interpersonal decision-making in a health-care context five years after college.

As you read the following excerpts from the interview and the researchers' analysis, ask yourself these questions: how do you judge Elicia's performance five years after college? Does she demonstrate complex, multi-dimensional learning outcomes? needed now and later? compared to what standards? to the level you expect? As you read, you will note Alverno researchers' analysis of the case (based on a Behavioural Event Interview and edited for confidentiality and clarity). Alverno researchers studied abilities through behavioural event interviews designed to demonstrate performance in everyday activities, and to capture an individual's performance in a particular context, including the setting, position, role and responsibilities (Mentkowski and Rogers, 1993). Alverno researchers synthesized and developed codes from effective performances that characterize outstanding performance of individuals from a range of successful organizations — abilities identified in our own and a host of independent studies of outstanding professionals — as well as Alverno faculty-defined abilities that all students demonstrate for graduation. Researchers independently coded 844 events from 211 five-year alumnae.

Example 1: Graduate as performer in work and civic life

Behavioural event interview

The alumna, Elicia (a baccalaureate nurse), is the new head nurse for a hospital floor. She describes a time when she effectively mediates a conflict. To wit, she analyses an unresolved problem — a long-standing conflict between two nurses in her unit — and takes persuasive action. This aspect of her performance illustrates key abilities from the Fourth Ability Factor, Analytic Thinking and Action.

In this event, a licensed practical nurse with two years of training (LPN) approaches Elicia about the conflict with a registered nurse with three years of training (RN). Elicia's questioning of her reflects her analytic approach.

> *The LPN came to me saying she couldn't work with this RN anymore. She refused to be demeaned. I said, 'Well,* I think we need to discuss this. What are your feelings? Why are you feeling demeaned? What can you tell me? What evidence can you tell me? *I can't deal with these broad statements.* I need to know some facts *and then I can tell you what action I can take.*

The LPN refuses to engage in direct dialogue with the RN. Elicia approaches the RN. She also refuses a face-to-face discussion. So, Elicia deals with them separately. After she gains an understanding of the problem, she actively persuades the nurses to resolve it.

> *I said, 'I* think that now you guys understand where each other is coming from, you may be able to work this out if you could have a positive attitude. *Do you think you could try it?' The LPN said, 'It's not that I don't like her. I think I could try it if she would try.' So, then I went back to* the RN and she said she would try if the LPN would try.

When she addresses these performance issues she is also, of course, demonstrating *Developing Others and Perspective Taking* (Ability Factor 3). Not only did she effectively confront them, she also *first* impartially listened to both sides of the story.

> *I said to the LPN, 'Since this is bothering you, I think it's only fair that the other person know that.' Then I told her I was going to talk to the RN, that I want to hear her story. I called the RN in and I explained to her that I needed to confront her with this and I needed to hear her side of the story. I said, 'This is how the LPN is feeling. What do you say about this situation and this situation and this situation and every fact?' And she had a completely different concept. And then she told me some things about the LPN that I'm sure the LPN had no concept about. I said, 'Okay, I'm going to go back and talk to the LPN about this and then we're going to work something out.'*

So, I ended up discussing what their job was. The RN as a professional, what was required of her. The LPN as the non-professional, what was expected of her. I just ended up having to tell them some expectations, *like I expect politeness.*

By connecting her values to her actions, she demonstrates a curriculum ability of reflective valuing, which is associated with *Developing Self and Acting With Integrity* (Ability Factor 2). For Elicia, fairness involves communicating openly, as when she says above, 'I think it's only fair that the other person know that.' Also associated with this Factor is the capacity to self-assess her own abilities accurately. Indeed, we see her reflectively abstracting her abilities beyond this individual performance:

I felt like that was one of the things that I do, keeping the staff flowing smoothly. *And if they can't do it themselves, I need to help them build the skills; I need to be able to come in and smooth things over.*

So far, our analysis of Elicia's actions has illustrated how her performance shows analytic thinking, integrity in action, and development of others. Elicia also demonstrates some abilities from Ability Factor 1, *Cooperative Organizational Thinking and Action.* You may have noted, for example, that when she confronted the RN she went beyond an immediate script called for by the situation, showing her initiative. Elicia also demonstrates a related ability, recognizing the key problem in this situation:

I feel that the problem between them was no communication. *Going back and forth between them made me feel that neither one knew what the other one was thinking. They both said that they really didn't dislike each other. But they had never had any open communication, so they kept being offended by each other, actually not meaning to. They each needed to know where the other one was coming from. They wouldn't do it themselves, so I did it for them. They had been at each other's throats for years before I got there. Now they're working together really, really well.*

Elicia does not spontaneously demonstrate in this event a more complex form of thinking that simultaneously involves several levels of abstraction. For example, she might have noted the implications of how an interpersonal conflict would reflect on her department. In another performance example, however, we do see evidence of how she thinks at an organizational level: She voluntarily takes on responsibilities for furthering the development of her profession.

Is Elicia performing to your expectations? You may judge this case quite differently than Alverno researchers did. However, what we discovered in factor analyzing 844 events from 211 five-year alumnae is one picture of what contemporary life requires.

Alverno five-year alumna Ability Factors

Cooperative Organizational Thinking and Action: Thinking and acting independently and within the interdependencies of the organization to achieve collective effectiveness.

Developing Self and Acting With Integrity: Self-reflecting for self-insight, for self-improvement, and for constructing integrity in action.

Developing Others and Perspective Taking: Compassionately and impartially understanding others and guiding their development.

Analytic Thinking and Action: Independently analyzing problems and persuading others.

These outcomes may be similar to what most colleges promise. The first Factor, **Cooperative Organizational Thinking and Action**, is somewhat unusual. It is related to career advancement. Graduates who judge Alverno preparation as more effective are more likely to demonstrate this Ability Factor and graduates who integrate their abilities are more likely to show it.

Performer in relation to the profession

We now turn to an analysis of Elicia as a performer in relation to professional expectations. You just read an example of her five-year performance, annotated according to the Ability Factors that Alverno researchers found for alumna performance when it was coded in relation to an integration of the highest ability standards researchers could find. Now, how does Elicia's portrait compare to a professional competence model developed by Alverno researchers from nurses who were not Alverno graduates? What pattern of nursing competences does Elicia demonstrate? We turn to an analysis of this same performance in relation to a set of broad abilities that are specifically related to the nursing profession (DeBack and Mentkowski, 1986). Elicia demonstrates — in her mediation of the conflict between the two nurses she supervises — most of the abilities in our model of nursing competence (bolded competences are associated with formal education).

Table 1

Competences of Nursing Professionals (Who Are Not Alverno Graduates)

Conceptualizes	**Reflective thinking**
Emotional stamina	Helping
Ego strength	**Influencing**
Positive expectations	**Coaching**
Independence	

Elicia *conceptualizes* the key to the interpersonal conflict as a lack of communication that leads to unintended offenses. Her *independence* in judgment and influence are inferred from how she persistently intervenes to resolve the conflict. Her *coaching* is more specifically illustrated in the work she does to ensure that the nurses take more responsibility for their performance, 'helping to build their skills'. Both coaching and influencing are associated with more education, but not more experience. Although Elicia demonstrates neither *ego strength* nor *reflective thinking* as described in the nursing competence code book, her performance in the rest of the interview is congruent with these kinds of abilities. For example, recall her reflective valuing in the behavioral interview event. Performance in relation to another profession-specific standard is also available. Elicia passed the state boards for nursing on her second attempt.

Example 2: Student as learner in the curriculum

Narrative transcript

[Now, how does Elicia's performance five years after college compare to nursing department judgments at graduation? To psychology department judgments at graduation? The case continues with Elicia's narrative transcript. Each graduate of the college receives a narrative transcript that summarizes her credits and learning outcomes — which is often read by prospective employers and graduate admissions committees. (For our purposes here, learning outcomes include the student as a knower and doer of the discipline in the context of a profession, which enables the graduate to perform at work and to contribute to civic life.) Elicia's transcript (edited for confidentiality) was developed by faculty from her nursing major and psychology support area.]

Elicia has demonstrated those professional characteristics required by the faculty of Alverno College for completion of the baccalaureate programme of study in nursing with a support area in psychology. These include the ability to apply the nursing process in a variety of situations, to respect the value systems of her clients, and to interact effectively with the health team.

Elicia adequately carried through the nursing process in a variety of settings — a nursing home, a neurological unit, a psychiatric unit, a semi-rural community hospital, acute care units, and non-traditional community health agencies. In selected settings, such as the psychiatric unit and a community agency providing service to children, she exhibited very creative problem-solving strategies. In establishing a therapeutic relationship with an adolescent client disturbed over her own sexuality, Elicia effectively designed interviewing strategies based on psychological theory. The staff acknowledged her ability by allowing her to work independently with the client. In working with a mother of two small children, her knowledge of family dynamics and child development enhanced her ability to analyse the effect of the mother's treatment on a ___ child. For each of the situations reported and within her clinical nursing experiences, she applied principles of environmental and learning psychology.

Elicia's consistent strength as a nursing student was her sensitivity to clients' needs. Throughout her clinical experience she acted as an advocate for the client. Her warmth and genuineness facilitated clients' confidence in her and allowed them to divulge their fears and anxieties. A particularly illustrative incident of her advocacy ability was her aid to a person suffering from ___, whose personality created a negative response from the staff. She worked with both the client and staff to assist the client to adapt to her illness and hospitalization. She also demonstrated managerial skills as she maintained channels to communicate the client's progress to the staff.

While collaborating with agency personnel, she acted as a resource for a ___ teacher as well as for health team members in an independent nursing clinic. Her creativity manifested itself in her teaching projects as she assisted clients to grow in their own health knowledge, and in the presentation entitled ___ for four and five year olds.

In her support area Elicia demonstrated the analytical and problem solving skills required of the psychology support area student. She applied learning theory concepts in analysing problem-solving and perceptual abilities of a historical figure. Although her course work was often descriptive rather than analytical, she demonstrated the ability to apply the various current theories of conditioning, problem solving and remembering. She also demonstrated the ability to generalize the principles of environmental psychology to their application in ___.

In group situations with health team members, Elicia was self-assertive and communicated her ideas convincingly. She actively influenced events and was persistent in reaching her goal. She was committed to professional nursing but her vitality and enthusiasm for nursing resulted in personal stressors that sometimes inhibited her effectiveness. She was aware of her capabilities and was very resourceful in planning alternatives to successfully further her nursing career.

Suffice it to say that, according to Elicia's narrative transcript, Elicia's teachers observed and judged her interaction with others during the first semester. They judged her analysis of an historical figure, and her collaborative project in the environmental psychology lab. They learned to observe and judge Elicia's treatment plan and how she carried it out in a psychiatric unit. They observed and judged how, in a community agency, she analysed the effect of a mother's treatment on her learning disabled child. They had to design assessments external to courses and invite other professionals besides themselves to participate in assessments at the end of general education.

A careful reading of the transcript shows that there are similarities and differences that can guide a department's discussion about what to assess. For example, nursing faculty say that Elicia does 'interact effectively with the health care team'. Psychology faculty note that Elicia's 'coursework was descriptive rather than analytical', but that 'she demonstrated the ability to apply the various current theories of conditioning, problem-solving and remembering'.

The practical benefit for us is that assessment helps us to **understand** the very complex learning outcomes faculty are trying to define and teach *and* that the student must eventually perform. This kind of comparison becomes another way to understand what knowing and doing a discipline and profession means — and what it might mean to demonstrate student achievement.

What is good assessment? What is good judgment? What is good evidence?

Elicia's case provides a range of judgments based on a number of performances, from multiple sources of evidence. What is good judgment? What is good evidence? Now we have a new problem. How do I *know* assessment that judges performance is 'good?' We take up this question because as scholars we are inherently interested in it. Assessment theory must be consistent with educational assumptions about what students should know and be able to do, and how students learn. Our theory of judgment also has to be consistent with our educational values and assumptions (Rogers, 1994). I have noted that judging performance can enable faculty to give feedback to Elicia to guide her learning and to understand the complex learning outcomes we want to teach for, such as *cooperative organizational thinking and action.* How do we do that well? And what is good enough? To deal with these questions as educators implies understanding 'wise professional judgment' about student learning. In my experience, it is professional judgment that leads to improvement ... judgment about what to improve, how to improve, and sustaining the improvement. So now, let us digress for a moment to a fundamental question that lies at the heart of using research and assessment to improve student learning: what is good judgment?

Can we trust complex human judgment, that it will be fair, that it will ultimately help students learn? Can faculty and students can have confidence in it? Can the public have confidence in it? In thinking about judgment, I did some self assessment. First, I began to realize that I was not always comfortable in situations that called for judgment rather than measurement. I also discovered that I did not appreciate the word 'judgment'. It seemed so final. Perhaps this concept of judgment has been most powerfully illustrated in Michelangelo's *Last Judgment.* Because I did not trust human judgment that much, I worried that judgment is inherently subjective or biased, and that I might impose a judgment upon someone else, and make a decision that was not based on past, accumulated evidence but on factors beyond anyone's persuasive influence. I was reminded of every student with a low grade point average who suffers from low marks from his early work, before he realized what college learning was all about.

Even when judgment was associated with righting major wrongs in society, such as the Judgment at Nuremberg, I was too often likely to associate the term with 'judges' and the court system. I knew my language often sounded 'wishy-washy' to outside audiences. It did not help that I was an academic psychologist. My husband, a law professor, would often comment, 'If you lay all the studies psychologists have done end to end, they would never reach a conclusion.' He implied that I have to commit to some kind of judgment. It helped to be reminded of this quote from Albert Camus: 'Do not wait for the last judgment. It takes place every day.' We constantly make judgments, in most everything we do. Henry James reminds us of the importance of independent judgment: 'Don't mind anything that anyone tells you about anyone else. Judge everyone and everything for yourself.' Perhaps, as educators, we should not be surprised that our colleagues from other disciplines, our students' employers, or programme accreditors insist on making their own judgments about the quality of a student's performance. An Alverno document, *The Proof is in the Performance,* was created, in part, so that outside audiences such as employers and funders could make their own independent judgments about Alverno graduates' achievement.

When developing assessment that serves each student's learning, and that lends itself to outside judgments of students' performance, I have to assume that professional judgment is central to wise professional practice. Can I assume that it lives within a discipline or profession and supports learning? Do persons outside the institution assume it? I submit two trial definitions to begin examining judgment: (1) expert judgment and (2) a community of judgment. For me, *expert judgment is the rigor and discipline of mind and heart that educators bring to judgment, based on their experience and education. It is a starting point for observing and judging complex performance.*

An even more difficult issue is to expand the group who makes the judgment about when the student's performance is meeting criteria, by including professionals who are not directly responsible for teaching the student. For example, our college had to learn to expand the group of assessors of student performance to include not only students and faculty, but community professionals who assess student performance or serve as mentors in internships. And ultimately, we also meet performance standards set by accrediting groups, disciplinary and professional groups, and colleagues from across the educational spectrum. We also have learned to better deal with the expectations of various publics: trustees, alumnae, campus visitors and workshop participants, scholarly reviewers and writers. We also consider the expectations of contributors, funding agencies, state and national groups, and education writers and journalists. For me, *a community of judgment is an interactive engagement of persons (joined by experience, expertise, role, responsibilities, educational values) in a process of evidence-based reflection and meaning making about their practice. Such a community can lead to ethical, insightful decision making about education. As a result, it can enhance learning. It invites substantive critique, and supports contributions to education in one's sphere of influence.*

A community of judgment, in its ideal form, assumes mutual trust, respect, and responsibility — such as one might find in a community of learning. It is a culture built on collaborative engagement in curriculum and assessment design and implementation, which leads to a culture where research and assessment improves learning. In such an exemplary setting, wise professional judgment is central to professional practice. One drawback to expanding a community of judgment along these lines is that, predictably, there are very different conceptions of what is a valid judgment, what expert judgment means, and what kinds of evidence should be the basis for judgment.

Kenneth Hammond (1993) argues that there is a lack of trust in the quality of human judgment generally. So, persons often do not put a lot of weight on judgment to start with, and are likely to downplay it as 'self-report' or 'subjective'. In my experience, academics often reserve their judgment because they may not have sufficient or appropriate information. Then their public audiences often assume that they are unwilling to take responsibility for student learning outcomes. Hammond's review of studies of human judgment does *not* support this lack of faith in human judgment. It is illuminating to explore different conceptions of judgment, and its corollary, evidence.

As academics, we are often caught up in the language of world views and paradigm shifts. Here are some different conceptions of judgment from that great authority, Microsoft's WordPerfect thesaurus.

Table 2

Conceptions of Judgement

conclusion	analysis	discernment
decision	belief	discretion
ruling	deduction	discrimination
sentence	estimate	sense
verdict	interpretation	taste
		opinion

Source: Microsoft WordPerfect 5.1

Imagine these various conceptions moving from left to right. It is apparent that the kind of judgment we want to use will depend very much on the context in which the student is performing. You are probably aware of the difficulties involved in using performance assessment created for the classroom or the curriculum in large-scale, state-wide assessment systems in the US. Many persons not directly involved in teaching and learning are more likely to expect conclusions and decisions (on the left side) rather than statements of analysis, interpretation, or estimates (in the centre), let alone the complex discriminations that are involved, for example, in judging that a student is ready for entering the major or a student is ready for an internship (on the right side).

Kenneth Hammond alerts us to two versions of 'truth' that can complicate faculty attempts to design student assessment of performance.

Table 3	
Theories of Judgement	
correspondence	**coherence**
consistency	cohesion
reliability patterns	
replication	profiles
(derived from "studies")	(derived from experience)
	Source: Kenneth Hammond

Often, faculty are asked for information that reflects a correspondence theory of judgment, that expects to match x with y, this performance with that one, this judgment with that one. Can you replicate the performance? Is the judgment reliable? That may be important in assessing beginning level skills; but for judging more complex performances, for example, of an intern in a psychiatric hospital, the faculty member and the hospital staff are looking for patterns in the students' thinking from one situation to the next, how they incorporate professional values into difficult situations, and respect the persons they are caring for from day to day. They are using a coherence theory of judgment. Because I lean more toward the coherence model of judgment in my research and assessment work, I have found it helpful to balance my own model by specifying the basis for judgment through performance criteria, and by working to articulate why we think one example of student performance is closer to these criteria than another. The criteria for judgment can be clarified on a dimension of explicitness, and the judgments about level of student achievement specified as to why they are informed, evidence-based, insightful, fair, and so on.

Let me return to the WordPerfect thesaurus for different conceptions of evidence. I have highlighted those that illuminate the shift in thinking we make with assessing complex skills.

Table 4		
Conceptions of evidence		
confirmation	**indication**	denote
data	sign	**exhibit**
proof	symptom	**illustrate**
testimony	token	**show**
	Source: Microsoft WordPerfect 5.1	

The struggle for us as practitioners is to communicate which conception of evidence we are working from — an exercise we take up when we discuss Elicia's performance as a community of judgment. In that community, we may apply some of the following criteria for evidence: Is evidence accurate and credible? comprehensive and representative? meaningful, in that it is contextual and grounded? drawn from multiple sources, perspectives, and settings? confirmed through study, experience, and practice? Is evidence compelling, and to whom? This kind of conversation can continue to probe what is meant by wise professional judgment.

Reflecting on our practice: how do emerging insights lead to improvement?

Let us continue with our map of questions, and include some that I believe can guide institutional and programme research and assessment that leads to improvement:

- Does teaching lead to learning?
- Does assessment lead to learning?
- Does this kind of learning last?

For example, does Elicia demonstrate important learning outcomes that faculty hope for? Does Elicia take responsibility for her own learning? To answer these questions, we turn to longitudinal studies of the learning, development, and performance of Alverno students and alumnae over a ten-year period (Mentkowski, 1988).

- From where they stand, Elicia and other students do become responsible for their own learning during college by participating in the curriculum. 320 rigorously analysed interviews of 82 students tracked their perspectives on learning in each of four years. Students linked knowledge and its application, and pinpointed causal aspects of the curriculum, such as feedback and self-assessment.
- The high value of accurate self-assessment was independently confirmed by our studies of the performance of outstanding professionals who are not Alverno graduates; self-assessment was also a key ability. On the whole, students describe learning as experiencing, reflecting, forming new concepts, and testing one's judgment and abilities in action.

Table 5

Components of self-sustaining learning

Student-attributed cause	Student outcomes
Instructor attention and empathy ⟶	Taking responsibility for learning
Feedback, self-assessment	
Experiential validation	Making relationships
Instructor coaching ⟶	among abilities and their use
Professional application	
Integration of abilities	
Practice, feedback	Using different ways
Modelling, peer learning ⟶	of learning

In Elicia's experience, by her own account, feedback and self assessment are feasible because they helped her connect what she learned with how she learned it. She learned to use faculty feedback to improve. She learned to self-assess, that is, to judge her own work. She forgot her test anxiety, and she began to judge herself in relation to criteria for effective thinking, for example, rather than to the person sitting next to her. In the case, it is apparent that her individual experiences with student assessment generated her motivation to perform to the best of her abilities. This student's perspectives are good news for faculty: the content faculty teach goes hand in hand with the student's skills and will to apply it.

These results have been encouraging. They have helped Alverno faculty develop self-assessment as a part of each student assessment experience, and to develop better ways to give students feedback on their performance. In fact, these and other findings led faculty to critique a whole series of student assessments. They noted where student assessments were weak in fostering self-assessment and where they were strong. The Alverno Student Assessment Council is now engaged in a reconceptualization of self- assessment based on ongoing research and experience in the classroom (Loacker and Mentkowski, 1993).

We have also become better at using performance examples such as those included in Elicia's case and *The Proof is in the Performance* to help illustrate the criteria for performance, and to use performance examples in assessor training, so that judges are more consistent in their judgments when that is required, and *coherent* in their judgments when that is required. When judges come to consensus, we can pinpoint when low agreement among judges is due to lack of clarity in understanding the criteria and the judgment process, and when it represents different perspectives on complex performance.

Does learning last? This question is important to test the long-term impact of a curriculum and whether the kinds of improvements observed day-to-day have lasting effects. It also provides insights into how learning happens across the life span and provides a picture of who is more or less likely to meet their potential as learners. In the recently completed ten-year longitudinal study, a general pattern of change on a battery of independently designed measures confirmed that student intellectual and moral growth during college were indeed linked to successful performance on Alverno assessments, even when other factors and entry scores were controlled. Patterns of change on measures include, for example, those based on William Perry's Scheme of Intellectual and Ethical Development; a measure of cognitive development based on Piaget's theory of cognitive development; James Rest's Defining Issues Test that measures development in judging moral issues; Jane Loevinger's measure of ego development; and Watson and Glaser's Critical Thinking Appraisal.

As one would expect, Elicia does not always fit the aggregate patterns. Elicia entered college similar to her classmates on most measures. Two and one half years after entering college, she showed a 'drop' on some of these external measures. According to her Perspectives Interview, she had a number of personal crises at that time, which could account for these changes. What is interesting is that a review of psychology faculty judgments are corroborated: 'her coursework was descriptive rather than analytical'. Nursing faculty judgments are corroborated: 'her vitality and enthusiasm for nursing resulted in personal stressors that sometimes inhibited her effectiveness'. For example, on the Perry scheme of Intellectual and Ethical Development, Elicia seems to recycle through less-sophisticated forms of thinking and decision-making and about her career. However, by five years after college, she again thinks in more sophisticated ways on the Perry Scheme. She bounces back.

These recycling patterns in some of the Alverno research on student learning led faculty to be less likely to assume that because students started at less sophisticated thinking and learning when they entered a new class or major, that the previous teachers had not taught well, or that students were not prepared. Rather, faculty are more conscious of the fact that students can 'begin at the beginning' when they enter a new major or professional field. A change in thinking about recycling in learning and development reflects how new understanding about student learning can lead to new ways of thinking about students' abilities and potential. Further review of Elicia's case reveals that the life events in her junior year led to a leap in personal growth during college, on Loevinger's measure of ego development. For most students this leap does not happen until after college. This kind of information can assist faculty in analysing their own judgments. Faculty judgments of Elicia's comparative immaturity in her junior and senior years were corroborated by her own account. In the long term, it seems that Elicia's difficult personal experiences during college, coupled with the fact that faculty held her to the standards of her discipline and her profession, challenged her to mature. What is notable is that, five years after college, Elicia's pattern of performance is comparable to effective nurses. Why do faculty care about these findings? They are now in a better position to question how intellectual development and personal growth walk hand in hand with performance five years after college over the long-term, and day-to-day at the level of the classroom (note 2).

Elicia's journey, by her own account, illustrates the value of the next question: how do emerging insights about student learning lead to improvement? Parker Palmer reminds us that developing a community of learning and judgment means creating public dialogue. For me, creating public dialogue means sharing discoveries about teaching-for-learning, making persuasive, evidence-based judgments so others can construct their own meaning about what works and what can make education better, creating processes for linking emerging insights with continuous improvement, and extending the conversation to various publics.

Reflecting on our practice: some challenges

The future of research and assessment for improving student learning across the curriculum, at the programme and institutional level, lies in enabling each person concerned to make wise judgments about teaching-for-learning on a dimension of responsibility: from faculty judgment of each student's learning to continued learning and effective performance by the graduate. Faculty keep the focus on student learning as they design and evaluate research and assessment processes that enable those judgments based on compelling evidence. As the public forum about education expands and grows, we as educators are in a better position to create public dialogue about what is good educational preparation and student performance.

In my view, when we publicly discuss both student achievement and our judgments about it, along with our nagging doubts and glimmers of insight — in a gradually more inclusive conversation — we can develop a community that is strong enough to take on the most intractable problems in education and in the public discourse around it. That can lead to realistic improvement of programmes and long-term benefits for students.

Research and assessment to understand, improve and demonstrate student learning across the curriculum is neither a fanciful landscape nor the coming storm. But there are challenges on the horizon. I included some at the end of this map. I have discussed two or three here. I leave the rest to you. Here are some challenges for departments and institutions:

- continually connecting research and assessment with teaching and learning;
- describing enquiry/research/assessment processes;
- demonstrating that education works for each student's learning;
- giving evidence that student learning is linked to curriculum;
- showing the use of feedback to improve;
- describing a culture of enquiry where research/assessment continuously improves learning;
- establishing credibility for educational innovations; demonstrating accountability for student learning outcomes; demonstrating institutional effectiveness, quality;
- sustaining commitment, effort, time, resources.

Here are some potential contributions if we take up these challenges:

- developing integrated assessments of complex learning outcomes in the contexts of the discipline, and related professions that demonstrate student achievement;
- connecting more summative, institution-wide efforts with ongoing, formative efforts by teachers in courses, and departments;
- connecting teaching, learning, and assessment through systems that are responsive to and responsible for students from diverse backgrounds who come to us with different ways of thinking and learning;
- discovering new learning principles and practices.

Are we up to these challenges? Yes, but it means becoming more explicit about our educational values — and our will to live out of them. It helps to keep in mind that the purpose of research and assessment is each student's learning and contribution after they leave us, and, through them, to those they ultimately serve. Research and assessment must stay connected with teaching and learning. I believe it stays connected as long as its fundamental purpose is transforming in nature — for the student, curriculum, institution or educational system. Connecting research and assessment with teaching and learning means considering new learning principles and their meaning for improvement so that learning happens. Connecting effectively means rethinking one's own role, judgment and expertise, in relation to that of others. The more we are unified around improving student learning, the better we can overcome challenges to uniting levels of research and assessment practice.

Notes

1. **Alverno assessment definitions**. Assessment is part of a dynamic learning system based on the educational principles and values underlying Alverno's mission and supported by structures that ensure coherence and continuing improvement. Student assessment-as-learning is a process integral to learning, that involves observation and judgment of each student's performance on the basis of explicit criteria, with feedback to the student for improving learning and to the faculty for improving teaching. It serves to certify student achievement in the development of academic knowledge and abilities required for graduation. Institutional and programme assessment are processes that contribute to improvement and shared learning by providing meaningful feedback to faculty, staff and various publics about patterns of student and alumnae performance on a range of educational outcomes. For the demonstration of programme and institutional effectiveness, the processes enable comparisons of performance both to standards and to evidence-based judgments of how students and alumnae benefit from the curriculum. This comprehensive assessment programme is possible because faculty and staff hold themselves responsible for the design, process, impact and ongoing evaluation and improvement of the teaching/learning/assessment programme at the college (Alverno College Faculty, 1994; Mentkowski, for the Alverno College Office of Research and Evaluation and the Research and Evaluation Committee, 1994).

2. **Alverno definition of practitioner-based enquiry**. Practitioner-based enquiry has played an important role in 'reflecting on our practice' at Alverno College. For us, practitioner-based enquiry is both a way of understanding how teaching relates to learning and an approach to improving teaching for learning. We use the term to refer to a process, prompted by questions that arise in teaching, of gathering, interpreting and using information that will illuminate how teaching enhances student learning. Practitioner-based enquiry is problem-based and capitalizes on educators' reflection about teaching (Alverno College Research and Evaluation Committee, Office of Research and Evaluation, and Additional Faculty and Staff, 1993; Alverno College Research and Evaluation Committee, 1987).

References

Alverno College (1993) *The Proof is in the Performance* (Alverno College 1992—93 Annual Report). Milwaukee, WI: Alverno College Institute.

Alverno College Faculty (1976, revised 1985, 1992) *Liberal Learning at Alverno College*. Milwaukee, WI: Alverno College Institute.

Alverno College Faculty (1979, revised 1985, 1994) *Student Assessment-as-Learning at Alverno College*. Milwaukee, WI: Alverno College Institute.

Alverno College Office of Research and Evaluation (1995) *Mapping Elicia's Journey ... From Entry to Five Years after College*. Milwaukee, WI: Alverno College Institute.

Alverno College Research and Evaluation Committee (1987) *The Alverno Educator as Researcher: Some Elements that Describe Teacher Inquiry that Improves Teaching*. Milwaukee, WI: Alverno College Institute.

Alverno College Research and Evaluation Committee, Office of Research and Evaluation, and Additional Faculty and Staff (1993) Reflecting on our practice: Practitioner-based inquiry to understand and improve teaching and learning across the curriculum. Paper distributed and discussed at the symposium, *Practitioner Research as an Evaluation Strategy in Higher Education* at the annual meeting of the American Educational Research Association, Atlanta, GA, 12 April 1993. Milwaukee, WI: Alverno College Institute.

Astin, A. W., Banta, T. W., Cross, K. P., El-Khawas, E., Ewell, P. T., Hutchings, P., Marchese, T. J., McClenney, K. M., Mentkowski, M., Miller, M. A., Moran, E. T. and Wright, B. D. (1992) Principles of good practice for assessing student learning. *AAHE Bulletin* **45**(4).

Consortium for the Improvement of Teaching, Learning and Assessment (1992) *High School to College to Professional School: Achieving Educational Coherence through Outcome-oriented, Performance-based Curricula* (Final Report to the W. K. Kellogg Foundation). Milwaukee, WI: Alverno Productions.

DeBack, V. and Mentkowski, M. (1986) Does the baccalaureate make a difference?: Differentiating nurse performance by education and experience. *Journal of Nursing Education* **25**(7), 275—85.

Hammond, K. (1993) Naturalistic decision making from a Brunswikian viewpoint: its past, present, future. In G. A. Klein, J. Orasanu, R. Calderwood and C. E. Zsambok (eds), *Decision Making in Action: Models and Methods*. Norwood, NJ: Ablex.

Holly, P. (1991) Action research: the missing link in the creation of schools as centers of inquiry. In A. Lieberman and L. Miller (eds), *Staff Development for Education in the 90's* (2nd edn) (pp. 133—57). New York: Teachers College Press.

Loacker, G. and Mentkowski, M. (1993) Creating a culture where assessment improves learning. In T. W. Banta and Associates, *Making a Difference: Outcomes of a Decade of Assessment in Higher Education* (pp. 5—24). San Francisco: Jossey-Bass.

McCombs, B. L. and Lambert, N. (eds) (in press). *Issues in School Reform: A Sampler of Psychological Perspectives in Learner-centered Schools*. Washington, DC: American Psychological Association.

McGovern, T. V. (1993) *Handbook for enhancing undergraduate education in psychology.* Washington, DC: American Psychological Association.

Mentkowski, M. (1988) Paths to integrity: Educating for personal growth and professional performance. In S. Srivastva and Associates (eds), *Executive Integrity: The Search for High Human Values in Organizational Life* (pp. 89—121). San Francisco: Jossey-Bass.

Mentkowski, M. (1994, January—February). How assessment practitioners who are educational researchers can contribute to assessment in higher education. In M. Mentkowski (ed.), How educational research can contribute to assessment in higher education. *Assessment Update* 6(1), 1—2, 10—11.

Mentkowski, M. (in press) Higher education assessment and educational goals: some issues, assumptions, and principles for discussion. In B. L. McCombs and N. Lambert (eds), *Issues in School Reform: A Sampler of Psychological Perspectives in Learner-centered Schools.* Washington, DC: American Psychological Association.

Mentkowski, M., for the Alverno College Office of Research and Evaluation and the Research and Evaluation Committee (1994, April) Institutional and program assessment at Alverno College. In W. Rickards (Chair), *Institutional Assessment across the Educational Spectrum.* Paper presented at a symposium conducted at the annual meeting of the American Educational Research Association, New Orleans. Milwaukee, WI: Alverno College Institute.

Mentkowski, M. and Rogers, G. (1993, Summer) Connecting education, work, and citizenship: how assessment can help. *Metropolitan Universities: An International Forum* 4(1), 34—46.

Nixon, J. (1987) The teacher as researcher: contradictions and continuities. *Peabody Journal of Education* 64(2), 20—32.

Rogers, G. (1994, January—February) Measurement and judgment in curriculum assessment systems. In M. Mentkowski (ed.), How educational research can contribute to assessment in higher education. *Assessment Update* 6(1), 6—7.

Zeichner, K. M. (1987) Preparing reflective teachers: an overview of instructional strategies which have been employed in preservice teacher education. *International Journal of Educational Research* 11(5), 565—75.

Zeichner, K. M. (1992, April) Developing reflective professional practice. In G. Handal (Chair), *Promoting Reflective Professional Practice.* Symposium conducted at the annual meeting of the American Educational Research Association, San Francisco.

4 Using research to improve student learning in large classes

Graham Gibbs and Lisa Lucas
Oxford Centre for Staff Development
Oxford Brookes University

Background

Perhaps the largest single threat to the quality of student learning in the UK over the past decade has been the rapid increase in student numbers without commensurate increases in resources. Student numbers have more than doubled on many courses while library provision, academic staffing and classroom facilities have increased little. Modularization and other forms of rationalization of course provision have also increased class sizes by combining all students studying similar courses into sometimes enormous first-year programmes. At Oxford Brookes University, which has expanded in a controlled fashion compared with some institutions, more than three times as many modules had more than 70 students enrolled in 1994 compared with a decade earlier (Gibbs and Lucas, unpublished). While class sizes have increased, student performance, in terms of degree classifications, have actually improved across the system as a whole (MacFarlane, 1992a). Politicians and some senior management have been able to argue that the effects of large classes and resource problems can be overcome through greater efficiency and effectiveness. And yet despite this huge change in one of the most visible features of students' and lecturers' experience and the political intensity of debate there has until recently been almost no research in the UK on the effect of class sizes on student learning. Policy decisions about funding and about patterns of course delivery have been made without understanding their consequences. Lecturers have been faced with enormous changes with little to guide them in their teaching, assessment and course design decisions.

In many courses decisions have been taken to increase the size of lecture audiences, increase the size of seminar groups, or hold them less frequently, cut back on the frequency of practical and laboratory work, replace coursework assessment with more economical exams or multiple choice question tests, and to abandon personal tutoring. But no-one seems to know what the consequences of these decisions have been and whether they have been appropriate decisions. Initiatives such as the Teaching More Students project (Gibbs, 1992, 1995) assumed that it was possible to teach effectively in large classes if new methods were adopted or at least that it was possible to minimize the damage caused by traditional methods being retained without the resources to implement them properly. In less than two years nearly 9,000 lecturers attended workshops to find out how this might be achieved which suggests at least a certain optimism that damage could be limited. But mostly people have assumed that large classes are a bad thing. This assumption has not been based on research or even on evaluation evidence.

Evaluation does not necessarily help much in these circumstances. Student feedback studies in North America suggest that in certain circumstances students actually like very large classes: the graph plotting ratings against class size is often 'U' shaped with students preferring small and very large classes to medium-size classes (Feldman *et al.*, 1984). However students' preferences are a poor guide to quality of learning and educational decision-making. Feigenbaum and Friend (1992) reported students preferring large classes for educationally dysfunctional reasons such as the low expectation of involvement or even being able to skip class unnoticed. Phenomenological studies have also highlighted the way that students with unsophisticated conceptions of learning may prefer teacher-centred methods rather than the kind of active learning involved in small classes (Van Rossum and Taylor, 1987).

American evidence on the effects of class size on student performance

Evidence of a negative relationship between class size and performance on individual courses takes two main forms. First, there are experimental studies in which students studying the same course are taught in different size groups and learning outcomes are then measured at the end of the course or on subsequent courses. Second, there are studies of classroom interaction in classes of different sizes which measure various qualities of student learning behaviour.

An example of the first type of study is that of Raimondo *et al.* (1990). They studied student performance on introductory and intermediate courses by randomly allocating students to different sized introductory classes. Students in a large introductory class performed as well as did students in a small class. Furthermore, students who had studied in a large introductory class performed as well in a subsequent intermediate class that did not require higher level cognitive skills as did students who had initially studied in a small introductory class. However students from the large introductory class performed significantly less well on a subsequent theoretical intermediate course which required higher level cognitive skills. In addition Lewis and Dahl (1972) found that class size did not have a negative effect on student assessment performance involving multiple-choice questions but did have a negative effect on performance in essay questions.

An example of the second type of study is that of Mahler *et al* (1980). Studying medical student interaction in parallel discussion groups of different sizes they found that the quantity of interaction declined as group size increased, the length of interactions declined and the cognitive level of interaction declined. In classes of 16 most interactions concerned clarification of factual information whereas in classes of four most interactions involved analysis and evaluation. This study provides no evidence of the effects of class size on learning outcomes but if the quality of the learning process changes as markedly as this evidence reveals then one would expect outcomes to be at least qualitatively different following experience of larger classes.

It seems likely that the negative effects of class size of student performance become apparent when a deep approach is required, through demands for higher level learning outcomes or through interaction, but possibly not when only a surface approach is required.

UK evidence on student numbers, module enrolment and student performance

MacFarlane (1992a, 1992b) examined the performance of the university system in the UK over 20 years as student numbers increased dramatically. He showed that, despite worsening staff—student ratios and declining resources as well as dramatic increases in the number and diversity of students in higher education in the UK, the performance of the system, measured in terms of degree classifications, has apparently improved markedly. The proportion of students who gained an upper second or first-class degree increased from 29% in 1969 to 48% in 1989. It is still increasing. From the perspective of the system as a whole, or an institution as a whole, more students apparently leads to better, not worse performance.

Lindsay and Paton-Saltzberg (1987) analysed data from 1,516 modules at Oxford Polytechnic from 1981/2 to 1984/5 and found a large negative effect of module enrolment on student performance. The effect was particularly marked in Social Science where students in classes of less than 10 were found to stand more than twice the chance of gaining an A grade, more than twice the chance of gaining a B+ grade and only half the chance of gaining a C grade, than did students in classes of more than 50. These are substantial differences. From the perspective of individual courses, more students means worse performance.

These two types of evidence are apparently contradictory and paradoxical. Much closer examination of what is going on within classes of different sizes is necessary to resolve this paradox.

The research study

In order to examine the effects of class size on student performance we analysed student performance on every taught module in every subject area within the Modular Course at Oxford Brookes University over a period of ten years. This course provided an ideal context for such a study because it is large (the analysis involved over 250,000 student grades on over 5,000 modules), long established, stable and consistent in its structure and regulations and especially in its assessment regulations. Modules are of an equal size in terms of learning hours (or multiples of a standard size) and contribute equally to students' final degree classification. Any gross variations in grade distributions are carefully scrutinized by an examinations committee and, if necessary, moderated, reducing any local variations which would invalidate comparisons or introduce unwanted variables. Much of the required data, including student performance, is readily accessible on a computer student management system and other data is available in archived form.

The study has involved several stages.

1. The administrative data base has been analysed to identify global effects of module enrolment on average marks and grade distributions over time and the differences between subject areas.

2. Patterns of assessment have been analysed in relation to module enrolment, student performance and changes over time in different subject areas.

3. A modified version of the Course Experience Questionnaire (Ramsden, 1991) has been administered to all students on matched pairs of small and large modules in each of ten subject areas, followed up by depth interview with students and informal interviews with the teachers involved.

4. Follow-up studies have been initiated within selected subject areas, putting together findings from stages 1—3 and local insights to explore various aspects of student learning in large classes within the different subject areas involved.

5. Parallel studies are being conducted at other universities with large modular courses where the effects of class size on student performance are an issue.

Preliminary findings of Stages 1 and 2 and the results of a pilot for Stage 3 were reported at the 1994 Improving Student Learning Symposium and advice was generated by Symposium participants concerning further analyses required and how to use this kind of research to improve student learning in large classes. A number of significant aspects of this advice have been acted upon and a fuller overall picture and further studies are reported below.

Module enrolment and student performance

Linear regression analysis was used to estimate the effects of module enrolment on average marks after allowing for differences between subject areas and for changes over time. It was found that module enrolment had a statistically significant effect on mean module marks after allowing for subject and year ($\beta = 21.95$, $df = 6,062$, $p < 0.001$). 42% of students on modules with less than 20 students gain grades of A or B+ compared with 34% of students on modules with enrolments of more than 70. A student is over 50% more likely to gain a C or F grade in a module of over 70 (Gibbs *et al.*, unpublished). These differences are not as marked as in the early 1980s by Lindsay and Paton-Saltzberg (ibid., p. 218). Fearnley (1995) has reported substantial differences between subject areas in the size of the relationship, but from a smaller data base and without taking into account the effect of increase in module size over time. These differences were again found here. Some subject areas had very substantial correlations between module enrolment and student performance (in excess of @ minus.5) with regression slopes showing a decline of 1% in average marks for each addition of as few as 12 students.

Coursework assessment and student performance

One of the most important differences between small and large enrolment modules is the pattern of assessment. Characteristically, expensive assessment methods have only been retained in small enrolment modules. At Oxford Brookes University there is a small but significant negative correlation between module enrolment and proportion of coursework assessment ($r = $ @ minus.12, $p < .001$): large enrolment modules use less coursework assessment. Modules with less than 30 students were almost twice as likely to have more than 75% coursework assessment than modules with more than 70 students, and only half as likely to have over 75% examination assessment (Gibbs and Lucas, unpublished).

The proportion of coursework assessment was found to be significantly correlated with student performance. Modules with more coursework produced higher average marks ($r = .36$, $p < .0001$) and subjects areas which contained courses with more coursework produced higher average marks ($r = .65$, $p < .0001$). Students are 51% more likely to gain a B+ grade on modules with 100% coursework than on modules with 100% examination, and only a third as likely to fail.

It seems that one of the main reasons students perform less well in large enrolment modules is that they are more likely to be assessed in a way that produces lower marks.

As student performance is worse on large enrolment modules a regression analysis was undertaken on the relationship between proportion of coursework assessment and average marks taking module enrolment into account. It was found that an effect of proportion of coursework on average marks exists independently of the effect of module enrolment (β= 15.99, $p < .00001$).

The proportion of coursework assessment contributing to students' marks has increased enormously over the past decade: from about 25% to about 75%. The size of the effect of this increase in coursework on average marks is sufficient to explain much of the increase in student marks for the entire modular course over the decade. If it had not been for this change in pattern of assessment the increase in module enrolments over the decade would presumably have led to a substantial overall decrease in performance.

Students' experience of small and large enrolment modules

Analysis of the quantitative data on module enrolment and performance does not tell us why students perform less well in larger enrolment modules and in modules with less coursework assessment or how students experience large modules. To explore this further we used a modified version of the 'Course Experience Questionnaire' (CEQ) (Ramsden, ibid.) supported by depth interviews. The CEQ was designed to identify those features of teaching of degree courses which were crucial to the quality of student learning. This questionnaire was specifically designed to be used as a performance indicator for courses. We needed to explore differences between individual modules within courses and simply replaced the word 'course' with the word 'module' on the questionnaire wherever appropriate and renamed it the Module Experience Questionnaire (MEQ).

In order to compare students' experience of small and large modules the MEQ was administered to 1,119 students studying matched pairs of small and large second and third-year modules in each of ten subject areas. The average enrolment of 'small' modules was 21 and that of 'large' modules 91. The return rate for the questionnaires was 69% for the 'small' modules and 53% for the 'large' modules.

The MEQ measures the following features of courses: good teaching, clear goals and standards, appropriate workload, appropriate assessment and student independence. These variables are likely to be affected by class size in the following ways.

Good teaching

Research evidence (Feldman *et al.*, ibid; Woods *et al.*, 1974) suggests that students will rate teaching less well in large classes.

Clear goals and standards

In smaller classes it is easier to negotiate and clarify goals and for students to check informally with tutors when they are unclear about goals and standards. It is predicted that smaller classes would have clearer goals and standards.

Appropriate workload

It is easier for teachers to calibrate task demands and workloads appropriately when they meet their students regularly and know how they are getting on. It is common when contact is limited to load students up with tasks to try and fill their independent study time. It is predicted that smaller classes would have a more appropriate workload.

Appropriate assessment

Assessment of large modules tends to involve exams, multiple choice questions and other mechanical methods involving little formative feedback and often measuring the achievement of low-level goals. Where the form of assessment does involve qualitative feedback the resulting marking loads often result in the feedback being very delayed. It is predicted that smaller classes would be perceived as having more appropriate assessment.

Student independence

Large classes are often characterized by strong central specification of assignments and reading, less opportunity to negotiate to meet individual interests or contexts and generally more teacher control and less student independence. It is predicted that smaller classes would have more student independence.

All the above hypotheses were confirmed (see Table 1). Students' perceptions of the 'small' modules were found to be more positive than that of the matched 'large' modules for every scale on the MEQ (t-tests, $p < .01$ in each case). Visual comparison with the norms from the CEQ (Ramsden, ibid.) shows the range of average MEQ scores for large and small modules to encompass the CEQ norms for every scale so it is unlikely that the sample of modules is atypical.

Table 1   *Comparison of ten 'small' and ten 'large' modules scores on the sub scales of the Module Experience Questionnaire (n = 1,119) together with norms from the CEQ (Ramsden, 1991)*

Module size	Average enrolment	Good teaching	Clear goals and standards	Appropriate workload	Appropriate assessment	Student independence
Large	91	3.2	3.0	2.8	3.3	2.6
Small	21	3.7	3.5	3.2	3.6	2.9
CEQ norms		3.2	3.3	2.9	3.3	2.6

Students' experience of large modules in this study was clearly inferior to their experience of small modules and this was reflected in interview transcripts. A number of students from each module volunteered to take part in the study and 30—40 minute interviews were undertaken. The interviews used questions on the MEQ as a prompt and then explored the students' experience of small and large modules more openly. The following extracts from transcripts illustrate the differences between students' experience of small and large modules in relation to each of the MEQ scales.

Good teaching

Large modules:

. . . he had a little timetable up on his door and he had about five blocks of time and if you got there quick enough you could put down your name. But he didn't seem to be around that much.

I think feedback is fairly limited . . . it would be nice to have an opportunity to discuss with staff more exactly what could have been improved because you could always have made things better even if you got a good mark.

I didn't have any tutorials I don't think. I suppose you could have gone and seen them but . . . you could see them at the end of the lectures I suppose. But I don't know of any of the times you could have gone and seen them.

Small modules:

It worked out quite well because not everyone wanted to talk to him at the same time in the practical classes and you could actually get to see him quite a lot when you wanted to.

It was in small groups . . . It was more sort of informal seminars rather than structured lectures . . . so it meant that you could actually ask more questions and it was more interactional. Most of it was sort of group work and . . . it wasn't actually that the person that was teaching us stood up there and sort of told us everything.

There was also scope for grabbing them in the break or after the session to talk about it if you were worried. There is always scope for that. It's nice to know that they've got enough time to answer questions.

Clear goals and standards

Large modules:

With regard to the coursework . . . he said on day 1 of week 1 this is the coursework. Write an essay on whatever . . . and then just hand it in. You don't get criteria of how it's marked so you're left in limbo.

. . . it was still a little bit of write down all that I know and hopefully it will be what he'll like . . . I don't think we had any criteria or anything, given a % of how the marks were going to go.

I felt that the practical staff didn't know any more . . . than us actually . . . I mean I spent a lot of time up there on the assignments and you'd have a problem and you'd be stuck because you couldn't find anyone that could help you.

This term it's quite difficult to understand . . . they've given no real guidelines, there's nothing specifically written down to say how we want it or what the critiques . . . or what the people marking . . . you were a bit unsure as to what you should be writing ..

Small modules

There were a few sessions when at the beginning they went round and said what are you doing your essay on. There was also scope for grabbing them in the break or after the session to talk about it if you were worried.

You get a lot of feedback on work you've done so for example, if you're sat there and you've got so far . . . then they are quite happy to sit there and spend 15 minutes with you . . . also having some kind of clinic or office hour or whatever you want to call it enables you to go and talk through work that you may have done, things that you may not have understood.

Appropriate workload

Large modules:

Well the exam's coming up next Saturday and up till now we've been working flat out. They seem to squash everything in so quickly and it all seems to be over before you know where you are and there isn't enough time at the end of it all to sort of compile your thoughts and get down to learning the stuff for the exam.

Small modules:

The coursework was fine. You had enough time to do it in.

It was a sod of an essay to write but it wasn't too much.

Appropriate assessment

Large modules:

It needs to be a bit more active. At the moment you just sort of turn up and you write notes in lectures and just sit quietly in the seminar and take notes . . . and then in week 10 everyone is cramming all this information into their heads.

I think you could do some cramming for the exam and get away with it because there's only seven lectures to learn . . . they're really bulky lectures . . . and there is actually quite a lot to learn. But I suppose you could get away with cramming.

Small modules:

I thought it had a good balance of implementation of a practical subject but also assessing other things as well.

You had to apply a certain amount of work to doing the (coursework). My first piece of work took a good 20 hours and the second piece was similar . . . so its physically impossible to pass the module and not do the things, so you can't just swot at the end, get through and forget everything . . .

Student independence

Large modules:

I've never really thought about you getting a choice of what you learn in the module. You pick the module and then that is what you learn. Whatever comes under it you learn it.

The coursework . . . essentially the format had to be the same and you couldn't interpret it too much. The first one it was basically saying this is the system that we want you to build and operate this, this and that . . . But there wasn't that much choice . . .

. . . it was all chosen for you. They chose a seminar group which you're meant to go in and they chose the article you had to read so you didn't have much option . . .

We don't have any choice . . . Well the coursework is six questions and you have to do those six questions. It's not like an essay it's just those six questions . . .

Small modules:

The whole course is like that it's very much self directed to what you want to look into. I mean if you've got particular areas of interests then you are able to look at those which is good.

It wasn't laid out . . . the coursework you had to design a window interface as opposed to having to type in commands . . . For the actual programme you could do anything as long as it was relevant to the topics the course was on.

We were given free rein. We had to choose a disorder and write about it. Yeah a huge choice.

It is very noticeable how much the assessment system dominates students' perceptions of almost every feature of the module and especially their perceptions of clarity of goals and standards, workload and independence. This underlines the importance of the differences in patterns of assessment between small and large modules identified in the previous stage of the research.

Students' approach in small and large modules

The MEQ includes surface and deep approach scales and can identify the extent to which students are adopting a surface and a deep approach to a module overall. It was found that students adopted a surface approach to a significantly greater extent on the large modules ($t = 3.38$, $p < .01$). Students adopted a deep approach to a greater extent on small modules, though this difference was not significant. The following quotes illustrate the approach students were taking. Again the assessment system and its perceived demands dominated their approach.

Surface approach

Large modules:
It's all meant to be based on what they've given us in the lectures so basically I'm just going to be spending a lot of time just picking up the facts from textbooks . . .

I try to understand a lot of the physiology and things like that but it's quite difficult sometimes and a lot of it is just memorising it all and being able to write it down on the day.

They want you to be critical but you've still got to be putting down facts. You are usually regurgitating everything you remember . . . about it and writing it down and hoping there's some marks in there somewhere.

Deep approach

Small module:
Just reading things off you'd get marks but if you could actually cross reference the different principles you'd get extra marks for showing understanding. It was more than just learning textbooks you had to show understanding.

Students' approach and course perceptions

Do students' reactions to the features of modules identified in the MEQ influence their approach to study? Students' scores on each of the MEQ scales concerned with perceptions of modules were correlated with their scores on the deep and surface approach scales. Every positive feature of modules was found to correlate positively with the extent to which students took a surface approach and negatively with the extent to which they took a deep approach (see Table 2, $p < .05$ in every case). The correlations between surface approach scores and module perceptions are higher than those between deep approach and module perceptions. The approach students take was closely linked with their perceptions of the modules they were studying: positive reactions appear to foster a deep approach and negative reactions a surface approach.

Table 2   *Relationship between students' perceptions of modules and the extent to which they took a deep and surface approach (n = 1,119)*

Approach size	Good teaching	Clear goals and standards	Appropriate workload	Appropriate assessment	Student independence
Deep	+.25	+.15	+.16	+.24	+.25
Surface	-.30	-.39	-.47	-.35	-.27

Students' approach and performance

The findings above show that students who have a more negative experience of large modules, take a surface approach to a greater extent in large modules, and take a deep approach to a lesser extent and a deep surface approach to a greater extent where their experience is positive. But does the approach they take make any difference to their marks? Both in a pilot study involving 281 students (but with a modest return rate of 30%) and in a sample of 144 students from the main study, students' scores on the surface and deep approach scales were correlated with their marks on the modules concerned. In each case there was found to be a small but significant negative correlation between the extent to which students took a surface approach and their marks ($r = @$ minus.31, $p < .01$; $r = @$ minus.17, $p < .05$): students who took a surface approach to a greater extent did less well. In each case there was also a very small positive correlation between the extent to which students took a deep approach and their marks, though these correlations were not significant.

This suggests that the approach students take makes a difference, though not all that much difference to their performance. However it is difficult to interpret these findings because larger modules use different forms of assessment than small modules, and in particular they use exams to a greater extent and coursework to a lesser extent. It may be that taking a surface approach in revising for exams is an adequately successful strategy on some large modules, as suggested in some of the interview extracts.

Variations between subject areas in student learning in large classes

While the findings reported above are fairly clear-cut the modest size of the correlations involved suggest that only a small proportion of the variance in student performance is accounted for by module enrolment alone. There is clearly a great deal else contributing to variance in performance. In particular there are large differences between subject areas, most of which were found to be stable over a decade, indicating distinctive and consistent patterns of teaching and learning. Even within subject areas individual disciplines display markedly different patterns of performance in relation to class size. For example within Social Science, while three subject areas displayed correlations between module enrolment and performance of @ minus.41, @ minus.44 and @ minus.53 respectively, a fourth subject area displayed no relationship at all: @ minus.01. These differences are not due to different student groups: many students would have been studying modules across subject boundaries and in particular students commonly combined the two subject areas with the two most extreme correlations. It is useful to understand how some subject areas avoid the negative effects of large classes most others experience. Studies undertaken collaboratively with lecturers in two subject areas, identified as A and B, are reported here as a contrast.

Students' performance in and experience of large classes in Subject A

Student performance in all 158 taught modules in subject A from 1984—94 was analysed along with module enrolment, the proportion of coursework assessment and the proportion of student learning time spent in class (as described in course documentation). Student numbers and class sizes increased markedly over the decade with three times as many modules enrolling more than 70 students in 1994 as in 1984 and only a third as many enrolling less than 20 students. The average proportion of coursework assessment increased from 35% to 79%. The proportion of total student learning time designed to be spent in class fell from 33% to 23%. Overall average marks remained unchanged over the decade, unlike for Subject A nationally over the same period which experienced a substantial increase in the proportion of good degrees (Chapman, 1994). It was found that there was no effect of module enrolment on student performance (B = +.10, n.s., multiple regression taking year and proportion of coursework into account). This is a very unusual pattern of performance.

Unlike the Modular Course at Oxford Brookes University as a whole, and unlike other Social Science subjects in particular, there was no tendency for large enrolment modules to use less coursework (B = +.22, n.s.; multiple regression taking year into account). Indeed every large module in Subject A used 100% coursework in 1994. In examining the methods Subject A had adopted as class sizes increased we began to understand some of the teaching, learning and assessment dynamics which have made Subject A so unusual.

Some of the larger enrolment modules had been broken down into smaller workshop groups and students did not experience a 'large class' even where module enrolment was large. To compensate for reductions in lectures there had been an increase in the use of learning packages and extensive course guides referring to a wider range of library and other reading resources. To compensate for an overall reduction in class contact time students' independent learning skills had been developed through a special first-year module and through a comprehensive skill development programme running through every module. To compensate for a reduction in the frequency of small-group teaching, much independent learning was undertaken in groups where students interacted without a tutor present. To compensate for less supervision of project work more projects were undertaken in groups and 'peer-supervised'. To compensate for larger seminar groups workshop-type methods had been introduced which involve sub-groups interacting actively despite large overall class size. And to help cope with increases in marking load, self and peer assessment methods had been introduced and extended and other economical ways developed of maintaining the volume of student work while retaining feedback to students in one form or another.

The effect of these changes in methods was identified by using the MEQ within a small and large module in Subject A. The large module, with 77 students, was found to have students taking a deep approach to a significantly greater extent than on the small module with 15 students ($t = 2.12$, $p < .05$): the only example we have identified of such a counter-intuitive pattern.

It has taken an enormous effort to introduce these changes and operating the current form of modules is more complex than previously and highly demanding. The introduction of each new major revision to the Subject A degree involved so much change that it was initially very disruptive with negative correlations between module enrolment and performance in the first two years of each five-year cycle of review (Gibbs *et al.*, 1995). It seems extremely unlikely that the success in improving student learning in large classes reported here could have been achieved without these extensive changes in process. Subject A was judged 'Excellent' in the Higher Education Funding Council's external Quality Assessment of Teaching.

Students' performance in and experience of large classes in Subject B

Subject B, within the same School as Subject A, experienced a similar rise in student numbers over the decade, with an increase in average module enrolment of 71%. However there had not been the same kinds of changes in teaching and assessment methods. While the overall proportion of coursework assessment had increased, examinations had been retained (or reverted to) in large classes and sometimes contributed 100% of the marks. The proportion of student time spent in class halved, from 45% to 22%. This means that while in 1984 each hour of class time was required to support about one hour of independent learning time, in 1994 it was required to support about three hours. However the nature of the teaching changed relatively little in order to achieve this, except that there was less of it, particularly in large enrolment modules, some of which had no seminar sessions at all. Perhaps not surprisingly in this context there was a large negative correlation between module enrolment and student performance of @ minus.44. Twice as many students in modules enrolling more than 70 gained grades of C or F ('Fail') as in modules enrolling under 20. Average marks dropped 1% for each additional 20 students on a module.

As module enrolment had increased so significantly and module enrolment was associated with such marked negative effects on student performance one might have expected overall performance to have declined over the decade. It had not. An obvious possibility was that there had been grade inflation and that this had covered up an overall decline in the quality of student learning. Subject B is now undertaking research into its marking standards to see if they have changed over the decade. A set of ten final-year student dissertations from 1984 and another 10 from 1994, with similar means, is being marked, and ranked on a series of scales, by a panel of internal markers and external examiners. If this study does indeed identify lower standards in 1994 than in 1984 then lecturers in Subject B will need to start examining aspects of their teaching and assessment methods. They may be able to learn from Subject A.

How can student learning be improved in large classes?

Our earlier work on student learning in large classes had involved student interviews and observations (cf. Gibbs and Jenkins, 1992) and the description and analysis of teaching and assessment options available to lecturers in coping with large classes (cf. Gibbs, 1992). It led to a very large scale national educational development project which included the training of nearly 9,000 lecturers (Gibbs, 1995). The most powerful conceptual tool which emerged from this work was a table, reproduced below, which summarized the way two contrasting strategies addressed the most common problems experienced by students in their learning in large classes.

Table 3

Problem area resulting from large classes	Characteristic methods adopted	
	Control strategies	Independence strategies
1 Lack of clarity of purpose Highly structured courses	Use of objectives	Use of learning contracts Problem-based learning
2 Lack of knowledge of progress	Objective testing Programmed instruction and CAL	Development of student judgement Self assessment
3 Lack of advice on improvement	Assignment attachment forms Automated tutorial feedback	Peer feedback and peer assessment
4 Inability to support reading	Use of set books Use of learning packages	Development of students' research skills More varied assignments
5 Inability to support independent study	Structured projects Lab guides Learning teams	Group work
6 Lack of opportunity for discussion	Structured lectures Structured seminars and workshops	Student-led seminars Team assignments
7 Inability to cope with variety of students	Pretests plus remedial material Self-paced study (PSI)	Variety of support mechanisms Negotiated goals
8 Inability to motivate students	Frequent testing High failure rates	Contracts, problem solving Group work

However while this conceptual framework formed the basis of much advice and training, and guided much consultancy work, it had little or no basis in research evidence concerning student learning in large classes. Our research is now bringing us back to this framework with new insights.

The first Improving Student Learning Symposium included a paper concerning the introduction of resource based learning in a degree programme (Blackmore and Harries-Jenkins, 1994). One large module which was part of this study, which enrolled 228 students, introduced extensive specially prepared resource materials and greatly reduced class and staff contact time involving one lecture every three weeks and supporting 'surgery' times, assessed with an exam after ten weeks. This course involved a number of the features listed in the 'control' column above such as use of objectives, a high degree of structure and the use of learning packages. It succeeded in reducing the average mark by 5% and more than doubling the failure rate. Students were found progressively to adopt an extreme surface approach and progressively to abandon a deep approach to studying the module. The factors the authors identified, from diaries, interviews and questionnaires, to explain this phenomenon, included those commonly identified by research to be associated with such problems (cf. Gibbs, 1992): an excessive workload, inappropriate and anxiety provoking assessment and a lack of opportunity for discussion.

In contrast 'Subject A' above had employed many of the methods in the 'independence' column in the table above and succeeded in fostering a deep approach to a greater extent in the large enrolment module studied than in the small enrolment module as well as producing at least as good student performance in large modules as in small modules. Both these contexts exploited resource based learning, but in a very different way: one to control students and one to support independent learning. Such methods can be emancipatory, releasing student potential to help compensate for resource problems, or restricting, reducing students to passive consumers meeting external requirements. Subtle features of course design can make all the difference (cf. Percival and Gibbs, 1994). It is not so much the specific methods lecturers adopt but the rationale for their adoption and the way students perceive these methods, which makes the difference. The 'control' strategies hold out the promise of managing large classes but the 'independence' strategies are probably necessary for quality in student learning. Perhaps we knew all along how to improve student learning in large classes but now we understand why a little better.

Provisional conclusions about using research to improve student learning in large classes

Our research is continuing and we have hardly begun to work with lecturers within subject areas to exploit and go beyond these findings to improve their students' learning. Nevertheless some provisional conclusions can be drawn:

- Students tend to perform less well in large classes, very much so in some subject areas. They perceive every course feature studied (Good Teaching, Clear Goals and Standards, Appropriate Workload, Appropriate Assessment, Student Independence) less positively in large classes than in small classes.

- Students take a surface approach to a greater extent in large classes and this helps to explain poorer performance in large classes as students who take a surface approach to a greater extent perform less well.

- Large classes tend to use less coursework assessment and this on its own helps to explain students' poorer performance in large classes as courses with less coursework produce poorer performance.

- It is possible to overcome many of the effects of increases in student numbers through changes in course delivery, teaching, learning and especially assessment methods. The study of exceptions to common patterns proved invaluable in identifying the key changes. The scale of change necessary may be disruptive in the short term.

- It is very valuable to use student performance data and to exploit existing administrative data bases in order to research student learning in large classes. Those within subject areas we have worked with were unaware of the large-scale effects our analyses identified even though they themselves had generated the data and had easy access to it — they had simply never analysed the data themselves. Sometimes they will not believe such analyses and will check them — which is productive. Sometimes the findings will prove to be the results of confounding variables and identifying what these are represents progress in understanding what is going on and gaining some control over it. Either way the raw data almost always provides an irresistibly engaging starting point for working with lecturers in researching their practice.

- Raw data concerning marks and class sizes needs to be combined with qualitative data, especially from case studies of individual courses and subject areas, if it is to be interpreted with insight. The conceptual framework concerned with students' approaches to studying and course perceptions proved very powerful in interpreting such qualitative data.

- The crude measure 'module enrolment' accounted for at most 28% of the variance in student performance and usually much less. There is a great deal going on which we either cannot measure or do not yet know how to measure. Discussing what these other variables might be, through exploring local idiosyncrasies and perceptions with the lecturers directly involved, is a valuable process.

- While it is possible to identify broad effects of class size across entire degrees or even institutions, differences between courses and subject areas are an important source of insight. It can be difficult to recognize what is going on within an individual course without reference to alternatives, especially for those who teach within that individual course. Lecturers from Subject B might not have considered their data all that surprising had not evidence from their colleagues' modules from Subject A been so profoundly different.

- Assessment (both formative and summative) and its effects on student learning behaviour are at the heart of making sense of student learning in large classes. Almost all students, in their interviews, referred to features of the assessment in discussing their learning within a module and they did so frequently, without prompting and with considerable awareness. Assessment is clearly something which very easily goes wrong in large classes and manipulating the assessment is clearly a powerful way of reorienting students' learning in large classes.

- The CEQ is a valuable tool which can readily distinguish between small and large classes and the ways they are perceived and experienced by students. It is easy to use, score and interpret and provides a simple framework for interviewing students.

- The kind of findings reported here have implications for institutional policy (e.g. about module enrolments and assessment regimes) as well as for lecturers selecting teaching and assessment methods. There are currently parallel studies under way at London Guildhall, concentrating on analysis of their modular course data base, and at Anglia Polytechnic University, concentrating on students' experience of small and large modules, both using almost identical methodologies to those described here. We suspect it will be the comparison of Oxford Brookes with other universities which will engage senior management in policy review.

References

Blackmore, M. A. and Harries-Jenkins, E. (1994) Open learning: the route to improved learning. In G. Gibbs (ed.), Improving Student Learning: Theory and Practice. Oxford: Oxford Centre for Staff Development.

Chapman, K. (1994) Variability of degree results in geography in United Kingdom universities 1973—1990: preliminary results and policy implications. *Studies in Higher Education* 19(1), 89—101.

Fearnley, S. (1995) Class size: the erosive effect of recruitment numbers on performance. *Quality in Higher Education* 1(1), 59—65.

Feigenbaum, E. and Friend, R. (1992) A comparison of freshman and upper division students' preferences for small and large psychology classes. *Teaching of Psychology* 19(1), 12—16.

Feldman, K. A. (1984) Class size and college students' evaluations of teachers and courses. *Research in Higher Education* 21(1), 45—93.

Gibbs, G. (1992a) *Problems and Strategic Options. Teaching More Students No 1.* Oxford: Polytechnics and Colleges Funding Council, Oxford Centre for Staff Development.

Gibbs, G. (1992b) *Improving the Quality of Student Learning.* Bristol: Technical and Educational Services.

Gibbs, G. (1995) National scale faculty development for teaching large classes. In A. Wright (ed.), *Successful Faculty Development*, Anker.

Gibbs, G. and Jenkins, A. (ed.) (1992) *Teaching Large Classes in Higher Education: How to Maintain Quality with Reduced Resources.* London: Kogan Page.

Gibbs, G. and Lucas, L. (1994) Does student performance suffer in large classes? *Teaching News*, Summer.

Gibbs, G. and Lucas, L. (1995) Coursework assessment, class size and student performance: 1984—1994.

Gibbs, G., Lucas, L. and Haigh, M. (in press) The impacts of course restructuring on student performance. *Higher Education Research and Development*, 14(2), 279–282.

Gibbs, G., Lucas, L. and Simonite, V. (in press) Class size and student performance: 1984—1994, *Studies in Higher Education*.

Lewis, D. and Dahl, T. (1972) Critical thinking skills in the principles course: an experiment. In A. Welsh (ed.), *Research Papers in Economic Education*. New York: Joint Council on Economic Education.

Lindsay, R. and Paton-Saltzberg, R. (1987) Resource changes and academic performance at an English polytechnic. *Studies in Higher Education* 12(2), 213—27.

MacFarlane, B. (1992a) The results of recession: students and university degree performance during the 1980s. *Research in Education* 49, 1—10.

MacFarlane, B. (1992b) The 'Thatcherite' generation and university degree results. *Journal of Higher Education* 16(2), 60—70.

Mahler, S., Neumann, L. and Tamir, P. (1986) The class-size effect upon activity and cognitive dimensions of lessons in higher education. *Assessment and Evaluation in Higher Education* 11(1), 43—59.

Percival, F. and Gibbs, G. (1994) *Course Design for Resource Based Learning in Technology.* Oxford: Oxford Centre for Staff Development.

Raimondo, H., Esposito, L. and Gershenberg, I. (1990) Introductory class size and student performance in intermediate theory courses. *Journal of Economic Education*, Fall, 369—81.

Ramsden, P. (1991) A performance indicator of teaching quality in higher education: the course experience questionnaire. *Studies in Higher Education* 16(2), 129—50.

Van Rossum, E. J. and Taylor, I. P. (1987) The relationship between conception of learning and good teaching: a scheme for cognitive development. American Educational Research Association Annual Meeting, Washington.

Wood, K., Linsky, A. and Straus, M. (1974) Class size and student evaluations of faculty. *Journal of Higher Education* 45(7), 524—34.

5 The impact of learning strategies on academic performance in an accounting undergraduate course

Angus Duff
Department of Economics and Management
University of Paisley

Introduction

Accounting is a popular choice of subject for undergraduate students with accounting courses offered as a first degree at 79 universities. Significantly, accountancy is a major employment destination for graduates, with over one in five graduates entering the accounting profession as trainee accountants. Typically students will seek traineeships with firms of chartered accountants, train as management or certified accountants with an industrial or commercial organization. A smaller number will work in public-sector organizations or local authorities and train as public finance accountants.

Chartered accounting firms have increased their share of the best graduates: in 1993/94 77% of the intake to the English Institute had a first-class or upper-second-class honours degree — compared to only 52% in 1988/89 (ICAEW, 1995). Interestingly, these employers chose to recruit non-relevant graduates at the expense of relevant graduates — nearly 80% of graduates recruited did not possess an accounting degree. Significantly Oxford and Cambridge universities who offer no accounting courses, provided 247 and 214 recruits respectively while the entire new university and college sector could provide only 337. This is despite the majority of accounting students being located in the new universities. Overall, the old university sector provided 90% of the total graduate trainee intake. While industrial and commercial employers are more flexible in their attitudes to the recruitment of graduates who train for other accounting qualifications, progression rates for these qualifications are typically much lower with the requirement on students to study for a demanding professional qualification in their own time.

Despite a ready supply of accounting graduates, accounting firms would appear to value the liberal traditions of old universities over the vocational and technocratic nature of the new universities. Given this selection criterion for entrants to the profession, a casual observer might imagine that employers (or their representatives in the accounting professional bodies) have little influence in determining the accounting undergraduate curriculum. This is not the case, with the professional bodies Board of Accreditation of Educational Courses (BAEC) responsible for reviewing the content, pedagogy and assessment procedures used in accounting undergraduate courses. Institutions are rewarded for following the BAEC's accreditation guidelines by providing exemptions for their students from individual institutes' professional examinations. Interestingly, despite the 'benefit' to students of having followed an accredited course, accounting students typically perform worse than non-relevant graduates in professional examinations.

Whatever the selection criteria employed by accounting employers, criticism of the accounting curriculum has been widespread.

Professional accounting education and its role in shaping the undergraduate curriculum

Todays's student and tommorrow's practitioners are saturated with a litany of rules and procedures that are supported by little other than expedient reasoning, ad hoc explanations and piecemeal rationalizations. Professional accounting education is certainly not a talkshop for exploring the meaning of social existence: rather it resembles a rote-learning process in which students are inculcated with the profession's party line by pendantic [sic] and legalistic methods.
(Tinker, 1985, p. xx)

In the US, Australia, New Zealand and the UK there have been calls to change both the accounting curriculum and the way in which it is taught. In the US, the AAA's Bedford Committee has been a driving force in the process of change, recommending the development of students' *learning to learn* as a primary objective (AAA, 1986). A subsequent paper issued by the largest accounting firms (the 'Big-Eight') in the US (Arthur Andersen *et al.*, 1989) called for broader intellectual development and change in the way accounting students are taught.

To implement the changes recommended by the Bedford Committee and the Big-Eight firms, the AAA formed the Accounting Education Change Commission (AECC). To date the AECC has issued five *Issues Statements* and two *Position Statements* to address relevant accounting education issues and to facilitate universities and colleges implementing changes in accounting education. In particular, the AECC has been influential in promoting the need to produce independent learners with good communication and interpersonal skills (Mathews, 1994).

Similar changes have been proposed in Australia by the Task Force for Accounting Education in Australia (Birkett, 1989) and the subsequent government-sponsored review of undergraduate accounting education identified a general lack of experimentation and innovation in teaching methods (Mathews, 1990). New proposals to include additional non-accounting and non-business studies subjects are likely to lead to an extension of the accounting programme by one year to a total of four years. The New Zealand Society of Accountants is changing from an emphasis on accounting and finance (with a reduced elective component) to four-year courses with greater emphasis on electives in the first two years.

In the UK calls have been made for education programmes that are broad and innovative rather than narrow and traditional (ICAEW, 1986, 1987 and 1993; Lothian, 1986). The UK is different in one important respect to these countries: the accounting profession recruits the majority of its trainees from non-accounting disciplines. Accounting has typically lacked academic status and prestige in the UK, being a relatively recent addition to the university curriculum. Up to 1957 only three full-time professorial chairs in accounting existed in English universities and two part-time chairs in Scotland. By 1912 only the universities of Birmingham, Leeds, Liverpool, Manchester and the London School of Economics offered an accounting element (Edwards, 1989). Since then the position has changed dramatically, with accounting degrees offered at 72 universities and seven colleges of higher education in the UK (UCAS, 1995). While Tinker's (1985) comments were directed at US education programmes, in the UK, professional accounting education places a similarly high premium on the passive acquisition of prodigious quantities of pre-packaged knowledge (see Sikka, 1987 and Ward and Salter, 1990). Despite the growth of accounting as an academic subject and the changing nature of accounting education in other countries, the impact of accreditation has grown with universities being made more to be accountable to the professional bodies. Pleas from US accounting academics who have taught to a highly structured accredited curriculum, have been unheeded (see Zeff, 1989) and innovative accounting educators are faced with trying to provide intellectually demanding and personally relevant courses in an increasingly uncreative environment.

Approaches to study and research instruments

In the higher educational literature a general consensus exists that students exhibit a number of different approaches to learning that are dependent on the context, the content and the demands of the learning task (see, for example, Biggs, 1987; Ramsden, 1992). They adopt a 'deep' approach when acknowledging the more abstract forms of learning that are demanded in higher education (Svenson, 1977) and intrinsically motivated by the relevance of the syllabus (Fransson, 1977). A 'surface' approach is taken when they encounter an overloaded curriculum and methods of assessment which empathize superficial properties of the material that is to be learned (Dahlgren and Marton, 1978). Approaches to study are measured using Schmeck *et al.*'s (1977) Inventory of Learning Processes.

Dunn *et al.* (1977) assert that a person's learning orientation is perhaps the most important determinate of their educational attainment. A learning style is described as being:

> *a description of the attitudes and behaviour which determine an individual's preferred way of learning. (Honey and Mumford, 1992, p. 1)*

Honey and Mumford (1992) describe learning as occurring in two substantially different ways: through formal structured 'taught' activities and from experience, often in an unconscious defined way — 'experiential' learning. They consider learning to be a continuous, iterative process — a learning cycle consisting of four stages: experiencing, reviewing, concluding and planning. Most individuals develop a preference for certain stages over others which may lead to a distortion of the learning process so greater emphasis is placed on some stages to the detriment of others. Learning styles are learned as an individual repeats strategies and tactics that were found to be successful, with unsuccessful strategies discontinued. Learning styles are measured using the Learning Styles Questionnaire (LSQ), a self-administered inventory consisting of 80 questions, 20 for each of the four learning styles.

Hypotheses

This section sets out the hypotheses tested in the present study and provides an explanation of the underlying rationale. As described previously, the undergraduate accounting curriculum is largely prescribed by the BAEC. This has the effect of making undergraduate programmes look similar to those of the professional bodies and hence emphasize the acquisition of knowledge, rather than understanding and techniques, at the expense of concepts. Typically, the curriculum introduces new subjects in all three years to meet BAEC requirements. This creates a lack of continuity in the curriculum, with students being constantly required to learn new subjects rather than consolidate, look beyond and elaborate on existing knowledge. In summary, it is contended, the accounting curriculum does not emphasize depth or elaboration in its construction. Furthermore, as students progress through the degree programme it is imagined that students will adopt and be rewarded for a deep-elaborative information processing type. This would be facilitated by assessment methods that encourage the understanding of concepts, relating ideas to previous knowledge and experience, examine the logic of arguments and relate this to their own practical understanding. It is widely accepted that the learning approach adopted by a student will be a function of the students' perception of the nature and the requirements of the task (Ramsden, 1992; Biggs, 1987). It is suggested that the nature of the accounting curriculum prohibits this personal and intellectual development.

Previous research (Tan and Choo, 1990) has suggested that accounting students who adopt a deep-elaborative approach to study are likely to outperform those students who adopt a shallow-reiterative style. This is confirmed by studies of other students in higher education (see Schmeck and Grove, 1979; Watkins and Hattie, 1981). This study will examine the pervasiveness of these results by subject and year of study.

Other studies have suggested that a significant relationship exists between learning style preference and the type of learning activities employed. In the field of accounting education, a significant body of knowledge already exists (see Gow *et al.*, 1994).

Further studies have examined sex differences in the performance of accounting students (Lipe, 1989) with conflicting results. However, no reference in the literature can be found to suggest that sex differences exist in relation to approach to study. The present study will therefore test accounting students' performance by sex and determine whether there is any significant difference between the sexes with learning style preference and approaches to study.

Although mature students are said to be deficient in study skills a consistent suggestion in research using questionnaires and inventories in study processes is that mature students exhibit more desirable approaches to academic learning (Richardson, 1994). Explanations for this include: (1) mature students are more likely to be motivated by intrinsic goals (Thacker and Novak, 1991); (2) younger students acquire a surface approach to learning in the final year of secondary education (Harper and Kember, 1986; Marton and Sãljö, 1976); and (3) the prior life experience of mature students provides a deep approach towards studying in higher education (Harper and Kember, 1986). A recent investigation of approaches to studying and academic performance found mature students significantly more likely to adopt a deep approach to their academic work than their younger counterparts. Given that a relatively high proportion of students following the accounting degree course are mature students (around a quarter in each year being at least 25 years of age) the effects of age on performance and the interaction with other intervening and background variables are examined.

The supposed effects of these 'background' and 'intervening' variables on student performance has lead to the development of the following hypotheses:

Hypothesis 1:   There will be no significant difference in information processing type across the three years of the course

Hypothesis 2:   Students who adopt a deep-elaborative information processing type will not significantly out-perform students who adopt a shallow-reiterative style

Hypothesis 3:   Students taking subjects which represent a continuation of prior study who adopt a deep-elaborative information processing type will not significantly out-perform those who adopt a shallow-reiterative information processing type

Hypothesis 4:   Learning style preference will have no significant relationship with performance

Hypothesis 5:   Background variables such as age and sex will have no significant relationship with performance

Hypothesis 6:   There will be no interaction between information processing type, learning style, age and sex

Method and results

Data collection and treatment of data

At the start of the year students were asked to complete the Honey and Mumford's LSQ and Schmeck's ILP in successive weeks. Background variables were available from the institution's students records. The students' combined scores on the Deep and Elaborative subscales of the ILP were ranked in descending order and divided into two groups by a median split. Those who scored in the upper half were grouped as deep-elaborative processors and those who scored in the lower half were grouped as the shallow-reiterative processors. The means and standard deviations were calculated and are shown in Table 5.1. These results are consistent with Tan and Choo's (1990) results and Schmeck's (1981, p. 384) remarks that students tend to adopt either a deep-elaborative or shallow-reiterative approach to study. Using a K-sample median test, membership of the two groups is examined with respect to year. No significant difference is noted suggesting no difference in the approach to learning across the three years. This is confirmed by a one-way ANOVA on the means of scores on the deep-elaborative subscale of the ILP by year of study.

Given normally distributed marks for individual subjects and homogeneity of variance between sub-groups of the independent variables, an independent sample t-test was performed with sex and age as the independent variables and coursework mark as the dependent variable. The results are reported in Tables 5.1 and 5.2. In year 1, females tend to out-perform males, significantly in the case of two subjects. In years 2 and 3 this difference is eroded to be negligible or non-existent by year 3. Age is not a significant predictor of performance in year 1, despite sizeable numbers of students aged over 25, but becomes so for two subjects in year 2 and for four subjects in year 3.

Table 1   Performance by sex and t-test on difference in means

	Female	Male	t-statistic
YEAR 1			
Accounting	54.80	46.76	
Economics	48.75	39.05	
Management	55.75	49.41	
Business Law	53.53	44.00	*p>0.01*
Quantitative Analysis	65.70	54.18	*p>0.05*
Financial Markets	43.68	36.79	
Languages	55.42	56.00	
YEAR 2			
Financial Accounting	59.11	51.75	
Management Accounting	59.74	45.94	
Company Law	51.06	51.25	
I.T. Management	51.53	50.67	
Money and Financial Institutions	55.77	52.22	
Languages	50.00	65.00	
YEAR 3			
Advanced Accounting	50.21	49.65	
Financial Management	46.90	50.30	
Taxation	46.69	49.19	
Auditing	46.45	43.45	
Investment Theory and Analysis	48.95	50.15	
Languages	55.43	56.00	

Table 2   Performance by age group and one-way ANOVA/Bonferroni test on differences in means

	(1) 17–20	(2) 21–24	(3) 25+	Significance
YEAR 1				
Accounting	49.08	59.67	50.71	
Economics	42.58	51.17	44.29	
Management	49.54	59.33	58.57	
Business Law	49.18	52.60	47.43	
Quantitative Analysis	58.96	66.50	60.14	
Financial Markets	36.47	52.00	41.67	
Languages	57.50	59.00	52.80	
YEAR 2				
Financial Accounting	54.00	53.69	63.29	
Management Accounting	46.87	52.15	69.86	(3)>(2),p<0.05
Company Law	50.58	47.86	57.00	
I.T. Management	47.71	48.92	62.14	(3)>(2),p<0.05
Money & Financial Institutions	49.33	56.00	60.60	
Languages	43.00	51.75	76.00	
YEAR 3				
Advanced Accounting	45.33	47.50	56.59	(3)>(2),p<0.05
Financial Management	51.33	46.92	51.95	
Taxation	55.33	46.76	55.27	(3)>(2),p<0.05
Auditing	45.33	43.15	49.68	(3)>(2),p<0.05
Investment Theory & Analysis	60.00	47.00	56.58	(3)>(2),p<0.05
Languages	–	56.22	52.44	

When the performance of the two information processing types is examined with respect to subject mark and year, no relationship is found in year 1, a significant relationship in three subjects is found in year 2 in three subjects and in two subjects in year 3. In only one subject (Business Law in year 1) do learners adopt a shallow-reiterative approach out-perform their deep-elaborative counterparts, with a very negligible difference (0.37) between the means. Therefore we must reject hypothesis 2, as deep-elaborative learners do out-perform shallow-reiterative students. Instances of deep-elaborative learners out-performing shallow-reiterative learners only occur when the subject of study represents a clear continuation of prior studies. Consequently we must reject hypothesis 3.

Table 3   Performance by information processing type and t-test on difference
in means

	Deep-elaborative	Shallow-reiterative	Significance
YEAR 1			
Accounting	53.00	48.88	
Economics	48.15	39.76	
Management	54.60	50.76	
Business Law	49.16	49.53	
Quantitative Analysis	63.40	56.88	
Financial Markets	43.00	35.10	
Languages	56.67	54.40	
YEAR 2			
Financial Accounting	60.30	52.30	*p>0.01*
Management Accounting	61.67	47.25	*p>0.05*
Company Law	55.40	48.07	*p>0.05*
I.T. Management	53.33	49.42	
Money and Financial Institutions	56.11	53.08	
Languages	62.25	49.00	
YEAR 3			
Advanced Accounting	54.16	49.81	
Financial Management	52.29	45.71	
Taxation	53.12	48.62	
Auditing	47.80	46.76	
Investment Theory and Analysis	51.93	50.44	
Languages	56.67	54.40	

Pearson moment correlation coefficients were calculated to establish the relationship between learning style and performance. Only a weak relationship is found and the only significant relationship is noted for a year 3 subject (Auditing) with a negative correlation between performance and those students preferring an activist learning style. We must therefore accept hypothesis 4.

ILP score						
Activist	-0.073					
Pragmatist	0.163	*0.198				
Reflector	0.054	**-0.416	-0.021			
Theorist	**0.303	*-0.192	**0.357	**0.416		
Sex	0.030	0.144	*0.198	-0.066	0.024	
Age	*0.224	-0.130	0.142	-0.032	0.153	-0.128
	ILP score	Activist	Pragmatist	Reflector	Theorist	Sex

The interaction between approach to study, learning style, sex and age is examined by means of a Pearson moment correlation coefficient matrix — see Table 4 (above). Significant relationships are noted between learning style preferences — these relationships are well documented and expected (see Honey and Mumford, 1992). However, a significant relationship is noted between approach to learning (as measured by score on the deep-elaborative subscale of the ILP), age and a theorist learning style preference. The significant positive relationship between age and score on the deep-elaborative subscale of the ILP confirms the findings in the literature and consequently we must reject hypothesis 6.

The relationship between approach to study, and learning style preference and age is examined by means of a stepwise multiple regression model. Despite a relatively low goodness of fit statistic (adjusted R2 = 0.108), this is believed adequate for such a model using cross-sectional data. The beta weight (0.27) given to the theorist learning style preference is significant ($p > 0.01$) indicating a strong relationship between approach to learning and a theorist learning style preference. Again we must reject hypothesis 6.

Discussion

In all but one of the 19 subjects in the curriculum, students in the deep-elaborative group outperformed their shallow reiterative counterparts. This confirms the findings of previous studies.

As students progress through the degree programme, they begin to be rewarded for adopting a deep-elaborative approach to study. This is particularly notable in year 2 where students follow courses in Financial Accounting, Management Accounting and Company Law, which represent a continuation of first-year studies in Accounting and Business Law. As expected, the extended nature of these subjects allows deep-elaborative students to make good use of their superior approach to study, having progressed from subjects introduced for the first time, which by their nature can only encourage limited amounts depth and elaboration in learning. However, this trend barely extends to year 3 where students are rewarded for a deep-elaborative approach in only two subjects: Financial Management ($p < 0.05$) and Advanced Accounting (only at $p < 0.1$), subjects which represent a continuation of prior study in years 1 and 2. This confirms expectations that the nature of the prescribed curriculum forces faculty to introduce new subjects throughout the degree programme — which limits students' intellectual development at the expense of prodigious knowledge acquisition. Only very limited evidence suggests that sex is a predictor of performance and only in year 1. Age however is significant in determining performance with students aged

25 or over outperforming their younger counterparts in two subjects in year 2 and four subjects in year 3. The reasons for this are less clear: mature students are significantly more likely to adopt a deep-elaborative approach to study, although mature students out-perform their younger counterparts in different subject areas to those which reward a deep-elaborative approach. A possible explanation is that intervening variables (other than a deep approach to learning) such as motivation are present which significantly influence their performance.

Finally, the noted interaction between approach to study, theorist learning style preference and age is particularly interesting. While age is a significant predictor of performance, as students progress through the programme, only a limited interaction is found between age and approach to study in individual subject performance.

In the multiple linear regression model, examining the relationship between the three variables (with approach to study as the dependent), a highly significant beta weight is given to those favouring a theorist learning style preference. Despite this finding, no significant relationship is noted between theorists and performance in any of the 19 subjects. It is likely this is attributable to the study process complex being made up of situational as well as personological factors, while a learning style preference is wholly personological (see Biggs and Rihn, 1984). Previous studies of the relationships between various study methods self-report inventories such as the ILP and LSQ using the technique of canonical correlation suggest only limited relationships between the factors the instruments purport to measure, suggesting the self-report devices are not measuring the same processes in the domain of learning behaviours and strategies (Ribich and Schmeck, 1979). Teaching techniques employed on the course are typical of those used on other undergraduate courses (Brown and Guilding, 1993), placing heavy emphasis on lectures, great reliance on textbooks and a relatively low emphasis on seminar work (compared to other business disciplines). This paints a picture of major reliance on didactic modes of instruction at the expense of student discussion. It is suggested this emphasis is likely to favour logic, objectivity and certainty at the expense of subjectivity, lateral thinking and hence favour a theorist learning style preference.

Conclusions

On the basis of this study, substantial evidence exists to suggest those adopting a deep-elaborative approach to study are rewarded in a number of subjects as they progress through the accounting programme. However, this finding is rather unreliable, given the nature of the curriculum which continually introduces new subjects over its three years. It is contended that this is a fault of the restrictive, prescriptive practices of the professional bodies' BAEC which effectively imposes a curriculum on institutions. Typically, professional accounting has been described as placing a heavy emphasis on an overloaded syllabi and promote 'cramming' at the expense of learning — conditions said to encourage students to adopt a surface-reiterative approach to learning. To maintain the quality and numbers of students entering accounting degree programmes, departments are required to adopt this curriculum to ensure students receive the maximum number of exemptions from professional examinations. This imposition is detrimental to accounting students intellectual development and leaves those students entering the accounting profession at a disadvantage compared to their 'non-relevant' degree holding counterparts. Many accounting employers actively prefer to recruit non-relevant graduates, leaving many accounting graduates holding an academic qualification with limited intellectual and vocational currency.

The pedagogy of an accounting undergraduate programme favours those with a theorist learning style preference. While no direct relationship exists between performance and learning style preference, a significant relationship exists between those with a deep-elaborative approach to study and a theorist learning style preference. Given this relationship, the study supports findings in the literature to make accounting programmes broader, more innovative or, in terms of educational theory, to adopt teaching methods which suit those with non-theorist learning style preferences.

Given a move by many UK higher educational institutions towards a modular, rather than a programmatic degree structure, the curriculum is likely to become increasingly disaggregated, increasing the lack of continuity in the largely uniform accounting curriculum. Further research is needed to determine the pervasiveness of these findings in three particular areas: (1) how the curriculum can be restructured to improve accounting students' intellectual development; (2) how assessment methods can be introduced to encourage learners to adopt a deep-elaborative approach to learning; and (3) how teaching methods employed in an accounting degree programme can encourage those with non-theorist learning style preferences to adopt a deep-elaborative approach to learning.

References

AAA Committee on the Future Structure, Content, and Scope of Accounting Education (Bedford Committee) (1986) Future accounting education: Preparing for the expanding profession. *Issues in Accounting Education* 1(1), 168—95.

Arthur Andersen & Co., *et al*, (1989) *Perspectives on Education: Capabilities for Success in the Accounting Profession*. New York: Arthur Andersen & Co., Arthur Young, Coopers & Lybrand, Deloitte Haskins and Sells, Ernst & Whinney, Peat Marwick Main & Co., Price Waterhouse and Touche Ross.

Biggs, J. B. (1987) *Student Approaches to Learning and Studying*. Melbourne: Australian Council for Educational Research.

Biggs, J. and Rihn, B. A. (1984) The effects of intervention on deep and surface approaches to learning, in J. R. Kirby (ed.), *Cognitive Strategies and Educational Performance*. London: Academic Press Inc., 279—93.

Birkett, W. P. (1989) *The Demand for, and Supply of Education for Professional Accountants*. Sydney: Task Force for Accounting Education in Australia.

Brown, R. B. and Guilding, C. (1993) A survey of teaching methods employed in university business school accounting courses. *Accounting Education* 2(3), 211—18.

Dahlgren, L. O. and Marton, F. (1978) Students' conceptions of subject matter: an aspect of learning and teaching in higher education. *Studies in Higher Education* 3, 25—35.

Dunn, R., Dunn, K. and Price, G. (1977) Diagnosing learning styles: a practice for avoiding malpractice suits. *Phi Delta Kappan* 58, 418—20.

Edwards, J. R. (1989) *A History of Financial Accounting*. London: Routledge.

Fransson, A. (1977) On qualitative differences in learning: IV. Effects of intrinsic motivation and extrinsic test anxiety on process and outcome. *British Journal of Educational Psychology* **47**, 244—57.

Gow, L., Kember, D. and Cooper, D. (1994) The teaching context and approaches to study of accounting students. *Issues in Accounting Education* 9(1), 118—30.

Harper, G. and Kember, D.(1986) Approaches to study of distance education students. *British Journal of Educational Technology* **17**, 212—22.

Honey, P. and Mumford, A. (1992) *The Manual of Learning Styles*. Maidenhead: Peter Honey.

ICAEW Education and Training Directorate (1986) *Effective Education and Training for the 21st Century*. Institute of Chartered Accountants in England and Wales.

ICAEW Education and Training Directorate (1987) *Training the Business Professional*. Institute of Chartered Accountants in England and Wales.

ICAEW Education and Training Directorate (1993) Chartered accountant — the future of our qualification. *Accountancy*, October, 131—2.

ICAEW (1995) *Education, Training and Student Salary Statistics 1993/94*.

Lipe, M. G. (1989) Further evidence on the performance of female versus male accounting students. *Issues in Accounting Education* 4(1), 144—52.

Lothian, N. (1986) *The CA in the 1990s — An Educational Profile*. Institute of Chartered Accountants of Scotland.

Marton, F. and Säljö, R. (1976) On qualitative differences in learning: I. Outcome and process. *British Journal of Educational Psychology* **46**, 4—11.

Mathews, M. R. (1994) An examination of the work of the Accounting Education Change Commission 1989—1992. *Accounting Education* 3(3), 193—204.

Mathews, R. (1990) *Accounting in Higher Education*. Report of the Review of the Accounting Discipline in Higher Education 1. Canberra: Australian Government Publishing Services.

Ramsden, P. (1992) *Learning to Teach in Higher Education*. London: Routledge.

Ribich, F. D. and Schmeck, R. R. (1979) Multivariate relationships between measures of learning style and memory. *Journal of Research in Personality* **13**, 515—29.

Richardson, J. T. E. (1994) Mature students in higher education: I. A Literature survey on approaches to studying. *Studies in Higher Education* 19(3), 309—25.

Richardson, J. T. E. (1995) Mature students in higher education: an investigation of approaches to studying and academic performance. *Studies in Higher Education* **20**(1), 5—17.

Schmeck, R. R. (1981) Improving learning by improving thinking. *Educational Leadership*, February, 384—5.

Schmeck, R. R. (1983) Learning styles of college students. In R. F. Dillon and R. R. Schmeck (eds), *Individual Differences in Cognition*. New York: Academic Press, 233—74.

Schmeck, R. R. and Grove, E. (1979) Academic achievement and individual differences in the learning process. *Applied Psychological Measurement* 3, 43—9.

Schmeck, R. R., Ribich, F. D. and Ramaniah, N. (1977) Development of a self-report inventory for assessing individual differences in learning processes. *Applied Psychological Measurement* 1, 413—31.

Sikka, P. (1987) Professional education and auditing books: a review article. *British Accounting Review* 19(3), 291—304.

Svensson, L. (1977) On qualitative differences in learning: III. Study skill and learning. *British Journal of Educational Psychology* 47, 233—43.

Tan, K. and Choo, F. (1990) A note on the academic performance of deep-elaborative versus shallow-reiterative information processing students. *Accounting and Finance*, May, 67—81.

Thacker, C. and Novak, M. (1991) Student role supports for younger and older middle-aged women: application of a life event model. *Canadian Journal of Higher Education* 21, 13—36.

Tinker, T. (1985) *Paper Prophets — A Social Critique of Accounting.* London: Holt, Rinehart & Winston.

UCAS (1995) Universities and Colleges Admissions Service University and College Entrance 1996. London: Letts & Co./UCAS.

Ward, J. and Salter, M. (1990) Law for professional accounting education. *The Law Teacher* 24(3), 208—28.

Watkins, D. and Hattie, J. (1981) The learning processes of australian university students: investigations of contextual and personological factors. *British Journal of Psychological Measurement* 15, 384—93.

Zeff, S. (1989) Recent trends in accounting education and research in the USA: some implications for UK academics. *British Accounting Review* 21(1), 159—76.

6 Approaches to studying and undergraduate well-being

Nancy Falchikov and Karen Thomson
Department of Social Sciences
Napier University
Edinburgh EH10 5DT

Considerable evidence has accumulated from studies of stress in students (e.g. McWilliams and Gerber, 1978; Punch and Tuettennum, 1989 and anxiety in lecturers and teachers (e.g. Savoy, 1990; Dunham, 1984; Kyriacou, 1987) to show that negative well-being pervades the academic environment. Such findings emphasize the urgent need to address the problem of anxiety and stress in educational establishments. Negative effects of stress are costly, not only in economic terms, but also in terms of emotional and physical well-being, as a potential health hazard, and ultimately as being detrimental to the individual's quality of life.

Student stressors

At least two classes of stressor exist for students: the academic and the personal. Not unsurprisingly, the major stressors for students have been found to be academic in nature. For example, Archer and Lamnin (1985) and Sarros and Densten (1989) identified size and number of assignments and other aspects of the workload, together with examinations and class presentations as the most frequently listed stressors. Archer and Lamnin's students were also troubled by financial and career worries, as were students in Falchikov and Heron's (1992) pilot study.

Effects and measures of stress

The health implications of chronic stress, such as cardiovascular disease and psychiatric disturbance, are well known. Psychosocial factors have been established as contributing to many forms of physical illnesses ranging from cardiovascular disease (e.g. Friedman and Rosenman, 1974; Steptoe, 1981) to dermatological disorders (e.g. Engels, 1985). Psychiatric manifestations of prolonged, excess stress are apparent across the broad range of disorders, including depression (e.g. Rabkin, 1982) in addition to disease categories which are, by definition, the result of stressful events (APA, 1982, 1987). Towers (1984) (see Everly, 1989), in a comprehensive meta-analysis of reports investigating the relationship between psychosocial factors and disease, was led to conclude that 'psychological well-being seemed to be most closely associated with cardiovascular disease and infectious processes . . . although there was a significant relationship with all diseases except complications of pregnancy' (p. 51). Recent work in the area of psycho-immunology, which examines the immuno-suppressive effects of stress, extends the area of influence of stress and illness to embrace infectious and degenerative diseases (Solomon and Temoshok, 1987; Kiecolt-Glaser *et al.*, 1986).

Non-morbid consequences of stress which are of particular concern to educators include their effects on cognitive functioning and academic performance. There is some support for the view that high levels of anxiety and stress may impede activities involving cognitive processing such as that encountered during academic work and decision-making (e.g. Reason and Lucas, 1982; Kane, 1987 in Reason, 1988).

Further evidence of a link between cognitive performance and stress may be derived from an investigation contrasting the effects of different anxiety management techniques with students (Thompson *et al.*, 1980). Experimental groups were matched on their scholastic aptitude scores and anxiety levels before undergoing a programme of treatment designed to reduce levels of academic stress. In general, the trend of results at three-month follow-up was for the intervention groups to show elevations in grade point averages with concurrent decreases in trait and state anxiety scores relative to the non-treatment control subjects.

Learning styles and strategies

Student learning has been conceptualized as being either explicitly developmental in nature (e.g. Perry, 1970) or as consisting of preferred styles, strategies or approaches (e.g. Pask, 1976; Entwistle and Hanley, 1977—78; Marton and Saljo, 1984). Whereas a developmental model such as that proposed by Perry emphasizes and encourages change, the individual style or strategy approach may be more resistant to it. Pask (1976) claimed that students normally prefer one of two types of learning strategy which he termed 'holist' or 'serialist'. However, there are some 'versatile' individuals who can act in either way depending on circumstance. The relationship between holistic and serialist (or what Svensson (1977) calls 'atomistic') strategies and Marton and Entwistle's 'deep' and 'surface' approaches to learning is made explicit by Laurillard (1984). The holistic approach entails those activities Entwistle designates as deep processing: the search for meaning, intention and relationships between the material and wider contexts. Similarly, the atomistic or serialist strategy resembles the surface approach to learning. Entwistle (1987) describes the broadening of Marton's two main categories (deep and surface approaches) and the addition of a third approach, the strategic (after Miller and Parlett, 1974).

A recent study of student learning using phenomenographic techniques tended to support the individual difference view of learning styles and strategies. Prosser and Millar (1989) found that students who actively sought to change their conceptions of the subject matter tended to do so, whereas those who sought only to reproduce did not change. However, there is some evidence to suggest that approaches to learning are not immutable (e.g. Duckwall *et al.*, 1991).

Approaches to studying and performance

There have been a number of studies investigating how the approach to studying, or the learning style or strategy adopted or preferred by students may influence their academic performance. Miller *et al.* (1987) found that students with high Grade Point Averages (GPAs) scored significantly higher on deep processing than did the average or low GPA groups. In contrast, ineffective learners with poor achievement have been found to attempt to reproduce information through repetition and practice rather than by means of thoughtful analytic deep processing (Schmuck and Crove, 1979, referred to by Miller *et al.*, 1987). A more recent study of the approaches to learning by undergraduate medical students by Duckwall *et al.* (1991) found that 'comprehension learning' was the best indicator of students being 'on' or 'off' track one and a half years into the programme.

Stress and learning style

While there is a substantial body of research into the relationship between approaches to learning and performance, less is known about the association between learning style and stress. Both Falchikov and Heron's pilot study (1992) and the present replication were devised to explore the relationship between approach to learning and stress in undergraduates.

Method

In the pilot study, the 80-item Approaches to Studying Inventory (ASI) (Entwistle and Hanley, 1977—78; Entwistle and Ramsden, 1983) and the General Health Questionnaire (GHQ28) (Goldberg, 1978; Goldberg and Williams, 1988) were completed by groups of second- and third-year Biological Sciences students during 1993 as part of their psychology course ($n = 33$ and $n = 35$ students respectively). The Biological Sciences degree course at Napier is unusual, in that it contains one-third social science (psychology and sociology). Furthermore, it should be noted that all Scottish honours degrees are of four years' duration.

The more recent study involved a mixed group of students from a variety of courses who had chosen either 'Introduction to psychology' or 'Film studies' as 'elective' modules during semester 2, 1995 ($n = 81$). They were predominantly in their first year of study, with small samples from years two ($n = 11$) and three ($n = 11$). They, too, completed the ASI (38 item version) and the GHQ28, as part of a wider investigation.

Treatment of results

1. Cronbach's alpha was used as a measure of internal reliability of the sub-scales of the Approaches to Study Inventory.

2. GHQ items were summed to give an overall index of psychological well-being, with low scores indicating positive well-being and high scores negative well-being (scores above 5 were regarded as indicating moderate to high levels of psychological distress).

3. Students who favoured a particular approach were determined using two methods: a simple cut-off point (absolute measure) and a relative measure. The absolute cut-off point represented students 'agreeing somewhat' or 'agreeing' with each item in a scale, that is to say, achieving a score of >60 for the earlier pilot cohorts and >40 for the more recent replication. Percentages of students who scored highly on each sub-scale were calculated. The second method involved inspection of the frequency distribution and definition of the top third as 'high scorers' (Tait, 1995).

4. Pearson product moment correlations were calculated for approach to study and psychological well-being.

Results

Cronbach alpha scores for each sub-scale and each cohort were calculated. In all cases except the surface sub-scale in year 3(92), Cronbach alpha values were high or moderately high (between 0.74 and 0.82). In the case of the year 3(92) surface sub-scale, inspection of the correlation matrix indicated a number of negative correlations. Moreover, one item in particular appeared not to 'fit in' with the rest, namely item 57, 'I don't often think about why I'm doing a piece of work — I just get on with it.' If deleted, this item would reduce the scale variance by only a very small amount, and increase the alpha value to 0.5712.

Percentages of students who scored highly using the absolute cut-off

Data from both the 92 and 95 cohorts suggest that there may be developmental differences in ratings of preferences for some approaches. Scores on the deep sub-scale, for example, are higher in year 3(92) than in year 2(92), and again are greater in the year 3 sub-set of cohort 95 than in years 1 or 2. However, given the small numbers of students in sub-sets in the more recent cohort (year 2, $n = 11$; year 3 $n = 11$), it is unwise to draw firm conclusions.

If the percentages of students from each group who fell in to the negative well-being category are considered, it is interesting to note that the highest percentages for GHQ scores occurred in year 2 in both cohorts. These scores suggest that year 2 students were suffering from considerable amounts of stress.

Pearson product moment correlations among the approaches to studying and GHQ

Correlations between deep and strategic approaches are positive in all three cohorts. This association is significant ($p < 0.001$) in Cohort 95. The deep approach correlates negatively with the surface approach in all cohorts (significantly in Year 2(92)). Correlations between deep approaches and GHQ scores are negative in years 2(92) and 3(92) groups. There is no relationship between GHQ and the deep approach in Cohort 95. Similarly, there appears to be little or no correlation between strategic and surface approaches. GHQ scores tend to be negatively correlated with both deep and strategic approaches and positively with surface.

Cross-tabulations of approach to study and psychological well-being with chi-square values were inspected for both absolute and relative classification methods.

Deep approach and well-being

In year 2 (92), 81.8% of the deep high scorers were classed as having positive well-being and 18.2% as negative. This difference was found to be significant (Chi-square = 3.96992, d.f. = 1, $p = 0.04632$). A similar, but statistically non-significant pattern was found in year 3(92) where 84.6% of deep high scorers had positive well-being. In cohort 95 the same pattern was also present, though in a less well marked form than in either cohort of the previous study. The use of relative categories appears to intensify trends apparent when using the absolute cut-off (apart from Cohort 95 where the two measures are identical).

Strategic approach and well-being

In year 2(92) the relationship between strategic approach and well-being closely resembled that between a deep approach and stress. Again, the association between positive well-being and a preference for a strategic approach was found to be significant (Chi-square = 3.96992, d.f. = 1, $p = 0.04632$). A similar pattern of association was found in year 3(92). In Cohort 95, 71.4% of the strategic high scorers fell into the positive well-being group, and 28.6% into the negative well-being group. These differences were found to be significant (chi-square = 4.54621, d.f. = 1, p = 0.03299). Some intensification of trend when using the more inclusive relative measure of classification, as observed above, was found in all cohorts.

Surface approach and well-being

The patterns of association between surface preferences and well-being are not clear, and use of the two classification systems does little to illuminate the issue. Absolute categories contain very small numbers indeed. However, it must be concluded that some students appeared to be happy using a surface approach. Only the relative classification pattern in year 2 (92) suggested otherwise, where the association between a surface approach and negative well-being was found to be significant at the p < 0.05 level.

Summary

Thus, except for the case of the surface sub-scale in year 3(92), the reliability of the ASI sub-scales was endorsed in the present study. Cronbach alpha values for the surface sub-scale were lowest overall, which suggests that further investigation of this sub-scale may be warranted. On the whole, students appeared to use a mixture of approaches rather than limiting themselves to one. Some students had low scores on all approaches, however. Percentages of high scoring students calculated by cohort suggested that there may be an increase in the tendency to use deep approaches as students progress through their courses, and a decrease in the use of surface approaches in later years compared with earlier years. A longitudinal study of approaches to studying and stress following three cohorts at Napier University is underway, which will shed some light on these questions. On the whole, stress appears to be negatively correlated with deep and strategic approaches to studying, and positively correlated with surface approaches, though the relationship between a surface approach to studying and well-being is not straightforward.

Discussion

The research reported here raises a number of issues.

1.   Can a strategic approach be regarded as coping behaviour?

An inverse relationship between GHQ (negative well-being) and the strategic approach is particularly clear, and it seems that students may be using this particular approach in order to deal with academic stressors. It should be noted that the Cohort 95 sample, where this trend was most marked, was composed predominantly of first year students. It may be that these students are particularly assessment oriented because of the necessity to score well in order to be admitted to second year and the rest of their academic career. It may equally well be that they are particularly cue sensitive as they attempt to learn to 'play the system', and that the strategic approach offers a practical way of dealing with a stressful situation.

2.   Is there a mismatch between the approach to learning and the teaching students encounter which is giving rise to stress?

Pask (1976) argued that mismatches between teaching and learning style could lead to 'grossly inferior performance and a pronounced failure to comprehend the principles underlying the subject matter'. These mismatches may also be giving rise to stress.

Mismatches may operate in a variety of contexts within the learning environment. For example, large numbers of Napier staff have claimed to foster deep learning (Falchikov, 1993), yet, in the earlier study reported here, about a third of all students agreed that 'improving my memory' was an important unmet need. The surface approach depends on memory to a large extent. It may be that some Napier students feel an obligation to attempt to adopt a surface approach to studying, and, as a consequence, feel the need to improve their memories. Certainly, Falchikov (1993) found a smaller group of staff, predominantly located in the Faculty of Science, who appeared to foster surface learning. These lecturers, in turn, may disadvantage deep learners. Mismatches between what lecturers say and what they do, or how they do it, are also possible, though Trigwell *et al.*'s study (1994) suggested that the teacher's intentions were more important than their teaching methods.

3.   Is the student's approach to study consistent or subject to change?

One of the main findings of Entwistle's early research was that students approaches to learning were 'relatively consistent individual differences' (1987, p. 17). Similarly, Prosser and Miller's (1989) research supported the individual difference view of learning styles. Our earlier study suggested that second and third year students differed in some respects. Second-year students were found to be particularly stressed, for example. However, this was a cross-sectional study, and cross-sectional research cannot provide definitive answers to questions of personal change or development. Nevertheless, Geiger and Pinto (1991) found that students exhibited some changes of learning style during the second year of study. This leads us to ask whether the second year is different from other years in some way. It may be fruitful to look at the coursework demands on these students, or at the degree of choice available to them. Now that our mode of course delivery to our students is by modules with credit ratings that are constant over their course of study, it would seem that coursework demands will be similar over the years. However, the earlier study was carried out pre-modularization, and the perception of students and staff involved with the year 2 courses was that coursework demands were particularly high. Similarly, in the second year of the 'old' biology course, only 10.8% of student time was spent on self-selected subjects, compared with 43.2% in third year. It may be that the high levels of stress observed in year 2 may have been due to the disappointing performance of some students during their first year rather than to their preferred approaches to studying. Certainly, Sarros and Densten (1989) found that poor results were rated as fourth most salient stressor for students.

4.   What is the meaning of low scores on all approaches to studying?

Entwistle *et al.* (1991) found that engineering students who failed the end of year examination displayed 'disintegrated patterns of study strategies and perceptions of the learning environment'. In our more recent study, 63.6% of the year 2 sub-sample showed no clear approach preference, and just under half of this group had positive well being. However, this sub-sample was very small. Nonetheless, the absence of a clear approach in such a large number of students is puzzling, given that a coherent outlook on the world carries advantages in terms of improving the ability to make predictions and thus reduce stress. We clearly need to examine the academic performance levels in our cohorts in order to see whether Entwistle's results have been replicated.

5.   What is the meaning of high scores on all approaches to studying?

How do these students differ from the versatile strategic scorers? Are the 'across the board' high scorers using a wide variety of strategies, or do their high scores represent a response bias in favour of an agreement with all statements? Further investigation of this phenomenon is desirable.

Conclusion

These studies seem to suggest that the approaches to studying adopted by students and the levels of stress they experience may be related. What the studies do not tell us is whether maladaptive learning styles and strategies give rise to increased levels of stress, or whether the direction of causation is reversed (or whether, indeed, a third variable intervenes). There are more questions raised by our research than answers provided. What we can say is that the levels of stress found in the present samples give cause for concern. Issues raised here must be addressed immediately if our students are to achieve their full potential.

Acknowledgements

Thanks are due to Peter Heron for work on the earlier study.

Note

A fuller version of this paper has been submitted for publication elsewhere.

References

Archer, Jr. and Lamnin, A. (1985) An investigation of personal and academic stressors on college campuses, *Journal of College Student Personnel* 26(3), 210—15.

Duckwall, J. M., Arnold, L. and Hayes, J. (1991) Approaches to learning by undergraduate students: a longitudinal study, *Research in Higher Education* 32(1), 1—13.

Dunham, J. (1984) *Stress in Teaching*. London and Sydney: Croom Helm.

Entwistle, N. (1987) A model of the teaching-learning process. In J. T. E. Richardson, M. W. Eysenck and D. W. Piper (eds), *Student Learning*, Milton Keynes: SRHE and Open University Press.

Entwistle, N. and Hanley, M. (1977—78) Personality, cognitive style and students' learning strategies. *Higher Education Bulletin, Institute for Post-Compulsory Education, University of Lancaster* 6(1), 23—43.

Entwistle, N. and Ramsden, P. (1983) *Understanding Student Learning*, London: Croom-Helm.

Entwistle, N. J., Meyer, J. H. F. and Tait, H. (1991) Student failure: disintegrated patterns of study strategies and perceptions of the learning environment. *Higher Education* 21, 249—61.

Falchikov, N. (1993) Attitudes and values of lecturing staff: tradition, innovation and change. *Higher Education* **25**, 487—510.

Falchikov, N. and Heron, P. A. (1992) *Approaches to Studying and Stress in Undergraduate Students: An Exploratory Investigation*. Social Science Working Paper No. 11, Edinburgh: Napier University.

Geiger, M. A. and Pinto, J. K. (1991) Changes in learning style preference during a three-year longitudinal study. *Psychological Reports* **69**, 755—62.

Goldberg, D. and Williams, P. (1988) *A User's Guide to the General Health Questionnaire*. Windsor: NFER-Nelson.

Kyriacou, C. (1987) Teacher stress and burnout: an international review. *Educational Research* **29**, 146—52.

Laurillard, D. (1984) Learning from problem-solving. In F. Marton, D. Hounsell and N. Entwistle (eds), *The Experience of Learning*. Edinburgh: Scottish Academic Press.

Marton, F. and Säljö, R. (1984) Approaches to learning. In F. Marton, D. Hounsell and N. Entwistle (eds), *The Experience of Learning*. Edinburgh: Scottish Academic Press.

Miller, C. D., Alway, M. and McKinley, D. L. (1987) Effects of learning styles and strategies on academic success. *Journal of College Student Personnel* **28**, 399—404.

Miller, C. M. L. and Parlett, M. (1974) *Up to the Mark: A Study of the Examination Game*. London: Society for Research into Higher Education.

Pask, G. (1976) Styles and strategies of learning. *British Journal of Educational Psychology* **46**, 128—48.

Perry, W. G. (1970) *Forms of Intellectual and Ethical Development in the College Years: A Scheme*. New York: Holt, Rinehart and Winston.

Prosser, M. and Millar, R. (1989) The 'how' and 'what' of learning physics. *European Journal of Psychology of Education* **4**(4), 513—28.

Reason, J. (1988) Stress and cognitive failure. In S. Fisher and J. Reason (eds), *Handbook of Life Stress, Cognition and Health*. Chichester: John Wiley & Sons Ltd.

Reason, J. T. and Lucas, D. (1984) Absentmindedness in shops: its correlates and consequences. *British Journal of Clinical Psychology* **23**, 121—31.

Sarros, J. C. and Densten, I. L. (1989) Undergraduate student stress and coping strategies. *Higher Education Research and Development* **8**(1), 47—57.

Savoy, L. (1990) Sources of stress on trainee lecturers for further and higher education. *Journal of Further and Higher Education* **14**(2), 94—104.

Svensson, L. (1977) On qualitative differences in learning: III study skill and learning. *British Journal of Educational Psychology* **47**, 233—43.

Tait, H. (1995) Centre for Teaching, Learning and Instruction, University of Edinburgh, personal communication.

Trigwell, K., Prosser, M. and Taylor, P. (1994) Qualitative differences in approaches to teaching first year university science. *Higher Education* **27**, 75—84.

7 Improving learner support for engineering students in learning to use learning logs: a case study

Roy Gregory, Lin Thorley and Christine Shepperson
University of Hertfordshire

Background

This case study is taken from work carried out on the MEng Engineering Scheme in the School of Engineering at the University of Hertfordshire. It includes looking at the use of student Learning Logs within the Management Skills Development Course. The work was carried out between February and June, 1995.

The MEng Scheme takes students from six specialist BEng schemes in the School of Engineering, drawing from a pool of approximately 450 students. The MEng provides students with a broader range of studies suitable for those with potential for engineering management.

Students are selected for the MEng and are chosen from those judged to be competent in their specialist studies but who also show potential for development in personal and management skills. The delivery of the scheme is designed to encourage personal development and the ability to be an autonomous lifelong learner. The scheme allows the students to obtain an MEng degree together with a specialist BEng degree in an overall time of four and a half years.

Use of learning logs in Management Skills development

In the first semester of MEng Studies one of the first MEng modules taken by the students is 'Management Skills Development'. The module seeks to improve the personal and interpersonal skills required for the management of people and also to model the type of learning progressively expected on the scheme. It not only supplements the theoretical management studies and the teamwork carried out elsewhere but also provides an opportunity to shift radically students' attitude to their own learning, and to inculcate the ethos of the course. In addition to providing an opportunity for recording and reflecting on the learning taking place, the learning log work becomes an important focus and indicator of how far a significant attitude change is achieved.

The Management Skills course is project-based and the students spend much of the time working in groups. The course includes two projects which require the use of a large range of skills in different and unfamiliar settings. This is supplemented by a number of workshops and seminars giving a theoretical framework for the self-development work (Gregory and Thorley, 1993).

The learning cycle and the way this can be used to learn from experience is introduced early in the course. Time is spent in developing the processes used in self-development and independent learning. Students are encouraged to use the learning cycle and to apply it in order to structure their own learning. Students are introduced to the Learning Styles Inventory and encouraged to identify their own preferred style and the implications of this for their own learning.

All the workshops and seminars provide opportunities for reflection and self-assessment. This starts early in the first week, with self-assessment of presentations based on negotiated criteria. Tutor, self- and peer-assessments are all used throughout the course and students become familiar and start to expect this type of approach. There is an emphasis on feedback and reflection after each exercise. The Belbin Inventory, Learning Styles Questionnaire and Myers-Briggs Type Indicator (MBTI) are used in the module to heighten self-awareness. The students also receive a 'Do-It Yourself Personal Skills Pack' (Thorley, 1992) with a questionnaire to identify potential skills development areas and a proforma for skills development.

Learning logs and assessment criteria are explained to students at the outset. The criteria attempt to describe the way high marks can be achieved by not merely reporting on the experiences but by reflecting on them through using their own and other people's observations, plus using various frameworks and models for interpreting behaviour. The log represents 40% of the overall course mark. Its place of importance rests on the assumption that consciously applying the learning cycle assists in the development of the personal skills associated with management.

Investigation

The course has run four times so far, student numbers varying from 11 to 21 per cohort. This year there were 11 male students from various engineering backgrounds on the course. This was a smaller group than usual and for the first time had no females (in the past females have been proportionally better represented than on the specialist schemes). None of this year's students had previous experience in writing a learning log.

Two learning logs are submitted: an interim log after about seven weeks followed by a feedback interview and a final log at the end of the course. Both learning logs are assessed: the interim log mark represents a quarter of the whole learning log mark. This year the learning logs were also analysed for insights into the attitude and processes of the students. The assessment was carried out by Roy Gregory. Lin Thorley and Christine Shepperson read the logs, commented on the assessment and provided input to final analysis and the relationship between scores.

The interview after the interim assessment was used as a tutorial and also to gain feedback from the students. A student summary of their reactions at that point was tape recorded for later analysis. A video film was made of the students reflecting on one of their projects during a group presentation. The Belbin Inventory, Learning Styles Questionnaire and Myers-Briggs Type Indicator results were also available for analysis. The qualitative nature of much of the data together with the small number of students involved has limited the extent to which conclusions could be drawn. The information does, however, provide the stimulus for useful insights which can form the basis of future course development.

A subsequent questionnaire was sent to the students as part of a wider study of learning logs involving both MSc students at the University of Hertfordshire and Occupational Psychology students from City University. This gives further information concerning the MEng students' attitudes. The results of this separate study were published earlier this year (Gregory and Hind, 1996).

Discussion

Student response to this module seems to be similar to previous years although there appeared to be a higher degree of difficulty with the more open-ended parts of the course than before. There did also appear to be more competitiveness and higher levels of insecurity concerning 'getting the right answer'. It did seem, at least superficially, that the absence of females in the group had some effect, although this is of course impossible to quantify.

Ten of the 11 students said they eventually found the learning log useful with four finding it very useful, saying they would continue the process. It is not known whether this has happened. These results are encouraging, although students' tendency to 'own' the work as a result of the effort involved can produce deceptively positive attitudes. One of the ten claimed to have benefited from the process, although on the basis of the learning log it seemed to the tutor that he never actually grasped what to do or why he did what he did. Another student who claimed not to benefit at all only made sufficient effort to pass and also seemed to have little idea of what he was doing.

On this small sample some correlation appears to be indicated between interim assessment marks and with certain MBTI profiles, but not with learning styles. The analysis on learning styles did not, however, extend to looking at the Kolb learning orientations of accommodator, assimilator, and so on because of insufficient data. There was also insufficient information to determine a correlation with Belbin categories.

The MBTI correlation observed (approximately 0.6) was between high interim learning log assessment marks and a combination of MBTI scores. These scores represent well-developed objective reasoning and conceptual functions, and a high tolerance for lower structure and ambiguity (i.e. high scores in the MBTI categories of Thinking and Intuitive functions and Perceiving attitude). A simple factor was devised to obtain this correlation by converting the four scores to a number above or below 100 as used in the Myers-Briggs literature. The factor is:

$$F = \frac{(S - N) \times (J - P)}{(T - F)}$$

where   (S - N) = score on Sensing-Intuition scale (above 100 Intuition)

                  (J - P) = score on Judging-Perceiving scale (above 100 Perceiving)

                  (T - F) = score on Thinking-Feeling scale (above 100 Feeling)

The factor is high when the students have high scores in Intuition, Thinking and Perceiving.

Students without the above MBTI combination expressed the most difficulties in knowing what was expected in learning logs and with appreciating the value of writing their thoughts down. Some evidence emerged from the interviews that 'expectations' of what learning was about affected attitudes to this reflective process. One student was dissatisfied by the whole course in that he was not able to 'come away with a good set of notes'.

After the interview/counselling sessions many students showed improvement when encouraged to use a well-defined structure for writing based on the learning cycle. The

MBTI correlation then became significantly weaker for the final assessment marks. The interviews/coaching sessions are resource intensive but appear necessary for some students to benefit from learning logs. For some, the 'Personal Skills Pack' was an important 'life-saver', a place to start; for others it was a constraint that tended to stifle creativity.

If some students naturally find the less structured written learning log easier and more helpful than others, this may imply that the latter would find an outcomes/evidence based approach more helpful. It is interesting to note that the MBTI scores of the course tutor (Roy Gregory) are similar to students with the higher assessment. There could be an inherent bias towards particular temperament types in the assessment criteria. This needs to be reviewed. A more varied approach to skills development, the way the learning log is structured and assessed may help in incorporating the way different temperament types prefer to learn.

The above implies a need for reconsideration of the way learning logs are introduced. This could include re-writing the written materials and the use of an even more structured workshop/exercises approach to the learning cycle process, aimed at assisting those who at present never really benefit from writing the learning log and at reducing the amount of staff intensive coaching. It is also worth considering whether more variety could be introduced into the method of recording learning to take account of different learning styles (e.g. videos, audio tapes, interviews).

The difficulty students experience when working in this area may also be partially due to the deliberate change in the teaching methods used for this course and also the change in handling situations and data of a different type and in different ways. The personal skills writing usually involves using more than one model for analysis, dealing with ambiguous and less certain qualitative data and having a reflection process focused on personal issues. Engineering and science based students have not been significantly exposed to this in higher education and probably not since leaving school. It is not then surprising that they express obvious difficulties in changing the way they view and analyse the world.

It is encouraging that some students do change, particularly as this is an important part of the challenge of the MEng. Since, however, the learning log is seen to be an indicator of the ability to change discipline paradigms, the real difficulty some students experience raises questions concerning the initial MEng selection procedure including whether this should focus more on the flexibility and comfort level in working in different discipline paradigms. In the future this selection procedure may be usefully informed by a framework involving learning styles and personality type indicators.

References

Gregory, R. and Hind, P. (1996) The skills of learning. *Occupational Psychology Conference Eastbourne*. Poster.

Gregory, R. and Thorley, L. (1993) Experiential learning: teaching meng students management skills. *Proceedings of the First UK Conference on MEng Degrees, Brighton.*

Kolb, D. (1984) *Experiential Learning*. New York: Prentice Hall.

Briggs Myers, I and Mc Caulley, M.H., (1993) Manual: A Guide to the Development and Use of the Myers-Briggs Type Indicator, Palto Alto: *Consulting Pschologists Press, Inc.*

Thorley, L. (1992) *Develop Your Personal Skills: A Do-It-Yourself Pack for Students*. D. and L. George.

8 The transition from high school to university at the University of the South Pacific

Roger Landbeck
Centre for the Enhancement of Learning and Teaching
The University of the South Pacific

France Mugler
Department of Literature and Language
The University of the South Pacific

Introduction

The transition from high school to first-year university can be a very difficult experience for many students. Simons, Parlett and Jaspan (1988) in their study of some United Kingdom students' first few weeks of university life suggested that many are disoriented at this formative time in their university experience. Given that evidence, with which many staff and students concur, it is important to see that the transition period is handled supportively so that students do not drop out at this early stage.

This chapter describes the experiences of students at the main campus of the University of the South Pacific in Fiji as they try to make the transition from school to university. It also makes proposals about how teaching staff could assist students to make the transition more smoothly and lead them towards more independent learning.

The description of the students' experiences comes from a larger study on students' approaches to learning (Landbeck and Mugler, 1994). The study was conducted in 1993 with a random sample of 16 students from a third-year linguistics course with an enrolment of 50. The interviews followed the phenomenographic approach developed in Sweden by Marton and Säljö (1976) and were tape-recorded and transcribed, then analysed by both researchers. In this chapter, interviewees are referred to by coded initials.

Since more Pacific students are enrolling in universities in Western countries the experiences and the backgrounds of these students and should be of interest to participants in this conference. However it is clear from the English study quoted earlier that the experiences of Pacific students are shared widely.

Background: the University of the South Pacific

The University of the South Pacific (USP) serves 12 nations: the Cook Islands, Fiji, Kiribati, the Marshall Islands, Nauru, Niue, Solomons, Tokelau, Tonga, Tuvalu, Vanuatu, and Western Samoa. The main campus is in Suva, Fiji, where teaching and research in Science, Social Sciences and Humanities take place. Another school and several small units are located in other member countries, and the university has an extensive distance education programme. The majority of students on the Suva campus come from Fiji, with smaller numbers of students from the 11 other member countries.

The USP first opened in 1968, before Fiji became independent (1970), and it has been strongly influenced by outside models, in particular the British system. Many members of the teaching staff were trained at Commonwealth institutions, and the secondary education systems in all USP member countries have been strongly influenced by those of Britain and New Zealand, and they have a significant influence on the students' approaches to learning.

Many students who have started their university studies through part-time distance learning face difficult learning conditions, ranging from lack of electricity and private space to lack of time because of family and community commitments, and even lack of understanding or support. Many on-campus students come from very small nations (Tokelau, the smallest, has only about 2000 inhabitants) and are intimidated by the size of Fiji's capital, Suva (pop. about 100,000). This includes students from rural areas or small towns in Fiji itself. English, the language of instruction at USP, is a second language for the overwhelming majority of students (the third or fourth for some), and although it has also been the official medium for much or all of their primary and secondary schooling, the proficiency in English of some is clearly not adequate for university studies. For all, the special skills required in a tertiary institution, the expectations of lecturers — often unstated — and the freedom and responsibility of university studies, are new challenges.

Some students are mature part-timers, and their responsibilities at work and at home, particularly for female students, have to be juggled along with their studies. Many new students feel homesick, which hampers their studying. Many of these problems are of course shared by university students elsewhere, but the unique regional nature of the USP and the vast discrepancies in background that are in part the result of the diversity of the South Pacific — a diversity which is also a rich resource and a source of strength — means that some students are faced with many difficulties at once.

The transition: from high school to university

Most of the students interviewed are very clear about the differences between learning in high school and at university. Their awareness of the teaching and learning styles prevalent in each environment is striking, as is the force of their opinions. Unfortunately in most cases their view is of a sharp dichotomy between rote learning in high school and independent learning at university. The gap between both types of institutions is considered so vast that the period of transition is often long and difficult. It is clear that some students in fact fail to adapt, even after several years at university. On the other hand the positive experiences of some students, either at high school or university, provide hope and indicate directions in which we, as researchers in student learning and as university teachers, can go to try to facilitate the students' adaptation to tertiary learning. A smooth and swift transition is surely the most promising sign of eventual success in the student's university career.

Learning in high school

Students paint a picture of teacher-dominated high-school classes, using such words as *'dictate'*, *'drilling'* and *'indoctrination'*. The most common term they use to refer to the process they went through is *'spoonfeeding'*. They consider that their role as high-school students was to accept whatever was presented to them by teachers and to *'regurgitate'*, *'give back the right answer'*, rather than to ask questions or try to work out original answers:

> *In the high school I just learn through probably imitation, indoctrination. (GB:16)*

> *Like, in high school, a secondary school teacher will practically drill into the students what he or she thinks is right, not leaving the students to form ideas of their own, to decide the way to weigh factors carefully. (OJ:11)*

> *Like, they are taught to be, like, quiet, put your heads down kind of thing, whatever the teacher says is, you know, that's the truth even though it might not be true, that kind of thing . . . (EV:21)*

One interviewee gives a specific example and, almost inadvertently, her reaction to the teacher's practice:

> *In high school it's mainly notetaking because teachers love filling up the board with notes and then disappear and then come back and — and we had to write them down. You'll be lucky if she decides to go over the notes or she might discuss the notes the other day, the following day. (GB:17)*

Some are perfectly aware that this teaching style often leads to students being afraid to ask questions, and one student describes vividly the effect as a kind of chain reaction cascading through the school environment:

> *I mean that's how it is, some people, you know, when they don't understand anything, they're so scared to go and ask their teachers — And you know in that way they don't perform very well and, like, the teachers get telling off in return, you know, you don't teach well, by the principal, and when the parents come to school, the parents ask 'what's my child's problem?' and then she goes 'I don't know because she does not come up to me'. I mean, a teacher would not have time to go to each individual — student. They should be the ones coming up and telling their problems. (EV:22)*

This interviewee goes on to say that she hopes that when she becomes a teacher, she will give students opportunities to ask questions. Others vow that they will try their best to break the mould and teach in a different way, saying they do not want their future students to have to go through the same experiences. A student describes *'pretty bad teachers'* who *'beat up the kids all the time'*. He adds:

> *That's why I want to start teaching, because I thought of those wrongs. (JE:14)*

Unfortunately, educational systems often discourage change - JE describes the one he went through as *'dogmatic'* — and new teachers in particular are under great pressure to conform to existing patterns of behaviour.

The result of this teacher domination must inevitably be to produce passive, dependent learners — the very opposite of what a university would wish to foster. It is hardly surprising that most students find the transition between high school and university difficult, the process of adaptation often taking a year or more:

> *It took me one whole year during Foundation. (NI:14)*

At least one student has evidently not been successful in this transition, often feeling distracted and homesick in class after three years at USP:

I spend now three years and I usually find difficulties with my concentration when I attend lectures. Usually I reflect back on my family. That's a problem to me, most of the time I'm dreaming and then I just try to recall again or concentrate on the lesson. (KF:4)

Two students had experienced more freedom in learning while in high school however, and did not find it so difficult to adjust to the university. One student had a very positive experience with a high school English teacher who encouraged independent learning and whose success she attributes to his consistently encouraging manner and to the interest he showed for each student, in and out of the classroom:

He was able to connect with the students . . . He was able to come and talk to us within groups and even to talk to us outside when we were having a recess. (NI:15—16)

The student from Western Samoa describes how a more questioning approach was introduced during his last year of high school:

Samoa has a Foundation course so we started this kind of learning in Samoa, learning how to critically analyse works and not take statements for face value. (JE:2)

These positive experiences are not typical of the group interviewed however, or even of the entire high-school experience of these two students. In fact the student who speaks so admiringly of her high- school English teacher is the one who says that it took her a year to get used to USP, and the Samoan student, in retrospect, feels *'betrayed'* and *'angry at the system for deceiving [him] for so long'*. (JE:15)

Learning at university

In contrast to the teacher-dominated high school, students describe the university as a place characterized by freedom, independence and responsibility, where you are expected to *'use your own initiative'*, *'think for yourself'*, *'find your own way'*, *'motivate yourself'*.

Like, in school we used to rely on our teachers. I mean, the teacher gives you everything. I mean, here you just have to do your own work and if you do it, you got it, and if you don't, well, too bad, you are down the drain kind of thing. (EV:22)

You get a lot of work, that's pretty obvious. But the pressure to study is, like, it's up to you to decide when to study and how you prepare your time and go about your studies, because no one is going to tell you what to do. (FA:1)

I feel the university is more, teaches you to think more for yourself rather than to, regurgitate what you've been programmed. (JE:1)

The student who describes copying what the high-school teacher writes on the blackboard contrasts this with notetaking at university and, again, her reaction to this kind of learning comes through:

But in here, basically lectures, I enjoy making my own notes — you just jot down a few points and go over them on my own. (GB:17)

Two students summarize the differences between high school and university as follows:

> At high school the teacher most of the time tells you what to do, spoonfeeding sort of thing. In here most of the time you have to be by yourself. (BR:8—9)

> Another difference that I found is that, you know, in high school, like, the teachers are always there to guide you, like, force you, I mean not force, tell you what to do, whereas here it's you, ourselves, we have to do what we, I mean the lecturers give us the work and it's our own initiative. (HC:1)

A former high-school teacher tries to clarify the interplay of expectations among teachers and students in high school and later at university:

> Learning at high school, we tend to give everything to the students, like we think that if I don't explain things, everything, they won't understand, they won't do it, and then we start to do that and in return the students expect to be spoonfed — Well, at university, you exercise your own freedom of choice. You attend lectures if you want. If you don't want, well you can go and do something else. But we know that if we don't attend lectures you miss something important. We have to use that choice wisely — And maybe we still expect to be spoonfed. Whatever we are doing to our students, we expect our lecturers to do to us. (AQ:15)

Except for one student who does not 'see any difference at all' between high school and university — 'it's the same sort of regurgitation, just giving back' (MH:8) — the interviewees also see the university as a place that encourages questioning and the search for alternative answers:

> Because usually in high school the answer given by the teachers is what is expected to be written back in the exam — and so we would consider that as the only answer. In here, in university, any answer is right if you provide evidence to support and it could be any answer you choose. (NI:13—14)

She explains further:

> Because you often feel that when you're in high school there is only one correct answer — and if you give another answer which might contradict what the teacher gives usually there is a big opposition from the teachers themselves. (NI:14)

Rote learning or independence?

Although they found it difficult to get used to, all students say that they prefer the independence offered by the university to the 'spoonfeeding' of high school. The freedom to go beyond what is being presented in class is highlighted by several:

> Well, you know, coming to the university, I know it's a tertiary institution, it's a big jump from high school to here. I mean, like, my knowledge has increased, broadened. I mean, in high school we didn't have that much interest to go further, I mean maybe because of the type of courses we are doing here and, like, we have to be independent. (EV:22)

> When I was in high school I'm always dependent on what the teacher tell us — and I'm more concerned at what the teacher wants us to learn from where she has given us. Now I'm able to, because we are given freedom to expand, and so when I'm given something just to study on a

particular thing, even though we study just on Japan for example, I'm also able to know from the readings that there were more to it than what is given in the lectures. (NI:13)

Several students associate the independence fostered by the university with maturity:

Like, they are not been made to think for themselves, like they are being spoonfed in high school, we were being spoonfed, so used to being patted on the back, but at university, one is taught to stand on one's own two feet and grow up. (OJ:11)

Being independent, you know, it kind of makes you feel mature, where you become a mature adult. (EV:22)

There is a point of life where you have to be independent. (BR:9)

Even the student who is still having serious difficulties coping with studies after three years on campus remarks that university has given him the chance *'to think and to learn deeply'*. (KF:16)

Easing the transition

The findings of this research project establish that the students recognise the differences between the teacher centred high school and the independent learning at university. Most prefer the independence of university learning, although they had to make their own often slow and painful adaptation to it. What can be done to make the transition smoother and faster, and to ensure that there are fewer casualties on the way?

A university has a distinct culture, with many of its conventions hidden. Simons, Parlett and Jaspan (1988) liken arriving at university to visiting a foreign country, pointing out that what is taken for granted by residents is not known to newcomers and that it is hard for residents to put themselves in newcomers' shoes. In another study of students' experience of academic life Parlett, Simons, Simmonds and Hewton (1988) identify five problems between teachers and learners in higher education. Among these are the psychological barrier between students and staff, underestimating the confusion experienced by students, and looking at an academic subject as the expert in residence without considering the point of view of the newcomer.

To clarify the nature of university culture, let us first consider some of the differences between high school and university.

1. Class size

Most students come from relatively small classes in high school, where they can receive close attention, to introductory classes at university which are often quite large and impersonal. Even the tutorial or lab groups offered in conjunction with these courses can still be large, so that this feeling of impersonality often persists.

2. The university lecturer and the school teacher

Students are aware that academic staff have greater qualifications than the school teachers they have known. They often feel that the gap between themselves and lecturers is much wider and therefore are more reluctant to ask questions in class than in high school, let alone go to a lecturer's office for assistance.

3.   Independent learning versus a directed approach

University staff often make it clear to students that independent *learning* must now replace the typical directed approach of high school. Unfortunately much of the teaching *continues* to be teacher-centred and opportunities for independent learning are not always provided. Fostering independence then takes the form of dropping students in at the deep end and watching them sink or swim.

4.   Academic writing and research skills

Academic writing requires longer and more elaborate discourses, evidence of research about the topic, and increased sophistication in arguing a point of view. Thinking skills are more advanced and arguments require supportive evidence. Students must realize that things are not black and white, right or wrong, and become able to hold differing viewpoints (Perry, 1970). Research skills are more highly developed, including the use of a much greater variety of resources than are available at high school. The information explosion requires more attention be given to helping students develop information literacy.

5.   The nature of academic disciplines

Schools teach 'subjects' but at university students need to be led to an understanding of the very nature of the academic disciplines they are studying, through questions such as 'what is the nature of history' and 'how do historians go about studying their subject'. Indeed they need to develop an understanding of the nature of research and of knowledge in general. This is often difficult for the 'residents' to articulate, since, as specialists in a particular field, they often take such issues for granted, yet this kind of understanding is indispensable to the students' intellectual growth.

Although some skills have been acquired at high school, ideally the undergraduate programme develops existing skills to a more sophisticated level, and fosters the creation of others which are specifically needed in university learning. The personal development in the students interviewed in the study reported here is impressive, and seems to have taken place in spite of the relative lack of attention paid by the institution to the issue of transition. One wonders how much more development would take place, and how many students would be prevented from dropping out early, if a conscious effort was made at easing the transition.

Practical suggestions

Academic staff need to develop a greater awareness of the hidden nature of much of the institution's culture, of the difficulties faced by newcomers, and of their own assumptions about students and the level of their skills. This requires, among other things, that they be prepared to get to know students and their background.

But awareness alone is not enough, and academic staff must be convinced that it is part of their brief to help acculturate the students to the university setting. They should, in particular, be prepared to teach students not only subject content but the conventions of their discipline and the skills required for effective learning in that discipline. Since conventions and skills needed vary substantially from one discipline to the next, this requires more than a general course in academic English or study skills.

1. Class size

To overcome the problem of conveying information about a course in a large class detailed class guides can be prepared (see Gibbs 1992b). These guides make the course more 'user-friendly' and enable students to develop independent modes of learning when class size makes it impossible for the staff member to relate effectively to each individual student. There is a close similarity between the detailed class guide and a distance learning package, as in both situations the lecturer is 'distant' in one way or the other.

2. Discussions

Staff frequently complain that students are reluctant to take part in small group discussions, but students often do not know the rules of participation, which should be clarified early on in the course. Pacific island students are not used to speaking their mind before elders, but with encouragement, in groups of two or three they will gradually learn to speak up. Discussion often works best when it is structured, and a free for all debate based on too general a question ('Discuss topic X') will often lead to silence and confusion. Questions can be planned which can get the discussion going and will lead smoothly to a general debate. They of course require more preparation on the part of the lecturer.

3. Research for assignments

The length of assignments set at university is often far in excess of anything the students have tackled before. Staff tell students that they need to go to the library to research an assignment but that is often the only direction that is given. A short assignment to help students learn how to use the library early in the semester can be arranged with library staff, and guidelines on how to get started with the research are also useful.

4. Academic writing

The nature of writing expected in a discipline can be a mystery to students and some clear direction is important, especially since in each discipline students are required to hand in different kinds of written work, each with its own convention and requiring different skills and styles (essays, lab reports, book and article reviews, etc). Successful assignments by previous students can provide models, and their variety makes the point that very different assignments can be equally successful and earn a good grade. A summary of what is expected for an assignment to get a particular grade (from A to E) provides direction (see Gibbs, 1992b). This can be given when the assignment is first set and when it is returned with a grade.

5. Meeting the standards

Students need to know early on whether they are meeting the standards so feedback on their work is essential. Unfortunately this is becoming increasingly difficult with large classes. Suggestions include defining the assignment clearly and listing the assessment criteria, which helps avoid time-consuming questions later, conducting tasks that can be marked in class, and enabling students to assess themselves and their peers (Gibbs 1992a).

6. Making the connections

As shown by the research at USP, students try to relate what they learn to their experience of the world, although some find this very difficult with some subjects, such as statistics. An important part of teaching is being able to relate the content of a course to the level of the students and to make it meaningful in their context.

7. Developing an understanding of the discipline

The nature of the discipline needs to be made explicit in first year introductory courses, not only in the first few weeks but throughout the year, so that students begin to experience what it means to think like a geographer or a mathematician.

Perhaps most important is to be prepared to make contact with students and try to understand the new situation they find themselves in. While this may be easier for some staff than for others, certainly all should be willing to make an effort to get to know their students.

Easing into independence

Many of these suggestions may seem like continuing the directed approach of high school and delaying the development of independence, but the differences between school and university are so great that not to provide students with guidelines on how to operate in the new culture is irresponsible. Furthermore, it is not a matter of spoonfeeding content but rather of assisting students to develop academic skills and an understanding of what the university expects of them. It is only once these skills start developing that students can begin to become independent learners. Students, for instance, are not used to evaluating their own learning because most of the time it is done for them by 'experts'. Jenkins and Pepper (1988) designed an essay self-assessment form, to be handed in with the essay itself, which required students to make judgements about how they performed in the essay according to a set of criteria. Using these criteria they had to answer a set of questions such as 'what are the best features of this work?' and 'how could it be improved?'.

Implementation

These suggestions can only be implemented with the cooperation of teaching staff, particularly those with first-year classes, who must be persuaded that helping students to adapt to university is part of their job and who must agree to make time to implement suggestions in their teaching. One approach is to have informal discussions in which studies about the early experiences of students is presented, and to encourage staff to talk to a group of their own students to find out for themselves their situation. Another is for the institution to recognise the importance of teaching and perhaps even reward particularly effective and innovative teachers.

In many universities, the suggestions presented here would require a major change in the way the institution in general and teaching staff in particular view their role. Such a change would no doubt be difficult.

References

Gibbs, G. (1992a) Assessing more students, Booklet 4, *The Teaching More Students Project*. London: The Polytechnic & Colleges Funding Council.

Gibbs, G. (1992b) Independent learning with more students, Booklet 5, *The Teaching More Students Project*. London: The Polytechnic & Colleges Funding Council.

Jenkins, A. and Pepper, D. M. (1988) *Developing Group Work and Communication Skills: A Manual for Teachers in Higher Education*. Birmingham: Standing Conference on Educational Development.

Landbeck, R. C. and Mugler, F. (1994) *Approaches to Study and Conceptions of Learning of Students at the USP*. Suva: CELT, the University of the South Pacific.

Marton, F. and Säljö, R. (1976) On qualitative differences in learning. II - Outcome as a function of the learner's conception of the task. *British Journal of Educational Psychology* **46**, 115—27.

Parlett, M., Simons, H., Simmonds, R., and Hewton, E. (1988) *Learning from Learners: A Study of the Student's Experience of Academic Life*. SCED Paper 54. Birmingham: Standing Conference on Educational Development.

Perry, W. G. (1970) *Forms of Intellectual and Ethical Development in the College Years*. New York: Holt, Rinehart & Winston.

Simons, H., Parlett, M. and Jaspan, A. (1988) *Up to Expectations. A Study of the Students' First Few Weeks in Higher Education*. SCED Paper 53. Birmingham: Standing Conference on Educational Development.

9 Using evidence of learning styles to improve student learning in photographic communication

David Matthews
Falmouth College of Arts

Introduction

Recent high application rates (450 in 1994 for 30 places) for the HND Photographic Communication Programme, raised discussions regarding the development of an improved selection process for candidates. Like many Art and Design programmes, selection is by interview and the presentation of a portfolio. Tutors are looking for a variety of personal attributes which students need to possess if they are to become successful professional photographers.

The specialist photographic element of the programme emulates experiences which a student would meet as a practising professional (as far as is possible within a college environment). Academic staff speculated that if the selection process could more precisely determine those candidates who had a behavioural pattern that closely matched the learning experience offered by the programme; then the selection process would be more efficient, and potentially produce a higher proportion of students who complete the course and successfully enter a very competitive profession.

Learning styles — an option?

There has been much research done on how people learn. Over the past few decades, this has perhaps been dominated by the work of Kolb. More recently however the work of Honey and Mumford has been accepted as a valid and practical method to determine the most appropriate learning experience for an individual. Honey and Mumford's research work has been undertaken mainly 'in the field'. Their background in management training and consultancy has provided the opportunity to collect and analyse data mainly from the commercial sector and the professions. They have not undertaken any research in the photographic profession, but the strategies they employ have been shown to be successful for most occupations.

Hypothesis

My research began as an investigation into the possibility that photographers have a particular and identifiable learning style. The methodology I used was based upon the work of Honey and Mumford. I used *The Manual of Learning Styles* and *The Learning Styles Questionnaire* (LSQ) as my research 'system'. My work has attempted to test the following hypothesis:

1. that there is a learning style profile which relates specifically to photographers;

2. that this profile can be discerned and defined;

3. that a system of analysis can reveal the profile.

If the hypothesis could be proved, I speculated that it would be possible to use my findings to devise a selection procedure which would more accurately match potential students with the experience offered by the programme.

The Learning Styles Questionnaire

Honey and Mumford identify four learning styles: activist, reflector, theorist and pragmatist. The extent to which an individual has a preference for each of these determines their particular learning style profile. The assessment of each learning style is accomplished by the completion and analysis of a single questionnaire (LSQ). This contains eighty questions, 20 linked to each of the four learning style preferences.

> *The LSQ is designed to discover general trends or tendencies running through a person's behaviour (Honey and Mumford, 1986, p. 6).*

The LSQ is completed by answering 'yes' or 'No' to each of the 80 questions. All the positively answered questions are collated to form a score for each of the learning styles. The weighting of the four scores indicating the persons learning style profile (activist, pragmatist, reflector or theorist).

Choice of student groups

Initially my research was conducted within my own College environment. In order to have a comparative range of groups, I collected data from several different programmes. A total of 242 students were in the study, from 7 programmes and 11 different groups of students; they ranged from FE to postgraduate level, and included two photography programmes (110 students).

1. ND Photography — Years 1 and 2

2. HND Photographic Communication — Years 1 and 2

3. HND Graphic Design — Years 1 and 2

4. HND Advertising — Years 1 and 2

5. BA Visual Communication — Year 1

6. BA Journalism Studies — Year 1

7. PgDip Radio Journalism

Both studio and academic based courses were represented, but in order to put my research in a professional context, I extended my data collection to include both photographic tutors and practising professional photographers.

Reliability and responses to the LSQ

Although the completion of the questionnaire is relatively straight forward, in order to avoid distortion by simple errors or mistakes, I made random checks that the LSQ scores had been collated and totalled correctly. Very few mistakes were detected, the data being accurate and consistent. Consistency and reliability checks were also undertaken by second sampling. This was done by asking a total of 97 students from four different groups to complete the questionnaire twice. There was a gap of five weeks between the two samples. A 'group mean' was calculated for each cohort of students, and the first and second group samples were compared with each other. The two sets of results were found to be remarkably consistent with each other. The activist scores were the least consistent with a comparison of 91% between the two means. Reflectors were the most consistent with a comparison of 97%. Theorists and pragmatists both compared at 96%. The number of questions answered, gave a comparison of 99% between the two sets of results. Looking at the findings overall, HND Advertising students on average answered 49 questions positively, the highest of all the groups. ND Photography and BA Visual Culture answered an average of 41 questions positively, the lowest, HND Photographic Communications students 46.5, and HND Photography tutors, responded with an average of 51 positively answered questions. The highest number of questions answered positively by any individual respondent, was 66, and the lowest 18.

Processing the data

Using Microsoft Excel 5, I designed a computer spreadsheet to undertake all the calculations, and to provide a method for comparison of the data. The individual learning style scores were used to determine a 'mean' for each particular 'study group', e.g. student year groups, tutors and professional photographers. The spreadsheet design included calculation of the group mean scores and automatic conversion to a learning style preference value, e.g. Very Strong Preference (VSP), Strong Preference (SP), Moderate Preference (MP), Low Preference (LP), and Very Low Preference (VLP). The results produced are displayed in tabulated form (Table 1).

TABLE 1 Group mean scores and learning style preference values

Programme	Learning styles mean scores					Learning style values			
	Activist	Reflect	Theoriest	Pragmatic	Average no. questions	Activist	Reflect	Theorist	Pragmatic
HND Photographic Comm yr 1	10.55	13.97	11.06	11.43	45.06	MP	MP	MP	LP
HND Photographic Comm yr 2	10.54	13.50	10.21	11.83	48.08	MP	MP	LP	LP
ND Photography yr 1	13.12	12.42	8.38	10.88	44.81	VSP	MP	LP	LP
ND Photography yr 2	11.87	11.13	8.33	9.80	41.13	SP	LP	LP	LP
HND Advertising yr 1	14.08	13.50	9.92	12.50	50.00	VSP	MP	LP	MP
HND Advertising yr 2	11.00	14.91	10.36	12.00	48.27	SP	MP	LP	MP
HND Graphic Design yr 1	10.90	13.58	9.63	10.20	44.36	MP	MP	LP	LP
HND Graphic Design yr 2	11.39	13.30	9.96	9.96	44.61	SP	MP	LP	LP
BA Journalism Studies yr 1	11.36	12.65	10.65	10.70	45.35	SP	MP	LP	LP
BA Visual Culture yr 1	11.06	13.67	8.56	7.72	41.00	SP	MP	LP	VLP
PgDip Radio Journalism	11.14	12.67	9.81	10.52	44.14	SP	MP	LP	LP
Tutors - HND P/graphic Comm	12.29	13.29	11.57	13.86	51.00	SP	MP	MP	MP
Professional Photographers	11.64	14.00	11.18	13.55	50.36	SP	MP	MP	MP
LSQ general norm	9.30	13.60	12.50	13.70	-	MP	MP	MP	MP

Honey and Mumford have calculated a 'general norm' using data collected over a long period of time and from a wide range of occupations. They have also produced 'Norms' for different 'occupational groups', for example, salesmen, engineers, production managers, etc. These are known as the LSQ norms. However, they have not produced a specific 'norm' for photographers. Therefore I have used the 'general norm' as a comparative benchmark for the groups in this study.

Representation of the data

Although Table 1 provides for comparison, it became obvious that it was difficult to evaluate the data accurately to form specific conclusions. Learning style values proved to be a poor method for accurate assessment, because the values are 'banded' these being determined by the research undertaken by Honey and Mumford since 1982 (see *The Manual of Learning Styles*). For example, the activist very low preference value (VLP) goes from 0 to 3.99, while the reflector (VLP) goes from 0 to 8.99. Other learning style values have similar numerical ranges and therefore overall it is difficult to compare one group mean score with another. One group could be at the top of one learning style value band while another could be at the bottom of the next band; each would have a different learning style value yet the scores may be only a faction apart numerically.

Honey and Mumford also used a radial graph charts to plot individual learning style scores. This pictorial representation proved to be the best way of analysing and comparing the data. However, I departed from Honey and Mumford's usual practice of plotting individual scores against the 'LSQ norm', to that of plotting 'group mean scores' against the 'LSQ norm' (Figure 9.1). This was because I was particularly concerned with understanding and identifying the behavioural pattern of specific groups rather than individuals.

FIGURE 1 Typical radial chart

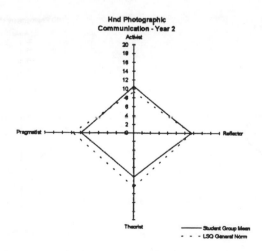

By comparing the shape of the plots on the radial graph charts, a consistent method of comparison could be made between the various study groups.

The HND Photography Programme and the Photographic Profession

In order to test my hypothesis fully, it was necessary to define the 'ideal' learning styles profile for photographers. I therefore extended my research to a group of practising professional photographers. These were drawn from a cross section of disciplines within the profession. My sample was relatively small (11 in all) due to the logistics of arranging and supervising the questionnaire, but the results threw up some interesting observations. Firstly, it identified that this group had a strong activist preference (SP). It further identified that they had a moderate learning preference value (MP) for the reflector, theorist and pragmatist learning styles. But when the radial graphs were compared, it was also evident that they also had a higher pragmatist learning preference than most of the other groups in the study (Figure 9.5), excepting that of the photographic tutors.

Can one identify different groups?

Because of the issues already discussed the assessment of the data has principally been done by analysing and comparing the radial graph charts for each group in the study. This revealed several different learning style patterns, notably, there was a marked difference between the National Diploma and Higher National Diploma Photography student profiles (Figure 2 and 3). The ND photography students had a very high activist score, and although the other learning styles were evenly matched they recorded relatively low scores for these styles. HND Photographic Communication students achieved higher scores for pragmatist, theorist and reflector preferences, making their learning profile more evenly distributed across the four styles and much closer to that of the LSQ General Norm (Figure 2).

FIGURES 2 AND 3

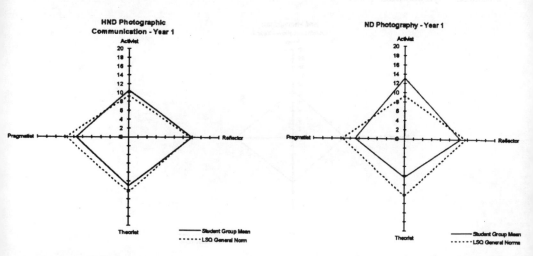

Although both programmes had their own specific profile, both first and second years in each, had remarkably similar profiles.

My results also indicated that the HND photography tutors and the professional photographers had almost identical behavioural profiles (Figure 4 and 5). These in turn were very similar to the HND Photographic Communication student profile, although the tutors and professional photographers were slightly more activist and pragmatic in their behaviour. However, there was no correlation evident between staff and students on the ND Photography programme.

FIGURE 4

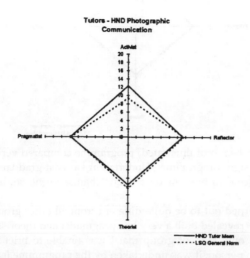

Tutors - HND Photographic Communication

The first-year Advertising group (not illustrated) had a profile similar to the ND Photography students; however the four scores of the former were overall higher, indicating a more rounded behavioural pattern. Both groups had a very high activist preference. Further results from the Advertising programme indicated that the activist preference waned somewhat in second year, bringing the profile more in line with that of HND Photographic Communication.

Both first- and second-year Graphic Design groups had very similar learning style profiles (Figure 7). A particular feature of these results were lower pragmatic and theorist scores when compared with both the HND Advertising and Photographic Communication programmes.

FIGURE 5

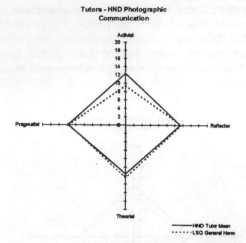

Tutors - HND Photographic
Communication

The PgDip Radio Journalism (not illustrated) programme compared very closely to that of the HND Graphic Design programme. Undertaking a post-graduate level vocational programme does not seem to have made a major change to the students learning style preferences.

BA Visual Culture turned out to be quite different from all other groups (Figure 6). The profile of these students revealed both a very low pragmatist and theorist preference (VLP). Curiously this was the only student group that I was unable to brief and supervise the questionnaire session in person; it was undertaken by the programme leader. These results merit further investigation, as it would seem unusual to have a theoretically based programme having a low theorist learning style. It may of course be due to many factors including the presentation and supervision of the LSQ.

FIGURE 6

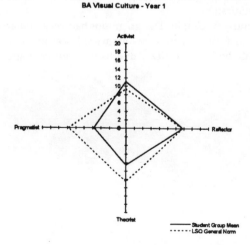

BA Visual Culture - Year 1

Is there a difference between the vocational and academic courses?

The BA Journalism Studies Programme (academic) had a profile very similar to HND Graphic Design (vocational), but my research revealed that both these two had an significantly lower pragmatist score than HND Photographic Communication (vocational). Apart from the unusual results from the BA Visual Culture programme, there seems to be no significant variation in the learning styles profiles of academic and vocational programmes.

Conclusions

There appear to be four different and quite identifiable learning style profiles within the groups in my study.

1. A very high activist preference, where all other styles are very low.
    ND Photography Programme (Figure 3)

2. Scores are more evenly distributed, although activism is higher than the other learning styles. This profile is very similar to Honey and Mumford's LSQ General Norm.
    HND Photographic Communication (Figure 2)

    HND Photography Tutors (Figure 4)

    Professional Photographers (Figure 5)

    HND Advertising Year 2

3. A relatively low pragmatic and theorist score.
    HND Graphic Design (Figure 7)

    BA Journalism Studies

    PgDip Radio Journalism

4. A very low pragmatist and theorist profile
    BA Visual Culture (Figure 6)

FIGURE 7

BA Visual Culture - Year 1

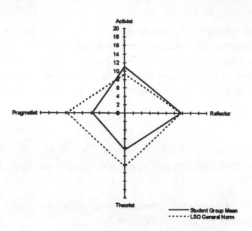

At this point, it is perhaps worth remembering the purpose of this research. I set out to test an hypothesis which suggested that there is a learning style specifically relating to photography, and that there is a system of analysis can reveal such a profile. The research has confirmed that it is possible to discern differences in student groups using learning styles profiles.

Both HND and ND Photography programmes reveal distinctly different profiles. No other group had a profile similar to that of ND Photography, yet the HND programme did have similarities with other groups. However, there is a correlation between the ND Photography 'group mean' and the 'norm' for 'A' Level/Diploma students documented by Honey and Mumford (*Learning Styles Manual*, 1993). Clearly there is room for further research in this area. Are the 'diploma level' profiles consistent across a range of courses and disciplines? Are the learning profiles at FE level different to that at HE level? etc.

The difference between the learning styles of the ND and HND photography programmes is even more intriguing when one considers that the students for the HND programme are recruited in the main from National Diploma Photography programmes. Are staff subconsciously selecting at interview students from ND courses, with a profile which this study has identified as being 'HND'? Do ND students join the HND programme and then have their learning style modified by their new environment or are there other factors?

Given that there seems to be similarity in the profiles of HND Photography students, HND Photography tutors and professional photographers, there is evidence to support the view that there is a learning style that can specifically be attributed to photographers. However, these findings need to be tempered with the knowledge that there are also similarities with the learning styles profiles of other student groups, and that the National Diploma Photography programme has a very different profile. Because this study has been just a 'snapshot' in time, the suggestion that the identification of learning styles could be used in the candidate selection process for the programme is somewhat premature. It does however point the way for further research which may clarify if it is possible to define learning style profiles more specifically.

Future action

I feel that my research has perhaps raised more questions than it has answered. It is clear that further studies need to be undertaken and in more depth. Given that this research has clarified my research and data analysis techniques, I feel that there is now an opportunity to refocus my work away from using the results for selection, and towards both individual students and programme development. Therefore further studies maybe directed in the following way.

- Monitor changes in individual student LSQ scores (HND Photography), and evaluate the connection with the programme teaching and learning strategies.
- Collect data from other photographic colleges for comparison with the Falmouth findings.
- Check the consistency and accuracy of results through larger group sampling of the learning style profiles of both photographic tutors and practising professionals.
- Investigate the differences and links between the learning styles of both the ND and HND photography programmes.

Bibliography

Bourner, T. and Barlow, J. (1991) *The Student Induction Handbook*. London: Kogan Page.

Daines, J, Daines, C. and Graham, B. (1992) *Adult Learning, Adult Teaching*. Nottingham: University of Nottingham.

Gibbs, G. (1988) *Learning by Doing*. London: Further Education Unit.

Hitchcock, G. and Hughes, D.(1989) *Research and the Teacher*. London: Routledge.

Honey, P. and Mumford, A. (1986a) *Using Your Learning Styles*, 2nd edn. Maidenhead: Peter Honey.

Honey, P. and Mumford, A. (1986b) *The Manual of Learning Styles*. Maidenhead: Peter Honey.

Honey, P. and Mumford, A. (1989) *The Manual of Learning Opportunities*. Maidenhead: Peter Honey.

Honey, P. and Mumford, A. (1990) *The Opportunist Learner*. Maidenhead: Peter Honey.

Honey, P. (1988) *Improve Your People Skill*. London: Institute of Personnel Management.

Kolb, D. A. (1984) *Experiential Learning: Experience as the Source of Learning Development*. New Jersey: Prentice Hall.

Personal and Learning Skills — A Sixth-Form Resources Pack. Institute of Chartered Accountants in England and Wales.

Personal Effectiveness: An Introduction to Self Development (1993) Bournemouth University.

Peterson, R. (1992) *Managing Successful Learning: A Practical Guide for Teachers*. London: Kogan Page.

Raine, T. (1993) *INSET by Discovery*. Devon County Council.

Riley, J. (1990) *Getting the Most from Your Data*. Bristol: Technical and Educational Services.

10 Research methodology and its usefulness in identifying barriers to learning

Chris Foggin and C. Rynners
University of Durban-Westville

Introduction

Towards the end of 1994 I was informed by the Head of the Department of Criminology that students were extremely disgruntled with both the content and methodology of the Criminology courses. It seemed that the major problem was the student perception that the pass rate was too low. This perception related to all Criminology courses in 1993. However some students were particularly distressed at the low 1993 Criminology 2 pass rate of 52%. It was those students who were studying Criminology 2 for a second time that comprised the majority of complainants. I was asked by the head of the department to research the legitimacy of the students' complaints.

In this chapter I elaborate on the methods I used to discover why many students of a course in the Department of Criminology had difficulty in passing it.

To ensure that the pass rate was indeed low I compared the following Criminology pass rates with the average pass rates in the majority of courses in the Faculty of Arts.

The pass rates for the following Criminology courses are given in Table 1.

TABLE 1 Tabulation of year and pass rate

YEAR	1993	1994
Crim 1	42%	59%
Crim 2	52%	70%
Crim 3	68%	80%

Student statistics for these years for the majority of courses in the Faculty of Arts are listed in Appendix A.

From the statistics listed in appendix A, it can be seen that the average pass rate for a second year course in the Faculty in 1993 was 63%. The Criminology pass rate of 52% was well below that average.

Demographics

The student demographics at this university present an interesting and dramatic picture. The university student population moved from being almost totally Indian to one of having a majority of black students in the space of a few years (see Table 2).

TABLE 2 Tabulation of year and race

Year	Demographics	
	% Black Students	% Indian students
1991	34	58
1992	38	55
1993	43	52
1994	48	47

An analysis of examination results in 1992 and 1994 reveals that the fluctuations in pass rates cannot be attributed to racial differences. The change in the average mark for 1992 and for 1994 does not differ much for each race group (see Table 3).

TABLE 3 Tabulation of year and average mark (%)

Year	Race	
	% Black Students	% Indian students
1992	48.8	56.4
1994	51.1	55.9

The picture in the Faculty of Arts is much more noticeable. In 1995 there were 940 Indian students and 1941 Black students.

In many other countries this classification may seem arbitrary; South Africa's infamous racial history however has meant that classifications are highly significant. The education system in South Africa was divided along racial lines in order to develop vastly different capacities in the people being educated. Education and training in South Africa has historically been based on conservative, authoritarian values espoused by a policy officially known as Christian National Education. Much of its purpose was to mould good citizens to fit into an ordered society and to be obedient to the state. Conformity was regarded as more important than developing skills necessary to cope in a working environment, or to study further at tertiary institutions.

In other words, education and training was considered to be transmission of facts with very little concern for insight or application. This was particularly true of black learners who were meant to provide a cheap source of semi-skilled labour and were not meant to compete with whites for highly skilled jobs. It is well-known that the development of the white population has until recently been largely at the expense of the black population. The Indian population has been better able to counter the discriminatory governmental educational policies and is largely an English-speaking race to boot.

Methodology

The methodology employed was that type of research usually associated with action research. That is, my intervention was situational, on a small scale, concerned with diagnosing a problem in a specific context and attempting to solve it in that context.

Specifically, the intervention was in the UDW criminology department; the problem being the fluctuating pass rates of undergraduate students over the past three years. The solutions would obviously be based on the findings of the study.

As part of the research the part played by student demographics was important as 65% of the student failures were black students. Indeed most of the student anger originated from this group.

The emphasis was on developmental research with the ultimate objective of assisting the Criminology department in their endeavours to achieve and maintain consistently high pass rates in all their courses.

One major point of concern was the fairly high pass rate that was produced in 1994.

In 1994 there was a dramatic increase of 17, 18 and 12% respectively in the Criminology 1, 2 and 3 pass rates. This was the year after the department had experienced their winter of discontent. Many of the variables one would associate with a change in pass rates had remained constant: staffing, marking criteria and methods of assessment were all the same over these years.

An inductive inference in the circumstances is that the department was more lenient due to sustained and defiant student pressure. This conjecture entails another research project and has not been an overt preoccupation of this project.

My first objective was to discover why the pass rates were low in 1993. It can be observed from Appendix A that the pass rates in Criminology fluctuate dramatically from year to year and this phenomenon was itself disquieting.

The following combination of research techniques were utilized:

1. one-to-one interviews;

2. small-group instructional diagnosis (SGID);

3. questionnaires (Appendix B);

4. statistical analysis of student profiles and data obtained from the above research techniques.

One of the problems experienced with research carried out in 1995 and not earlier was the question of how to contact and meet students who had studied Criminology 2 in 1993. Fortunately 17 of the students who failed Criminology 2 in 1993 resat the examinations in 1994, passed it and were studying Criminology 3 in 1995. In order to collect data about the 1993 course from these students we wrote to the 164 students who studied Criminology 2 in 1994 and requested that they meet with us. In this way we would be contacting those students who had failed Criminology 2 in 1993 and were resitting it in 1994 as well as those students who had studied the course for the first time. The latter group of students would be capable of informing me of their assessment of the course without being prejudiced by past failure of it.

The response rate to our first letter was extremely poor and we wrote to these students twice after that. A few of the practical problems experienced were the following:

1. securing permission to access student addresses (this was not a major obstacle but one to bear in mind);

2. ensuring that student addresses were printed on self-adhesive labels (when only one or two researchers are involved small logistical problems can become major ones);

3.   ensuring that most of the statistical information required from the administration was requested at much the same time (this is to avoid ongoing requests for data).

One of the reasons why only 33 of the 164 students (or 20%) responded may be related to the text of the letters sent to them. We were extremely wary of prejudicing the informants and did not specify in the letters the fact that we needed to interview them on their experience of the Criminology Course. Instead I stated that we wanted to find out how they felt about their courses in general (Appendix B).

In the first few interviews students were allowed to express their thoughts on all their courses. The approach used was one of informality and ease. The interviewer introduced himself as an educational researcher who wanted to improve the quality of courses at the university and was interested in their experiences of the courses they had studied. They were then asked to comment freely. At that stage we did not have a list of specific questions and the informants were free to relate their experiences. The first five informants were unaware that we were interested only in their opinions on the Criminology 2 course. These interviews were audio-taped with the students' permission. After the first four interviews we decided to modify our *modus operandi* by informing students of the precise reasons we were conducting research and we also began recording their thoughts in writing rather than on tape. This was a consequence of discussions held with colleagues at a meeting on research methodology. It was felt that being completely open with the students was more desirable for ethical reasons.

We began writing down interviewees' responses as the time taken in transcription became prohibitively long and we felt that it did not add to the quality of the responses. Students in the main were not reluctant to talk about their experiences. They knew they would remain anonymous and that the information they gave may improve the quality of courses being offered by that department.

The interview as a research technique proved immensely valuable; it allowed me to probe issues and to expand on topics that would not have been possible with a questionnaire. A clear thread of grievances began to emerge after six or seven interviews. Each of the 33 interviews finally completed occupied between 45 and 60 minutes and the quantity of data was large. Each informant, in addition to corroborating the information provided by preceding interviewees, also provided their own interpretations of phenomena readily available to all students.

It was soon apparent that there was indeed a number of serious problems with the Criminology 2 course curricula. To show that these problems were acting as barriers to learning however would not be easy to prove.

Small-group instructional diagnosis

Another structured way of gaining information about the learning experience of students was through small-group instructional diagnosis.

Students who have been grouped in clusters of five were asked during a lecture or tutorial to spend two minutes on each of the following questions:

(a) What has helped you improve your learning?

(b) What limits or hinders your learning in this class?

(c) What suggestions can you make for improving your learning?

We were only able to do this once and it was moderately successful in that some groups volunteered information and some did not.

Instead of using a lecture period we had access to the last portion of a double lecture (one lecture = 45 mins). The students were obviously quite eager to leave the classroom promptly. Nevertheless some interesting suggestions were made but the data collected were not of the same quality as that collected through interviews. This was to be expected as the time spent interviewing was far greater.

After an analysis of the data collected from both the one-to-one interviews and the small-group instructional diagnosis, a questionnaire was constructed drawing heavily on the common issues raised by the interviewees (Appendix B).

Analysis of student profiles

It was feasible that demographic data could have had an impact on the disparity of results achieved by students taking Criminology 2 in 1993. Consequently, this data had to be analysed. It was possible that one cause of the high failure rate in 1993 was a significantly lower student matriculation aggregate in that particular year. Upon investigation, however, it was found that the average aggregate in 1993 was only two points higher than in 1994. The Indian aggregate was six points higher than the Black aggregate in 1993 and five points higher in 1994. Not much of value could be extracted from these differences due to the differences in the secondary education systems under which each racial group studied.

As far as the average aggregate was concerned it is clear that there was little difference between the two years.

Conclusions

The part played by student demographics seems significant.

It has been mentioned that 65% of the students studying Criminology 3 in 1995 and who failed Criminology 2 in 1993 were black students. The percentage of black students who studied Criminology 2 in 1993 was 29%. Not all of these students have been interviewed. The majority of those that have been interviewed do not blame themselves for their failure but believe that components of the Criminology curriculum are in need of revision.

A corollary to this investigation has been the clear correlation between black school-leaving certificate results and success at university. It has long been the view in South Africa that it is extremely unwise to use these school certificates or matriculation results as indicators of competence at university. This view is prevalent because the educational system which has spawned these results has been severely neglected by the former governmental system and is thought to be incapable of producing accurate reflections of student ability. More research is being done in this area with some researchers now contradicting that view (Sharwood and Rutherford, 1994).

These later findings have been borne out by our research in the Department of Criminology. Of the 17 students who failed Criminology 2 in 1993 and who in 1995 are studying Criminology 3, 88% achieved less than a D average on their school certificate failed Criminology 2 in 1993.

The research conducted reveals insufficient evidence that the low pass rate is a result of the difference in student demographics over the years. Although there are significant changes in the racial composition of the university over these years they do not correlate with the changes in the pass rates.

The earlier inference that the fluctuation in pass rates is a function of inconsistent marking practices must be taken seriously.

Bibliography

Cohen, L. and Manion, L. (1994) *Research Methods in Education*. London: Routledge.

McKay, R. (1994) *SGID Interviews: Helping Teachers and their Students Develop Learning Environments*, mimeograph. New Zealand: Educational Research and Development Unit, University of Canterbury.

Powney, J. and Watts, M.(1987) *Interviewing in Educational Research*. London: Routledge.

Richardson, J. T. E., Eysenck, M. W. and Piper, D. W. (1987) *Student Learning: Research in Education and Cognitive Psychology*. Milton Keynes: Society for Research into Higher Education and Open University Press.

Sharwood, D. W. and Rutherford, M. (1994) DET results do predict the students' chance of success: a new model for selection.

In *SAAAD Conference Proceedings* (University of Natal, Durban, South Africa.)

Vulliamy, G. and Webb, R. (1991) Teacher research and educational change: an empirical study. *British Educational Research Journal* 17(2), 219—36.

Appendix A: Subject statistics, 1993 and 1994, University of Durban-Westville

Student % passed 1993 and 1994

1   Afrikaans
1: 54 ... 51
2: 42 ... 54
3: 92 ... 78

2   Anthropology
1: 73 ... 72
2: 73 ... 89
3: 95 ... 91

3   Criminology
1: 42 ... 59
2: 52 ... 70
3: 68 ... 80

4   Drama
2: 68 ... 70
3: 92 ... 86

5   Theatre and Film Practice
1: 36 ... 65

6   Theatre and Film Studies
1: 38 ... 22

7a English
1: 64 ... 46
2: 87 ... 78
3: 79 ... 74

7b English
1: 54 ... 53
8a Fine Art
1: 92 ... 81

8b History of Art
1: 56 ... 91
2: 94 ... 94
3: 90 ... 87
4: 100 ... 88

9   History
1: 62 ... 56
2: 84 ... 80
3: 86 ... 86

10 French
1: 52 ... 53

2: 50 ... 50

3: 100 ... 100 (2 students)

11 Philosophy
1: 69 ... 73
2: 61 ... 70
3: 75 ... 75

12 Political Science
1: 73 ... 71
2: 72 ... 80
3: 86 ... 81

13 Psychology
1: 51 ... 66
2: 46 ... 44
3: 94 ... 78

14 Science of Religion
1: 66 ... 82
2: 83 ... 64
3: 86 ... 88

15 Social Work
1: 85 ... 100 (60 students)
2: 90 ... 96
3: 88 ... 96

16 Sociology
1: 55 ... 63
2: 92 ... 89
3: 88 ... 96

17 Zulu
1: 85 ... 92
2: 80 ... 94
3: 95 ... 97

1993: Average first-year result = 1065 - 17 = 62.6%
1993: Average second-year result = 1022 - 14 = 73%

Appendix B: Criminology 2 Evaluation Questionnaire, University of Durban-Westville

We are trying to evaluate the quality of this course and would like you to answer the following questions as honestly as you can.

Last school attended ....

Please state your home language ....

Year in which you matriculated ....

Age ....

This is a departmental questionnaire and therefore questions refer to your experiences in the department as a whole.

Responses:
-2 = strongly disagree
-1 = disagree
 0 = neutral
 1 = agree
 2 = strongly agree

	-2	-1	0	1	2
	Percentage of response				
1. There were sufficient comments made on our tests and projects	25.00	31.25	15.62	21.87	6.25
2. There were too many parts to the Criminology 2 course		15.62	18.75	40.62	25.00
3. Lecturers made sufficient use of overhead projectors (transparencies) and other visual or audio-visual aids	28.12	40.62	18.75	9.37	3.12
4. In some courses one did not need to attend the lectures because all the information was in the coursepack	6.25	18.75	6.25	37.50	31.25

5. There was too much information in the coursepacks

6.25   6.25   12.50   25.00   50.00

6. The information in the coursepacks was well structured and easy to find

18.75   40.62   12.50   18.75   9.37

7. The coursepacks were easy to understand

25.00   21.87   25.00   21.87   6.25

8. The skills necessary to use the information in the course pack have not been taught

3.12   12.50   18.75   28.12   37.50

Have you any other comments to make about the coursepacks?

....

....

9. I attended almost all of the Criminology lectures

3.12   9.37   12.50   40.62   34.37

10. If I failed a Criminology course I attributed that failure to myself. (Ignore the question if you have not failed a course)

18.75   9.37   3.12   6.25   62.50

Please say why you think so?

....

....

11. The lectures were well-presented

31.25   34.37   31.25   3.12

12. The standard of marking was not good

6.25   18.75   28.12   28.12   18.75

13. There was enough interaction between lecturers and students in lectures

25.00   21.87   25.00   21.87   6.25

14. The time between handing in a test and its return was too long

6.25   15.62   15.62   25.00   37.50

15. In essays, tests and
other assignments, my
opinion was considered even
though it may have been
different to my lecturer's   15.62 21.87 25.00 34.37 3.12

16. The course did not
deal with relevant issues   12.50 31.25 18.75 25.00 12.50

17. If some lectures were
very similar to the notes
in the coursepacks I still
attended those lectures   6.25 6.25 6.25 40.62 40.62

18. The test questions were
not clear   15.62 50.00 28.12 6.25

19. The lecturer was
usually available during
consultation times   31.25 28.12 15.62 15.62 9.37

20. The content of the
course was not enjoyable   15.62 43.75 18.75 15.62 6.25

21. The examples used by
the lecturers were relevant
to my own experiences   9.37 18.75 37.50 28.12 6.25

22. The department ought
to provide me with more
guidance about the course
requirements   6.25 6.25 12.50 37.50 37.50

23. I do not have difficulty
taking notes in lectures   12.50 18.75 18.75 37.50 12.50

24. It was easy to understand
what was important and what
was not important in this
course   28.12 31.25 15.62 18.75 6.25

Please state anything else you wish to about the Criminology 2 course last year.

....

....

....

....

11 From theory to reality: research in practice and on action

Mike Heathfield and Sue Bloxham
Department of Applied Social Sciences
University College of St Martin, Lancaster

This chapter reports an action-research project on innovation in higher education. In one sense it is a narrative of how staff development leads to action, and how that action cannot develop without drawing in more and more elements of the educational process. In another sense, it illustrates the reality of attempting to be innovative in higher education against the long-standing background of student expectations, staff traditions and organizational processes. We have found that once the ideological decision had been made to start the journey of improved student learning, we could not retreat or contain it as the ramifications became increasingly complex and extensive. Like throwing a pebble into a pond where it's impossible to avoid disturbing the surrounding water, the consequences ripple out extensively from the original site of the action.

Therefore, although it is a personal account, the analysis of the experience also provides important, general points for the introduction and development of methods for improved student learning. The chapter will provide a description of the rationale for the initial innovation and what actually happened over the three years. Finally, we will extract the key themes in the implementation of student learning that emerge from our experience.

Background

In 1992 various things coincided to provide the impetus for innovation. A one-year post-graduate programme required revalidation in order to make it accessible to part-time students, our institution offered funds to enable staff to introduce 'flexible learning' into their courses, and we attended a seminar by the Oxford Centre for Staff Development on improving student learning. Fired up by the ideas from the seminar (Gibbs, 1992) which coincided with many of our intuitive ideas about learning; motivated by the offer of reduced teaching while we worked on new ideas, and driven by the need to create a course which required less staff-student contact time, we set out to design a radically changed student programme. It may be the case that we had a 'head-start' in HE innovation, because we teach in a field — youth and community work — where traditionally there has been an emphasis on student-centred approaches to learning, particularly in relation to activity and interaction.

The principles, values, and beliefs that implicitly underpinned the innovation are as follows:

- a belief in education as empowerment;
- a critical awareness of one's own work;

- a desire to improve and change things for all;
- a desire to maximize the number of students gaining benefit, motivation and depth of learning;
- a desire to encourage student independence, activity, creativity, problem-solving and challenge;
- a desire to reduce one's own 'expert' role;
- a desire to produce better, more skilled, competent, professional youth and community workers.

An important factor which cannot be separated from the outcomes of the innovation is the parallel research effort. Research has been used to monitor, evaluate and develop the work. It has involved the normal processes of staff and student evaluation (for example course evaluation sheets, log books, assessment of student work, staff discussion and external examiner reports), but there has also been a major formal element of research in each year. The research on this innovation has taken place over three years with various different cohorts of students. In the first two years the focus of research was in-depth interviews with students on the new post-graduate programme, but in the third year we also included a questionnaire study among first-year undergraduates. The detailed results of this research can be found elsewhere (Bloxham and Heathfield, 1994, 1995 and 1996; Bloxham, 1995).

The following model attempts to provide a framework for understanding how the innovation developed, and how the experience and research from one year influenced the development of the ideas in the following year. It also illustrates how, although students and staff were immediately affected by the change, it wasn't long before there were wider institutional ramifications.

Figure 1 An illustrative model of the growing impact of an innovative scheme

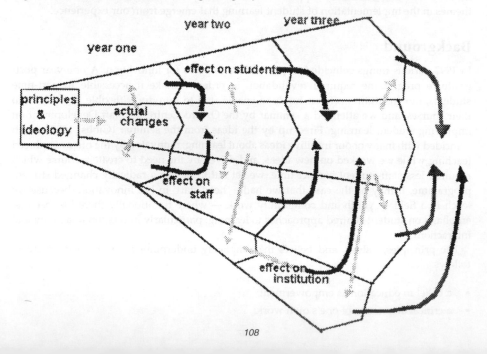

The practical changes and their impact on others

It would seem appropriate initially to itemize the practical changes we made to the curriculum and the way in which it was delivered and assessed. The consequences of these changes and developments will then be reviewed in terms of the effects on three constituencies. Firstly, a key source of data about the effects of these changes came from students participating in the courses concerned. Their view of the courses and our evaluation of the meaning of their data continually informed the progress of developments. Secondly, the changes have, obviously, had an important impact on departmental staff and, in turn, staff have influenced the passage of events. Lastly, from the second year of this research and development programme onwards, there were also institutional consequences that were linked to the practical developments within our department, and these form the third area of interest in this brief narrative of our research..

The starting point for our innovations was the preparation period for the 1992 intake of our courses. Initially three units on a six- unit one-year post-graduate programme were altered by reducing contact time, restructuring the programme and radically altering the nature and content of assessment. Assessment was the lever by which we attempted to change student approaches to learning, using it to encourage motivation, interaction, activity and structure (Biggs, 1989). We reformulated the tutor role as 'engineers of the learning experience' rather than the more usual 'transmitters' of knowledge. At a practical level this meant injecting considerably more student-led activity both individually and in groups.

The first students to encounter the new course in 1992 entered a significantly different learning experience to their previous degree programmes. Generally there was greater depth in learning, with more curriculum content retained specifically for practical professional use. The experience was busy, intensive and stressful with too much work. Students relied on each other a great deal which led to some difficulties when there were problems in group work or where deadlines were too distant. For a few students the new design was perceived as a lack of support resulting in demotivation or fear of losing their direction. Our learning from the students not able to benefit from our new design led to the shift in focus for the practical changes we made to the courses for the next intake.

For the staff concerned, the initial changes, while intensive in advance preparation time, did lead to a 30% reduction in teaching contact time throughout the first year of the programme. However, some of this time went on marking more assessed pieces and learning to mark more diverse and complex items. This marking complexity was particularly evident in group work pieces where there was great difficulty in discriminating between individual student achievements. Both staff and students felt that in some group work weaker students were being carried and stronger students were being penalized.

Our learning from the research programme on these initial developments led in the second year (1993/4) not only to a general expansion of these developments but also a slight shift in focus. Our original redesigned structure and assessment models were transferred across the whole six unit programme and into some undergraduate teaching programmes. In some cases this required revalidating courses with newer forms of assessment. Feedback from many of the new group work items indicated we needed to provide much more support for students undertaking group work based assessment items; and we attempted to do this through better induction, support and preparation for students and assessment tools that validated the group work process as well as the product. We also attempted to reduce the workload for students.

The results of these developments were measured by the research programme which produced a mass of data about the student experience. Their workloads were still incredibly heavy, they covered and were assessed on considerably more of the curriculum than students on the old programme and they were more active and responsible for a far greater proportion of their own learning. For most group work was highly motivating and productive and the quality of the learning outcomes was high. The placement experience provided a confidence booster and helped many process their college-based learning. Many students rationalized their workloads and assessment grades to manage their learning successfully. A small minority of students were still not able to benefit from the initiatives and were demotivated in many different ways; too heavy workloads, too much autonomy, too high staff expectations, lack of induction and preparation and resistance to new experiences. All students felt they had received less teaching in the unchanged units; the ones that actually contained more tutor contact time. The whole year was an intensive and emotional experience for the majority of students.

Staff found during the second year of the programme that they were more skilful in some areas such as managing group crisis situations and providing meta-cognitive support to vulnerable students. More significantly, our understanding also changed in that we realized that teacher philosophy was a crucial element in the success of the changes and this is discussed below. This led to the recognition that when new staff appointments were being made within the department, it was important to ensure that we were appointing staff with similar pedagogic ideologies and that all staff needed to spend more time discussing and sharing their educational philosophies.

Our focus on the curriculum and the comparisons we made between different elements of the new design also led us to conclude that curricula have embedded differences that can both hinder and assist efforts to introduce improved student learning.

As previously mentioned, the ever-increasing ripples caused by these developments also generated institutional responses. The relative success of the programme led to the development of a college-wide strategy to encourage similar innovations across the campus. This positive response was not, however, fully evident in validation panels where some changes met with resistance which, unsurprisingly, focused on modes of assessment. It also became clear that the fabric of the institution was not geared to teaching and learning in newer modes. Different student work patterns required different access arrangements to rooming and resources.

The experience of all three parties — students, staff and institution — influenced the changes introduced in the third year of the development programme (1994/5). Further courses on the undergraduate programme were affected by the innovations, but our attention was more directed towards induction and preparation for students about to experience the new courses. We made some attempts to reduce the workload but this remained limited by the assessment driven nature of our developments.

At this point our attention also began to focus on the nature of learning through placement experiences. All our professional courses had a substantial fieldwork placement element (30%). The findings from our first-year research programme (Bloxham and Heathfield, 1994) had indicated that placement experiences were a significant learning point for the majority of students. Consequently we began to look at new assessment procedures for placements and new student preparation materials for fieldwork experiences. As the influence of the changes spread wider more staff were involved in the teaching which meant time had to be invested in clarifying some of the basic principles behind the developments.

Staff training was also introduced for placement supervisors to familiarize them with new procedures and to test out the validity of our initiatives with field practitioners. The focus of these practical changes has remained the same for the current year of the development programme (1995/6). Induction and preparation were adjusted in the light of research evidence and an even greater investment was made in all the areas pertinent to placement assessment.

The research in the third year indicated that the focus on induction and preparation was having some effect on the student experience; group work became less contentious and problematic for the majority of students, meta-cognitive awareness was clearly articulated and on the undergraduate programme the drop out rate was reduced from the previous year. There were clearly identified gains for students on the newer induction programmes in comparison to other students on campus; better IT and library skills but no increase in their reported confidence in transferable skills. The new induction course was not valued by students equally with their other courses, it was still seen as an additional support course rather than a fundamental component of the whole training programme. Students also spent more time in detailed placement allocation procedures leading to a sharper perception of learning required from their practical experiences.

The new emphasis on procedural areas of knowledge such as placements had important affects on staff during the third year. While piloting new systems and tools for placement learning and assessment, we realized that all internal procedures needed to be made more consistent and more staff training was going to be required to develop consistency of judgement. Since, for the first time, we would be passing detailed placement performance judgements to students, we needed actually to define an agreed concept of 'good professional practice'.

The specific research in the third year on the new induction programme provided college-wide evidence of the positive effect of such innovations. On an institutional level, this led to senior management making a commitment to skills training for all students and requests to provide induction for new lecturing staff and staff development for all other academic staff in the college. Despite strong resistance to any innovations of this nature from a small number of staff, placement assessment procedures were validated for a full pilot in 1995/6 and the institution planned to set up a new learning resource centre with specific group work spaces available to students. In our most recent quality audit (HEQC 1996) the training of students to assess their own placements was featured and highly commended as good practice worthy of wider dissemination.

Discussion

Three theoretical themes emerge for us from the analysis of the narrative above. These are firstly, the shift from structural and pedagogic changes to student preparation as the driving force for changing student approaches to learning; secondly, the importance of institutional support and investment; and thirdly, the issue of maintaining control and direction of the innovation as it ripples out to wider constituencies of interest.

From course design to student preparation

The theoretical impetus for our initial changes was that teaching and assessment methods directly affect students' approach to learning. Various features such as passive methods and unseen examinations are considered to encourage a 'surface' approach, and other features such as student activity, interaction, and problem solving are seen to encourage a 'deep' approach to learning with greater understanding and enjoyment of learning (Ramsden, 1992). However, our early interviews with students indicated that although changed course structures and pedagogic approaches had the desired effect for many students, they were actually disempowering for others who, retaining a teacher-centred approach, felt resentful and did not benefit.

In the second year we addressed this issue by continuing with the course design changes, but building in a clear explanation of the course methodology during the induction period. This helped the students to understand the intention behind the course design, but it didn't actually help them do it. Tutors continued to find themselves giving considerable support to students who struggled with both the content and the process of the programme. Therefore, in the final year of the project, we introduced a fairly intensive induction programme to both our post-graduate and undergraduate courses. The purpose of the programme was to help the students both understand the purpose of the teaching methods, but more importantly, develop the skills to put it into practice. Team work skills are an excellent example of this need for careful preparation of students so that the vast majority can enjoy the benefits that only some students gain if they are left to work it out by their own devices. Other elements of the induction have included very practical skills such as library search, information technology, personal organization, presentation skills and writing for different audiences. However, it has also included a considerable emphasis on students increasing their metacognitive awareness to help them recognize and develop their conceptions of learning. Student conception of learning has been shown to predict the quality of their learning (Van Rossum and Schenk, 1984).

There is no doubt for us that this emphasis on induction and preparation for learning appropriate to the course design is essential to the implementation of improved student learning. Transferable learning and interpersonal skills should not merely be built into courses as a beneficial side effect, but they should become key topics in themselves. Experience (Gibbs *et al.*, 1994) has suggested that study skills courses are unlikely to be taken very seriously or have much affect if they are seen as independent of the 'real' business of learning and thus the challenge is to integrate them adequately into the 'content' of a programme so that students do not reject them as irrelevant.

Institutional support and investment

A review of the progress of this innovation indicates that although the impetus came from tutor attitudes and motivation, it was enhanced by institutional support and investment. Conversely, it suggests that however keen institutions are at a strategic level, to improve students' learning, there has to be commitment, understanding and motivation at grassroots (tutor-teaching-course) level.

The major rethink of course design and preparation of independent and group study materials, which was required in order to implement features of improved student learning, was aided because there were funds available to free staff to do the work. It allowed time, but also suggested that the initiative was valued. Staff drawn in to the innovation at later stages have not had the same support and have had to innovate under the pressure of normal workloads. It takes a strong sense of deferred gratification to invest hours of time into new course designs and materials on the basis that there will be a long-term payoff in terms of independent study by students and improved learning. Our experience also illustrates how institutions can work against themselves as exhortations to increase 'flexible' learning are countered by continuing pressure for examinations, the building of fixed seating lecture theatres and the lack of provision for student teams to work together.

Likewise, our efforts at top-down implementation of changes indicated that this was not possible without all the tutors concerned having assimilated a shared understanding with us of the philosophy and theory underlying our intentions. Indeed, it was interesting to discover that the students' perceptions of different units of the course varied considerably, and consistently, regardless of whether they were students who appeared to benefit or not. While this is not surprising in itself given that the units had different tutors, it is surprising in that a number of students complained that some courses had not had as much teaching as others, when in fact all units had had similar or less contact time than the criticized units! Analysis of the data suggests that students equated teaching with the amount of clear framework that was provided to help them learn, rather than the actual amount of contact with a tutor. Therefore, where tutors had altered their contact time in order to use it primarily to set up, monitor and evaluate independent and group learning tasks, students were happier with the teaching time devoted to the unit. Where tutors had tried to squeeze their normal amount of teaching input into reduced contact hours with additional assignments, students felt that they had insufficient teaching and demonstrated less active personal engagement with the content.

There is a possible lesson here regarding the development of innovative pedagogy. It cannot be done without almost going back to the first principles of the course and rethinking how the various learning outcomes can be met in a more open way. Tinkering with existing courses may satisfy no-one. Trigwell, Prosser and Taylor's (1994) work on lecturers' intentions suggests that change in teaching techniques will only follow where there is a complementary change in intention on the part of the tutor: 'As long as teaching staff hold transmission intentions in teaching, suggesting student focused strategies will be a futile and misunderstood pursuit' (p. 83). Therefore, it may be the case that some staff involved in the programme reported here have a general sympathy with increasing levels of student activity and interaction, but have retained an intention behind their teaching which retains elements of 'teacher focus' and information transmission. An implication of this inference is the need to provide a strong theoretical basis to staff development in regard to improved student learning. Providing lots of examples of techniques will be unsuccessful without sufficient understanding to encourage an appropriate change in intention. In this, our experience reflects the debate about 'competency' approaches to professional training with their emphasis on technical competence rather than understanding (Jones and Moore, 1993).

Control and direction

The innovation described above began with two tutors making major changes to the courses that they organized, taught and marked. Consequently, we were able to maintain control of the translation of principles and ideology into action. However, we soon wished to expand the innovation to elements of the student programme that involved other staff. This seemed important in order to offer students a consistent learning experience and fortunately our course leadership posts gave us the power to introduce appropriate structural changes across the student programme. But, the more staff were involved, the more we felt a loss of control over the work, and concern that our ideas were being misinterpreted or watered down. The institution has become involved and wishes to extend a version of our induction course to all first year undergraduates. Are their 'intentions' different? Will they interpret the ideas and techniques as they were intended?

Furthermore, we are involved with professional training and so it has become obvious that the principles inherent in the college-based elements of the course should be extended to students' on-the-job learning. However, fieldwork is generally managed and facilitated by personnel external to the higher education institution. The day-to-day learning experiences of students while they are completing the work-based elements of their courses are normally the responsibility of practice teachers, supervisors or mentors, employed by the placement agencies. Influence over the philosophy and approach of such staff is extremely difficult to ensure.

Clearly there is an unpredictable element to innovation in HE as staff and institution are interdependent and student experience cannot be radically changed without the different component parts changing together. Furthermore, as tutors, there is a fear that others will do it badly and it may have been better to leave them alone to do what they do well. For example, is it preferable to have tutors deliver well-organized lectures and request conventional essays, than do unthought-through group-based teaching and assessment which have the effect of making students disenchanted with the whole business of independent and active learning?

In a sense, the further away from the original course planning that the learning takes place, the greater the risk of dilution or misinterpretation. As illustrated by the metaphor in the introduction, where the pebble hits the water, the effect is strong and clear. However, as the ripples move away from the centre, the forces become dissipated. As innovators, we need to have realistic expectations about what is achievable in terms of improving student learning, otherwise we are bound to be disappointed.

Conclusion

This chapter, although largely a personal narrative, indicates a number of factors which influence efforts to develop improved student learning in higher education.

- Course design changes of a structural and pedagogic nature need to be accompanied by programmes designed to prepare and support students in the development of learning skills and metacognitive awareness. However, such support initiatives need to be carefully integrated into the main course programme in order to avoid students' perception that they are insignificant.

- Innovation is enhanced by a combination of institutional investment and tutor commitment and understanding. One without the other will limit possibilities.

- Realistic expectations of the scope for improvingstudent learning in a given situation need to take into account the vast range of people and processes involved.

References

Biggs, J. B. (1989) Does learning about learning help teachers with teaching? Psychology and the tertiary teacher. In *Supplement to the Gazette* **36**(1), 20 March.

Bloxham, S. (1995) *Integrating Learning Skills Training: An Evaluation*. Unpublished report.

Bloxham, S. and Heathfield, M. (1994) Marking changes: innovation in the design and assessment of a post-graduate diploma in youth and community work. In Gibbs, G. (ed.), *Improving Student Learning*: Theory and Practice. Oxford: OCSD.

Bloxham, S. and Heathfield, M. (1995)Rejecting the theory/practice dichotomy in youth and community work training. *Youth and Policy* **50**, Autumn, 35—48.

Bloxham, S. and Heathfield, M. (1996) The unexpected outcomes of critical professional learning. In Tait, J. and Knight, P. *The Management of Independent Learning*. London: Kogan Page/SEDA. Higher Education Quality Council (1996) *The Quality Audit Report of St. Martin's College Lancaster*. Birmingham: HEQC.

Gibbs, G. (1992) *Improving the quality of student learning*. Bristol: Technical & Educational Services Ltd.

Gibbs, G., Rust, C., Jenkins, A. and Jaques, D. (1994) *Developing Students' Transferable Skills*. Oxford: OCSD.

Jones, L. and Moore, R. (1993) Education, competence and the control of expertise. *British Journal of the Sociology of Education* **149**(4).

Ramsden, P. (1992) *Learning to Teach in Higher Education*. London: Routledge.

Trigwell, K., Prosser, M. and Taylor, P. (1994) Qualitative differences in approaches to teaching first year university science. *Higher Education* **27** 75—84.

Van Rossum, E. J. and Schenk, S. M. (1984) The relationship between learning conception, study strategy and learning outcome. *British Journal of Educational Psychology* **54**, 73—138.

12 Encouraging research into learning in a subject-related context

Barry Jackson
Middlesex University

Introduction

The Improving Student Learning symposium provides us with an opportunity to bring together researchers and teachers.

It also provides an increasing number of reports by teachers of their own research into their own teaching and course delivery. Consequently, when you look at the papers for this symposium, when you meet colleagues here, it 's very easy to relax into the view that the campaign to research into ways of improving student learning is being won. Here we are all, broadly, working towards the same ends, with an agreed, and agreeable sense of shared values and purpose.

Back at the workplace however, things always seem a little different ...

This chapter seeks to explore the role of managers in encouraging research into learning within a particular discipline area: that of art, design and the performing arts.

It has three goals:

1. to outline the context and to highlight the reasons why practitioner research is less common than might be assumed (section 1: Context);

2. to describe a small research project intended to throw light on staff attitudes and perceptions about practitioner research (section 2: A case study);

3. to suggest ways in which managers might encourage practitioner research (section 3: What can be done by managers?)

1. Context

A little history

There is indeed plenty of evidence of a growth of concern about student learning over the last two or three years. Most of this might be reasonably attributed to the dramatic changes in the size and diversity of student groups with which teachers now work. But prior to these changes some teachers had already begun to look at ways of improving teaching practice in relation to models of student learning which were emerging during the previous decade.

In 1991 the CNAA funded a project, managed by Graham Gibbs, called Improving the Quality of Student Learning (Gibbs, 1992). This project consisted of case studies of teachers, who, with support from the Oxford Centre for Staff Development, tried innovations and evaluated their outcomes, using frameworks which were then comparatively unknown but which are now fairly commonly understood.

This project gave rise to the present series of symposia. It encouraged teachers to research their own practice, and it provided an introduction to appropriate research methodologies, such as action research.

There was only one case study from art and design in that project, provided by myself and a colleague at Falmouth School of Art & Design (Davies, 1992). It is interesting to note that at this 1995 symposium there are no less than five presentations stemming from art and design backgrounds, a subject area which has been rather conservative regarding innovations in teaching.

While this is encouraging, it would be more so if all five presentations were not linked in some way with the institution or people who provided that first case study. There is increased activity, but it appears to be limited to pockets rather than built into the whole fabric of teaching in the discipline.

The reasons why practitioner research has not yet spread very widely may not be difficult to understand, if one looks at the working circumstances of most teachers in higher education today. Although they are urged to learn different ways of teaching, the context in which this happens is mostly characterized by those features which we know to encourage a surface approach to learning: namely, excessive workload, lack of choice over content and process, assessment schemes which provoke anxiety and/or reward a surface approach (staff appraisal schemes spring to mind . . .)

Two further substantial changes have occurred which have held back the continued development of improved learning through practitioner research:

The Research Assessment Exercise

Following the 1992 RAE the significance of good research ratings became apparent to higher education institutions. In a period of increasing financial hardship for HEIs the possibilities offered by research funding were substantial. Those departments which had not seriously attempted the exercise, and who therefore stood by, watching other institutions reap the benefits set about vigorously making sure that in the next exercise they would have a share. Those who had benefited set about making sure that their share was better than before.

As a consequence institutional and management attention appears to have moved back to encouraging research. Although policy statements, and mission statements say otherwise, it is a view commonly held by teaching staff at many universities that their institution values research above teaching.

What is certain is that the institutional concerns to do well in the RAE provide a useful cover to those teachers who are inclined anyway to value research over teaching, and who do not see teaching (and therefore learning) as needing any improvement.

It has a further impact, because research is now only valued if it can fit within the RAE framework of definitions. Within this framework, educational research appears to become the province of education departments. What value is there in a subject teacher undertaking research into teaching if it is not going to count in her departmental ratings?

There is a particular significance for the creative arts and design here. A very large proportion of lecturers in these subjects are part-time or fractional posts. The majority of teachers see themselves first of all as artists, designers etc., rather than as teachers. The RAE encourages this practice, and staff are now valued (again) for the amount and quality of their practice as artist. Teaching expertise, notwithstanding mission statements, has comparatively low currency in comparison.

More and different students

The second important factor is the changes associated with the developments towards a mass higher education system.

One outcome of this is that while there is now a greater level of activity associated with educational development, it is increasingly focused on extrinsic problems resulting from government policy, such as that of greater student numbers.

The agenda for improving learning is now increasingly directed towards the 'solution' of these pressing problems, overshadowing other issues.

This activity seems to be increasingly technocratic and operational, and does not always seem to be grounded in a secure theoretical framework about student learning.

In these circumstances teachers, increasingly hard pressed, perceive their managers' exhortations to improve teaching to be merely a response to larger student numbers. In this context the offer of staff development to improve teaching can seem like a threat, and staff can feel increasingly devalued, therefore increasingly insular and suspicious of change.

Practitioner research

The value of practitioner research has been stressed already at this symposium, and is a value shared, I suspect, by most of us here. We believe it is important for a number of reasons:

- involvement in developing one's own practice leads to intrinsic motivation, and
- it is more sensitive to local context, including the particular values of particular subjects.

Practitioner research is a form of action research. Zuber-Skerrit makes no distinction:

> *(action research) may be defined as collaborative, critical enquiry by the academics themselves (rather than expert educational researchers) into their own teaching practice, into problems of student learning and into curriculum problems. (Zuber-Skerrit, 1992)*

The action research paradigm is a valuable one for practitioner based research, because it stresses action , thus ensuring that the knowledge gained from research activity is put to use (unlike much traditional research, which can be written up in obscure journals, never to be read, let alone have any impact). Action research prioritizes **relevance** over **rigour**.

However, this emphasis on action is also the weakness of action research, since it reduces its currency in a wider domain, and specifically within a RAE oriented culture. It is not necessarily highly valued by most teachers or their managers.

The gap widens

There is a developing 'surface approach' to innovation in teaching and learning. In this approach teachers undertake activities and change their practices not because of an intrinsic motivation to improve learning, but because of extrinsic motivation — the desire to remain employed, perhaps. Research into learning will not flourish in this climate.

In summary, there appears to be little incentive to teachers to undertake educational research, while at the same time there is plenty of incentive to do other things, e.g. subject research or head-down, get-through-the-day teaching.

2.   A case study

Introduction

In the context outlined above it has become increasingly important to look at the role of managers. The attitudes and perceptions which managers hold, will affect whether, and in what ways they can, or will wish to, encourage research into learning.

This is the subject of a research case study which is presented here, which I began in order to improve my understanding of my own situation.

For me the starting point has been an attempt to understand the factors which block teachers' willingness to innovate and evaluate their practices. The contextual elements outlined above are clearly significant in this. I was aware also that teachers within creative arts and design often perceive themselves to be different in kind from teachers of other disciplines. My hypothesis is that there is an innate resistance to the importing of innovations from other disciplines, amounting to a conservativeness, which the discipline itself does not recognize.

There seemed to be an inertia or resistance to changing teaching methods (notwithstanding certain notable exceptions), which could be improved in my view if teachers were researching the impact of their teaching, using frameworks such as SOLO, approaches to learning, etc.

Starting with the assumption that there is a need for subject based research into learning, I hoped to explore what factors supported this inertia.

Aims of the study

The aims of the initial study were:

- to explore the issues related to subject-based educational research;
- to seek hypotheses as to the reasons for inertia;
- to throw light on colleagues' perceptions, attitudes and conceptions of educational research;
- to explore the apparent distinctiveness of the subject discipline;
- to start to identify points in the organizational structure at which management efforts might be better able to encourage change.

Methodology

To explore these questions I tried to find views on a number of issues. This was done principally by questionnaire, with supporting evidence from some interviews.

For the questionnaire I took as my target groups academics at two levels of the management organization in art, design and performing arts (ADPA hereafter) in my own university. These groups were heads of school, who are senior mangers, responsible for a discipline- based school such as Fine Art or Dance and set leaders, generally principal or senior lecturers, responsible for a specific programme or set of modules. (Each school on average might have two set leaders).

The same questionnaire was used for both groups and also for the equivalent groups outside of ADPA.

The questionnaire was concerned with respondents' views about subject-based educational research. The terms used were defined on the questionnaire (see illustration), and further opportunity was taken on the covering memo to stress the distinction between educational research and 'straight' subject research.

Respondents were asked to rate their agreement/disagreement with a few statements and were further asked to identify any educational research that was ongoing in their school.

The response rate to the questionnaires was 100% for art, design and performing arts heads of school. Set leader responses in ADPA were also reasonably high, over 60%. Returns from heads of school and set leaders outside the faculty were less comprehensive, being under 50% in both cases.

The differential response rate is perhaps a lesser problem in interpreting the results of the questionnaires, than the fact that the total number of respondents within the faculty is very small, amounting to nine heads of school (or equivalent) and 15 set leaders. The quantitative results must therefore be treated with considerable caution. Nonetheless it is possible to use the data as indicative or supportive of certain views rather than of others.

Main outcomes

The questionnaires revealed interesting attitudes and perceptions held by staff. The results seem to support the view that ADPA teachers do have different perceptions about the role of educational research from the norm. There is also evidence that senior managers appear to value educational research more than set leaders. This might be expected, perhaps, and is discussed more fully below. There is evidence of confusion about funding council views, and institutional views. The responses also seemed to reveal a confusion between educational development and research.

Art, design and performing arts characteristics

In comparison with other disciplines there seems to be a greater variety of response from ADPA staff about the importance of research into learning. There is a less coherent view, indicating perhaps less certainty about the importance, in the minds of both heads of school and set leaders.

There is less agreement that research into learning is as valuable in ADPA as it might be in other disciplines.

Although there is majority agreement within ADPA heads of school that learning research is as valuable as subject research, there are divergent views, apparently to a larger extent than the norm.

Unlike heads of school elsewhere in the university who showed a high score in the 'no strong opinion' category when asked whether the university valued learning research, ADPA heads were clear, but split — some very firmly believing that the university did value it, while others were very much more doubtful.

The views of ADPA staff at both levels regarding HEFCE's position on subject-based research into learning were not distinguishable from those expressed in other disciplines.

More detailed discussion of significant points raised under particular questions follows.

Question 1: Research into learning is valuable in my discipline

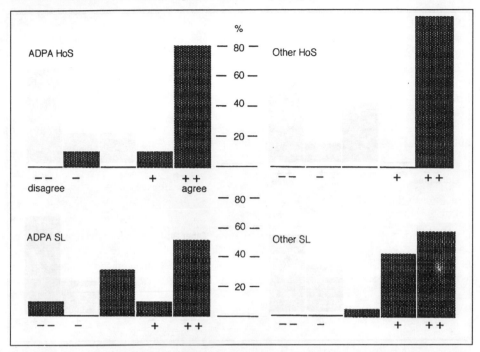

There appears to be a stronger, and clearer agreement with this by heads of school than by set leaders. This might reflect the fact that senior managers are more likely to give a 'management view'. This is particularly noticeable outside ADPA. Within ADPA there is evidence of a certain attraction towards 'non-management' views.

Set leaders in ADPA are similarly not as convinced of the value as their equivalents in other disciplines

Question 2: Research of this kind is as valuable in my discipline as in others

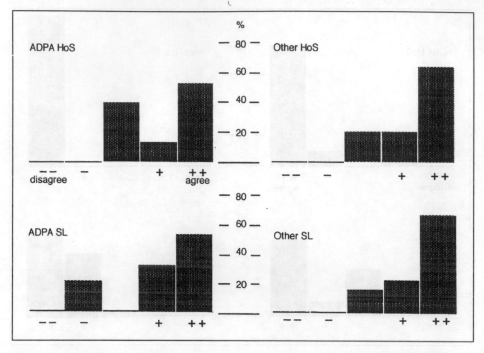

The intention behind this question is to explore colleagues' views about relative values.

Both levels of staff outside ADPA hold similar views — with a small amount of 'no opinion', all are in agreement.

In ADPA there are significantly higher 'no opinions' among heads of school. No set leader demonstrates the same lack of opinion. While the majority do agree, there are a small number who believe that ADPA benefits less, or has less need than other disciplines. This result is interesting in relation to other disciplines: none of which responded negatively.

It may be worth noting that an answer of 'no strong opinion' may be associated with a professed ignorance about the needs of other subjects.

Question 3: Research of this kind is as important as research into the subject itself

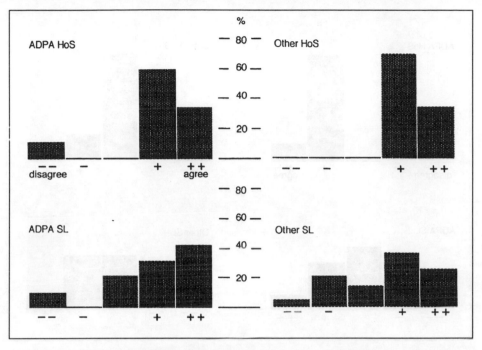

Unlike heads of school of other subjects, there is an element of disagreement within ADPA heads of school.

No heads of school, in or out of ADPA, fails to have an opinion on this. Set leaders however are more diverse in their views. Although the majority agrees on the equal importance of pedagogic and subject research, there is a certain amount of uncertainty both within and outwith ADPA, reflected in the spread of scores and the presence of 'no opinion' scores.

The area of uncertainty represented by these 'no opinion' scores may be the most fruitful area on which to focus for encouraging change.

Question 4: Research of this kind is valued by the university

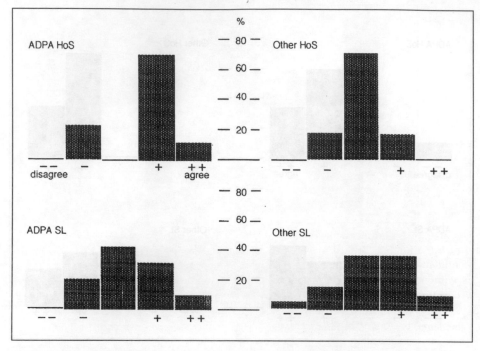

The ADPA heads of school stand out here as the only group who have no doubts — the majority believing that the university does value it, but a significant minority believing the opposite. There are no 'no opinion' scores. This is unlike the other groups, heads of school responses are most clearly characterized by lack of certainty, with only weak displays of certain agreement or disagreement.

Here there seems to be evidence of the institution's view not being understood, even by senior managers, with any confidence.

There is scope for improvement here, perhaps.

Question 5: *Research of this kind is valued by HEFCE*

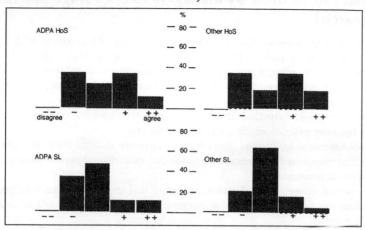

For all groups of respondents there appears to be considerable uncertainty about the value which the funding council may put on educational research. Heads of school feel more confident than set leaders that such research is valued, but not by a large margin. No group is without significant scores in the 'no strong opinion' or 'disagreement' answers. There seems to be evidence of a similar pattern of answers between ADPA and other disciplines.

Question 6: *Part of my job responsibility is to encourage and support this kind of research*

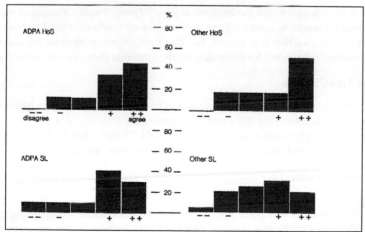

The majority of heads of school agree that encouraging pedagogical research is part of their job responsibility.

More surprisingly a significant number of set leaders also accept some responsibility for this. This is more surprising because set leaders have no formal management responsibility.

This outcome should be perhaps tempered by views expressed in comments which indicate that there is confusion in the minds of several staff between pedagogical research and more general educational development.

3. What can be done by managers to encourage practitioner research?

There is an analogy between teachers improving the quality of students' learning and managers improving the quality of teachers' teaching. A teacher who wishes to improve the quality of students' learning is attempting to provide opportunities for the students to take a deep approach, and to restructure their understanding of some aspect of the world. Similarly, managers who wish their colleagues to change, should encourage them to take a deep approach; should help their understanding of the need for, and the nature of, the changes to teaching practice which are being encouraged.

This encouragement for change starts from a reflective view of their own practice. The manager's first responsibility therefore becomes the encouragement of reflective practice — a step towards action research.

The survey and interviews undertaken as part of this small project have helped identify possible areas in which action by management can help to encourage and support practitioner research.

Resourcing

Providing targeted resources, in terms of time particularly, is a key means by which management can support research activity. Although resources are increasingly difficult to divert, it may be possible to divert research funding to practitioner research, if outcomes are clear enough.

Clarify the institutional view

Making clear to colleagues that the institution (even if only the department, at worst) does value practitioner research, even perhaps expects it of all teachers, would be helpful. Some staff may never believe that it is valued, but there are clearly a considerable number who simply are unclear. Clarifying for them may be the stimulus they need to become engaged.

Clarify the HEFCE view

The HEFCE do allow that pedagogical research in particular disciplines can be submitted as part of the research return for the discipline, providing that it is not simply curriculum development or the preparation of learning materials. Clarification of this might have the same effect as above, and also provides a route into research funding bids.

Try to organize a context for teachers which takes account of approaches to learning

If teachers are to learn new ways of teaching they need to do so by taking an engaged, deep approach. Managers might seek ways to encourage the features which are associated with deep approaches:

- motivation — (wanting)
  what are the ways in which staff can be encouraged to **want** to undertake research into their own learning?

- action — (doing)

  how can the reflective and planning stages of action research be made an activity which staff engage in readily?

- interaction with others — (talking)

  how can staff be encouraged to offer each other support and share their learning?

- building a firm knowledge base — (digesting)

  what means can be provided for staff to build their growing understanding into a coherent conception of teaching and learning?

Clarify research as distinct from curriculum development

Quotes from respondents to the survey demonstrated a range of understandings about the nature of research. Many people reported as research activity the kind of activities more usually associated with staff development, and few had any framework within which innovation was guided.

Clarification of this would help the the process of support and funding, making it clear that financial support from research budgets can be legitimately spent on research, where there is a public outcome.

Action research support

Teachers could be better supported in carrying out action research, and could be helped to externalise their learning in the form of reports and other outcomes.

Many more teachers might undertake research into their own teaching if they can be helped to see that their everyday practice can be a starting point for reflection and innovation. It may be that there is already considerable activity which needs only to be more thoroughly reflected upon and reported to become valuable action research. Exploring, understanding and using the model of the Kolb learning cycle will be an important staff development strategy.

Managers have an important role to play here, as do educational and staff development personnel.

Undertake action research themselves

Managers who undertake action research on the teaching of their colleagues are likely to gain a better understanding of their practices and how they might be improved. The project reported above has helped me in this way.

References

Gibbs, G. (1992) *Improving the Quality of Student Learning*. Bristol: Technical and Educational Services.

Davies, A. (1992) Encouraging reflection and independence on a graphic information design course. In Gibbs, G. *Improving the Quality of Student Learning*.

Zuber-Skerrit, O. (1992) *Action Research in Higher Education*. London: Kogan Page.

13 Evaluating a student-centred course through participative action research

Gary Rolfe
Principal Lecturer, School of Health Studies
University of Portsmouth

Melanie Jasper
Principal Lecturer, School of Health Studies
University of Portsmouth

Introduction

This chapter has two aims. The first is to offer a participative action research methodology for course evaluation, and the second is to present and discuss some of the findings generated from the application of that methodology. The course to be evaluated was a shortened Common Foundation Programme (CFP) in nursing for graduates, run by ourselves, which the students studied for alongside a Masters' degree. What was required was an indication of the students' feelings about being on the course; that is, a measure of process rather than outcome, and of course structure and learning methods rather than content, since the latter were already being assessed in a number of other ways. The course was designed along student-centred lines, with course members participating in content and process decisions, and we wanted the evaluation to reflect the same philosophy.

Unfortunately, our previous experience of course evaluation, both as students and teachers, has been generally disappointing. Most evaluations utilize tools generated by the teacher, which effectively ignore the students' agenda. The information generated is often of little practical use, with the focus being either too general or too specific, and students are usually not briefed to write constructive and useful criticism.

Furthermore, response rates are often disappointingly low, reflecting both a lack of ownership of the findings, and the belief that whatever feedback the students give will not be acted upon. And since evaluations usually occur at the end of courses, students often feel that even if action is taken, it will be too late to be of benefit to them. This often results in a 'see-saw' effect in which changes suggested by one intake to the course are reversed by the following group. In short, our experience of course evaluation has been of an unthinking ritual with little commitment by the teachers to act on the information generated.

Research methodology

In attempting to rectify some of these problems, the research project adopted several principles:

- Evaluation should be an ongoing, integral part of a course, and not just a retrospective exercise.

- Curriculum planning should likewise continue throughout, based on findings from regular evaluation sessions. In this way, the course will retain its flexibility and respond to the needs of the students.

- The students should play an active role in the process of evaluation. Course evaluation is part of the education process, and the students can learn and practice high-level cognitive skills through participation in the evaluation of their course.

- All evaluation is by definition subjective, so there is little point in searching for objective methods or bringing in outside evaluators. Rather, we should embrace the subjectivity of the evaluation process and collect a variety of perceptions of the course, not just those prescribed by the teacher.

Clearly, the above principles lend themselves perfectly to a participative action research approach in which:

> *all those involved contribute both to the creative thinking that goes into the enterprise — deciding on what is to be looked at, the methods of inquiry, and making sense of what is found out — and also contribute to the action which is the subject of the research. (Reason, 1988)*

This approach implies not only that the 'subjects' of the research play an active part in every stage of the project, but that the findings are immediately acted upon, thereby bringing about direct change in the organization or process under investigation.

Thus, the students were seen as equal partners in, and joint owners of, the project, with the intention that the material generated should be of direct benefit to the people who provided it. It was therefore considered important that evaluation should start at the beginning of the course, with immediate application of the findings.

The role of the teacher in the early stage of the evaluation was that of enabling the students by constructing a framework in which the process could evolve. In psychological terms, this involved adopting an attitude of permissiveness and non-judgementalism, acknowledging the importance of the evaluation, and ensuring that the students understood its purpose. In practical terms, it required the provision of space in the timetable for the evaluation to take place, and ensuring that the students had the necessary research skills for the task.

An overview of the evaluation process

An initial meeting with the students was called in order to engage them in the project and to present the philosophy of participative research. In the second meeting, the students divided into small groups of four or five to pursue specific areas of the evaluation. Students were given a completely free hand to choose which aspects of the course to evaluate and the methods they would employ. In allowing the students this freedom, we made the assumption that they would choose issues that had personal meaning, importance and significance to them, and that they would therefore invest high emotional energy in their chosen areas. We might expect, then, that their evaluations would be highly subjective, even biased, despite their best efforts at objectivity. However, this is seen as an advantage, since their findings will reflect issues of relevance to them as individuals.

At this stage, the research strategy split into two parallel streams. The students proceeded to investigate their chosen aspects of the course in five small groups, examining areas such as the effectiveness of self-directed learning, communication, and the use of groupwork. All five groups chose to use questionnaires to collect their data, the main reasons being those of speed and simplicity, although a wide range of methods was open to them.

The material generated by the questionnaires provided a rich source of information about the issues that were relevant and important to the students, but it is by definition surface information, reflecting their immediate perceived needs. The course teachers held a philosophy of group dynamics based on the work of Bion (1961), who argued that as well as a surface agenda aimed at meeting their stated needs, in this case the need for education, all groups also have a deep and usually unconscious agenda of which their members might be totally unaware.

Therefore, at the same time that the students were administering their questionnaires, the course teachers were attempting to probe the deeper group issues by analysing and deconstructing the research instruments. This involved trying to get underneath the surface meaning of the questions to look for deeper motivations. It is recognized that what this produces is a subjective impression by the teachers of what the unconscious group issues might be, and therefore this analysis was then used to construct an interview schedule for a depth interview with each group in order to validate the teachers' hypotheses, and to attempt to bring the unconscious group agenda into the conscious awareness of the group members. A flow chart of the full research process is shown in Figure 1.

1 Flow chart of the research process

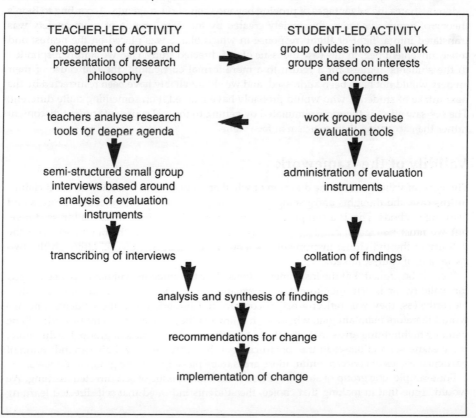

TEACHER-LED ACTIVITY	STUDENT-LED ACTIVITY
engagement of group and presentation of research philosophy	group divides into small work groups based on interests and concerns
teachers analyse research tools for deeper agenda	work groups devise evaluation tools
semi-structured small group interviews based around analysis of evaluation instruments	administration of evaluation instruments
transcribing of interviews	collation of findings

analysis and synthesis of findings

recommendations for change

implementation of change

This process, although time-consuming, generated a very rich fund of information about all aspects of the course. On the one hand, we had the information collected by the students themselves concerning the issues which they saw as important, and which they wanted addressing in time to benefit them on their course. On the other hand, we hopefully gained access to the hidden agenda of the group, to the feelings, attitudes and anxieties of the course members based on the material from the group interviews.

The final task of the teachers and students was to integrate the findings from the students' inquiry with the material from the interviews into a broad and holistic evaluation of the course, and to negotiate ways of acting on the students' recommendations while at the same time addressing their feelings and anxieties.

This can raise problems, since the two agendas often appear to conflict. For example, many of the students on the course were having difficulty in setting their own objectives and directing their own study, and this was reflected in their evaluation by a request for a return to more formal teaching methods. However, the group interviews uncovered a great deal of anxiety about the examination at the end of the course and the depth of knowledge required to pass it. What emerged was that it was not the process of self-directed study that was causing difficulty, but a perceived lack of information and guidance about the content and format of the exam, which was resolved very simply by providing information and reassurance.

This was a very different intervention from that originally requested by the students, and it demonstrates the advantages of probing beyond their surface agenda. According to Bion's theory of group dynamics, the anxiety created by the deep agenda of exam anxiety was translated into a 'fight or flight' response in which blame was placed on the nearest and most convenient peg, in this case the issue of self-directed study. Had we simply responded to the students' request for a return to a more formal curriculum, the real cause of their anxiety would not have been addressed, and would inevitably have been resurrected by the next intake of students, who would probably have blamed it on something quite different. The see-saw effect is therefore eliminated by getting to the real source of student discontent rather than accepting their criticism at face value.

Validity of the framework

The issue of validity raises the question of whether an instrument measures what it claims, in this case, the thoughts and feelings of the students about issues of course process and learning methods. This is a complex and difficult area that cannot be fully addressed here, but we must be careful not to confuse the validity of the research framework with the validity of the individual instruments generated from that framework, although the two issues are, of course, linked.

It could be argued that the instruments devised by the students will not have been tested for validity, and that therefore the information they yield will be of limited value. Nevertheless, they will reflect areas of concern and importance to the students, and we would therefore maintain that, whatever instruments they construct, the framework will be valid by highlighting areas that are relevant for that particular student group. Furthermore, the weaknesses and biases in the construction of the instruments will give an indication of particular issues of concern within those areas to be picked up in the group interviews.

For example, one group of students chose to look at the issue of self-directed learning. We would argue that in making that choice, the students indicated that self-directed learning was a particularly relevant issue to them, and this assumption was later borne out in the group interview. Furthermore, the students' questionnaire contained several leading questions and was, by conventional standards, poorly designed. Nevertheless, an analysis of the content and intention of those questions highlighted possible issues of concern within the area of self-directed learning, and again these leads were followed up during the interview. This revealed that the students had believed their questionnaire to be fair and bias-free, and they were genuinely surprised that we had managed to uncover specific problem areas which would otherwise have gone unnoticed.

Thus, although the student-generated tools within the evaluation framework will almost certainly lack validity, their purpose is to raise issues of importance as much as to collect data, and they are therefore to some extent a means to an end. However, we would argue that the overall framework can be said to be valid in that it uncovers areas of concern, it is a vehicle for the students to express their thoughts and feelings about course structure and process issues, and it can provide a forum to address deep issues which might be acting as a block to learning.

Some selected findings

This part of the chapter reports on some of the findings from the first intake to the course, and examines the material generated by a group of six students who chose to look at the issue of student-centredness. The group designed a questionnaire for completion by all the students on the course (22 in total), which addressed areas such as levels of achievement, self-motivation, objective-setting, preferred learning styles, perceived problems of self-directed study and use of time. The small-group depth interview with the course teachers explored the selection of the topic and probed the issues identified by the students.

Levels of achievement

The students considered themselves to be sufficiently well-motivated and skilled to achieve the expected workload, but identified the need for greater tutor input to the definition of goals and objectives. One student commented:

> *you don't know quite how much depth to go into ... everyone's different ... some people want to do well, others are perfectionists, but is there a set standard?*

and another said:

> *you might be achieving the right level, but you are not confident of the fact that you are.*

Students constantly compared themselves to the non-graduate students undergoing the full-length CFP, and were anxious to be seen to be achieving the same accomplishments and knowledge-base. In particular, they felt the need for prescribed levels of achievement and focused on the needs of assessment.

This highlighted the differences between the teachers and the students in their perceptions of the purpose of course assessment. The teachers had constructed the assessment strategy as integral to the course, and therefore providing the students worked consistently throughout the course, there would be little likelihood of failing the assessments. In particular, there was no need to 'cram' or rote learn, as the examination w based on a continually updated portfolio, testing the ability to apply knowledge rather than to reproduce it. The intention of this strategy was to free the students from exam stress and to enable them to identify their own learning needs and strategies to accomplish these within the prescribed outcomes of the course, motivated by their intrinsic need for growth.

The students, however, tended to be assessment-driven, relying on the extrinsic motivation of deadlines for course work and the examination to structure their learning, and as a result they became frustrated and anxious by the lack of 'knowledge' targets which they could 'learn' in order to pass the course. This reflected the students' previous experiences of higher education, where courses tended to be dominated by examination success, but which did not reflect the philosophy of this course.

Learning styles

The apparent paradox between the students' perceptions of their ability to be self-motivated, and their need for motivation from externally directed objectives highlighted the differences in learning styles amongst the students. Comments from students reflected these differences, ranging from 'we need specific guidelines and clear goals' (tutor-dependent) to 'group work and self-directed learning is an excellent way of learning, but too much is tiring and stressful'. The general opinion of the students was that student-centred learning was a good thing, but that it needed to be supported by a strong infrastructure in terms of organization, and by clarity in terms of 'knowing what was important' and 'depth of achievement and goals'.

Some of the students saw the student-centred approach to teaching as imposing more rather than less stress, with their perception of student-centred as being anything done by the teachers to make learning easier, for example, lectures, handouts, articles photocopied, and so on. Mostly, though, the students' interpretation of student-centred appeared to tread a middle road between the extremes of teacher- and student-centred methods. Most students valued the presentation of knowledge in lectures and seminars, but also appreciating the flexibility of small group work and individually set objectives. The degree of stress appeared to lie not so much in the self-directed nature of the course, but more in the perceived gap between the identification of what the students needed to learn and the means by which they were expected to learn it.

Students' needs

It is evident from the previous discussion that in some ways the course design was not fulfilling the students' needs. Why might this have been so? In part, it reflected the different expectations of the students and tutors. Students' concerns appeared to be around the need for a structured knowledge base, whereas the tutors took a broader approach in stressing the importance of the development of nursing practice based on both theory and reflection on clinical placements. The added stress of coping with the demands of two courses, one of them abbreviated, also added support to the demand for work to be clearly directed by the tutors. Students often limited the amount of work they did to what was perceived as the bare minimum. For example, one student said:

> t the MSc to think about, which is taking over. I don't want it to because I came here to be a
> ut I feel that it's easier to sit down and write an essay than to teach yourself nursing, so
> direction I'm going in, which I fear is counterproductive to what I want to be in the end.

d that a compromise needed to be established between the creation of cognitive dissonance as a motivation for learning, and the point at which this becomes stressful and inhibits learning. Students' suggestions for maintaining a balance related primarily to enabling the students themselves to organize their own learning by providing a more tangible support system within which they could define and achieve objectives. One student acknowledged that 'people do learn from self-directed learning, but they just feel so safe in a lecture situation because that is what they are used to', and another said 'I think the course is on the right lines, but people need reassurance', with a third commenting 'the emphasis is on "do-it-yourself" and "this is your own course", and sometimes you can forget that there are objectives there'.

In fact, both formal and informal opportunities for on-going support were a planned feature of the course and were available to the students throughout. The use of small group workshops and reflective practice provided regular timetabled opportunities for peer support facilitated by a teacher, and all students were allocated to both an academic and a personal tutor whose roles were to provide support on request from the student. The lack of use of this latter facility perhaps again reflects the students' previous experience of tutorial support as 'only there if you are in trouble or falling behind', or seen as an 'admission of being unable to cope'.

Modifications to the course

Two issues stand out from the evaluation in relation to the student-centred learning components of the course. Firstly, the lack of explicit, externally set objectives caused anxiety in the students, which at best took up valuable time in worry, and at worst interfered with their learning. Secondly, many of the students had doubts about their ability to self-motivate sufficiently to succeed on the course.

Modifications to the process of student-centred learning, in line with the recommendations of the students, included the formal identification of learning objectives to tie in with the weekly themes of the course, and the creation of a work-book. The work-book provided a unifying strand for theory, practice, identification of students' needs, objective planning and reflective practice through the use of critical incident analysis. Another strategy to be implemented was the use of student teams (Gibbs, 1992) to establish interactive learning.

A formalized structure for tutorial support was also established, with students required to meet with their tutors at least monthly in order to review learning accomplishments and to set objectives for the coming months. Another modification was to construct a support system at the beginning of the course to help the students feel safe and in control of their learning. These strategies appear to date to have rectified the problems identified by the evaluation study, but are themselves in the process of evaluation.

Conclusion

This chapter has outlined a strategy for a student-centred approach to course evaluation drawing on collaborative inquiry and action research techniques. Although specifically designed for a CFP in nursing, we believe that this method is applicable to any course in further or higher education. It requires a reappraisal of outmoded and redundant notions about the role of evaluation within educational courses, and has, we believe, several advantages over traditional methods. Firstly, it gets below the surface issues and highlights the underlying causes of problems and difficulties; secondly, teachers and students are made aware of issues of importance which might interfere with the process of learning as they arise; thirdly, students are put in touch with, and are therefore more able to deal with, their own feelings and anxieties about the course; fourthly, it results in real and effective changes during the life of the current intake to the course; and fifthly, the evaluation process itself could help to develop analytical skills and high-level cognitive functioning in the students.

On the negative side, an evaluation of this kind can be extremely threatening to teachers, since it involves a loss of control over the evaluation process, a result of which is that they are left exposed to criticism by the students. It also demands a prerequisite attitude of student-centredness in the course teacher, and a great deal of commitment to look critically at both their course and their teaching. Finally, it might appear to be an extremely time consuming approach to evaluation, but in fact it need take only about one hour per week, and in our experience, this has been well spent time which has contributed greatly to the ongoing development of our course.

References

Bion, W. R. (1961) *Experiences in Groups.* London: Routledge.

Gibbs, G. (1992) *Improving the Quality of Student Learning.* Bristol: Technical and Education Services.

Reason, P. (1988) *Human Inquiry in Action.* London: Sage.

14

A different kind of R&D? Combining educational research and educational development

Liz McDowell
Educational Development Service
University of Northumbria at Newcastle

Introduction

Many universities employ educational development staff, working in departments such as an educational development unit, teaching and learning service or learning methods unit, with the primary aim of improving teaching and learning within the university. Typically, educational developers undertake formal staff development and training; act as internal consultants to individuals, course teams and departments; provide information and access to resources about teaching and learning; and sometimes work with students in relation to study skills and/or learning difficulties. The extent to which they are involved in educational research varies, but most will be involved at some level in investigations into teaching and learning. This chapter describes and evaluates ways of combining educational research and educational development based on the experience of the Impact of Assessment research project in the Educational Development Service at the University of Northumbria.

Educational research and educational development: contrasting activities?

Educational developers are often stereotyped as confirmed pragmatists offering practical advice and suggestions, impatient with research and theory. Their clients may view educational research as irrelevant and unhelpful because it tends to illuminate complexity and provide provisional answers, whereas decisions and choices about teaching and learning have to be made immediately without waiting for further research to be done. Webb (1992, p. 352) highlights the issue:

> The practical has been valued over (and often defined in opposition to) the theoretical, and especially the philosophical. In short, practitioners tend to want answers, rather than further questions.

However, as academics, educational developers often do derive their practice from a basis of knowledge, understanding and theory and wish to contribute to the development of their discipline.

There are differences between educational research and educational development, some of which are summarized in Table 1. Educational development aims to change practice in teaching and learning. Educational research may also aim to do this in the long run, but its primary aims are to understand teaching and learning and to explicitly address theoretical issues. Educational development tends to concentrate on supporting clients and meeting their needs, and this often results in diverse, fragmented and apparently *ad hoc* activity. Research, in contrast, tends to be rigorously planned and has a different focus and set of clients within a research community. Researchers aim to develop knowledge which is as accurate and truthful as possible.

Table 1 Some contrasts between educational development and educational research

	Educational Development	Research into teaching and learning
Aims	Changing practice	Understanding practice
Relationship to theory	Theory used in a distilled form	Intention to develop and critique theory
Methods	Diverse, eclectic	Planned, methodical
Focus/area of concern	Client needs	Understanding, knowledge, truth
Primary clients/ audiences	Local clients (lecturers and students)	Research communtiy

Although a number of distinctions between educational development and educational research can be made, in practice the two activities are often combined. Action research and practitioner research are most frequently recommended and promoted as means of linking the two. These involve the practitioners or lecturers themselves in researching their own practice, enabling research and practice to be continuously interlinked. In its fullest form, action research involves the collaboration of a group of lecturers and a cycle of research and development, though some people would allow for the possibility of single action researchers working alone. However, practitioner and action research appear to be more common in sectors of education other than Higher Education (Kember and Gow, 1992 p. 299), although the level of activity may be underestimated since such activities are not always formally published. Where they are, the focus is often on process rather than outcomes (for example, Schratz, 1992) with some notable exceptions such as Gibbs (1992).

However, action and practitioner research are not the only ways of combining educational research and development and they have some problems and disadvantages. For example, there can be a long lead time while lecturers become familiar with the way of working and with appropriate research methods and relevant theories. External publication may be inappropriate or difficult, and this is a significant consideration in the current UK climate where educational research activity in universities must increasingly take into account the need to provide evidence for periodic research assessment exercises, whether or not the research contributes to local improvements in teaching (Jenkins, 1995). It is therefore worthwhile to consider whether other research approaches can also support educational development. We have addressed this question in the Impact of Assessment project and are now in a position to review how the project has operated.

The Impact of Assessment Project: key features of the research process

The project, based in an educational development service, is investigating the impact on student learning of innovative assessment methods, via a series of case studies of assessment in practice at the University of Northumbria. We are using a case- study approach, mainly collecting data through observation and interviews with both staff and students, to illuminate instances of assessment. Our research approach could thus be described as conventional, within the broad spectrum of qualitative research approaches. Case studies undertaken so far have covered a range of subjects and a variety of forms of assessment including: assessment by group project, oral presentation, poster presentation, open book exam, a formative assessment programme to develop essay writing skills, and examples of self and peer assessment. The management of the project by educational developers has affected the way in which it has been conducted and organised throughout.

Choice of research topic

Our choice of research topic did not stem from a theoretical debate or some particular aspect of the research literature, but from our awareness as educational developers that assessment was a matter of crucial importance and concern within our own university and beyond. Reasons for this include: increasing student numbers, new demands being placed on assessment systems from quality assurance perspectives and the need to consider new purposes for assessment in HE such as the assessment of competence. Our research focus was therefore determined by what we judged to be relevant and important to our client community. We were also aware that we had played our part in promoting innovative methods of assessment and that it was timely to take a genuinely open-minded and critical look at the impact of such innovations.

Nature of the project

We expected the outcomes of the project to be of use within our own university and higher education more generally. We would not have felt justified in undertaking a project which did not have this aim. However we were definitely intending to conduct a research project rather than a development project or the provision of case studies of good practice. This stemmed from a belief that educational development should be underpinned by research, and that undertaking our own research would be helpful to local clients. In terms of the wider HE community, we expected to produce work which could be externally published and contribute to the development of research and theory concerning teaching and learning.

Research methods

Our approaches to data collection, analysis and interpretation are similar to those used in many other examples of qualitative, case study research. We mainly gather data using a variety of types of interview, including interviews with staff and students, at a number of stages in an assessment task. We also use observation and documentary sources, and sometimes the work students produce for assessment and the marks and feedback received. Multiple sources of evidence and the varying perspectives of different people involved in the assessment process are important in building up a rich, contextualized picture of what is happening. Our case studies are short and intensive, in contrast to the extended ethnographic style of case study, but because we are part of the university we are able to be flexible. We do not have to complete the fieldwork in a short period of time but can adapt our data collection to match significant points in the assessment process being studied, and we can almost always return to collect more data if it is necessary.

Like all researchers, we have to negotiate with the people, chiefly lecturers and students, involved in our research. We cannot research what is going on without their agreement, and the methods to be used need to be clear and acceptable to them. Nevertheless, unlike a collaborative action research project, we retain the final say in important decisions about the research, and ownership of the data collected.

Relationships between researchers and researched

The examples of assessment practice which we study are located in a variety of ways. Sometimes lecturers become aware of the project and offer an example from their own practice, in other cases, we make the first approach. Either way, because we are well known within the university as educational developers and because we are well-informed about what is going on in the faculties, the process of locating case studies is made easier.

We then negotiate with the lecturers concerned exactly how the case study will be conducted, when interviews and observation will take place and so on. We are willing at this stage to take into account any particular questions which the lecturers themselves would like the research to address as long as it does not prevent us from addressing our own research questions or fall too much outside the scope of our aims. Subsequently students are also involved but always on a volunteer basis. Although we also have to negotiate with them on issues of access, confidentiality and anonymity, we have not found that the we need to vary the usual practices and approaches used in this type of research. It is in the relationships with lecturers that rather different issues arise.

Lecturers readily recognize some positive outcomes for themselves from their involvement in this research. At one level it is interesting to have their practice, and their students' learning, investigated. Gibbs (1995, p. 155) notes that lecturers like to be asked to talk about their teaching and we have found that this also applied to being part of a research project and discussing an aspect of their practice with a researcher. It provides a form of recognition for lecturers' achievements, although we also have to be aware that all of them will also experience some level of anxiety about having their practice studied by an outsider.

Many lecturers view the research as a kind of free consultancy and hope that it will help them to develop and improve their practice. There can be much more of an expectation that advice and support will be provided than would otherwise be the case in a research project, because of our link to educational development. There can be a problem in maintaining the balance between the level of detachment we would aspire to as researchers and the support we would wish to offer as educational developers. Fortunately we have been able to deal with this by adopting different roles within the research team. Normally, the research assistant, who is not a permanent member of the Educational Development Service is the person most responsible for data collection and for providing a descriptive report to individual lecturers. The two educational developers on the team can therefore be identified as the ones who will subsequently discuss outcomes and possibilities with the lecturers and provide advice and suggestions.

Reporting back to lecturers

One of the most important things that lecturers gain from their participation in the research is a detailed, confidential report from us on the main findings from their particular case study. It is our first priority to report back to the lecturers involved quickly, even when we are short of time. External publication takes second place, and in-depth analysis of data over a lengthy period of time comes after the initial work of analysing, interpreting and reporting the data for the individual case study. These priorities have certainly been influenced by our position as educational developers.

The report to lecturers is a summary of the evidence we collected in the case study, particularly what students did and said and how their learning was affected. This is informed by the views of the lecturers themselves, their aims, activities and so on. From a research point of view, the report helps to validate research findings; lecturers can and do let us know if they think we have been misled or misinterpreted some evidence, and we consider their comments seriously. After all, they know the students and the situation better than we do. Nevertheless, we still retain the right to make our own judgments and interpretations. We do not normally refer to previous research or educational theory in these reports although our interpretation of the data is naturally influenced by our knowledge of these, particularly work on deep and surface approaches to learning. This is something we need to consider further as we may be wrong in making the assumption that overt references to research and theory may not be acceptable to lecturers.

Lecturers normally hope to learn something and improve their assessment practice as a result of receiving our report. Some say that they do not mind how critical a report is; it will still be useful. Nevertheless we take great care in how reports are written, both to safeguard student anonymity and to ensure that critical comment is not presented in such a way that it could be damaging to the lecturers receiving it. For example, we always begin by reporting on the positive outcomes before highlighting the problematic areas. Aspects of the report which could be construed as critical are carefully phrased. There is the danger that if we are too guarded, lecturers will miss the point, but we believe that the danger of being over-critical is much greater. Although these reports are confidential, many lecturers wish to share them with colleagues and we must bear that in mind.

In addition to the main part of the case-study report we include some suggestions for changes in assessment practice, clearly identified as coming from our perspective and experience as educational developers. These would not normally form part of a research account but we have found that lecturers expect and welcome such suggestions from us. Of course, they are merely suggestions and it is the lecturer concerned who decides what action to take, if any. A report may be followed up by a discussion between an educational developer and the lecturer concerned. A face-to-face discussion is often a better context in which to discuss some of the more problematic areas which will have been raised, but perhaps not adequately dealt with, in the written report.

External publication of the research

We place considerable emphasis on reporting back to lecturers involved in our research but also aim to publish it in the usual ways. This requires us to undertake a more rigorous and in-depth analysis across case studies, and to report for an external audience using a rather different style and language. Since reports for external publication are always cross-case study rather than focusing on one example and we try as far as possible to anonymise the courses involved, we do not feel the need to clear such publications with lecturers. They are aware of this practice from the beginning of their participation in the project and this has not been problematic. We also inform the Head of Department where the case study is taking place at an early stage, telling them what is happening and of the agreement about publication.

Combining research and educational development: advantages and disadvantages

Having discussed some of the key features of our research approach I would now like to suggest the main advantages and disadvantages for both the research process and the educational development process which have been identified. Some comparison will be made with action research but there is no intention to suggest that one approach is necessarily better than the other in all circumstances. We have been involved in action research in the past (for example, McDowell, 1991) and hope to be involved again in the future, but on this occasion we deliberately chose a different approach.

Use of time and expertise

Research in the Impact of Assessment project is carried out by a team who have experience in educational research methods, and a knowledge of the literature and theories of student learning. We do not have to train lecturers for their involvement before we start as Gibbs (1992) did in his action research project where lecturers needed to learn about appropriate research methods and access theories of student learning. We do not have to spend a lot of time and energy maintaining the commitment of lecturers to the project since their input is relatively limited whereas with an action research project a considerable amount of sustained effort would be required. Having said this we acknowledge that lecturers may gain more from action research, particularly in their abilities to continue with research and development once the formal project has ended.

In this project we put our efforts into doing the research rather than supporting other researchers but a major outcome for lecturers is our report to them. As educational developers, we would not normally have the time to prepare such a report about one instance of practice and probably, without the imperative of a research project to complete, we would not undertake such detailed, careful data collection and analysis. Through the report and our subsequent discussions, we are not very different from the 'critical friends' (Carr and Kemmis, 1986, p. 161) who support action researchers.

Distance

I would not wish to claim that our research is objective and prefer the notion of distance. I believe that the distance which researchers maintain from the situation they are studying, and their attempts to study it in an open minded way are useful. A particular difficulty which lecturers experience in conducting their own research is that of obtaining student views. Students are always aware of their lecturer's role and power as an assessor and where assessment itself is the focus of research, this problem may be serious. An outside researcher may obtain more open and honest views from students although it is always possible they will misinterpret what they hear or be deliberately misled by students. It is an advantage here to be educational developers with a good knowledge of the context.

Setting aside problems arising from the power relationship between lecturers and students, it is not easy for anyone to distance themselves from their own work, to collect and interpret evidence in an open-minded way rather than to confirm pre-existing views or personal beliefs and hopes. As researchers we too have our biases and prejudices, but nevertheless it is not our own work which is being analysed in this project. We also adopt research procedures to maintain distance. We use multiple sources of evidence, cross-check interpretations among the research team, relate our findings to previous work and explore discrepancies. Since we are involved in a number of case studies, not just one, we can gradually refine our methods and develop our own understanding and insight.

Data analysis and interpretation

In the Impact of Assessment project, our initial analysis is done on the basis of a single case study and carried out relatively quickly for reporting back to the lecturers concerned. Some would consider that this first analysis could be too impressionistic and inaccurate. It is the case that later work undertaken in more depth on a cross-case study basis may lead us to revise some of the interpretations made. Whilst it is important to be rigorous, and to verify and cross-check interpretations, in ongoing research, data is continually being reinterpreted and all public statements are, in that sense, provisional. Early reporting and later re-thinking is therefore not too much of a concern. When we write for external audiences, copies are sent to the lecturers involved in the project, so at least they have the opportunity to read our later thoughts and reflections on the project in general if they wish to do so.

Analysing qualitative data is always problematic. Researchers are often recommended to ensure that they approach the data at different levels and from a variety of perspectives. Our approach requires us to undertake at least two levels of analysis, at the level of the individual case study and then an analysis where we draw on data from across case studies. We also have the advantage of at least two genuinely different audiences to consider, namely individual lecturers and their colleagues, and the educational research community. To enhance the variety of our perspectives we also have two ready-made roles to step into as researchers and educational developers.

Benefits to lecturers

Lecturers clearly gain something from involvement in our project. Some feel that the status of their practice in teaching and assessment is enhanced because it is considered worthy of being researched. The value of the reports lecturers receive has been emphasized but, even before that, some lecturers seem to be motivated by simply articulating their views and practices to us as the case study progresses, and learn a lot from this. We hope that they will gain some new ideas from the report they subsequently receive from us, not just ideas of the 'hints and tips' variety but some new insights and perspectives on their assessment practice and their students' learning, since we support the view proposed by Ramsden (1993) among others, that educational development is not only about changing what lecturers do but, perhaps more fundamentally, also about changing lecturers' understandings of what they do. What lecturers do not gain from our project, as they might do from participation in an action research project, is an enhanced ability to carry out research in future into their own practice. However, we know that some individual lecturers have been stimulated by our project to undertake further developments in their assessment practice and monitor the outcomes.

Impact on practice

Our research for each case study is carried out over a period of a few weeks, months or a semester, but we provide the main report at the end, after the assessment exercise has been completed. This could be a source of concern as it may seem too late then to have any useful impact on practice. However in most cases the lecturer will continue to teach and assess similar groups of students in future. The particular instance of their practice we studied developed from something and will develop into something else in future. There is therefore the potential for some influence on future practice. In addition, unlike other researchers who may quickly move on, we have an ongoing responsibility towards the lecturers involved who are our educational development clients.

The impact on practice is only a potential one however, since the lecturers themselves decide whether to do anything as a result of what they have learned from the research, and they may do nothing or something that we feel is mistaken. As educational developers this is a situation which is well-known to us since we can usually only advise, support, promote and encourage. We are rarely able to direct or instruct! However we know that some lecturers involved in our project have developed their own ideas, used them creatively and appropriately and in some cases involved their colleagues in the process. Others undoubtedly have read our report with initial interest and then filed it away, carrying on as before.

The nature of educational change

If we consider our project as being ultimately about promoting educational change, a principle important to educational developers, it is possible that we may be concentrating too much on the micro-level. We are looking at specific instances of assessment. We hope to improve our understanding of what goes on when students are assessed using the newer methods which are becoming increasingly widespread in HE. We even make recommendations about how assessment might be improved to the individual lecturers involved. However, if the aim is to promote change in assessment practice within higher education are there important variables and issues within the wider system which we are failing to consider? Are we too prone to remain within the confines of what currently seems to be politically and socially acceptable and possible?

This is may be a trap which educational developers are particularly likely to fall into with their tendency to emphasise practical developments on the ground. We may be reluctant to propose ideas which we know 'just won't work'. As researchers, it is our responsibility to look more widely when it comes to interpreting the outcomes of our research, but we might be reluctant to go so far as Becker (1968) and his colleagues whose early work on assessment is so often cited, in proposing the virtual abolition of assessment systems because of their pernicious influence on learning. As researchers within an educational development service we might be unwilling to be so radical.

Conclusion

In the Impact of Assessment project we have found that the relationship between educational research and educational development is mainly positive, although there can be some confusion between the two roles and it certainly helps to have a research team rather than a single researcher. We are able to draw on expertise and strengths from the two approaches. In practical terms, the educational development base assists the research by providing access and contacts, and it also ensures that the research is in touch with real practice and communicates with local audiences. The research perspective adds increased rigour, depth and distance to educational development practice which often suffers from pressures to deal with immediate problems and concerns. Most importantly, our local clients, the lecturers, do clearly benefit from the research by having their assessment practice valued, by receiving some advice and suggestions but also by being given the opportunity to examine the issues in more depth and see some aspects of what they do in new ways.

References

Becker, H., Geer, B. and Hughes, E. C. (1968) *Making the Grade. John Wiley & Sons.* New York.

Carr, W. and Kemmis, S. (1986) Becoming Critical: Education, Knowledge and Action Research. *Falmer Press.* London.

Gibbs, G. (1992) *Improving the quality of student learning.* TES. Bristol.

Gibbs, G. (1995) *The relationship between quality in research and quality in teaching.* Quality in Higher Education *1(2), 147—58.*

Jenkins, A. (1995) *The Research Assessment Exercise, funding and teaching quality.* Quality Assurance in Education *3(2), 4—12.*

Kember, D. and Gow, L. *(1992) Action research as a form of staff development in higher education.* Higher Education *23, 297—310.*

McDowell, L. (1991) Course Evaluation: Using Students' Experiences of Learning and Teaching. *CNAA/Newcastle Polytechnic.* Newcastle upon Tyne.

Ramsden, P. (1993) *Theories of learning and teaching and the practice of excellence in higher education.* Higher Education Research and Development *12(1), 87—97.*

Schratz, M. (1992) *Researching while teaching: an action research approach in higher education.* Studies in Higher Education *17(1), 81—95.*

Webb, G. (1992) *On pretexts for higher education development activities.* Higher Education *24, 351—61.*

For further information on the Impact of Assessment project please contact:

Liz McDowell
Educational Development Service
University of Northumbria
Newcastle upon Tyne
NE1 8ST

The Research Team consists of:

Liz McDowell, Sally Brown, Graham Mowl (until August 1994) and Kay Sambell

15 Exploration of evaluation and research methods for improving student learning in art and design

Allan Davies
Worcester College of Higher Education

Introduction

This chapter is a comment on the problematics of evaluating an ongoing project on the impact of a self-and peer assessment programme on art and design students' approaches to their learning.

During the past four years I have been engaged in developing strategies, through curriculum and assessment design, that are intended to improve the quality of student learning in art and design. This development work is based on research evidence that clearly demonstrates that the approach that a student takes to learning has an impact on the quality of that learning. Much of the research evidence comes from a pilot project, directed by Graham Gibbs at Oxford Brookes University, which began in 1991. This project had its roots in work carried out in the early 1970s in Sweden and Australia by such educationalists as Ference Marton, Roger Säljö and John Biggs.

At the heart of this research work is a recognition that there are two extremes that a student might take when studying — a deep or a surface approach. In short, a deep approach is characterized by the student's attempt to make sense of the subject. Students taking this approach try to relate concepts and use evidence and rationality to make personally meaningful judgements about their understanding of the subject. Knowledge and understanding gained in this way is often longer lasting. A surface approach is characterized by students trying to remember and recall what they have been taught. They have a conception of learning that distances themselves from making sense of what they are learning. There is a heavy dependence on the teacher to provide the goods. Knowledge is often short-term.

Another characteristic which has to be taken into account is to do with the conceptions students have about what learning consists in.

According to Gibbs,

> *when students were asked what they thought good teaching consisted of some of them thought that the teacher should do all the work and make all the decisions. The teacher should select the subject matter, present it in teacher controlled classes, devise tests and mark students on how well they have learnt the material which has been presented. What is to be learnt and what learning outcomes should look like is completely defined by the teacher. Others think that while the teacher has the responsibility for setting the learning climate, for making learning resources available, and for supporting students, all the responsibility lies with the student; responsibility for selecting learning goals, devising appropriate learning activities and for judging when learning outcomes are satisfactory. (Gibbs, 1992)*

The former is regarded as a 'closed' conception of learning and the latter as 'open'. It is not surprising, says Gibbs, that the 'closed' conception of teaching is held almost exclusively by those students who take a surface approach, while the 'open' conception of teaching is held by those who take a deep approach.

My research and that of others has led me to the firm conclusion that the nature of the assessment of the subject being studied is likely to have more effect on the student's approach to and conception of learning than any other single feature of their curriculum. No matter how interesting and challenging the content of the subject might be during the course of study and no matter how deeply the student engages in the subject, it is quite possible for the assessment and its procedure to vitiate the whole enterprise. There is good evidence to show that whatever approach a student takes to a subject at the outset, they will take an increasingly surface approach as the assessments get nearer.

As a consequence of this I have designed an assessment programme which is intended to avoid those aspects of conventional assessments which promote a surface approach. This programme involves students using explicit criteria to assess their work and that of others. The criteria are presented under a series of domains which cover the range of activities in art and design practice. They are also structured in increasing sophistication, based on Biggs' SOLO taxonomy, (Biggs and Collis, 1982), from a surface to a deep approach. When students assess themselves using the criteria they are effectively commenting on and establishing the approach they have taken to their learning.

The project, which began as a general investigation into the impact of self- and peer-assessment on student learning, has now crystallized into a three-year action research, case study of a group of students following a joint honours course in art and design. This project is to be initiated during the coming academic year with a cohort of first-year students.

During the past twelve months I ran small-scale pilot project with a group of 40 first-year students in order to evaluate the effectiveness of particular methods of data generation.

What I want to know is whether students, as a result of experiencing the self-and peer-assessment, have changed their conceptions and approaches to learning. Implicit in this question is that I take a phenomenographic approach to the evaluation. As I need to know what students' conceptions of learning are, traditional quantitative data collection methods appear to be inappropriate.

The context

In any phenomenographical analysis (Ballantyne and Bruce, 1994) it is important to identify features of the context which may make a contribution to the foreground of the research. Several of the features identified below have emerged as significant as a result of the administration of two questionnaires to the pilot study group.

The study group is 40 first-year art and design students following a joint honours modular degree programme. There are certain characteristics of the programme that differentiate this programme from other art and design courses. Firstly, the majority of students following the programme have come directly from secondary school having completed their A-levels. Most other art and design courses recruit students from art foundation courses which offer a year of 'diagnostic' tuition prior to their applying to specialist institutions for specific courses. While there is little evidence of research in the sector of the impact of foundation courses on students' conceptions of learning it is reasonable to assume that the expectations of students following a foundation course would be somewhat more modified or transformed than those students who have not had that experience. Certainly, in interviews I have conducted with first-year students who have attended foundation courses they tend to have clearer expectations of what higher education should provide than those who have not attended foundation courses. However, students who have moved directly from A-levels to school tend to have firm conceptions of what learning and teaching consists in. Most significantly, many students report that their A-levels were teacher centred and the learning experience was about cramming in knowledge and regurgitating it during examinations. Their experience of assessment was that it was something that was done to them in somewhat mysterious circumstances. They handed in their work and a grade or mark was given by the teacher often without explanation.

A feature of the art and design course at Worcester is that it is intended to be explicitly student-centred. The projects are problem based, students work throughout each module as a member of a learning team which meets regularly to review each other's work and each student keeps a learning journal which is intended to enable students to demonstrate what kind of approach they are taking to the work set. Students are made aware that, as the course progresses, they are expected to move towards an increasingly more independent mode of working. A section of the assessment criteria refers specifically to students' personal and interpersonal skills.

The first year, and particularly the first semester, is a significant period of transformation for many students as they are asked to move from a teacher-centred (closed) conception of learning to a more student-centred conception (open).

Making this transformation is very difficult for some students. While no student reported that they did not understand the purpose of the self- and peer-assessment, some student's responses to other questions indicated that they had difficulty accepting the transformation. Much of the concern was about the operation of the process of self- and peer-assessment. Making sense of and applying the criteria was a reported difficulty of one or two students. The commitment of some students to the process was another. While these problems diminished somewhat in the second semester as students reported a greater understanding of the process, it is clear that student anxiety about the processes of the assessment could cloud their conception of its worth and therefore vitiate their reports of their experiences. Students who had a negative experience of the process tended to report a negative response about the assessment's value.

However, although the art and design programme may be attempting to promote a deep approach to learning through student-centredness, it is not necessarily the case that the other subjects that the students are following are so doing. The influence that some subjects might have on students conceptions of learning should not go unregarded. There is much evidence to show that teacher-centredness has been a characteristic of many higher education courses. Some students could be having their initial, closed, conceptions of learning reinforced by these other subjects. How do students deal with these mixed messages? What impact would it have on the research that is looking particularly at art and design?

The questionnaires

At the end of each semester of their first year students were required to complete a questionnaire. Both questionnaires allowed students to reply anonymously. The purpose of this was to minimize the possibility of students making responses they felt I wanted them to — a strategic approach. At the end of the first semester they were asked:

Questionnaire 1

What do you think the purpose of the self and peer assessment was?

Was the purpose satisfied in this particular assessment? If so, how and why? If not, why not?

Was the process of the assessment clear to you? If not why not?

How could the process be improved?

How did you feel about assessing yourself?

What were the difficulties in assessing yourself?

How did you feel about assessing your colleagues?

What were the difficulties in assessing your colleagues?

How did your experience of this assessment differ from your previous experience of assessment?

Has the experience of this kind of assessment changed your approach to learning? What do you do now that is different?

If you were to be assessed in the same way for your next project would you approach your work differently? If so, what would you do that was different?

Out of 40 questionnaires administered 15 were completed and returned. This is clearly not a sufficient number for the questionnaire to be statistically significant in relation to a quantitative analysis.

At the end of the second semester the same students were asked:

Questionnaire 2

Has your approach to learning in art and design changed as a result of the self- and peer-assessment process? If so, how?

Can you give a specific example of how your experience of the assessment has changed your approach to learning?

How can the self- and peer-assessment be improved?

When I constructed the first questionnaire I was keen to find out not only what the student's conceptions of, and approaches to, learning were but also how they had adapted to the processes and what might be changed as a result. It struck me at the time that each student's response to all the questions could provide broad evidence of their approach. By applying

Bigg's taxonomy to the replies I felt it might be possible to determine, co-incidentally to the information, what the general orientation of the group was.

On reflection, and in the light of some of the responses, I'm not convinced that the evidence is so reliable as to fulfil this wish. Firstly, as the questionnaire was anonymous, I was unable to investigate further any issues that needed to be explained or substantiated. There were a number of these. The issue of anonymity did not confirm that students were not writing to please me although nothing confirmed the opposite either. The issue of sincerity will be key in a future exercise.

Secondly, the number of questions asked seems to have encouraged some students to return one-word answers to some of the questions. I am not convinced that this necessarily reveals a surface approach but it wasn't particularly helpful. Also, students found themselves giving responses to questions which were more appropriate to subsequent questions. Hence, any opportunity to collate and relate focused responses was lost. Each questionnaire had to be taken as a whole.

Consequently, the second questionnaire was different. The fact that it was different, however, prevented other possibilities. The most obvious being the opportunity to compare like with like.

Below are examples of students' responses to the first questionnaire. I have provided instances, where possible, of a 'positive' and 'negative' response. While the questionnaire provides me with an illumination of the general view of the success of the assessment programme and possibly specific instances where practice can be modified and improved, it does not provide me with clear-cut examples of students' conceptions of learning which can be acted upon in any meaningful way:

1. **What do you think the purpose of the self- and peer- assessment was?**

    Peer assessment enabled me to see aspects of my work which I had not appreciated; to see my ideas in the context of what others were doing and to work as part of a team in evaluating a project in which we were all personally involved.

    Self-assessment — forced me to 'believe' in what I had produced, to re-evaluate ideas and work and think about how I could have done it differently or, if I had succeeded conveying ideas.

    Initially, I thought that the purpose of the exercise to be a way of easing the work load of the lecturers concerned. I now realise that it was a learning process.

2. **Was the purpose satisfied in this particular assessment? If so, why and how? If not, why not?**

    I felt that this purpose was satisfied in the last assessment because the peers assessing my work were able to tell me why they awarded marks for an aspect of the assessment and suggest ways to improve my work to achieve a higher mark. Hearing other peoples views sometimes makes one aware of other ways of approaching the work.

    We were able to give and take ideas and evaluations, and to compromise amicably. I found it generally a reinforcing experience, and I think that others did too, in that we accepted each others judgements, and appreciated each others work.

    The weakness with this assessment at the moment is that it's totally new to everyone. In my own personal experience I've never been encouraged to give or think about my own opinion, which takes a while to get used to. Especially as the majority of people are frightened of offending others or don't feel 'qualified' to give our view. As a result of this there wasn't much questioning of views or 'positive' criticism.

3.   **Was the process clear to you? If not, why not?**

On firstly reading the assessment criteria notes I was a little puzzled with the personal development sections, but after the first time my assessment group met, we got the general idea of the process. The second assessment session, which included self, peer and tutor assessment, was a lot easier and quicker from the experience we gained from the first time.

The process also became clear when discussions in the assessment team took place, before the assessment procedure.

4.   **How could the process be improved?**

Perhaps displaying work after assessment to see what other people have done to achieve the grade they were given. This would also help to moderate the marks as all students would then know what was expected for a certain grade.

I think tutor assessment should play a larger part as the tutor should have a better understanding of how to assess and grade the work than the students do.

5.   **How did you feel about assessing yourself?**

Uncomfortable. I have always had a low opinion of my work despite grades and my current position. The criteria helped me realise how good my work was without it there would have been an even larger gap between the grade I'd given myself and what I was given by the group.

I took it more lightly than I should have. Although I'm never usually happy with my work I didn't want to give myself a low grade. Perhaps I need to be more honest.

6.   **What were the difficulties in assessing yourself?**

Occasionally I assumed that I had fulfilled part of the criteria when really I had not. To successfully assess my own work I had to try and look at it as though for the first time, and only mask what was actually there, not what I thought was there — this was quite difficult.

I didn't see the need to spend so long on the assessment (suggested time — 1 hour).

7.   **How did you feel about assessing your colleagues?**

I felt under pressure to give them good grades even when their work wasn't worth them.

I was worried about making certain comments about my group. They seemed the types to be easily offended!

8.   **What were the difficulties in assessing your colleagues?**

That the most dominant in the assessment group tended to lead the marking and others in the group found it difficult to argue their own opinion of someone's work.

Fear by them, caused by the belief that these grades would effect their future, led to anger and being argumentative. I feel a less formal and SECRETIVE PROCESS would be of benefit.

9.   **How did your experience of this assessment differ from your previous experience of assessment?**

Complete contrast. In the past 'teacher' always assessed ie handwork in one week, returned with grade the next week, and if lucky 'teacher' gave a comment.

It was very difficult for instead of working towards the teachers goals and that of the rest of the class, I was working to keep in line with that of my assessment group.

I also see my grade as not being worth much as it was given to me by people on the same course instead of a teacher. I think many other people feel the same way.

10.   **Has the experience of this kind of assessment changed your approach to learning? What do you do now that is different?**

I now write down, in more detail, the thoughts that are going round in my head — previously many were overlooked as insignificant to my work but I now realise that ideas which lead nowhere, or that are complete disasters, are very valuable in the learning process.

Not really, because my art work is still the same standard as it was at 'A' level. The only thing that differs is that I now have to look at Art history which has broadened my knowledge of art and makes me think more about what I am drawing.

11.   **If you were to be assessed in the same way for your next project would you approach your work differently? If so, what would you do that was different?**

I think looking at the work of other artists helped me a lot in the last project. I think I would use this approach next time but perhaps consider what the artists have done in more depth.

Not really as I adjusted my way of working after our very first assessment.

The second questionnaire, which has so far elicited 17 replies, seems to make much the same contribution as the first. It is helpful in a general sense and whilst it provides clear cut examples of areas that can be developed it still does not provide the kind of qualitative data that would be useful in resolving my initial problem.

At the same time as I sent out the second questionnaire I included the Approaches to Learning Questionnaire. The intention was to see if there was any relation to be found between the open ended questions and the students' orientation to learning identified by the ALQ. There was a surprising correlation despite my doubts. As the students had been inducted into the concepts of deep and surface learning as part of the degree programme and also their assessment, I felt inclined to think that they would easily identify the structure of the questionnaire and take a strategic approach. Whilst, on the whole there seemed to be a reasonable consistency there also seemed to be some rather glaring anomalies. One or two students identified themselves as extremely high on the meaning orientation but their responses suggested otherwise.

Conclusion

The above account may not appear particularly successful in relation to its intentions but nevertheless, as far as the long- term project is concerned, it has proven very useful. Eliciting students' conceptions of learning in art and design has not so far shown to be straightforward in any formal and systematic way. This does not mean to say it cannot be done. Students are regularly providing examples through their learning journals and their practical work. The task is to be able to harness this evidence in a way which demonstrates improvement or change.

One of the major difficulties in evidencing change is that the art and design programme of study in question makes very explicit to students at the outset of their studies what it is intending to do in relation to deep and surface approaches to their learning. What is emerging from the research is that this very act of explication enables those students who take a strategic approach to their learning to contaminate any questionnaire exercise.

Another difficulty is that of being able to isolate or differentiate the object of the exercise — self- and peer-assessment — from all the other features of the curriculum which contribute to students taking a deep approach to their learning. It may be that questionnaires do not lend themselves easily to determining exactly which features of the curriculum make the improved contribution. When responding to questionnaires, how do students know themselves which part of the curriculum is making what kind of contribution? How can we guarantee that their reports, no matter how sincere, are accurate or reliable.

Finally, phenomenographic approaches to eliciting students conceptions of learning tend to be post-experiential (Fleming 1995) and therefore reports after the event may well be influenced by the final outcomes of the event, in this case, for example, a good or bad grade. *When* we elicit students' conceptions of their approach to learning may be as important as *how* we elicit them.

What remains constant in all of this is, of course, those students who consistently take a surface approach to learning. There is evidence from the questionnaire exercise that there are some students who still take a surface approach despite the nature of the curriculum they are following. One fruitful strategy, therefore, might be to identify those students who take a surface approach at the beginning of their programme of study and follow their progress using a range of methods; questionnaires, learning journals, practical work, interviews and so on. By focusing on those students who are most likely to show sincere evidence of change, it might be possible to extrapolate an hypothesis which relates to the whole cohort.

References

Ballantyne, R. and Bruce, C. (1994) *Phenomenography: Philosophy and Practice*, QUT.

Biggs, J. B. and Collis, K. F. (1982) *Evaluating the Quality of Learning*. Academic Press. New York, Sydney.

Fleming, W. (1995) Methodography: the study of student learning as situated action. In Gibbs, G. (ed.), *Improving Student Learning Through Assessment and Evaluation*. Oxford: Oxford Centre for Staff Development.

Gibbs, G. (1992) improving the quality of student learning, *Times Educational Supplement*.

16 Coursework assessment: what are tutors really looking for?

Lin Norton, Tom Dickins and Neil McLaughlin Cook
Liverpool Hope University College
(formerly Liverpool Hope Institute of Higher Education)

Introduction

The success of three symposia on improving student learning is testimony to the change that is slowly growing in higher education. This change is all about how the quality of student learning can be enhanced, in spite of ever-increasing student numbers, increased administration for academic staff and the pressure of a market economy ethos. Improving the quality of student learning has taken several different paths both in the research and in practice, but one of the major influences has been the seminal work by Marton and Säljo (1976) on the distinction between deep and surface learning, where a deep approach reflects the intention to understand and a surface approach reflects the intention to memorize. The importance of encouraging students to take a deep approach has been widely promoted by Gibbs (1992; 1994; 1995). Now, although it is widely accepted that encouraging students to take a deep approach to their work is beneficial, it seems that it is not always easy to achieve and one of the reasons according to Boud (1990) is that the assessment in higher education does not always reward students for taking a deep approach.

At Liverpool Hope University College, there has been a concerted effort over the last three years to improve the quality of psychology students' learning in their first year as undergraduates. This has been done not only by putting on learning to learn courses for the students, but at the same time encouraging tutors in the department to set essay and examination questions which test a deep approach and to reward students when they do so. A detailed account of these interventions is reported in Norton and Crowley (1995), Norton and Dickins (1995) and Norton, Scantlebury, Duckmanton, Dickins and Richardson (submitted for publication) but briefly, one of the main purposes of these courses was to make absolutely explicit to students what the tutors' marking criteria for coursework essays were.

This stemmed from a finding by Norton (1990) that there was a mismatch between students' perceptions of the criteria tutors used in marking their essays and the actual criteria that tutors said they used. Students believed that tutors would be looking for content and knowledge in their essays but the tutors said they were primarily interested in how students put together an argument to answer the question. Such a mismatch seems to indicate the fundamental difference between a surface and a deep approach to the task of essay writing. Therefore, the idea in the learning courses was that if the students were told that the department expected them to take a deep approach in their written work and rewarded them for doing so, then students would show a demonstrable shift from a surface to a deep approach. As was reported in Norton *et al.*, however, the latest study showed that while students did decrease their surface strategies they did not significantly increase their deep strategies by the end of the learning course. More worryingly there was evidence to suggest that the psychology tutors were not consistently rewarding a deep approach in the students' written work.

One explanation for this finding and one that we wanted to investigate in this study is that perhaps a hidden curriculum as suggested by Bergenhenegouwen (1987) operates in higher education. This idea of a hidden curriculum suggests that tutors explicitly make their marking criteria clear to their students but then actually go on to mark their work according to a different, implicit set of criteria. For example, students might not take a deep approach to an essay when explicitly told to do so by their tutor, because they know that this particular tutor sets a high store on seeing her own views put forward in that essay. This predilection might not be explicitly stated by the said tutor, and indeed she might not even be very aware of it. Yet somehow, students seem able to pick it up and pass it on to other students in the same department, so that it becomes an implicit 'rule'. It may be then that there are two sets of rules in academic departments — those that tutors set out and state explicitly and the implicit — those that tutors are not seemingly very aware of but *students* are. This then raises the question: if tutors do not formally communicate these implicit rules, who does? Our hypothesis is that it is the students themselves.

The aim of this research was to establish whether or not such implicit rules, related specifically to essay writing, exist and, if they do exist, what are they? These implicit rules have been called 'Rules of the Game' (ROGs) to distinguish them from explicitly stated criteria that students are told will enhance their chance of getting a good mark. The research reported here is explorative and is in two stages:

* Stage 1 was an investigation using students from Liverpool Hope Psychology department only.
* Stage 2 was a follow up study using students from two other departments in Liverpool Hope (the department of English and the department of Environmental and Biological Studies) and another sample of psychology students from the neighbouring John Moores University.

Stage 1

Aim

In this stage it was intended to find out what psychology students thought were Rules of the Game and whether or not they would admit to ever having used any of them.

Method

A detailed account of the procedure is reported elsewhere (see Norton, Dickins and McLaughlin Cook, 1996), but briefly it went as follows. An open-ended questionnaire was used in which 70 second year psychology students were asked to generate as many student tactics as they could think of. Their responses were then content analysed, refined and eventually reduced to a list of 25 items which formed the body of the questionnaire which we have used in both stages of this research.

To be included on the questionnaire as a ROG, the student generated tactics had to meet the following criteria:

- be mentioned by at least six students;
- be implicit, not explicit;
- not be a cheating strategy;
- not be a study skills strategy.

The questionnaire was then constructed in two parts. Part 1 listed the 25 ROGs and asked students to simply indicate whether they had ever used any of them. Part 2 asked them to list any ROGs not covered in Part 1, including ones they had used themselves and ROGs they had not personally used but knew that other students had. The questionnaire was checked for test-retest reliability on a sample of 35 second years which gave a correlation coefficient of 0.89 significant beyond the 0.005 level.

The questionnaire was then given to 182 first years and 101 third years in the psychology department.

Results

The main findings from this stage suggest that there are 25 tactics, shown in Table 1, that were identified by second-year psychology students as being ROGs.

TABLE 1

ROG No	Description of ROG
1.	**Got to know the tutors socially in order to favourably influence them** (eg by spending time with them outside lectures, asking them about their interests/hobbies/familes, having a drink with them)
2.	**Put your greatest effort into getting a high mark for the first submitted essay in a course** (because of the 'halo' effect)
3.	**Made your essay visually exciting** (eg used 'fancy' designs for headings, underlined in a different colour from the text, used pictures/diagrams)
4.	**Found out who would mark the essays so that you could choose the title set by the easiest marker, or the tutor you get on best with**
5.	**Avoided criticising your marker's views and/or research in the essay**
6.	**Asked tutor for help so s/he will approve of you and think you are a keen student**
7.	**Chosen the easiest title to give you a good chance of getting a high mark**
8.	**Tried to reflect your tutor's opinions/views/style as closely as possible**
9.	**Used big words/technical terms/jargon to impress your tutor**
10.	**Avoided writing anything controversial in the essay**
11.	**Invented studies/research/articles to include in the essay**
12.	**Played the role of a good student** (eg keen/enthusiastic/motivated)
13.	**Acted extra 'nice'/asked for sympathy to get an extension for your essay**
14.	**Chosen an essay title nearest to the tutor's subject or research area**
15.	**Handed the essay in before the deadline to create the impression that the assignment was mastered without difficulty/to show eagerness**
16.	**Used up to date/interesting references/lots of references/contradictory references in your essay**
17.	**Wrote a lot/wrote big/made the essay look longer/exceeded word limit**
18.	**Chosen a difficult title in the hope of being given extra credit**
19.	**Presented a false bibliography** (ie one that is long, but you have not consulted all the books on it)
20.	**Tried to include information not covered in the lectures/obscure references**
21.	**Chosen an unpopular essay title so that your answer is distinctive**
22.	**Changed dates of old research to make it look like up to date research**
23.	**Avoided putting simple/basic textbooks in the bibliography even though you have used them**
24.	**When feeling confident, argued a position regardless of your tutor's views in order to appear insightful/clever etc.**
25.	**Put a theorist's name against your own point/criticism/comment to make it look erudite**

As this table shows, these ROGs ranged from what could be described as cheating strategies (e.g. items 11, 19 and 22) to strategies designed to impress or flatter tutors (e.g. items 5, 6, 8 and 15).

Analysing the responses of the first- and third-year psychology students to the questionnaire showed that every tactic had been ticked by at least one student from each sample, with some items being ticked by as many as 90% of the students. One way of looking in a little more detail at the pattern of responses obtained is shown in Table 2 which presents the six most popular ROGs identified by the first year sample.

TABLE 2

ROG No	Description of ROG	Percentage
7	**Chosen the easiest title**	73
20	**information not covered in lectures**	67
12	**played role of good student**	51
16	**up to date/interesting/ contradictory references**	48
17	**wrote a lot**	36
9	**big words/ technical jargon**	35

As can be seen, nearly two-thirds of the first-year students said that they had chosen the easiest title (item 7) to give them a good chance of getting a high mark. Presumably this is the strategy of students who take a surface approach, where they are hoping that they do not have to show too much understanding in the essay.

The next most popular ROG (item 20) asked if they had tried to include information not covered in the lectures or used obscure references. This tactic might at first sight seem like the type of strategy that tutors would want to encourage, but the concept of a ROG is that it is used to make a good/favourable impression on the marking tutor, not that it is a study skills strategy. Such an interpretation is supported by comments made on the original open-ended questionnaire given to the second years, where some students actually said that the reason why they went for obscure information was to plagiarize it and precisely because it was obscure, they hoped that the tutor would not be able to track it down.

The third most popular ROG (item 12) was playing the role of a good student. Here, our interpretation is that the most important word to consider is 'role' — meaning it is an act to get the tutor to think that the student is really keen and clever.

The fourth most popular ROG (item 16) is about students using up to date/interesting/contradictory references. This is again like item 20's reference to obscure material in that it is a strategy designed to impress the tutor with how hard-working the student is so that hopefully the said tutor will give the essay a really high mark.

The next ROG (item 17) is particularly interesting in the context of this particular psychology department where there is a rigorous procedure for word limits with stated penalties for exceeding them. In spite of this, however, 36% of the first year students claimed that they had actually set out to write a lot, write big, try to make the essay look longer and to deliberately exceed the word limit!

The 6th most popular ROG (item 9) shown in this table was where students would use big words/technical terms/jargon to impress their tutors. Quite clearly this is an indication of a concentration on surface rather than deep strategies when writing their essays.

Table 2 only shows the six most popular ROGs as identified by the first-year sample. When ranking the responses of the third-year sample, the same six items appeared but in a slightly different order, with the most popular being item 16, where 90% of the third years who completed this questionnaire tried to impress their tutors with the references they cited. (The other ROGs in order of importance were: items 20, 7, 17, 12 and 9.)

Presenting a list of the six most frequently mentioned ROGs is of course only one way of describing the data. What is important to remember is that all 25 items were identified as having been used by students in both our samples. So the findings from this stage of the research would suggest that the students in this psychology department certainly do use these ROGs when writing their essays.

Since ROGs by their very nature are not explicitly communicated by tutors, they must presumably be communicated by students. It would seem reasonable to suppose, therefore, that the longer students are in a particular department, the more ROGs they are likely to pick up from their peers. To test this, a comparison was carried out between the first- and third-year samples on the number of ROGs they claimed to have used. A *t*-test showed that, as predicted, third years claimed to have used significantly more ROGs than first years students ($t = 5.22$, $p < 0.005$).

Conclusions

Stage 1 of the research has shown that ROGs do exist in this particular psychology department and they are used by the students. Also it has been shown that students used more ROGs the longer they were in the department.

These conclusions raise some more questions — specifically would students in other departments and other institutions respond in the same way? To answer these questions, stage 2 of this research was set up.

Stage 2

Aims

The main aim of this second stage of the research was to make sure that the ROGs established in Stage 1 were not peculiar to Liverpool Hope University College or peculiar just to psychology students.

Method

The first step of this second stage was to give the same questionnaire to a sample of third-year psychology students at the neighbouring John Moores University. Next, the questionnaire was given to third-year students in the Environmental and Biological Sciences (EBS) department and in the English department, at Liverpool Hope.

In this way it was possible to compare the responses obtained in stage 1 from 100* third-year psychology students with the pattern of responses from 63 third-year psychology students at another institution, and from 20 third-year EBS students and 71 third-year English students in the same institution. (*One student had to be dropped from the original sample of psychology students at Liverpool Hope because of an incomplete questionnaire.) By choosing departments from different disciplines we were also able to find out if the same profile would emerge regardless of whether students were from a science, arts or social sciences discipline.

Results

To begin with, the frequency of response for each ROG was recorded per group. This was then converted to percentage data for ease of comparison as the group sizes differed somewhat (see Table 3).

TABLE 3

ROG No	John Moores: Psychol Dept (N= 63)		L'pool Env.& Biol.Dept (N= 20)		L'pool English (N= 71)		L'pool Psychol Hope: Dept (N= 100)	
	raw data	percent age	raw data	percent age	raw data	percent age	raw data	percent age
1	5	8	1	5	3	4	3	3
2	19	30	7	35	21	30	23	23
3	18	29	11	55	9	13	18	18
4	26	41	11	55	12	17	27	27
5	17	27	3	15	19	27	15	15
6	13	21	2	10	17	24	20	20
7	45	71	11	55	53	75	72	72
8	24	38	3	15	28	39	25	25
9	23	37	6	30	36	51	39	39
10	14	22	3	15	14	20	22	22
11	11	18	2	10	7	10	11	11
12	34	54	9	45	43	61	45	45
13	19	30	3	15	11	16	29	29
14	13	21	4	20	9	13	16	16
15	13	21	4	20	6	9	8	8
16	49	78	19	95	44	62	92	92
17	27	43	10	50	29	41	48	48
18	4	6	1	5	3	4	12	12
19	26	42	7	35	28	40	28	28
20	45	71	16	80	49	69	89	89
21	12	19	4	20	14	20	11	11
22	2	3	1	5	1	1	5	5
23	21	33	3	15	26	37	25	25
24	15	24	5	25	26	37	36	36
25	6	10	3	15	14	20	15	15

From this percentage data ROG profiles were drawn up. These profiles represent the data as continuous, which it is not, but it was felt that this would be visually more helpful than a crowed bar chart or histogram. Figure 1 shows the profiles from the two psychology departments at Liverpool Hope University College and John Moores University.

Figure 1

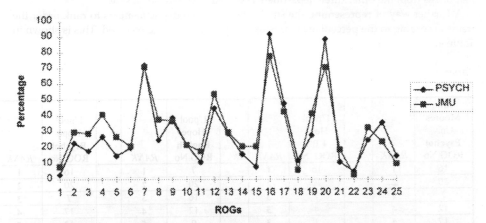

Viewing these two profiles together, it can be seen that there is a distinct similarity in the patterns exhibited by both psychology departments. This suggests that the ROGs employed at two different institutions by psychology undergraduates, were very similar.

Turning now to the representation of responses of all four departments together as shown in Figure 2, there is again a very tight pattern of response with good matching for peaks and troughs. This would seem to indicate a strong similarity between different subject departments in the same institution as well as between different institutions but with students studying the same subject.

Figure 2

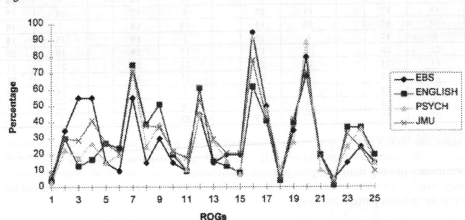

These profiles are a helpful way of comparatively analysing this group data because they indicate how individual items are rated in relation to one another within a group. The immediate point to note is how similar the overall shape for each department is apart from items 3 and 4 where the profiles seem to drift with the EBS department showing a much larger frequency of scoring. Such a difference may have been due to chance or it may be revealing something peculiar about this particular department, especially since the responses from the other three departments seemed to cohere so closely.

A further way of representing the similarities between departments is to rank order the items according to the percentage of positive responses each one received. This is shown in Table 4.

Table 4

John Moores Univ **Psychol** ROG No	RANK		L'pool Hope **EBS** ROG No	RANK		L'pool Hope **English** ROG No	RANK		L'pool Hope **Psychol** ROG No	RANK
16	1		16	1		7	1		16	1
20	2		20	2		20	2		20	2
7	2		7	3		16	3		7	3
12	4		4	3		12	4		17	4
17	5		3	3		9	5		12	5
4	6		17	6		17	6		9	6
19	7		12	7		19	7		24	7
8	8		19	8		8	7		13	8
9	9		2	8		24	9		19	9
23	10		9	10		23	9		4	10
13	11		24	11		2	11		8	11
2	11		21	12		5	12		23	11
3	13		15	12		6	13		2	13
5	14		14	12		21	14		10	14
24	15		25	15		25	14		6	15
10	16		23	15		10	14		3	16
15	17		13	15		4	17		14	17
14	17		10	15		13	18		5	18
6	17		8	15		3	19		25	18
21	20		5	15		14	19		18	20
11	21		11	21		11	21		21	21
25	22		6	21		15	22		11	21
1	23		1	23		1	23		15	23
18	24		18	23		18	23		22	24
22	25		22	23		22	25		1	25

Again this shows strong similarities. For instance, the top three slots are filled by the same items — 7, 16 and 20. More importantly, only the English department altered the order of occurrence placing item 7 in pole position. With increased numbers of students this effect may well have altered and fallen into line with the rest of the departments - but it is not far from the general pattern any way.

Conclusions

Both the profiles and the rank ordering of ROGs in stage 2 of the research have shown that certain question responses peaked consistently across different learning environments. This indicates that ROGs are not peculiar to one psychology department, nor are they peculiar to one institution. They are widespread which suggests that they may be culturally mediated either directly through student gossip or rumours, or indirectly due to the demands of HE delimiting possible strategies for 'playing the game', or possibly a combination of both.

It would be interesting to take this research further and run the analysis over many more departments from different institutions to extract information about within-discipline effects and overall HE effects. It would also be illuminating to see if tutors do actually reward students for adopting ROGs when writing essays, as at this stage of the research, all we can assert is that students believe this to be the case.

Implications for assessing essays

The findings from both stages of this research highlight what may be a thorny problem of tutors saying, even believing themselves, that a deep approach to essay writing is crucial, yet at the same time their students are believing (and acting upon this belief) that tutors will give credit for a whole range of tactics that have nothing at all to do with a deep approach.

In terms of the implications, the evidence seems to be accumulating that the way tutors assess students has a profound impact on whether or not they take a deep approach to their studies (see for example, Biggs, 1989; Boud, 1990; Montgomery, 1994). This research has suggested that students are acutely aware of all messages passed on by their tutors with regards to essay assignments and are very ready to play whatever 'game' they think is necessary to get a good mark. Perhaps then as tutors, we need to look more closely at whether our own current practices in setting and marking essays actually encourage or discourage a deep and independent, approach to learning. We also need to be more aware not just about how discipline specific conventions in essay writing such as those described by Lukeman (1992) can lead to student misconceptions, but also how the unstated, implicit messages can be transmitted to the student body (see for example, Ramsden, 1979). Without such an awareness, it may be that any attempts to help students produce good essays are likely to be seriously hampered.

References

Bergenhenegouwen, G. (1987) Hidden curriculum in the university. *Higher Education* **16**, 535—43.

Biggs, J. (1989) Does learning about learning help teachers with teaching? Psychology and the tertiary teacher. Supplement to *The Gazette* **26**(1), University of Hong Kong.

Boud, D. (1990) Assessment and the promotion of academic values. *Studies in Higher Education* **15**(1), 101—11.

Gibbs, G. (1992) *Improving the Quality of Student Learning*. Bristol: Technical and Educational Services.

Gibbs, G. (ed.) (1994) Preface to *Improving Student Learning. Theory and Practice*. Oxford: Oxford Centre for Staff Development.

Gibbs, G. (ed.) (1995) *Improving Student Learning. Through Assessment and Evaluation*. Oxford: Oxford Centre for Staff Development.

Lukeman, H. (1992) First year student essays in humanities and social sciences: The need for new paradigms.*Education in Rural Australia* **2**(2), 37—40.

Marton, F. and Sâljo, R. (1976) On qualitative differences in learning. I. Outcome and process. *British Journal of Educational Psychology* **46**, 4—11.

Montgomery, D. (1995) Critical theory and practice in evaluation and assessment. In Gibbs, G. (ed.) (1995) *Improving Student Learning. Through Assessment and Evaluation*. Oxford: Oxford Centre for Staff Development.

Norton, L. S. (1990) Essay-writing: what really counts? *Higher Education* **20**, 411—42.

Norton, L. S. and Crowley, C. M. (1995) Can students be helped to learn how to learn? An evaluation of an Approaches to Learning programme for first year degree students. *Higher Education* **29**, 307—28.

Norton, L. S. and Dickins, T. E. (1995) Do approaches to learning courses improve students' learning strategies? In G. Gibbs (ed.), *Improving Student Learning. Through Assessment and Evaluation*. Oxford: Oxford Centre for Staff Development.

Norton, L. S., Dickins, T. E. and McLaughlin Cook, A. N. (1996) Rules of the Game in essay writing. *Psychology Teaching Review*, 5, 1, 1-13.

Norton, L. S., Scantlebury, E., Duckmanton, S., Dickins, T. E. and Richardson, P. (submitted for publication) Helping psychology students to become more expert in their learning strategies.

Ramsden, P. (1979) Student learning and perceptions of the academic environment. *Higher Education* **8**, 411—27.

17 Academics as learners: issues for courses in the study of higher education

Peter Taylor and Carol Bond
Griffith Institute for Higher Education
Faculty of Education, Griffith University
Australia

Lee Andresen
(retired, University of New South Wales)
Consultant on Higher Education and Academic Development
Sydney, Australia

Introduction

The movement towards increasing 'professionalization' of academics in the UK and Australia includes a drive towards the compulsory accreditation of staff as university teachers.[1] The question of how to provide appropriate opportunities for the achievement of teaching qualifications poses significant challenges for those engaged in academic development in higher education. In this paper we explore some of those challenges in the context of an existing programme: the Graduate Certificate in Higher Education.[2]

One of the guiding questions that influenced the design of this programme was:

[h]ow can academics-as-learners be located at the centre of their own learning where that learning is focused on their academic practices?

We use this question as a focus to highlight issues which became evident in our reflections on our experiences in teaching this course during 1995. Some issues have become evident during the progress of the course. For example, participants are also our colleagues, some with more experience than us as academic teachers and holding more senior appointments. It is not these that we wish to address here, but other less visible issues, related to our initial

---

[1] In the UK there are calls from the Association of University Teachers 'for universities to follow the example of professions such as accountancy, law and architecture by introducing formal and compulsory accredited qualifications for academics' (Utley 1995, p. 52). In Australia, the contents of the Hoare Report (1995) exemplify this movement.

[2] The Griffith University Graduate Certificate is a two semester part-time course designed to provide a basic educational qualification for university teachers. It consists of two subjects, Professional Workshop and Learning and Teaching in Higher Education which are taught through a programme of workshops and independent work, supported by resource materials, learning groups and relatively unlimited access to the course lecturers – Carol and Peter. Lee continues to provide consultancy support for its development.

question, and which we feel are both more fundamental and theoretically challenging. Our intention is to indicate both how we have sought to implement a programme which was focused on the exploration of participants' conceptions of teaching and learning, and to share critical reflections on how we implemented that focus. In so doing we hope to contribute to the development of strategies for academic staff development which, while they are consistent with the extensive knowledge base on conceptions of teaching and learning, are not pre-determined by it.

The chapter is written in three parts. In the first we introduce what we see as three *orthodox* foci for academic staff development, represented as: a focus on skills development; a focus on developing a knowledge base on effective teaching; and a focus on conceptual change. In the second part we discuss the approach that we have adopted — a hybrid of these three foci. We indicate our rationale for this approach, together with some of the strategies we have used. In the final part we critically reflect on some of the assumptions underlying this hybrid, exploring some implications of our reflections and identifying changes that we expect to implement in 1996.

Part 1: Orthodox foci

At the outset it is important to make several acknowledgments. First, we do not use the term *orthodox* in any disapproving sense. What we are seeking to explicate are three relatively distinctive foci, each of which is well justified and supported in the literature. Second, we present them here as relatively distinct foci, in part because their relative strengths are often lost in discussions or practices which blend or merge them. Third, we acknowledge that most academic staff development practices involve a blending of all three. In fact we move to discuss our work in terms of all of these foci in the second part of the chapter.

One kind of response to the question which framed our course might involve a focus on the development of the skills required (Cox, 1994) to undertake academic practices effectively. To be aware that effective practices are skilful practices is significant. It involves recognition that, for most, becoming a teacher means acquiring particular capabilities (or skills), rather than merely drawing upon some existing, taken-for-granted capacities that people are assumed to bring with them by virtue of having studied a subject to an advanced level or because of their 'natural talent' or genius. We perceive that the process of identifying these skills has given considerable impetus to efforts to value teaching, and to challenge the assumption that 'good teachers are born not made': an assumption which has been used, in the past, as a justification for ignoring the professional development of teachers. We can see traces of this focus in many of the discussions of quality assurance which explicitly address issues of teaching. In particular, we see it in the movement towards the identification of a 'standard' or 'perfection and consistency' in the quality of teaching (Harvey and Green, 1993). Focussing on skills permits the quantification of some aspects of teaching, and allows the discussion of teaching to focus on specific issues, rather than lapse into unconvincing claims that 'teaching is an art', or 'while we can't tell you what great teaching is, we recognize it when we see it'. Thus, a focus on the development of skills as a way of locating academics-as-learners at the centre of their own learning could be both appropriate and politically expedient within the context of concerns for quality assurance. Our problem with this approach is the lack of a 'critical rationale' which underlies responsible practice (Brookfield, 1990) — a rationale, for example, which enables a teacher to respond to the unexpected from an informed position.

A second kind of response might overcome this concern. It would be to focus on sharing what we know about effective teaching — the knowledge base on effective teaching that has resulted from research on teaching and learning generally, and in higher education in particular. This knowledge base has expanded rapidly, and is formalized in a range of publications, including Ramsden (1992). Given that the majority of academics in disciplines outside of education studies have had little contact with this knowledge base, there would appear to be obvious benefits from introducing them to an education studies perspective on their academic practices. The adoption of an educational perspective has particular value for two reasons. First, the knowledge base has been developed to identify principles of effective teaching in higher education (Ramsden, 1992, pp. 96—103), principles which could provide a very appropriate conceptual platform for reflecting on, designing, and evaluating teaching practices. Second, the base has been explored and elaborated in the context of the teaching of numerous disciplines. Thus, it provides contextualized understandings as well as abstract principles for effective teaching.

However, despite its obvious attractiveness, we consider that this response, when used alone, is also problematic. It is probably very effective in introducing the university teacher to new knowledge and skills which they can access to improve their educational practice. But, returning to the original question: would it locate the academic as a learner in their own practice? Our sense is that it might not. Indeed it may, in certain situations, have the opposite effect — the knowledge could remain inert (Bereiter, 1990).

A third response to the question might be to focus on the notion of conception and conceptual change. Graham Gibbs (1995) refers to this approach in ways that both indicate its development, and imply its centrality to current 'directions in staff development'. He introduces the literature on 'students' conceptions of learning' (pp. 22—5) and 'teachers' conceptions of teaching' (pp. 26—8), in both cases providing an overview of the conceptions and their relationships. Most discussion of conceptions of teaching, including that of Martin and Balla (1991), Bruce and Gerber (1995) and Gibbs (1995), indicate a hierarchy of conceptions, with a clear implication that the higher conceptions are preferred. Gibbs also briefly explores the relationship between students' conceptions of learning, and their preferences in terms of approach to teaching. However, neither Gibbs nor the other sources cited explore in any sustained way the relationship between conceptions of teaching and the actual practice of staff development.

Thus, while there is much reference to the need for conceptual change as a central feature of academic staff development, that literature appears to provide little assistance for those who wish to make it a feature of their pedagogical practices. In particular, while it provides quite detailed empirical evidence on the nature of these conceptions, it fails to provide complementary discussions (in either nature or detail) of *how* these conceptions should be *treated* as pedagogical foci, or suggestions on appropriate strategies in terms of that pedagogy. Rather, some of these discussions could be read as implying that it should be a feature of the knowledge base on teaching learning, that is a central piece of information in the second response. At this stage, we see this third focus as underdeveloped in the literature on higher education in terms of strategies for its implementation.

Part 2: Our hybrid approach

Our approach to the question incorporated elements of all of the foci outlined above. We provided advice on skills development when requested, and required all participants to videotape and analyse a segment of their teaching. We modelled 'good practice', including videotaping our own teaching and inviting participants to act as 'critical friends' to our critical reflections on the recording. We set a text which overviewed the research base on teaching and learning in higher education (Ramsden, 1992), and provided a set of readings for each subject in the course. Those readings provided a focus for workshop discussions. That is, we introduced participants to the knowledge base on effective teaching in higher education, and to an educational perspective on higher education.

However, our approach to teaching substantially reflected the third focus. It was based on our understandings derived from both the constructivist and phenomenographic literature. Those understandings form the basis of our rationale for this hybrid approach. In particular, our approach draws on the constructivist literature as a source of strategies for implementation.

Some of our understandings

Constructivism suggests that learning is both an individual and a social process, and is determined primarily by what we (implicitly and explicitly) know and how we feel about what we know. Both the constructivist perspective (for example see Hollingsworth (1989), and the professional development literature, represented by work such as Bromme and Tillema (1995), discuss 'conception' in terms of the interaction between prior-understandings, understood as beliefs, and the 'new' information being presented through engagements intended to promote learning. This interaction is understood primarily as a cognitive activity. Research from a constructivist perspective indicates two key points here: that, for a specific content area, only *a limited number* of alternative conceptions can be identified; and, that conceptions are developed over time, in *a relatively uniform sequence*. In this perspective a conception constitutes one part of a wider network — the conceptual framework (Demastes, Good and Peebles, 1995). It is through this framework that the learner understands a topic. Thus learning is characterized as *a series of cognitive restructurings* in which the conception/conceptual framework undergoes change, with the intent of these restructuring being for each learner to sequentially develop more 'advanced' conceptions.

Constructivist research on conceptual change has studied the teaching of science as represented in the work of Vosniadou (1991), Stofflett (1994), and Demastes *et al.* (1995). In this field researchers have found that students tend to hold prior understandings of many scientific concepts and that those understandings are resistant to change, largely because many of the terms, such as energy, light, gravity, rock, atom, star, environment, plant, and so on, used to represent these concepts are also used in everyday language. Importantly, this research has also indicated that these *prior conceptions* may pose a significant *impediment* to the achievement of intended learning outcomes. For this reason research from a constructivist perspective has tended to move to the exploration of concept development and change. Moreover, the limited number, and sequential development, of alternative conceptions of a concept has led to the development of teaching strategies which are intended to promote the development of *preferred* conceptions; conceptions which are more consistent with those held by scientists (see Stofflett (1994) and Vosniadou (1991) for examples of these strategies). Research on these processes suggests that students tend to change their prior conceptions only when they 'become dissatisfied with their existing conceptions, as well as find new concepts intelligible, plausible, and fruitful' (Stofflett, 1994, p. 787). However, what Stofflett also found is that, while those conditions for conceptual change are important, and while her application of conceptual change strategies was successful in changing pre-service teachers' conceptions of teaching, it was the actual teaching experiences of her subjects which determined whether those changes in conceptions were evidenced in their teaching practices. Thus her work suggests that 'operationalization' of 'new' conceptions is dependent on the existence of appropriate contexts for their enactment in practice.[3]

Our work was also based on understandings drawn from the phenomenographic perspective (see for example, Marton, 1981; and Marton *et al.*, 1984). This research seems to have been taken most seriously by researchers in academic development in higher education, particularly in the United Kingdom and Australia. One of phenomenography's major contributions to education is its adoption of the perspective of the learner rather than that of the researcher or teacher. It, like constructivism, also suggests that, for any one phenomenon, there are only a limited number of ways that it might be understood, i.e. 'conceptions' of the phenomenon. While there is little reference in this literature to the temporal development of conceptions, the hierarchical arrangement of conceptions in some studies suggests a developmental sequence. However this notion of conception differs from that described in relation to constructivism. In phenomenography, a conception is understood to be the relation which exists between an individual and a phenomenon (Ekeblad and Bond, 1994). It is the experience or understanding that is constituted by the dynamic interaction between a person and that phenomenon. For example, a person's conception of learning is the way in which they understand or experience learning (in a particular context). In this way of thinking about learning conceptual change is assumed, learning is conceptual change.

Phenomenography uses the terms experience and understanding in common with constructivism but, contrary to it, does not regard 'conception' as being a mental entity. Phenomenographic research seeks to avoid the mind—body dualism that is evident in the kind of model of conceptual change which derives from constructivism.[4] The teaching strategies associated with conceptual change theory often focus on beliefs in ways which imply that knowledge can be decontextualized, thus encouraging mind—body dualism. The strategies use context primarily as a backdrop: a source of experience upon which understandings are based, or against which predictions can be tested. Here, the focus is on the belief in abstraction from its greater substance and history. On the other hand, the implicitness of context in the notion of the phenomenographic conception (Ekeblad and Bond, 1994) has the potential to overcome this problem.

Strategies used to enact these understandings

Whether we respond to our opening question from either the constructivist or the phenomenographic perspective, enacting these understandings would involve inviting students to express their existing conceptions of, for example, knowledge, teaching and learning, and then to challenge them — e.g. as useful, adequate, consistent, etc. — in various ways. This represents a quite focused approach to the challenge of having learners activate their prior knowledge, compared to the strategies suggested by some research on professional development. For example, Tillema (1995) reports a study into changing the

---

[3] *Demastes et al. (1995, p. 659) provide additional evidence in support of this suggestion, arguing that 'often conceptual change is not an exchange, but can include instances when two competing conceptions are held and applied'.*

[4] *We should point out that our understanding of constructivism as a research orientation, particularly that variation which has a more social and cultural orientation, such as that discussed by Alexander, Schallert and Hare (1991) and Demastes et al. (1995), suggests that this dualism is not fundamental to it.*

professional knowledge and beliefs of teachers which was based on three 'training models': concept-based training, which involved a focus on presentation of the new knowledge (similar to the second focus identified above); concept-based/diagnostic training, which involved the provision to the trainers of diagnostic knowledge on the learners' prior knowledge and beliefs; and experience-based training, which involved discussions and peer-interactions stimulated by case studies (p. 294). While our strategies placed great importance on discussions and peer-interactions, we explicitly invited participants to identify the beliefs which we believed would be central to those discussions and interactions prior to such engagements. In so doing our understandings anticipated Tillema's (1995, p. 312) conclusion that:

> *the knowledge structures of professionals are very difficult to change by mere presentation of information. Conceptual change, and training as a means to achieve it, needs to engage the pre-existing ideas, orientations, ways of thinking and perspectives of professional teachers; otherwise the hegemony of those knowledge structures will remain unchallenged. Challenging beliefs ... as a confrontational approach to knowledge restructuring promises to be more successful than an incremental training approach aimed at the gradual accretion of new information and tuning of existing knowledge structures, at least where professional 'learners: are concerned.*

We chose to focus on the explication and exploration of participants' beliefs about a range of issues, including their conceptions of higher education, knowledge, learning and teaching. We invited participants to articulate their conceptions formally through the use of directed written responses and personal diaries. We then sought to have them 'challenge' these through discussion of relevant research literature in our regular workshops (for example: Boyer, 1990; Martin and Balla, 1991; Ramsden, 1992). We assumed that access to the relevant literature and discussions of it would provide considerable opportunity for participants to develop an awareness of preferred approaches and to make comparisons between these and their own beliefs. We chose not to indicate 'preferred' approaches or beliefs explicitly but in our role as their 'teachers' we hoped that our practice advocated those preferences.[5] Inevitably, those preferences became much more visible once we began negotiating the criteria for assessment with the participants. In that context our preferences were quickly identified, and participants invited us to justify them.

We sought to acknowledge and to respect the range of beliefs about concepts such as knowledge, teaching and learning that individuals brought to the course and to invite participants to clarify and elaborate these through critically reflecting upon them. This lead to a strong sense of collegiality within the workshops, in which opportunities to discuss the perspectives and practices were welcomed, and in which openness was respected. However, within those discussions we attempted to maintain a meta-focus on the beliefs which underlay participants' academic practices. In essence we were attempting to ensure that our practices avoided the theory—practice binary, which privileges theory in the context of most formal educational programmes (Bromme and Tillema, 1995). Our focus on beliefs was intended to help participants locate our discussions of the assigned reading within the context of their own practices. Thus, this way of thinking about the contextual relatedness of learning gets closer to the heart of our question, but does it adequately answer it?

---

[5] *For us, the communal and explicit confrontation of a 'wrong' conception posed an ethical dilemma. First, the notion of conception as a world view or a way of seeing is very personal and second, we were working in a context in which we were trying to encourage the notion of individual difference and respect for that difference. Intentionally, therefore we did not require participants to share their conceptions with us or with each other unless they chose to do so voluntarily. Instead, we focused on the notion of competent practice in context.*

Part 3: Some reflections on our hybrid approach

Before we move on to discuss these reflections we need to make it clear that, in the main, participants in the 1995 Graduate Certificate course were very happy with it and report having achieved a range of valued learnings. For example, one participant expressed delight at having become capable of engaging in discussions of educational practices with educators, rather than remaining silent because she lacked the necessary language and the confidence to use it. Another spoke of his growing understanding of his own practices — why they did or did not work — and the pleasure of being able to design more effective strategies. A third spoke of his surprise that while he had set out to introduce new strategies, which emphasized process aspects of his teaching, he had in fact dealt with a 'content' in greater breadth and depth than he had in his traditional strategies. Finally, one student reported on her lecturing strategies in terms of their considerable value in supporting student learning. Those strategies included chanting of recalled information, listing of 'things you have learnt during this lecture' and explicit behavioural contracting with the students, with her agreeing to teach in ways which were consistent with their expectations. In turn, and deliberately, she challenged some of our preferences concerning the practices of quality teaching.

What we have found

We have gained an increasing awareness that our participants' expectations of us as teachers and of our approach to teaching and learning in the course were consistent with their conceptions of learning. They defined the learning context of the course in relation to their own conceptions of learning and teaching: accordingly their expectations of and their approach to the learning experiences appeared to derive from these 'conceptions'. In turn, these became the basis for evaluating the value of that experience and, in some cases gave rise to a quite explicit challenge to the value of our 'preferences'. However, we now see that, while we succeeded in having participants reflect on their beliefs and understandings in relation to teaching and learning, they often continued to do so from a position in which they located 'learning' explicitly as an issue for their students rather than for themselves as learners or teachers. This phenomenon is similar to that described by Stofflett (1994).

Our reflections have helped us to identify a number of ways in which the hybrid response differs from the third focus. First, and in line with phenomenographic research, it is based on an understanding of 'conceptions' as a complex inter-relationship which represents the individual's way of understanding their world. In addition a 'conception' is relational, and includes information that is available only through participation in a setting. This meaning is related to the view of knowledge discussed by Alexander *et al.* (1991) who refer to the socio-cultural knowledge in terms of 'ways of talking, ways of thinking, ways of conceptualizing' (p. 325), and to knowledge as being 'fluid and dynamic' (p. 324): a statement made in the context of a discussion of the distinction between tacit and explicit knowledge. The authors were indicating that 'any particular 'known' does not exist in one or other state exclusively' (p. 324), and that the accessibility of knowledge is more a function of contexts and circumstances than of the knowledge itself. This view of knowledge is presented here in the framework of constructivism but it illustrates the dynamism and complexity of the interaction between teacher, learner and knowledge. Other authors, such as Lave and Wenger (1991), take this issue further, arguing that what is constructed may continue to depend on the knowledge held by others, or information provided by the environment. That is, the construction remains a 'situated' artefact,[6] rather than an individual one.

Second, while constructivist conceptions are seen as developmentally sequential, with the implicit valuing of the more completely developed conception over prior-conceptions, this hybrid response should allow 'conceptions' to be valued in terms of other, more contextual and cultural, dimensions. Thus, the degree of cultural and contextual awareness and sensitivity would be significant indicators of the value of a 'conception', as would an ethical dimension. Our point here is that this response should not, *a priori*, privilege any particular conception. Thus, even though some phenomenographic research has discussed conceptions of teaching in ways that suggest a hierarchical relationship, our sense is that it may be pedagogically inappropriate to attach preferences to those conceptions in ways which ignore either the intentions or the practices and expectations that are associated with its operationalization. By implication, then, it would also be possible to make judgements about the relative and contextualized value of particular expressions which might in some more global sense be seen as similar 'conceptions'. Clearly we are moving away from a view that expertise is a uni-dimensional construct. Like John Biggs' (1994), we see the simplistic binary of 'deep' versus 'surface' approaches to learning and the related notions of 'good teaching' as problematic, and are beginning to question whether his challenge on cultural grounds should be extended to involve disciplinary and institutional issues.

We have likened the effect of our growing awareness to Bereiter's notion of the hall of mirrors.[7] We are coming to acknowledge, in ways that we had not considered sufficiently, that our participants' interaction with the course is contextualized within their own conceptual framework rather than simply 'conceptions' of teaching or learning of the kind which have been described previously. In this we should emphasize that we are not advocating the limited notion of an internal cognitive, conceptual framework. Rather we liken conceptual field to Gurwitsch's (1964) notion of thematic field from which the theme (conception) emerges and in which it is embedded: the complex contextual ground. Thus, it is becoming increasingly clear to us that 'conceptions' are both more functionally important in terms of participants' expectations of and responses to our teaching, and more deeply interrelated within the context of their practices than most constructivist or phenomenographic approaches have yet suggested.

Implications for future course design

We now see the need to acknowledge and work with our participants' conceptual framework and to explore how we might respond to their contextualized understandings of learning and teaching in ways which both value and challenge their views. Our growing understandings appear to have many similarities with issues discussed by Demastes *et al.*

---

[6] *Lave and Wenger (1991, p. 33) refer to situatedness as indicating an 'implied emphasis on comprehensive understanding involving the whole person rather than "receiving" a body of factual knowledge about the world; on activity in and with the world; and on the view that agent, activity, and the world mutually constitute each other'.*

[7] *Bereiter (1990), drawing on the earlier work of Cronbach (1975), uses this expression to signal difficulties in addressing issues of interaction within the functionalist approach to education research. While we are not seeking to make that point, Bereiter's general point that 'process theories must demonstrate that they can do more than produce better shopping lists of variables to pay attention to. They ought to tell us something about how to think about the variables that, for the most part, we already know are relevant', (p. 607) remains very salient to this discussion.*

(1995), who speak for the need to see conceptions as located within a broader set of understandings and commitments — *a conceptual ecology*. They suggest that this ecology includes issues such as 'the learner's epistemological commitments, anomalies, metaphors, analogies, metaphysical beliefs, knowledge of competing conceptions, and knowledge from outside the field' (p. 638), and their 'goals, emotions and motivations' (p. 661). Their research focused on students' conceptions of evolution, a conception which, by its very nature, was likely to have strong interrelatedness with the elements of the conceptual ecology that they nominate. It seems reasonable to speculate that other conceptions, such as of light or gravity, might have fewer and/or weaker interractions, and for that reason be more open to change through the sorts of relatively straightforward strategies discussed by Vosniadou (1991) and other constructivists. We believe that the conceptions with which we are dealing are located within a very complex ecology, and that within this complexity it is clear that 'mere presentation of information' (Tillema, 1995, p. 312) is not going to result in significant learning.

Further, we are coming to consider ways in which we can provide a safe environment in which participants can explicitly focus on and explore their conceptual ecologies as a prior issue to the consideration of their academic practices. These considerations give rise to a series of questions.

- How do we both respect participants' conceptions while seeking to explore those conceptions and the implications they hold for their approach to teaching?
- Further, how do we help participants to recognize the role of those conceptions in their thinking about the conceptions of learning that their students might bring to their classrooms?
- That is, what conditions do we provide to encourage participants to explore the implications of their own conceptions in relation to the different conceptions held by others.
- More importantly, and in keeping with the recognition that many of the terms which we use have multiple meanings given their use in everyday language, in what language do we communicate with each other when use of our own 'conceptual' language masks the very differences that we wish to highlight?

Some elements of a possible response include:

1. the need to extend the initial exploration of each participant's *conceptual ecology*, as a prior issue to the consideration of their academic practices;

2. that this exploration would need to explicitly address issues of context, including students' and colleagues expectations, the expectations of professional bodies, cultural and organizational norms, and discipline-specific considerations, including the nature of the learning outcomes which are to be achieved; and

3. that these issues of context need to be explored relationally, from within, and as parts of, each participant's *conceptual ecology*.

While not dissimilar to the approach we adopted this year, the meta-frame would need to be different, addressing situated conceptions rather than individualized beliefs. The clear implication is that the issues of preference can then be addressed in terms of the *ecological intelligibility, plausibility and fruitfulness* (to draw on the three conditions for conceptual change noted by Stofflett, 1994, p. 787) of any particular conception.

Conclusion

This chapter reports the progressive examination and development of our thinking in relation to a programme which offers a professional qualification to university teachers. In doing so we have described how we approached the design and preparation of the programme and also the way in which we tried to create a discursive context for our students. Our thinking is itself contextualized and in communicating it in this linear medium we risk a simplification that may misrepresent our intentions. Our thinking has been significantly influenced by the phenomenographic and constructivist research perspectives. Each of these offers a rich ground for the exploration of new approaches to teaching. They embody a way of thinking about teaching which focused on what Boyer (1990) referred to as the scholarship of discovery (of specific conceptions) and the scholarship of teaching (about the approach). In this discussion we have sought to extend that scholarship to issues of integration (with other areas of research), and application (to pedagogical practices), a process which has led us to challenge some of our earlier understandings and examine the implications of the approach we adopted. This represents, for us, a rediscovery of the value of scholarship — of formalizing and sharing our thinking. This process has been our fundamental strategy in teaching the Graduate Certificate and in seeking to make our understandings explicit we have had our students explicitly challenge them. We, as well as they, are the beneficiaries.

What we seem to be working towards is an elaboration of participants' understandings such that much of what is currently implicit, and therefore unexamined, within their 'conceptions' is opened to critical reflection. We are not seeking to formalize those understandings as an end in itself. Rather, we are seeking to ensure that the value of any particular conception is identified and clarified in context. The educational literature would provide a language and rules for such a discussion, together with methods to research aspects of the formerly taken-for-granted understandings. That is, 'challenges' would not be posed in terms of *'a priori* ideals', but in terms of the value of testing the *intelligibility, plausibility* and *fruitfulness* of particular conceptions within the overall situatedness of each participant's conceptual ecology.

As teachers of the Graduate Certificate Program we would no longer have a role as advocates of particular preferred conceptions, but would become critical friends to the process of elaboration and evaluation. Rather than act as agents for conceptual change, we would seek the development of conceptual clarity and cohesion, along with a much sharper recognition of the likely impact of each participant's practices on the approaches their students might adopt to learning. Thus (and unexpectedly) we find reasons to agree with Pratt's (1992, op. 218) conclusion that:

> *it would be wrong to conclude that some conceptions are better than others. Each has philosophical and epistemological roots which are consonant with particular people, purposes, and contexts. Indeed, it is entirely consistent with these findings to expect that exemplary teachers can be found for each of these conceptual categories, as long as judgements of quality have regard for the internal consistency between actions, intentions, and beliefs and the contexts within which individuals are operating.*

Further, as Pratt goes on to note, 'we must see our own conceptions as problematic'. We too are learners who must focus our learning on the conceptual ecology underlying our academic practices.

References

Alexander, P. A., Schallert, D. L. and Hare, V. C. (1991) Coming to terms: how researchers in learning and literacy talk about knowledge. *Review of Educational Research* **61**, 315—43.

Biggs, J. (1994) What are effective schools? Lessons from east and west. *Australian Educational Researcher* **21**, 19—39.

Bereiter, C. (1990) Aspects of an educational learning theory. *Review of Educational Research* **60**(4), 603—24.

Boyer, E. L. (1990) *Scholarship Reconsidered: Priorities of the Professoriate*. New Jersey: The Carnegie Foundation for the Advancement of Teaching.

Bromme, R. and Tillema, H. H. (1995) Special edition: fusing experience and theory. *Learning and Instruction* **5**(4).

Brookfield, S. (1990) *The Skilful Teacher*. San Francisco: Jossey-Bass.

Bruce, C. and Gerber, R. (1995) Towards university lecturers' conceptions of student learning. *Higher Education* **29**, 443—58.

Cox, B. (1994) *Practical Pointers for University Teachers*. London: Kogan Page.

Demastes, S., Good, R. and Peebles, P. (1995) Students' conceptual ecologies and the process of conceptual change in evolution. *Science Education* **79**, 637—66.

Ekeblad, E. and Bond, C. (1994) The nature of conception: questions of context. In R. Ballantyne and C. Bruce (eds), *Phenomenography: Philosophy and Practice*. Brisbane: Queensland University of Technology.

Gibbs, G. (1995) Changing lecturers' conceptions of teaching and learning through action research. In A. Brew (ed.), *Directions in Staff Development*. Buckingham: SRHE and Open University Press.

Gurwitsch, A. (1964) *The Field of Consciousness*. Pittsburg: Duquesne University Press.

Harvey, L. and Green, D. (1993) Defining quality. *Assessment and Evaluation in Higher Education* **18**(1), 9—34.

Hoare, D. (1995) *Higher Education Management Review: report of the Comittee of Inquiry*. Canberra: Australian Government Printing Service.

Hollingsworth, S. (1989) Prior beliefs and cognitive change in learning to teach. *American Educational Research Journal* **26**, 160—89.

Lave, J. and Wenger, E. (1991) *Situated Learning: Legitimate Peripheral Participation*. New York: Cambridge University Press.

Martin, E. and Balla, M. (1991) Conceptions of teaching and implications for learning. In B. Ross (ed.), *Teaching for Effective Learning*. Research and Development in Higher Education, 13. Sydney: HERDSA.

Marton, F. (1981) Phenomenography — sescribing conceptions of the world around us. *Instructional Science* **10**, 177—200.

Marton, F., Hounsell, D. and Entwistle, N. (1984) *The Experience of Learning*. Edinburgh: Scottish Academic Press.

Pratt, D. D. (1992) Conceptions of teaching. *Adult Education Quarterly* **42**, 203—20.

Ramsden, P. (1992) *Learning to Teach in Higher Education*. London: Routledge.

Stofflett, R. T. (1994) The accommodation of science pedagogical knowledge: the application of conceptual change constructs to teacher education. *Journal of Research in Science Teaching* **31**, 787—810.

Tillema, H. H. (1995) Changing the professional knowledge and beliefs of teachers: a training study. *Learning and Instruction* **5**, 291—318.

Utley, A. (1995) AUT calls for accreditation. *The Times Higher Education Supplement*, 10 November, 52.

Vosniadou, S. (1991) Designing curricula for conceptual restructuring: lessons from the study of knowledge acquisition in astronomy. *Journal of Curriculum Studies* **23**, 219—37.

18 Triple-mode theory as a context for effective teaching and learning

Peter Radloff
Behavioural Health Science, School of Nursing

and Alex Radloff
Academic Staff Development
Teaching Learning Group
Curtin University of Technology

Introduction

Once one accepts that behaviour involves actions, feelings and thoughts, it becomes apparent that all three must be separately addressed if we are to help students become more effective learners and communicators since all three modes are components of both written and oral communication skills. However, actions, feelings and thoughts have not been considered a useful theoretical trinity in research on student learning in general or for the development of communication skills, in particular. This is especially the case in research on student learning emanating from a cognitivist perspective. Behavioural triple-mode theory offers a useful alternative to cognitivistic views of learning which have dominated discussions of student learning in recent years. In this chapter, we describe triple-mode theory; outline theoretical and research evidence mainly from the clinical intervention literature to support its usefulness in promoting behaviour change; provide evidence for the importance of well developed communication skills; and suggest ways in which triple-mode theory can be used to help students develop their oral and writing skills as part of regular subject learning.

Origins of triple-mode theory

Malott, Whaley and Malott (1994) define behaviour as 'anything a dead man cannot do'. Considering this definition, and the range of a non-dead man's capability, we must recognize three separate modes or domains which comprise behaviour. Any experience is made up of **actions**, **feelings**, the subjectively judged pleasant and unpleasant; and **thoughts** involving cognitions, self statements or expressible ideas. This representation is sometimes known as triple-mode theory (Evans, 1986; Eifert and Schauss, 1993). Educators will be familiar with these categories since they know the three domains of Bloom's (1956) educational objectives: the cognitive, affective and psychomotor, to use the order in which they are usually stated. This order seems also to represent the relative importance usually accorded each objective. Some reflection may tempt you to change the order to psychomotor, affective and cognitive, and even, perhaps, to refer to actions feeling and thoughts when addressing objectives. Whatever the terms used, the categories are common, and have a long history which includes one of the older classifications of behaviour into rational or voluntary actions, the emotions or passions and cognitions. These basic components of behaviour management can be found in vernacular theories in different cultures and throughout history so what may be thought to characterize current versions? Can any central feature of the current behavioural triple-mode approach be identified to distinguishes it from other approaches, and from earlier theories. It is not just the classification of behaviour into different modes which lends this approach importance: it is the analysis of events over time, and the recognition that what follows a particular behaviour is what controls it. This ABC of the method we owe to Skinner.

Skinner (1963) emphasized that it is the selection of behaviours by consequences which distinguishes his approach. This can be compared with (and may be seen as a subset of) the Darwinian law of survival of the fittest. Those species which are fit, i.e. produce surviving offspring, will continue developing and adapting to their ecological niche. 'Behaviour is a function of its consequences' is the equivalent of this selectivity of species law in that those behaviours which are favoured by consequences will survive. Behaviour management has this law at its core. To provide a framework to make this law of functional relationships easy to apply in practice, any behaviour is considered in terms of its origin, the details of its occurrence and the consequences which follow. The A-B-C mnemonic reminds users that any behaviour has **Antecedents** including setting conditions, the **Behaviours** (comprising Actions, Feelings and Thoughts) and **Consequences** which follow. Recognizing that consequences are important, and that the sequence of a particular experience has relevance to its future probability of occurrence makes it easier to record experiences in terms of the A-B-C standard, and to pay attention simultaneously to the components of the behaviour, to the actions, feelings and thoughts (AFTs) involved. The advantages of such a multi-faceted viewpoint must be argued since its seeming complexity goes against the view, currently popular, which has most people considering that a single all-encompassing theory is the ideal.

Alternativism and how to use three modes in practice

Reductionism has been accepted as false by many, perhaps most behavioural scientists, but there is less agreement as to how to proceed in a discipline which necessarily includes different levels or modes of analysis. Instead of promoting eclecticism which fudges the divisions between fields, or holism, a modernized version of the same thing, any tendency towards agglomeration must be resisted for less restrictive options. The sensible alternative would be to become better at working across the different modes or levels while preserving their distinctiveness. One way of achieving this is to recognise that one never uses one mode in isolation from others. Theoretical pluralism, and alternativism promotes just such an approach.

Feyerabend's (1965, 1975) solution to the problem of reduction requires openness to alternative theories to avoid the inconsistencies and contradictions which follow attempts to use a single theory. The clarity of his analysis has become vital in an environment which has constructivists use his phrase 'anything goes' but give it a twist implying that no constraints are needed and that any constructed approach is acceptable. It is important to recognize that using alternativism requires care, and understanding.

So how should the actions, feelings and thoughts of triple-mode theory be dealt with? Are these part of a single behavioural paradigm, or have they to be considered as forming separate paradigms? On theoretical and metatheoretical grounds, as well as on the basis of some outcome studies, it appears that each should be considered a separate paradigm with all three coordinated to produce any final (triple-mode) application. Thus when using the triple-mode approach, if one intervenes to modify feelings, changes follow in both action, and thought modes. Working on thoughts yields changes to actions and feelings, and so also for actions when feelings and thoughts become influenced. The question which has to be answered is: 'How is one to represent, with consistency, interventions which involve one or more of these triple-mode components?' The low correlations for measures across these modes (Evans, 1986) instead of causing puzzlement, should be recognized as part of the distinctiveness, the independence or orthogonality among them.

Aiming to produce a single theoretical language to describe change embracing more than one mode will, at first, appear to succeed. It is only later that accumulating contradictions and inconsistencies will require the promising foundations to be abandoned. If, instead of attempting to smear the three modes together to make one language, each is kept separate, confusion is avoided, and development can be continuous. With care it may even be possible to successfully carry out and interpret multivariate analyses across modes provided each is considered separately to ensure that one does not misinterpret results through the confounding of independent with dependent variables.

Usefulness of triple-mode theory

The triple-mode approach has proved useful in clinical settings. This behavioural approach has contributed to clinical outcome methodology, including replication, and the insistence on short term (e.g. 6 months) and longer term (e.g. 2 years) follow-up assessment before pronouncing on treatment effectiveness. Studies aimed at changing client behaviour using a triple-mode approach have included attention to all three modes and have usually led, as shown by meta-analysis, to improvements beyond that obtained with alternative methods.

The approach has also proved useful in sports psychology where training and coaching has focussed on helping athletes to manage feelings, thoughts and actions in imagined virtual performances so as to achieve peak outcomes in competition. It has also changed the whole approach to the field of psychopathology where behavioural methods have been shown to be prescriptive for a range of disorders. Watson and Tharp (1993) provide a self-management handbook using this approach to manage depression, anxiety and daily hassles among other issues, and in the process covers effectiveness, measurement and design issues as well.

In educational settings, the effectiveness of small group activities as exemplified by the jigsaw method and reciprocal teaching among others, can be understood in terms of the triple-mode approach. Learning activities which acknowledge the role of feelings and actions in learning, in addition to thoughts, and which encourage students to participate in activities beyond the classroom, result in effective and enjoyable learning experiences.

Triple-mode theory and communication skills

One of the most important educational goals is the development of communication skills. Effective communication skills are important for communicating new knowledge and ideas. Employers and professional bodies value and seek graduates with well-developed communication skills, especially writing and oral skills. But they are often disappointed with the level of skills which they encounter (Australian and Employers, 1993; Cowen, 1993; Harvey, 1993). Tertiary teachers regularly complain about students' communication skills especially writing and oral skills (Bate and Sharpe, 1990; Cowen, 1993) and their concerns are growing with the increased diversity of the student body. Although there is an ongoing debate as to whether the 'literacy' skills of school leavers are increasing, declining or static, there is general agreement that the expectations for higher levels of these skills are growing in university courses and as career and work demands change and become more complex (Radloff and Samson, 1990; Wickert, 1989).

Communication skills are not only important for demonstrating what has been learned. They are part of the learning process. For effective learning to occur, students need to be actively engaged with the subject matter and learn with and from others. Students who are actively engaged with the subject through talking and writing about it, are more likely to gain personal meaning; achieve deep learning and apply learning outside the classroom.

Students who have well-developed oral and writing skills learn through peer and group discussion, questioning, and debating, and by means of note-making, summarizing, expository writing and journalling. But many students do not come to university with such skills already well developed. As a result, they are unable to take full advantage of the opportunities to participate in learning activities which require them to speak or write. Furthermore, they are at a disadvantage when assessment involves class presentations, student led seminars, essays and examinations. Oral and writing skills are also important for managing the learning process. Students who are confident about their speaking and writing skills are likely to ask questions and seek help from others, and to use journalling and other forms of writing to regulate and reflect on their learning. Students who lack confidence in these skills, are less likely to use them for learning.

How can we best help students develop their communication skills both as a tool for learning and for demonstrating their mastery of new knowledge? Our experience suggests that the triple-mode approach is useful for understanding and managing the development of both writing and oral skills.

Traditionally, cognitivist models of student learning have focused on cognitive and metacognitive processes and strategies and have largely ignored both actions and feelings. Actions have been conceptualized as emanating or flowing from thoughts. But both research and common sense tell us that the relationship is much more complex than that. Just thinking or knowing something, 'knowing that' (declarative knowledge), is no guarantee that one can apply such knowledge, that is, 'knowing how' (procedural knowledge), in a learning situation. A good example of this lack of congruence between thought and action comes from (Mahalski, 1992, p. 129) who, when she examined students' use of study manual advice on writing, noted that, '"knowing" is not easily translated into "doing"'. We have found a similar discrepancy between students' knowledge of what constitutes good writing and their ability to produce such writing. These examples of (unedited) responses to the question, 'What is good writing?' from a group of first-year Design students illustrates the point:

> *Good writing is the ability to express ideas and facts that can be understood by the reader clearly. When writing about a particular topic or subject, a good writer will not loose focus of their aim of expressing this on the page yet be able to keep the work interesting to the reader.*

> *Good writing consists of group of facts or ideas put together in a fluid way. It is when a reader can gaze effortlessly across paper and be involved and interested about what he or she is reading.*

Good writing is writing with correct grammar, spelling and communicates well. ie gets the message across to the reader. Whether it be an idea, informing someone something etc. It must be well structured according to the type of writing desired. ie with proper sentences and paragraphs.

The students' comments capture the essence of good writing — audience awareness, coherence and structure, and appropriate language — but they also illustrate the difficulty students have in achieving these goals in their own writing. Undergraduate Education students also show this discrepancy between thought and action, between knowing and doing, when they regularly tell us that any piece of writing must have a beginning, a middle and an end but often fail to include these basic components in their own essay and report writing.

Actions must be considered in any model of learning, especially if we are to address the problems associated with adopting new strategies and changing established patterns of response. Actions are also crucial if we are to increase the likelihood of 'transfer of training' of new knowledge and skills over time and beyond the classroom to new situations and tasks.

Feelings have also been neglected in discussions of learning. As Pintrich (1994) points out, models of learning based on cognitive science generally have not dealt with affect or feelings very adequately. But feelings play an important part in learning as recent research has shown. In reviewing some of this research, (Boekaerts, 1993, p. 150) notes that in the last ten years, 'a vast amount of evidence has convinced even the strictest cognitivist that there is an interplay between cognitions and emotions'. Both thoughts and feelings have to be considered if we are to understand how students learn.

Feelings play an important role in communication, both written and oral. For example, students often express negative feelings about writing. They report feeling anxious about having to write (Nightingale, 1986; Radloff and Samson, 1991) and not enjoying writing (Emmitt and Bradford, 1993). Moreover, these problems are not limited to undergraduates as Torrance, Thomas and Robinson, (1992) found when they surveyed full-time social science masters and doctoral students. Responses to their questionnaire revealed that 34% of the students found writing highly stressful. It is probably not surprising therefore, that one of the most commonly expressed problems with writing which our students report is avoidance through procrastination — any writing which can be delayed, will be delayed.

Students also report feelings of anxiety when having to speak in class or present a seminar (Radloff, 1995). They are not the only ones who experience such anxiety. It is probably a truism that most people are more afraid of public speaking than of dying. Certainly, anxiety, and sometimes phobia, about speaking in a group may seriously jeopardize students' academic progress and achievement. It came as no surprise to us when we incorporated a presentation requirement into a communication course for Physics students that three students withdrew when they discovered that they would have to present a paper at a student conference as part of the assessment for the course. Those students who remained in the course, reported that the 15 minute presentation was the most anxiety-provoking task they had to do even though their performance attracted a mere 10% of their final mark for the course.

Clearly, if we are to understand how students develop communication skills and to provide appropriate support for their development, we must recognize the role of actions, feelings and thoughts. The triple-mode theory provides an alternative model of learning which acknowledges the interaction of all three and offers strategies to deal effectively with each to achieve desired learning.

Using triple-mode theory to develop communication skills

Over the past few years we have been using triple-mode theory to support the development of student oral and writing skills in the context of their regular subject learning (Radloff and Samson, 1993; Radloff, 1994; Radloff, 1995). Strategies for helping students develop their oral skills have included an emphasis on acknowledging and dealing with negative feelings, understanding the factors which contribute to an effective presentation, and repeated graduated exposure to reinforce skill development and manage anxiety. Students practise oral presentations over the course of a semester and are helped to plan, manage and evaluate their own efforts within a supportive peer group setting. Students are encouraged to recognize the role which feelings, thoughts and actions play in the development and use of communication skills and to develop strategies to manage the process effectively.

Strategies for helping students develop their writing skills have involved a simple heuristic — the Five by Three Writing Model (Samson and Radloff, 1992) — which unpacks the complex writing task into five steps:

Preplan	define task identify audience establish purpose
Plan	gather information decide on issues select format and structure
Compose	speak – express ideas aloud write – write to 'see' ideas monitor – 'Is that what I mean?'
Review	check validity of content check structure and format edit for mechanics
Evaluate	'Did I answer the question?' 'Were my strategies effective?' 'How well did I carry out the task?'

The steps are described and modelled by the teacher and are practised by students individually and in groups as they work on their set assignments. The model focuses on feelings associated with writing and helps students to manage these. It emphasizes thoughts through discussion of the process of writing and of common beliefs and myths about good writing and how to achieve it. Finally, the model reinforces action by requiring students to set writing goals, to write regularly and to rewrite in response to audience feedback.

We have refined our strategies for supporting the development of oral and writing skills in response to student performance and feedback using triple-mode theory. Thinking about communication skills from this perspective has helped us to recognize the need to address explicitly each mode when we plan teaching and learning activities. It has also provided students with insight into how they develop oral and writing skills and practical strategies to manage the process. Triple-mode theory provides a useful basis for supporting the development of communication skills as part of regular classroom teaching.

References

Australian Association of Graduate Employers (1993) *National Survey of Graduate Employers*. Sydney: Author.

Bate, D. and Sharpe, P. (1990) *Student Writer's Handbook*. Sydney: Harcourt Brace Jovanovich.

Bloom, B. S. (1956) *Taxonomy of educational objectives. Handbook I: Cognitive Domain*. New York: McKay.

Boekaerts, M. (1993) Being concerned with well-being and with learning. *Educational Psychologist* **28**(2), 149—67.

Cowen, K. (1993) Responding to the writing crisis in universities: Writing across the curriculum. Paper presented at the *Queensland Branch HERDSA Conference*, Brisbane, Queensland, 15—16 April.

Eifert, G. H. and Schauss, S. L. (1993) Unifying the field: Developing an integrative paradigm for behavior therapy. *Journal of Behavior Therapy and Experimental Psychiatry* **24**, 107—18.

Emmitt, M. T. and Bradford, C. (1993) First year preservice teacher education students' attitudes to reading and writing. Paper presented at the *Australian Teacher Education Association Annual Conference*, Fremantle, Western Australia, 11—14 July.

Evans, I. M. (1986) Response structure and the triple-response-mode concept. In R. O. Nelson and S. C. Hayes (eds), *Conceptual Foundations of Behavioral Assessment*, New York, NY: Guilford Press.

Feyerabend, P. K. (1975) *Against Method*. London: New Left Books/Boston.

Feyerabend, P. K. (1965) Reply to criticism: comments on Smart, Sellars and Putnam. *Boston Studies in the Philosophy of Science* **2**.

Harvey, L. (1993) *Employer Satisfaction: Interim report*. Warwick: Quality in Higher Education, University of Warwick.

Mahalski, P. A. (1992) Essay-writing: do study manuals give relevant advice? *Higher Education* **24**, 113—32.

Malott, R. W., Whaley, D. L. and Malott, M. E. (1993) *Elementary Principles of Behavior*, 2nd edn. Englewood Cliffs, NJ: Prentice-Hall.

Nightingale, P. (1986) *Improving Student Writing*. Green Guide No. 4. Kensington, NSW: Higher Education Research and Development Society of Australasia.

Pintrich, P. R. (1994) Continuities and discontinuities: future directions for research in educational psychology. *Educational Psychologist* **29**(3), 137—48.

Radloff, A. (1994) Writing to learn, learning to write: helping academic staff to support student writing in their discipline. In *Proceedings of the Thirteenth International Seminar on Staff and Educational Development*, Cape Town, South Africa.

Radloff, A. and Samson, J. (1990) Literacy and open learning. In R. Atkinson and C. McBeath (eds), *Opening Learning and New Technology*, pp. 283—9. Perth, WA: Australian Society for Educational Technology, WA Chapter.

Radloff, A. and Samson, J. (1991) Expository writing at tertiary level. Paper presented at the *HERDSA Annual Conference*, Brisbane, Queensland.

Radloff, A. and Samson, J. (1993) Promoting deep learning: using academic writing to change the learner's epistemological stance. Paper presented at the *5th European Conference, EARLI*, Aix-en-Provence, France, 31 August—5 September.

Radloff, P. (1995) Managing student presentation anxiety. Paper presented at the *Teaching Learning Forum '95*. Joondalup, Western Australia: Edith Cowan University.

Samson, J. and Radloff, A. (1992) *In Writing: A Guide to Writing Effectively at the Tertiary Level . . .* Perth, WA: Paradigm Press.

Skinner, B. F. (1963) Behaviorism at fifty. *Science* **134**, 566—602.

Torrance, M., Thomas, G. V. and Robinson, E. J. (1992) The writing experiences of social science research students. *Studies in Higher Education* **17**(2), 155—67.

Vines, G. (1995) Is there a database in the house? *New Scientist* **148**, January, 14—15.

Watson, D. L. and Tharp, R. G. (1992) *Self-directed Behavior: Self Modification for Personal Adjustment*, 6th edn. Pacific Grove. CA: Brooks/Cole.

Wickert, R. (1989) *No Single Measure: A Survey of Australian Adult Literacy*. Summary report, Canberra, ACT: Commonwealth Department of Employment, Education and Training.

19 Individual differences in the autonomy-related psychological characteristics of undergraduates

Della Fazey
University of Wales
Bangor, Wales

Introduction

Higher education increasingly is expected to facilitate the development of autonomy-related behaviour (see for instance, Stephenson and Laycock, 1993). Recent discussions about the outcomes of higher education across Europe have highlighted the important link between the characteristics of graduates, life-long learning and the perceived needs of employers and economic growth (see for instance, CBI, 1994; Biatecki and Domanski, 1995; Fuente, 1995; Teichler and Kehm, 1995). Higher education has to provide its students with opportunities to develop attributes and skills which are complementary to the acquisition of narrow expertise if these employment needs are to be met. Although the relationship between higher education and employment is important within the autonomy context, and was undoubtedly the stimulus for funding of this research by the (then) Employment Department, the educational implications of autonomy in learning are undeniably important for well-being in a wider context.

Learner autonomy is discussed within this chapter which reports studies investigating changes in some psychological characteristics of undergraduate students hypothesized to relate to autonomy in learning. Of particular interest were the sex and age differences in beginning students compared with a 'control' group of students who were identified by staff as being 'self-regulated' (study one), and changes in self-reported characteristics following intervention (study two). The research was limited to a description of psychological characteristics without measuring behaviour or controlling environmental variables.

Psychological characteristics of autonomy

Deci et al. (1991) consider that 'autonomy refers to being self-initiating and self-regulating of one's own actions' (p. 327) describing it as a basic human need which we seek to satisfy along with competence and relatedness. It involves elements of personal control (Doyal and Gough, 1991) and intention to act in a way which meets personal needs. Autonomy cannot be achieved without the mediating effect of other variables such as self-efficacy (Bandura, 1989b), skill (McCombs and Marzano, 1990), locus of causality (Ryan and Connell, 1989) and sense of self (Deci and Ryan, 1985, 1990; McCombs and Marzano, 1990; Koestner, Bernieri and Zuckerman, 1992) and volition (Corno, 1993). This research investigated three major psychological elements of learner autonomy — academic motivation, locus of control and perceived competence.

Motivation

Motivation relates to the intrinsic and extrinsic reasons for the initiation and regulation of behaviour. Intrinsically-motivated behaviour is self-initiated, congruent with the individual's sense of self (aspirations, values and beliefs), self-satisfying and self-regulated (Deci and Ryan, 1985). An autonomous person has an intrinsic orientation to motivation. Extrinsic motivation is that which stimulates action for instrumental reasons, and which is therefore perceived as being initiated by an event external to the positive notion of 'the self'. The continuum from intrinsic motivation, through identified regulation, introjected regulation to extrinsic regulation describes a shift from total self-determination to an externally determined regulatory functioning. The extent to which individuals' reasons for behaving are internalized, owned and valued determines the extent to which they are able to behave autonomously, although there are other factors which interact to affect the demonstration of autonomy (see Ryan and Connell, 1989; Ryan and Stiller, 1991).

Locus of control

The element of choice and control is important for autonomy, with a perceived internal locus of control describing this characteristic of the autonomous person. Those who are not considered to be autonomous would perceive their behaviour and its outcomes to be controlled by factors external to themselves — an external locus of control. These two extremes are proposed by some to be predispositional characteristics (Rotter, 1966) or situationally specific and therefore not predispositionally fixed (e.g. Deci, 1980; Hyman *et al.*, 1991). Autonomous behaviour in learning can only be achieved by those who perceive themselves to be in control of the outcomes of their efforts and who do not attribute their success, in particular, to influences beyond their control. Attributing failure to external influences may be a short-term measure for maintaining self-esteem but in the longer term it is important for learners to accept responsibility for reducing deficits. By accepting responsibility for positive and negative events learners perceive themselves to be in control of future outcomes and can prevent a repetition of failure (Lachman and Burack, 1993).

Self-perceived competence

Self-perception of competence in the academic domain will affect the achievement-related behaviour of the student. People with high perceived competence will challenge themselves, persist in their attempts to succeed, will explore and take risks and will expend extra effort to secure success. Those with a low perception of competence are less likely to demonstrate these achievement-oriented behaviours (see for instance, Harter, 1985; Bandura, 1989b). A perception of competence can be applied in a broad sense (e.g. in relation to academic work generally) or more specifically to an activity (e.g. writing an assignment). Sufficiently high perceptions of competence in the academic domains must be possessed by students, and nurtured by the higher education environment, to enable them to behave in ways which lead to achievement.

Autonomous learning: two studies

The research reported here investigated three of the psychological characteristics (motivation, locus of control, perceived academic competence) hypothesised to underpin behaviours which were identified by higher education staff at Bangor and elsewhere as self-regulated. The questions asked in two separate studies were:

Study One: What characteristics do first-year students possess and how do these compare with those of a group of students identified by staff as 'self-regulated'?

Study Two: Do the motivation, perceived competence and locus of control scores of first year students change following interventions to support self-regulation?

Instruments

Three validated questionnaires designed for use in higher education were used:

1. The Academic Motivation Scale (Vallerand *et al.*, 1992)

This questionnaire measures students' perceptions of their reasons for studying using five categories of behaviour regulation: intrinsic motivation (sub-divided into 'to know', 'to achieve' and 'to experience stimulation'); identified regulation; introjected regulation; extrinsic motivation; and amotivation. Students responded to statements about 'Why do you go to university?' on a 7-point Likert-like scale. For each factor, a mean score is derived and the 'Relative Autonomy Index' (RAI) calculated by weighting the first four categories as follows: intrinsic motivation +2; identified regulation +1; introjected regulation -1; extrinsic motivation -2.

2. The Self-Perception Profile for College Students (Neeman and Harter, 1986)

This questionnaire measures students' self-perceptions of self-worth (self-esteem) and competence in discrete domains. For this study self-worth and the domains of scholastic competence (ability to undertake academic study), and intellectual ability (perception of intelligence) were measured. Using a forced choice format students rate their perceptions of competence and self-worth as in the example of a self-worth question shown in Figure 1.

FIGURE 1 Example of a self-worth question

Really true for me	Sort of true for me			Sort of true for me	Really true for me
◯	◯	Some students like the kind of person they are	BUT Other students wish that they were different	◯	◯

The answers are scored from left to right 4, 3, 2 and 1 respectively, with 4 indicating high and 1 indicating low self-esteem or perceived competence. A mean score for each domain and for self-worth is calculated.

3. The Academic Locus of Control Scale (Rossouw and Parsons, 1995)

In a composite measure of students' perceptions of the degree to which they have control over their successes and failures in academic work students are asked to say whether statements about reasons for success and failure in studies correspond with their own reasons. Using a 7 point Likert-type scale students' internal, external and unknown loci of control for success and failure are then described as a mean score for each factor.

Study One

Subjects

Group 1 was a cohort of 394 randomly selected first-year students who volunteered to complete questionnaires immediately after initial registration. Of these 206 were female (38 mature and 168 traditional) and 188 were male (52 mature and 136 traditional). Mature students were defined as those who were 21 years of age or over at registration.

Group 2 consisted of 70 students (42 females — 21 mature and 21 traditional; 28 males — 22 mature and 6 traditional) who were identified by staff as 'self-regulated'. These second- and third- year students from a variety of schools were contacted by post and asked to fill in and return the questionnaire booklet. They were told that they had been randomly selected to take part in the survey and were unaware that they had been nominated by a member of staff.

Results

A 2 x 2 x 2 MANOVA (group x sex x age) was used to analyse the three questionnaires separately (motivation, perceived competence and locus of control). Table 2 presents the results for variables in which there was a main effect for group. Group differences at the 5% level were not found in any variables other than those shown in the table.

Sex and age main effects

Motivation

In the variable 'intrinsic motivation to experience stimulation' a main effect for sex was revealed ($p < 0.04$) with females scoring higher than males. This was mainly due to the high score recorded by mature females in Group 2.

Main effects for age were revealed as follows:

- *'intrinsic motivation to know'* ($p < 0.008$) with mature students significantly higher than traditional students overall;
- *'identified regulation'* ($p < 0.05$) with traditional students higher than mature students;
- *'extrinsic regulation'* ($p < 0.051$) with traditional students higher than mature students;
- *'total intrinsic motivation'* ($p < 0.03$) with mature students higher than traditional students;
- *'Relative Autonomy Index'* ($p < 0.02$) with mature students higher than traditional students.

Perceived competence

There was a **main effect for sex** in *Scholastic Competence* ($p < 0.03$) with males significantly higher overall than females.

Locus of control

There were no sex or age main effects or significant interactions in the locus of control data.

Interactions

In **motivation** the following interactions were noted:

*Table 1 Means for Group 1 (first-year students)
and Group 2 ('self-regulated' students)*

Factor	Group 1				Group 2			
	female		male		female		male	
	mat.	trad.	mat.	trad.	mat.	trad.	mat.	trad.
Perceived competence and self-worth								
Self-worth	2.93	2.79	2.85	2.95	2.34	2.32	2.20	2.58
Schol. comp	2.60	2.51	2.74	2.66	2.33	2.23	2.41	2.54
Intellect. abil.	2.48	2.53	2.69	2.78	2.04	2.05	2.02	2.17
Academic motivation								
Total intrinsic	4.76	4.29	4.49	4.67	3.29	3.55	3.36	2.65
Identified reg.	5.03	5.65	4.89	5.15	4.99	5.66	4.88	5.00
Introject. reg.	4.74	4.31	4.51	4.18	4.10	4.88	4.38	4.54
Extrinsic reg.	4.22	4.79	4.06	4.67	3.00	3.41	3.17	3.38
Total extrinsic	4.66	4.92	4.49	4.67	4.03	4.65	4.14	4.31
Amotivation	1.18	1.23	1.33	1.34	3.10	3.55	3.06	2.96
Rel. aut. index	0.48	0.07	0.89	0.19	1.47	1.06	0.89	-0.99
Locus of control								
Internal	5.05	4.94	5.14	4.88	3.52	3.61	3.47	3.60
External	2.98	3.01	2.84	2.99	3.99	4.03	4.09	4.13
Unknown	2.51	2.45	2.39	2.17	2.93	2.83	2.80	3.46

Table 2 Group main effects (1,456) DF: comparison of first-year undergraduates (Group 1) and 'self-regulated' students (Group 2)

Variable	Hypoth. SS	Error SS	Hypoth. MS	Error MS	F	Sig of F	High Grp
Perceived competence and self-worth							
Self-worth	11.706	129.422	11.706	0.284	41.243	0.000	1
Schol. comp.	2.748	111.815	2.748	0.245	11.205	0.001	1
Intell. ability	13.468	154.907	13.468	0.340	39.646	0.000	1
Academic motivation							
IM to know.	145.536	694.679	145.536	1.523	95.53	0.000	1
IM to accomp.	483.969	665.331	483.969	1.459	331.699	0.000	1
IM stimulation	67.876	938.069	67.876	2.057	32.995	0.000	1
Extrinsic reg.	62.657	1029.401	62.657	2.258	27.756	0.000	1
Amotivation	156.521	315.552	156.521	0.692	226.208	0.000	2
Total int. mot.	74.100	512.665	74.10	1.124	65.910	0.000	1
Total ext. mot.	7.22	593.741	7.122	1.302	5.47	0.02	1
Locus of control							
Internal loc	91.941	261.164	91.941	0.573	160.532	0.000	1
External loc	53.307	303.128	53.307	0.665	80.190	0.000	2
Unknown	17.029	509.127	17.029	1.117	15.252	0.000	2

Key: Motivation: Intrinsic Motivation to know; Intrinsic Motivation to accomplish; Intrinsic Motivation to experience stimulation; Extrinsic regulation; Amotivation; Total intrinsic motivation ('to know' + 'to achieve' + 'to experience stimulation'); Total extrinsic motivation (Identified + Introjected + Extrinsic Regulation). Perceived Competence: General self-worth; Scholastic competence; Intellectual ability. Locus of control: Internal locus; External locus: Unknown control

- *'intrinsic motivation to experience stimulation'* — a **sex x age interaction** ($p < 0.05$) which was largely due to high scoring traditional females in Group 2;
- *'intrinsic motivation to experience stimulation'* — a **group x sex interaction** ($p < 0.04$) due mainly to the high score of traditional females in Group 2;
- *'introjected regulation'* — a **group x age interaction** ($p < 0.05$). Traditional students were higher than the mature students in Group 2 (with a very high male score and a low female score) but the mature students scored higher than the younger students in Group 1.

In **perceived competence** there was a **sex x age interaction** ($p < 0.05$) in *Self-worth* with traditional females lower than traditional males but mature males lower than mature females.

Discussion

It was hypothesized that Group 2 would score higher on autonomy-related measures than would the randomly-selected first year students. As Table 2 indicates this hypothesis was not supported. Internal motivation (the three separate variables as well as the total measure), perceived competence, self-worth and an internal locus of control are proposed to be indicators of autonomy. On all these measures, contrary to expectations, Group 1 scored significantly higher than did Group 2. The significantly higher scores for Group 2 on amotivation, external and unknown locus of control measures support the conclusion that students in Group 2 perceive themselves to be less autonomous than do those in Group 1. It would appear that first-year students perceive themselves to be more intrinsically motivated, have higher perceptions of their academic competence and self-worth, and feel that they are more in control of the outcomes of their work than do the more experienced students, despite the selection of this second group as 'self-regulated'. The picture, however, is less easy to interpret when the extrinsic regulation and total extrinsic motivation (identified + introjected + extrinsic regulation) scores are considered. On all of these variables, which indicate **lack** of autonomy, Group 1 scores significantly higher than does Group 2.

The dearth of evidence to support the original proposal might be explained in three ways:

- the identification of self-regulated students may be more problematic than was at first assumed with university staff having very different perceptions of what is meant by 'self-regulated';
- first-year students at registration may perceive themselves to be highly autonomous and that, over time this perception is depressed; this seems to be a likely explanation, at least in part, as beginning students have been actively involved in making a decision to come to university and probably have high expectations of their academic studies;
- that the proposal that autonomy can be measured using the instruments in this study is fallacious. Certainly the definition of autonomy (see Doyal and Gough, 1991) involves more than motivation, locus of control and perceived competence and must include the sense of self with its framework of beliefs and attitudes.

The age differences revealed in a number of the variables provide some support for the notion that an active decision to study, related as that is to perceptions of internal control and intrinsic motivation, is a characteristic of mature students. Although the overall pattern is not easy to interpret, mature students score significantly higher on intrinsic motivation and the Relative Autonomy Index than do the traditional students but there is no age difference in the locus of control data. The traditional students score higher than the older undergraduates on identified regulation — the 'extrinsic' measure which is closest to intrinsic motivation on the continuum from extrinsic to intrinsic motivation — and are also highest on extrinsic regulation. While a high score on identified regulation suggests that traditional students are more motivated than mature students to study for personal reasons (which may be instrumental rather than purely intrinsic) they are also more highly motivated by factors external to themselves. This is a confusing pattern and suggests that the theoretical proposition that intrinsic and extrinsic motivation are bipolar might have to be re-considered.

While there were some sex differences and interactions between sex and age, there were no patterns that enable any definitive statements to be made about sex differences in student autonomy. Although males usually score higher than females in perceptions of competence (see for instance, Harter, 1985), apart from scholastic competence, the students appear to be more homogeneous as a group than might be expected. The sex by age interaction for self-worth indicates that both types of individual difference need to be recognized.

Overall this study produced some unexpected results which indicate that first-year students are more highly motivated to study, perceive themselves to have more control over their academic work and have a higher perception of their academic competence than do students who were identified by staff as self-regulated. Further investigations will consider whether or not the first year cohort will later report the relatively low scores of the more experienced students when that cohort reaches the same stage of study.

Study Two

The second study measured students who were first years at the same time as students in Group 1 but who were involved in interventions designed to increase their sense of autonomy.

Subjects

Group 3 consisted of 53 first-year students who were involved in curriculum and personal tutor initiatives to enhance their self-assessment skills. The group consisted of 36 females (12 mature and 24 traditional) and 17 males (9 mature and 8 traditional). The students were measured at two points — pre and post semester.

Results

A $2 \times 2 \times 2$ repeated measures MANOVA (age x sex x test), with repeated measures on 'test' was used to identify changes across time and in relation to age and sex for the data from each questionnaire separately.

Three main effects for test were revealed, with an increase over time in each case:

Scholastic competence ($p < 0.02$); Intellectual ability ($p < 0.03$); Intrinsic motivation to accomplish ($p < 0.03$).

Age main effects were as follows:

• *Intrinsic motivation to know ($p < 0.008$) with mature students scoring higher;*

Table 3 Group Three mean scores at pre- and post-test

Factor	Pre-test					Post-test				
	All Ss	Females		Males		All Ss	Females		Males	
		Mat.	Trad.	Mat.	Trad.		Mat.	Trad.	Mat.	Trad.
Perceived competence and self-worth										
Self worth	2.84	2.96	2.69	3.02	2.90	2.93	3.04	2.77	2.98	3.21
Schol. competen.	2.56	2.50	2.46	2.75	2.75	2.74	2.69	2.68	2.78	2.97
Intellect. ability	2.63	2.58	2.45	2.94	2.91	2.84	2.77	2.74	2.83	3.25
Academic motivation										
IM to know	5.07	5.50	4.85	5.56	4.53	5.30	5.94	5.15	5.22	4.88
IM to accomplish	4.29	4.42	4.17	5.14	3.50	4.69	5.15	4.54	5.06	4.03
IM for stimulation	3.68	4.02	3.57	4.06	3.09	3.91	4.58	3.73	3.97	3.34
Identified	5.02	3.71	5.67	4.97	5.06	5.12	4.19	5.50	4.89	5.63
Introjected	4.09	3.40	4.38	4.50	3.78	4.31	3.83	4.63	4.42	3.94
Extrinsic	4.28	2.98	4.83	3.94	4.94	4.25	3.06	4.53	4.36	5.06
Total intrinsic	4.35	4.65	4.20	4.92	3.71	4.63	5.22	4.47	4.75	4.08
Total extrinsic	4.46	3.36	4.96	4.47	4.59	4.56	3.69	4.89	4.56	4.88
Amotivation	1.43	1.08	1.54	1.00	2.13	1.31	1.29	1.14	1.56	1.56
Rel. aut. index	1.07	3.65	0.02	2.42	-1.2	1.57	4.67	0.76	1.25	0.27
Locus of control										
Internal	5.00	4.91	5.03	5.24	4.75	5.15	4.98	5.17	5.37	5.09
External	2.87	2.29	3.05	2.58	3.52	2.80	2.23	2.87	2.57	3.71
Unknown	2.34	1.65	2.78	1.72	2.72	2.27	1.81	2.49	2.11	2.50

- *Intrinsic motivation to accomplish* ($p < 0.002$) with mature students higher;
- *Identified regulation* ($p < 0.003$) with traditional students higher;
- *Extrinsic regulation* ($p < 0.004$) with traditional students scoring higher;
- *Amotivation* ($p < 0.043$) with traditional students higher;
- *Total intrinsic motivation* ($p < 0.004$) with mature students higher;
- *Total extrinsic motivation* ($p < 0.005$) with traditional students higher;
- *Relative Autonomy Index* ($p < 0.008$) with mature students higher;
- *Extrinsic locus of control* ($p < 0.0001$) with traditional students higher;
- *Unknown control* ($p < 0.003$) with traditional students higher.

There was only one **main effect for sex** which was in *extrinsic locus of control* where males scored higher than females ($p < 0.02$)

Interactions

A **sex x age interaction** occurred in *introjected regulation* ($p < 0.05$). Mature males and traditional females scored highest on this variable.

An **age x test interaction** in *amotivation* ($p < 0.003$) occurred as mature students increased on this measure over time while traditional students' scores decreased.

Discussion

Three variables related to autonomy increased from pre- to post-test (scholastic competence, intellectual ability and intrinsic motivation 'to accomplish') and none of the negative variables (e.g. amotivation) significantly increased. The table of means (Table 3) indicates that variables related to autonomy tended to increase while those which would suggest declining autonomy tended to decrease. The lack of a significant increase in some of the variables related to autonomy, while disappointing, might be due partly to high scores at the pre-test point. These students rated intrinsic motivation 'to know', identified regulation and an internal locus of control high before the intervention and also recorded a moderately high Relative Autonomy Index (RAI)score at this point.

The RAI is an interesting measure. Calculated by weighting intrinsic and identified regulation positively and introjected and extrinsic regulation negatively and then summing the scores for all four variables, it gives an overall motivation score which, when positive, indicates that students are clustered more around the intrinsic motivational end of the continuum. The very high mean scores for mature students and relatively low scores for traditional students results in the age main effect which was revealed. It is rather confusing to note that there was also an age by test interaction in amotivation with mature students increasing on this measure over time while traditional students decreased. As amotivation scores indicate that students are not interested or stimulated by their studies, this increase over time is not a positive finding. However, traditional students still score significantly higher than do mature students on amotivation overall.

As in the first study the results do not provide a clearly defined answer to the question being asked — in this case the nature of autonomy-related changes which occur over time and in relation to an intervention. Again there are individual differences related to sex and age. Mature students in this study score higher than the younger students on those variables proposed to be associated with autonomy but both age groups have benefited similarly from the intervention. It seems that committed, skilled tutors can influence students' perceptions of competence and their motivation to be successful in their work. Although increases in locus of control measures seem to be more difficult to achieve this might indicate that this characteristic is more stable than are the others.

Conclusion

The very surprising difference between Groups 1 and 2 in the first study needs to be investigated further. A longitudinal study of the first-year cohort is being undertaken and will allow comparisons to be made between Group 2 and Group 1 students at a similar point in their studies. The very high scores recorded by the first years may, in fact be typical of a group which is just beginning higher education. It would be disappointing to find, however, that students perceived themselves to have less motivation, competence and control as they progressed through their studies. Hopefully that will not be the case. The intervention study produced a more positive picture, indicating that the teaching and support which these students had experienced created some important and significant increases in characteristics related to positive achievement behaviours. While the methods used to help these students acquire self-assessment skills were diverse, it seems that they were successful, at least in part, in increasing autonomy-related attributes of undergraduate students.

References

Bandura, A. (1989) Perceived self-efficacy in the exercise of personal agency. *The Psychologist: Bulletin of the British Psychological Society* **10**, 411—24.

Biatecki, I. and Domanski, H. (1995) Employment opportunities in Poland's changing economy. *European Journal of Education* **30**(2), 171—86.

Confederation of British Industry (1994) *Thinking Ahead: Ensuring the Expansion of Higher Education into the 21st Century*. London: CBI.

Corno, L. (1993) The best-laid plans: modern conceptions of volition and educational research. *Educational Researcher* **24**(3), 14—22.

Deci, E. L. (1980) *The Psychology of Self-determination*. Lexington, MA: Heath (Lexington Books). Cited by E. L. Deci and R. M. Ryan (1985) The general causality orientations scale: self-determination in personality. *Journal of Research in Personality* **19**, 109—34.

Deci, E. L. and Ryan, R. M. (1985) *Intrinsic motivation and self-determination in human behavior*. New York: Plenum Press

Deci E.L. and Ryan, R.M. (1991) A motivational approach to the self: integration in personality. In R. Dienstbier (ed.), *Nebraska Symposium on Motivation: Vol 38. Perspectives on Motivation*, pp. 237—88. Lincoln: University of Nebraska Press.

Deci, E. L., Vallerand, R. J., Pelletier, L. G. and Ryan, R. M. (1991) Motivation and education: the self-determination perspective. *Educational Psychologist* **26**(3 and 4), 325—46.

Doyal, L. and Gough, I. (1991) *A Theory of Human Need*, London: Macmillan Press.

Fuente de la, G. (1995) Higher education and employment in Spain. *European Journal of Education* **30**(2), 217—33.

Harter, S. (1985) Competence as a dimension of self-evaluation: toward a comprehensive model of self-worth. In R. Leahy (ed.), *The Development of the Self*. New York: Academic Press.

Hyman, G. J., Stanley, R. and Burrows, G. D. (1991) The relationship between three multidimensional locus of control scales. *Educational and Psychological Measurement* **51**, 403—11.

Koestner, R., Bernieri, F. and Zuckerman, M. (1992) Self-regulation and consistency between attitudes, traits and behaviors. *Personality and Social Psychology Bulletin* **18**(1), 52—9.

Lachman, M. E. and Burack, O. R. (1993) Planning and control processes across the life-span: an overview. In M. E. Lachman (ed.), *Planning and Control Processes across the Life-span: International Journal of Behavioral Development Special Issue*. Hove, UK: Lawrence Erlbaum.

McCombs, B. L. and Marzano, R. J. (1990) Putting the self in self-regulated learning: the self as agent in integrating will and skill. *Educational Psychologist* **25**(1), 51—69.

NIACE (National Organisation for Adult Learning) (1993) *An Adult Higher Education: A Vision*. Leicester: NIACE.

Neeman, J. and Harter,S. (1986) Self perception profile for college students. University of Denver.

Rossouw, P. and Parsons, P. (1995) An exploration of the association between students' approaches to learning and their perceived locus of control. In G. Gibbs (ed.), *Improving Student Learning through Assessment and Evaluation*. Oxford: Oxford Centre for Staff Development.

Rotter, J. B. (1966) Generalized expectancies for internal versus external control of reinforcement. *Psychological Monographs* **80**(1, Whole No. 609).

Ryan, R. M. and Connell, J. P. (1989) Perceived locus of causality and internalization: examining reasons for acting in two domains. *Journal of Personality and Social Psychology* **57**, 749—61.

Ryan, R. M. and Stiller, J. (1991) The social contexts of internalization: parent and teacher influences on autonomy, motivation and learning. In P. R. Pintrich and M. L. Maehr (eds), *Advances in Motivation and Achievement: Vol.7. Goals and Self-regulatory Processes*, pp. 115—49. Greenwich, CT: JAI Press.

Stephenson J. and Laycock, M. (1993) *Using Learning Contracts in Higher Education*. London: Kogan Page.

Teichler, U. and Kehm, B. M. (1995) Towards an understanding of the relationships between higher education and employment. *European Journal of Education*, **30**(2), 115—32.

Vallerand, R. J., Pelletier, L. G., Blaise, M. R., Brière, N. M., Senêcal, C. and Vallières, E. F. (1992). The higher education academic motivation scale: a measure of intrinsic, extrinsic and amotivation in education. *Educational and Psychological Measurement* **52**, 1003—17.

20 Action research to help post-graduate research student and supervisor learning

John Fazey
Staff Development Unit
University of Wales
Bangor

Introduction

Progress is reported in a scheme related to the general need to re-establish research cultures which feed into and take from teaching in the university. The project is offered as an example of how we can use creative, flexible learning and teaching approaches to cope with particular examples of the changing nature of some universities.

The thing that makes universities unique is that they are involved in transforming people through their teaching and transforming knowledge through their research. The demands on new staff who have had no formal training in one or other of these activities represent a significant wave of change. Ensuring the reality of the claim about what makes universities unique in the face of waves of change probably demands highly skilled surfing rather than just hanging on or riding out the next thundering breaker. This chapter is about helping staff from the Faculty of Health Studies, members of pan-university project teams and others become increasingly autonomous about their own research education and supervisory skill development. They can then begin to enjoy surfing the waves.

Within the context of the theme of this volume this chapter is about the development of research skills and interests for staff as a direct way of enhancing their contribution to the wider learning community of the university. It is also about applying, as well as communicating, the products of recent research in the way we create a better learning effect for students. The distinction between students and staff as learners has become blurred. Increasingly staff come to teaching (and other) roles in the university by diverse routes. This is a report about a collaborative scheme amongst staff and students that is a conscious attempt to apply what we know about learning from the products of research and the synthesis of professional expertise.

Increasingly voiced demands are for higher education (HE) to turn out graduates who are self-regulated, if not autonomous, in their learning. Such graduates should be at least flexible, if not creative, in their approach to problem-solving. They should also be able to operate and communicate reasonably well in a variety of settings if not actually transferring all their highly developed learning skills to new situations. It always strikes me that the above are the very qualities to be valued in an academic taking up a research and teaching commitment in a university. Of course, once our current attempts to change the learning experiences of students have been successful, and graduates with such attributes permeate the system, all of our new colleagues can be expected to portray those characteristics. It is a feature of change to which we might look forward, though we had better not hold our breath.

A current, major responsibility in staff development is to ensure the survival of an ethos within which there is a strong commitment to strategic use of different approaches to learning (cf. Entwistle, 1988) and an orientation of learning goals which seeks a theoretical framework within which to understand our professional activity (Marton and Såljö, 1983. Volet and Chalmers, 1992). It is surprising and disappointing to see how little attention is paid to some basic principles of learning (let alone a theoretically based approach). Many attempts to use research as a part of the student experience even in postgraduate research training (cf. Biggs, 1994) are not supported by a strong framework of principles. This is especially so given that the distinctive feature of universities is a supposed strong link between the pursuit of disciplined research and the induction of newcomers (usually students) to a disciplined view of the world in which they wish to operate.

It is also part of the claim to distinctiveness that universities make that they are institutions that research what they teach. That claim now makes two demands on academics. The first is that of a discipline — the commitment to scholarship in a given academic field. It has to be balanced with the second — an increasing expectation of commitment to much higher levels of professionalism as a teacher.[1]

It is obviously difficult to hold on to the ethos implied by the claim for distinctiveness if the demands of the university situation seem to far outweigh each individual's current capacity. It is made even more difficult when the arguably rapidly changing culture of the university denies the appropriate opportunities for the continuing professional development of some members of the institution. The problem is often exacerbated when the progress that is sought by implementing rapid changes to structures, or by expanding the range of activities, of an institution brings in a relatively large body of people expected to function as academics but who have little direct experience of the university setting. In our case, as apparently has been true in a number of institutions in Australia and elsewhere, this was a consequence of the reorganization of nursing education. That move established a Faculty of Health Studies with some 80 teaching staff, all highly qualified professionals and all trained as teachers (which was, and still is, rare outside of schools of education). Only 12 had research degrees but there was an expectation that they would all embrace the university ethos of combining research and teaching. There are also at Bangor a number of university-wide development projects located in a quasi-administrative departments. These are staffed by experienced and well-informed academics who are isolated from the academic study of their area because of their own institution-wide development brief. The Computer Assisted Learning team and the Staff Development Unit serve as examples.

This chapter presents observations and comment on the outcomes of an action research innovation to develop self-help groups of beginning post-graduate research supervisors and their students at the University of Wales, Bangor.

---

1. *Although some may not agree that it is the appropriate generic label the term teacher will have to suffice here. It is used in the broadest sense and encompasses all the titles given to academics who have a responsibility for supporting the learning of others whether in formal student/tutor roles, in the mentorship or advising of colleagues or in the professional leadership role of a professor and head of department.*

Intentions

The intention was twofold. First it was decided that initial and continuing development of both research and supervisory skills should be accelerated and second, that by setting group objectives and establishing a collaborative ethos in the groups, research productivity could be enhanced. Both would be reflected in submissions for publication and the rate of participant progress toward completion of research training degrees.

The context for each group was similar but born of different backgrounds. The Faculty of Health staff are new to the University and the recent departure of two of the key members of their small research division left a large number of staff registered for higher degrees through the research route without supervisors. The few remaining staff with research degrees, but little supervisory experience, were faced with a large group of colleagues and students to support. Financial constraints indicated that early replacement was unlikely.

The CAL group is a Teaching and Learning Technology project team. It has a project leader with a Master's degree, a technical officer with a shiny new PhD and a recently graduated project worker. In Staff Development three staff, one with an MPhil, one with an MA, and one with a BSc wished to pursue higher degrees. There was one experienced and qualified supervisor.

In the psychology department the health-oriented group were somewhat isolated and disadvantaged. The active member of staff had a large teaching load and little access to research funds and other support. There were three potential students.

The formal guidelines for supervisory practice lay down committee and operational procedures to safeguard research students but are clearly predicated on a one-to-one, hierarchical system of supervision and reporting. This assumes a ratio of qualified and experienced staff that was completely absent in the groups involved. A solution was sought in developing a collaborative supervision scheme. The formal requirements are met by recognizing that peer support can remove a good deal of the need for close supervision and since everyone concerned has entered into the spirit of the scheme there have been few problems with the formalities thus far.

The principles

The principles are relatively straightforward. They stem from ideas about learner centredness. They are constructivist in that they demand active learning whilst recognizing that much of the activity has to be cerebral (Biggs, 1995). They acknowledge the importance of the principles of Social Learning Theory and stress the need to promote and allow for success, for emotionally satisfying outcomes (e.g. Bandura, 1989) . They build in the ideas of action learning sets and action research (Schön, 1983) and they promote a methodology which shares ownership and responsibility among the participating learners (Deci, Vallerand, Pelletier and Ryan, 1991). They are designed, in short, to promote autonomous learning in a collaborative framework (Fazey, 1996).

The key principle in facilitating learning is the application of the notion that skill development requires practice (Fazey and Fazey, 1995). Continued practice needs motivation and support. Learning as progression, invention and improvement that sticks requires practice of the two functional requirements of success. Learners have to get to know two things: how to do something and how to judge it. This is much more profound than it might first appear. Not only do learners have to internalize the facility to produce they have to internalize the criteria of performance. The two are logically but probably not functionally separable. In this case the learning is about being a researcher. It is about being a researcher in a university. The process to be mastered usually ends with writing up and the emphasis is often on the learner doing and the supervising teacher checking. It is of course not over until the writing up has appeared in print. Even then the checking is done by reviewers and editors. The theoretical view and the practical application in skill development suggest that any learning programme has to include practice of all the elements of conducting research, writing, critically reviewing, editing and publishing. Doing it with and for peers seems an obvious way to proceed — doing it holistically, for the practice also seems like a good strategy for learning (Topping, 1992). Unfortunately many students only ever get to do things once.

The principle of learning how to do something better by learning how to do a related but different activity is not without theoretical or practical foundation in the field of motor skill development. It is arguable that the many failed attempts to demonstrate such transfer in cognitive skills is probably more to do with the way in which the investigations are conducted than an erroneous theory. Suffice to say here that the most rapid enhancement of writing skills for beginning postgraduate science students seem to be associated with the experience of `playing' at reviewing and editing draft journal submissions by real scientists. The principle is simple. The process of making judgements demands a full understanding of criteria to be applied. Most beginning authors do not know enough about the criteria to be able to know what differences make a difference.

Given that there were two original learning objectives, one to learn how to be a researcher and the other how to supervise research training, the situation offered an opportunity to try out the related idea that training to learn could be achieved simultaneously through learning to train. It is not new at all. All teachers glibly support the hypothesis that the best way to really learn something is to teach it. Much of that must be to do with getting to understand more clearly the criteria for success.

The innovation

The groups of staff mentioned above break down to relatively small numbers:

- In the Faculty of Health they are: School of Nursing 12, School of Radiography 6, Post Registration 6;
- Computer Assisted Learning Project (CAL) 3;
- Health Psychology 3;
- Staff Development Unit 4.

The scheme works through monthly meetings held as workshops and seminars to which all participants are invited and separate monthly meetings for each theme group. These meetings alternate at two weekly intervals. Needs are continuously being identified. Proposals are being made in formal and informal modes. Papers are being written and participants are acting as peer reviewers. They met regularly for a semester to establish independent research groups with overlapping interests in health professions, health psychology, teaching and computer assisted learning. The health psychology group members have not been able to sustain their activity and two members have migrated to other groups.

A key innovation is the focus provided by the planned intensive Summer School in 1996.

This will be a week-long event presenting, reviewing, editing and publishing, as theme group collections, the papers arising from individual and collaborative research topics. This has been opened up to other research students and staff who want to contribute to the process and the experiment. A planning group is taking that forward with administrative support from Staff Development.

Interestingly, in the autumn of 1995, all departments were expected to introduce core and transferable skills modules for beginning post-graduate research students. As a consequence of this the Bio-Chemistry Department have decided to join in with the summer school programme. It will represent the culmination of a key element of their foundation year work. They still have a traditional pattern of supervision but intend to participate in the intensive Summer School with their own theme group of 16 participants.

Problems

The main problem is maintaining the impetus in the face of apparent lack of management support. Making the development activity a priority is not, it seems, as important as expressing the difficulties of timetabling, resourcing and financial pressures. Some institutional practices, especially at departmental level, actually work against the scheme. Where staff are still `managed' in a framework which looks more like the National Health Service, rather than a University, they have little opportunity for exercising autonomy and are subject to very tight control measures. These are breaking down as staff recognize and begin to adopt the practices of their colleagues in other Faculties. There is of course a good deal of inertia to overcome.

Successes

After six months eight participants have submitted their first attempts to publish and one stalled thesis has been completed and submitted. Two collaborative, major bids for funding have been submitted to external agencies. A key orientation in these bids is the idea of training to learn through learning to train which is at the centre of the collaborative supervision scheme. Three participants are using the group as part of their action research in our Teaching in Higher Education Scheme.[2]

While the health psychology group has not really got off the ground two members have submitted abstracts for the Summer School and still participate in sessions and workshop meetings. Interestingly they are not the only ones who are migrating to other themes. From within the health group a significant proportion will contribute to either the CAL theme or the Learning Development theme at the Summer School although their proposed papers retain a Health flavour.

---

2. *The Teaching in Higher Education (THE) Scheme is a University of Wales, Bangor qualification in teaching. It is now compulsory for all newly appointed beginning teachers. It is based on the SEDA scheme and uses action research cycles as the vehicle for demonstrating competence.*

The quantifiable outcomes are (after two semesters):

- five draft submissions for publication by first-time authors;
- three formal presentations of proposals for PhD studies;
- reasonable attendance rates;
- 32 abstracts for the Summer School;
- a theme group formed in the Department of Bio-Chemistry.

Additional outcomes include:

- a recognition of what is possible within the structures of the university;
- a working party development of a networked computerized personal profiling (self-appraisal) system for research staff modelled on the system produced for undergraduates.

Practical academics

A feature of teaching and learning in the present climate of instability created by the convergence of successive waves of change is the apparent ease with which some proposals for change can be implemented whilst some obvious improvements never get implemented. A general strategy is to help people learn not just how to ride the waves (of change) in a passive, hang on to the lifebelt style, but to help them become skilful surfers. They need the expertise that allows them to spot waves coming, the confidence to select good ones to ride and the skill to adjust their angle as they hang in on an exhilarating ride to where they want to go. Skilful, flexible performance presupposes that we know where we want to go, and that given particular circumstances, we can decide to wait, try for it, give up, get ready again and ride the wave we choose. It is about flexibly adjusting tactics and strategies in the face of apparent instability by learning the features of the system that allow us to predict with sufficient certainty the short-term future so that we can influence longer term outcomes. The collaborative research training groups are an example.

Teaching academics to be teachers and researchers in an ever- changing university demands that they become the best strategic learners that we can develop. Teaching professionals and teachers to become researchers demands a similar approach. It is therefore imperative that the theoretical models we apply, and ask them to use, are also the best that we can develop. Understanding how to develop learning and enquiry skills is an intellectual challenge that provides many with a board with which to surf the waves. It is of course paramount that those who espouse such approaches also provide models of their use.

References

Bandura, A. (1989) Perceived self-efficacy in the exercise of personal agency. *The Psychologist: Bulletin of the British Psychological Society* **10**, 411—24.

Biggs, J. (1994) Student learning research and theory where do we stand? In G. Gibbs (ed.), *Improving Student Learning. Theory and Practice*, pp. 1—19. Oxford: Oxford Centre for Staff Development.

Biggs, J. (1995) Constructivism and assessment. In *Proceedings of the 20th International Conference on Improving University Teaching, Hong Kong*. University College, University of Maryland.

Deci, E. L., Vallerand, R. J., Pelletier, L. G. and Ryan, R. M. (1991) Motivation and education: the self determination perspective. *Educational Psychologist* **26**,(3 and 4), 325—46.

Entwistle, N. J. (1988) Motivational factors in students: approaches to learning. In R. R. Schmeck (ed.), *Learning Strategies and Learning Styles*. New York and London: Plenum Press.

Fazey, D. M. A. and Fazey, J. A. (1995) How students acquire research skills: Shaping a degree at Bangor. In B. Smith and S. Brown (eds), *Research Teaching and Learning in Higher Education*. London. Kogan Page. SEDA Series. 139-151

Fazey, D. M. A. (1996) Learner autonomy. In McNair, S. (ed.), *Handbook of the Guidance and Learner Autonomy Projects*. Chapter 1. Sheffield: Department for Education and Employment.

Marton, F. and Säljö, R. (1984) Approaches to learning. In D. J. Hounsell and N. J. Entwistle (eds), *The Experience of Learning*, pp. 36—55. Edinburgh: Scottish Academic Press.

Schön, D. A. (1983) *The Reflective Practitioner: How Professionals Think in Action*. New York: Basic Books.

Topping, K. J. (1992) Cooperative learning and peer tutoring: an overview. *The Psychologist* **5**, 151—61.

Volet, S. E. and Chalmers, D. (1992) Investigation of qualitative differences in university students' learning goals based on an unfolding model of stage development. *British Journal of Educational of Educational Psychology, 62, 17-34*

21 Examining action research to improve seminars through assessment

Paul Hyland
Head of School of History
Faculty of Humanities
Bath College of Higher Education

Introduction

Of all the kinds of educational research that are currently undertaken, few, if any, are as fundamentally and explicitly wedded as is action research (AR) to the idea of improving educational practices. By its very nature, according to Kemmis, AR 'expresses a commitment to the improvement of educational practices' (1988, p. 46). That commitment dates from the original formulations of AR by Kurt Lewin and Stephen Corey in the 1940s, and was already strong enough by 1957 for Hodgkinson to pronounce that 'the main reason for action research is the improvement of practice' (p. 137). When, due in particular to the work of Stenhouse in the 1970s, AR became more widespread in the 1980s, Cohen and Manion offered what they called 'a conventional definition' of AR as 'small scale intervention in the functioning of the real world and a close examination of the effects of such intervention' (1994, p. 186). Such a definition might well be reckoned broad enough to encompass many kinds of research that are often rejected or derided by some action researchers. But ten lines later Cohen and Manion are more pointed: 'the ultimate objective' of action research, so they declare, 'is to improve practice in some way or other'. Similarly, Elliott states: 'The fundamental aim of action research is to improve practice rather than to produce knowledge' (1991, p. 49).

Following the schisms that have developed within the AR movement (or 'Salvation Army', if you prefer (Gibson, 1985)), its definition has become harder as usage of the term has grown both more common and more varied. It may be easier, as Barrow and Milburn's *Critical Dictionary of Education Concepts* (1990, p. 12) declares, for commentators 'to state what those who practice action research are against than what they are for', and it may also be argued that such a dialectic is at least implicit in the definition of all concepts. Yet even those practitioners who stress that AR 'means different things to different people' (Zuber-Skerritt, 1991, p. 2), and that 'there is no correct way of doing action research. Nor is there a "true definition" of action research' (McNiff, 1992, p. xviii) still insist upon the practitioners' commitment to improvement. This emphasis upon improvement — of the self and of the group — becomes even more pronounced when we consider how little agreement there is now over so many of what might have become the distinctive features or characteristics of AR. So, for example, there are substantive disagreements among scholars about whether or not AR must be a collaborative activity; the role (if any) of the professional researcher or facilitator; whether AR ought to have a 'formal' or 'dialectical' method; how empirical or naturalistic it should be; whether it should resist or attempt to contribute to the development of teaching and learning theories; the extent to which it should be socially and personally liberating or 'emancipatory', and so on (Whitehead and Lomax, 1987; McKernan, 1988; McNiff, 1988). These and many other well-known differences over methodology turn even Nixon's claim that 'action research is nothing if not eclectic' (1981, p. 7) into something rather more ironic than surely he would ever have intended. I want to focus, however, not so much upon the characteristics or 'family resemblances' of AR that are the subject of so much contention, as upon how that common and fundamental commitment to improvement can be examined.

The idea of improvement is, of course, embodied in all teaching and learning, and in every kind of research, theorising and discussion about them. We may well disagree about what constitutes 'improvement', how to achieve it and how to measure it, but it is ever-present and pervasive in our thinking. Nobody can speak against it; only for it from some other point of view. This is obvious, as is the difficulty (if not impossibility) of thinking about improvement without some corresponding sense of dissatisfaction and/or idealism. For most leading advocates of AR, the feeling or recognition of dissatisfaction is clearly focused upon what they see as the irrelevance, the invalidity, and the undemocratic and exploitative nature of 'conventional' educational research (Hammersley, 1993), whereas idealism is located in the conviction that AR will prove personally illuminating and liberating, and ultimately lead to the creation of a more just and rational (democratic) society.

More particularly, however, for the practitioner-researchers, dissatisfaction must be grounded in some aspect of their own educational practices, in their understanding of those practices, and in the contexts in which they take place (Kemmis, 1988). The identification of that shared concern or 'problem' drives the action-reflection cycles or spirals, through which experience (therapy) the group undergoes a continuous process of improvement. There is no pre-determined point of closure or completion of research, and there are no 'external' criteria for assessing what each group deems as progress or counts as evidence of improvement (Carr and Kemmis, 1983). But according to Kemmis and McTaggart, each group will be able to monitor changes (improvements) in its actions/practices, in its use of language/discourses, in its social relationships/forms of organization, and in the connections between these registers. So, for example, the group's practices will become more justifiable, its discourses more orderly, its forms of organization more suited to its educational aspirations, and the connections between these more consistent (Kemmis and McTaggart, 1988).

Context of innovation

An action-research project was begun among the historians at Bath CHE in 1985, and has been sustained by various members of the group through periodic bursts of 'activity' since that date. The original aim of the group of five (now ten) full-time tutors was to review the effectiveness of teaching and learning strategies employed by staff and students in the classroom, though most attention was soon focused upon the need to improve the quality of seminars, which tutors and students both regarded as the heartbeat of the History programme. In particular, tutors wanted to find ways of raising levels of student preparation, participation, enthusiasm, and sense of achievement in seminars, which then (as now) constituted over half of the teaching schedule for all courses. Although all tutors had several years of teaching experience, none was well versed in AR, either in terms of reading or of practice. An 'outside' researcher from the Education Faculty was therefore asked to act as a facilitator: overseeing the video-recording of several of each tutor's classes, audio-taping confidential interviews with students afterwards, briefing staff at review and 'play-back' sessions, and providing agreed reports for the group's progress and planning meetings (Preston, 1988).

In conducting this kind of teaching review, the assistance of a 'facilitator' or 'consultant' was essential, and may well have contributed 'to the improvement of practices, practitioners' understandings, and the situations in which practice occurs', as Kemmis concedes. However the distinctions that Kemmis and others made between 'technical', 'practical' and 'emancipatory' forms of AR (based largely upon what they regard as the more or less intrusive role of the facilitator) were by no means evident in this work. For the use of a facilitator did not inhibit the group's development of 'collaborative responsibility for practices' or reduce its sense of common 'ownership' of research, as Kemmis feared (Elliott, 1988). Rather, the relationship here established between practitioners and the 'outsider' enabled several tutors to undertake further research in the manner that they wished.

A second phase of research, less intensive but of longer duration, was begun in 1987 and continued for three years. Building upon the findings of the teaching review, the aim was to promote greater student preparation and participation in seminars by ensuring that all students not only had constant access to the historical sources and critical readings selected for seminar discussion, but also were able to prepare individually or in self-help groups by working through a series of preliminary exercises for each session. Feedback from students on the design, use and value of the course material was gathered through questionnaires and group interviews, and used through action-reflection cycles to develop resource-based learning throughout the undergraduate curriculum (Wisdom and Gibbs, 1994, pp. 42—5).

Following a rapid expansion of student numbers and the appointment of new staff, a third phase of research was conducted by those tutors responsible for first-year courses in 1991—92. The aim was to improve tutor and student understanding of the relationship between teaching and learning in seminars. Tutors kept accounts of what they believed to be the objectives and outcomes of each session, and of any changes they were making to their usual practices. Students recorded their views about their learning achievements and problems in personal diaries at the beginning and end of every meeting. At regular intervals, students were asked to lend their diaries to the facilitator to prepare anonymous transcripts for comparison with tutors' journals. Transcripts, journals and returns from Ramsden and Entwistle's ASI (1983) provided the main sources of information for action-reflection cycles.

Rationale for innovation

In retrospect, and in this kind of summation, it is easy to portray the first three phases of research as considerably more coherent than they were during the experience or process. However, despite many contradictions and questions (akin to Whitehead, 1989) that had surfaced within and between individual tutors' views and practices, collective research and self-critical reflection on seminars had, by 1992, produced agreement on the need to assess student seminar presentations throughout the undergraduate programme. Although tutors were broadly familiar with research on the importance of assessment in terms of its influence on how and what students learn in higher education, the lack of precedents for assessing seminar presentations in other History departments, and the prospect of a Teaching Quality Assessment visit by HEFCE in 1993, urged conservatism and caution. So, too, did what appeared to be a deterioration in some of the contexts of teaching and learning; most notably, as a rise in student numbers pushed the normal size of seminar groups from fifteen to over twenty. The decision to change the assessment scheme was therefore taken very much within the department in the light of its own investigations and readings of research on student learning, rather than in response to external promptings, and it was based upon the following propositions:

- Students should be rewarded for making an active contribution to what they and tutors widely regarded as the central medium for achieving the most-prized goals of higher education (Jacques, 1984; Boud, 1990; Ramsden, 1992).

- Student-centred learning should be promoted by students playing an important role both in selecting the topics and criteria for their own seminar assessments, and in contributing to the assessment of their peers (Wittrock, 1986).

- Deep learning should be facilitated by assessments that encouraged students to work more collaboratively, and that enabled them to exercise greater choice and control over their learning (Biggs, 1987; Gibbs, 1992).

- The development of students' interpersonal and transferable skills should be explicitly encouraged and rewarded in presentations (Rogers, 1978; Elton, 1991).

- Tutors should foster student autonomy in learning by promoting self-critical reflection by all members of the group, and by encouraging open and democratic forms of discussion and decision-making (Boud, 1988).

Problems of innovation

Having agreed these propositions, attention was focused upon practical concerns and problems:

1. Should the assessment of seminar presentations be instituted immediately for all courses and year-groups, or be introduced incrementally, say, beginning with the first-year intake?

2. Should some marks be awarded for each student's contribution to seminars throughout a course, or solely on the merits of her/his particular presentation?

3. What proportion of the total marks for each course should be allocated to presentations?

4. In cases of student absence or sickness, should presentations be re-scheduled or should an alternative form of assessment be requested?

5. Would newly appointed staff be sympathetic to this form of assessment, and what experience would they need before they were proficient in its use?

6. If the average marks awarded for presentations were frequently and significantly (say, ±5%) higher or lower than for other forms of assessment, should they be 'moderated'?

7. Should students and tutors each allocate a proportion of the marks, and should there be a clear distinction between the criteria to be marked by students and those to be marked by tutors?

8. How should 'joint' presentations by two or three students be assessed?

9. To what extent should tutors lead discussion in assessment and, particularly in cases of disagreement or appeal, determine the final mark awarded?

The first three questions were resolved without great difficulty on the grounds that: (1) a three-year cycle of implementation allowed more scope for staff and students to learn by trial and error, and would not disrupt the patterns of assessment and seminar work familiar to continuing students; (2) the majority of tutors and students thought that any element of continuous assessment would prove unmanageable, or would produce an 'artificial' learning context in which some students were constantly in search of marks, thereby inhibiting 'open' discussion and interaction; (3) since most students would work hardest at assessments that were most rewarded, the importance of seminar presentations should be signalled by the equal weighting of presentations (20%), essays (20%) small projects (20%), and the double weighting of traditional examinations (40%) on all courses. It was also soon agreed in relation to questions (4) and (5) that, wherever possible, presentations should be re-scheduled in order to prevent some students from opting for an alternative assessment, and that the induction programme for new tutors would need to be revised in consultation with them. Similarly, in relation to question (6), a decision would have to be deferred until evidence was gathered from internal monitoring and external examiners, who would attend some sessions. However, since presentations were in part designed to test and promote the development of abilities and skills that would otherwise go untested and unrewarded, standards of achievement and of marking could not be determined by the simple comparison of students' marks over different methods of assessment.

Reaching agreement over responses to the final questions proved more difficult as they raised what appeared to be intractable problems over the impartiality and ability of students as assessors, and the role and responsibility of tutors. Some of these problems were resolved by drawing upon various kinds of self- and peer-evaluation sheets to produce a seminar assessment form that could be used throughout the History programme (Hyland, 1995, p. 143), and by a new section in the student handbook which set out advice over such matters as choosing criteria for assessment, and ways of organising a discussion. It was also agreed that each seminar group should set its own ground rules or conventions over such matters as whether or not any supporting papers could be handed in, whether presenters should leave the room during the actual marking, and whether the tutor or group as a whole would 'moderate' all marks at the end of the semester. However, in order to respect the diversity of opinion and to maintain all tutors' enthusiasm for the change, the vexed question (7) over the manner and extent to which students would determine the marks awarded was left to each tutor's discretion. This was intended to be a provisional decision, enabling tutors to maintain or modify their chosen practices in the light of self-monitoring over a three-year period, by which time all students would have experience of seminar assessments and an evaluation could be conducted.

Nature of evaluation

In 1995 it was agreed to evaluate the use of presentations primarily through an anonymous questionnaire to be posted to all UK based students (287) who had studied History on varying degree programmes in the previous year, and through individual interviews with all History tutors (10). The student questionnaire was designed to gather anonymous responses to thirty-five questions under four main headings:

- Your Experience as a Seminar Presenter;
- Your View of the Tutor's Role;
- Your Experience as an Assessor of Seminar Presentations;
- Your Experience of Different Methods of Assessment.

A fifth section invited students to provide a brief statement of their general observations about seminar presentations, and a sixth section asked for information to facilitate classification by year-group, age (over/under 25), sex, the number of presentations given, and whether the marks awarded were generally higher, lower, or about the same as for coursework essays. Further information (e.g., about student marks for different year-groups and for different methods of assessment) was gathered from departmental records in order to compare with student responses. So, for example, 18% of respondents said that their marks for seminar presentations were generally higher than for essays, 17.4% claimed that they were lower, and 64% said that their marks were about the same (no response: 0.6%). These claims can be corroborated from departmental records, though there are some significant variations by course and year-group.

After pilot studies, responses from 172 students who returned their forms were processed independently, and checked for their reliability by computer services. Broadly, the returns were representative of the student population (see Table 1).

Table 1 Evaluation Data

Total population of students surveyed:		287	(100%)
Respondents		172	(60%)
Non-respondents		115	(40%)
Age:	under 25 year-olds,	103	(60%)
	over 25 year-olds,	69	(40%)
Sex:	female,	123	(72%)
	male,	49	(28%)
Year-Group:	first,	74	(43%)
	second and third,	98	(57%)

Semi-structured interviews with all staff were conducted in June by an educational researcher who produced transcripts from and commentaries upon the audio-taped discussions.

Interpretation of student opinion

In reflecting upon the design of the evaluation, and particularly the creation of the student questionnaire, it is difficult not to regret the largely consultative role allotted to the students. Not only might more imaginative methods of gathering information have emerged from greater student participation, but, as yet, no students have been involved in the interpretation of the collected data. This may seem unimportant, especially as scholars have not paid much attention to the nature and impact of the various kinds of relationships that action researchers in higher education may establish with their students (Wengraf, 1995). Yet at Bath, one of the greatest (and largely unexpected) benefits to emerge from aiming to work with students as equal partners in research has been a gradual re-evaluation of some of the traditional distinctions between staff and students as 'the teachers' and 'the learners'. In part, this may be indicative of a general shift towards a more student-centred curriculum. But in accounting for that change, the transformations that may take place in staff-student, as well as staff-staff and student-student, relations when all learn about one another's needs and problems, should not be forgotten. What follows is therefore one among many readings of the information collected from the initial triangulation of staff, student and facilitator opinion.

For those readers seeking assurance of the validity of the propositions underlying the decision to assess seminar presentations, the aggregated responses to the student questionnaire provide some useful evidence. In describing their experiences as seminar presenters (Table 2), 70% of all students reported an increase in their sense of control over their learning (cf. Booth, 1993); over half claimed an increase in various personal and communication skills; 85% felt that their knowledge and understanding of history had been increased; and 77% reported a growth in their ability to apply historical knowledge in other situations.

Table 2 Students as Seminar Presenters

Please describe your experience of giving history seminar presentations. Tick one box on each line below.

		greatly increased	slightly increased	no change	slightly reduced	greatly reduced	(no reply)
	How has your experience as a seminar presenter affected:						
a)	*your self-confidence*	19.8%	48.8%	24.4%	4.7%	2.3%	0.0%
b)	*your enthusiasm for learning*	25.0%	33.1%	37.2%	3.5%	1.2%	0.0%
c)	*your verbal communication skills*	17.4%	54.1%	26.7%	1.2%	0.6%	0.0%
d)	*your ability to work as a member of a team*	9.3%	41.9%	45.9%	2.9%	0.0%	0.0%
e)	*your ability to work independently*	23.3%	34.9%	40.1%	0.6%	1.2%	0.0%
f)	*your ability to use your initiative and to lead others*	12.2%	43.6%	41.9%	1.7%	0.6%	0.0%
g)	*your knowledge and understanding of history*	40.1%	45.3%	13.4%	0.6%	0.6%	0.0%
h)	*your ability to apply historical knowledge in other situations*	32.0%	44.8%	22.7%	0.0%	0.6%	0.0%
i)	*your sense of control over your own learning*	29.7%	40.1%	26.2%	2.9%	1.2%	0.0%
j)	*your desire to do well academically*	42.4%	26.2%	28.5%	2.3%	0.6%	0.0%

A majority also noted increases in self-confidence, enthusiasm for learning, and academic motivation. In several respects, student perceptions of how assessed seminar presentations affected the role of tutors (Table 3) can be used to corroborate these findings.

Table 3 Student Views of the Tutor's Role

Please indicate the extent to which you agree or do not agree with the following statements. Tick one box on each line below.

		strongly agree	agree	don't know	disagree	strongly disagree	(no reply)
	Seminar presentations help:						
a)	**tutors to stimulate class discussion**	22.7%	54.7%	4.7%	16.9%	1.2%	0.0%
b)	**tutors to understand student learning problems**	10.5%	41.3%	23.3%	22.1%	2.9%	0.0%
c)	**tutors to relate to student as individuals**	19.2%	51.7%	10.5%	15.1%	3.5%	0.0%
d)	**tutors to establish a good rapport with students**	20.3%	47.1%	14.0%	16.9%	1.7%	0.0%
e)	**tutors to motivate students to do their best**	13.4%	41.9%	17.4%	25.0%	2.3%	0.0%
f)	**tutors to keep students informed of their progress**	9.3%	44.2%	16.9%	25.6%	3.5%	0.6%
g)	**tutors to make good use of seminar time**	10.5%	44.2%	16.3%	22.1%	5.8%	1.2%
h)	**tutors to get students to think for themselves**	43.0%	47.7%	2.3%	5.2%	1.7%	0.0%
i)	**tutors to enable students to actively contribute to the course**	43.0%	47.1%	4.7%	3.5%	1.2%	0.6%
j)	**tutors to achieve the objectives of the course**	11.0%	45.9%	27.3%	12.2%	3.5%	0.0%
k)	**tutors to become better teachers**	1.7%	16.9%	50.0%	25.0%	6.4%	0.0%

For, 90% of the respondents thought that presentations helped tutors both to get students to think for themselves, and to actively contribute to the courses. Large majorities also believed that presentations helped tutors to stimulate class discussion, to relate to students as individuals and to establish a good rapport with them. In reflecting on the impact of peer assessment (Table 4), two-thirds of students reported that the experience of assessing others had helped them to become more self-critical.

Table 4 Students as Seminar Assessors

Please indicate the extent to which you agree or disagree with the following statements.
Tick one box on each line below.

		strongly agree	agree	don't know	disagree	strongly disagree	(no reply)
a)	*Students can play a valuable role in helping to assess presentations*	12.2%	37.8%	14.0%	27.3%	8.1%	0.6%
b)	*I have been fair and honest in assessing other students*	16.3%	49.4%	24.4%	8.1%	0.6%	1.2%
c)	*Assessing other students has helped me to think more critically about my own work*	24.4%	41.9%	18.0%	11.0%	3.5%	1.2%
d)	*Marks for seminar presentations should count towards the final assessment for each course*	31.4%	43.0%	9.3%	9.3%	7.0%	0.0%
e)	*The quality of seminar presentations would be reduced if marks did not count towards the final assessment for each course.*	43.6%	29.7%	15.1%	8.7%	2.9%	0.0%

In comparing different methods of assessment (Table 5), students did not rate presentations as highly as coursework essays in terms of raising enthusiasm for learning, being personally rewarding, and increasing depth of understanding.

Table 5 Student Views of Different Methods of Assessment

Please list in order of priority (1,2,3) your views about different methods of assessment (examinations, essays, seminar presentations). Fill in all boxes by entering 1, 2 and 3 on each line below.

		coursework essays (mean scores)	unseen examinations (mean scores)	seminar presentations (mean scores)
	Which method of assessment is			
a)	*most stressful*	2.77	1.31	1.81
b)	*most likely to make you work hard*	1.75	2.03	2.01
c)	*most likely to produce rote learning*	2.29	1.29	2.30
d)	*most likely to raise your enthusiasm for learning*	1.36	2.83	1.71
e)	*most personally rewarding when you do well*	1.52	2.52	1.83
f)	*most helpful in increasing your depth of understanding*	1.20	2.82	1.88
g)	*most fair*	1.19	2.50	2.18
h)	*most likely to produce high marks*	1.26	2.84	1.83
i)	*most likely to help you to develop your personal skills*	1.80	2.86	1.25

But presentations were no more likely to produce rote learning, and were clearly reckoned most likely to promote the development of personal skills. Moreover, on all these counts, the mean scores for essays and presentations were far better than for traditional examinations.

From this kind of evidence it would not be difficult to prepare a *prime facie* case for seminar presentations having fostered many elements of active and deep learning. It is more interesting, however, to consider why so many students did not always share the perceptions of a majority of their peers. For largely unarticulated reasons, several tutors had expected that the main divisions of student opinion would reflect differences of age, sex, and year-group in the student population. Yet, from extensive computer searches, very few significant relationships could be established on these grounds. Mature students were slightly less inclined to believe that presentations helped tutors to understand student learning problems and to make good use of seminar time. One in ten of the female students (and no males) felt that the experience of presenting seminars had reduced their self-confidence, though they were also more likely to state that presentations had greatly increased their leadership abilities. Most striking, perhaps, was the fact that throughout the questionnaire there were no significant differences between the views of first, second, and third-year students. Nor, on the basis of sampling, did differences in A-level scores, degree programmes, and marks awarded for presentations reveal any underlying patterns.

These are useful findings, if only because they help to eliminate some preconceptions about the influence of such factors in this context. More pressing, however, are the numerous correlations between responses; such as those showing that the 22 students who felt in one or more ways adversely affected by giving seminars also felt that presentations were most unlikely to induce hard work and were most unfair. The nature and causes of these relationships cannot, of course, be logically determined, but some clues may be detected in the students' verbal statements.

At the close of the questionnaire, students were asked to provide a brief summary of their views on seminar presentations. Of 163 students who responded, usually in 80—130 words, none made any mention of age or gender, and very few recorded that their views had changed during the course of their experiences. Just over half the students made more than one 'approving' comment: most commonly commending presentations for stimulating class discussion and cooperation, developing personal skills and confidence, and raising interest and enthusiasm for the discipline. However, whether expressing approval or disapproval, hardly any judgements were unconditional. So, for example, a third of all students wrote of their anxiety on giving presentations, often using words like 'nerve-racking', 'traumatic' and 'frightening' to convey their strength of feeling (cf. McDowell and Mowl, 1995). About half of these students attributed their stress to fear of public humiliation; typically, 'of looking stupid in front of class', as one reported; though very few instances of embarrassment due to peer or tutor remarks were actually recorded. Moreover, despite the strain of their experience, 'like visiting the dentist', it did not prevent many students from stating that on reflection they also found the exercises 'very satisfying', 'enjoyable' and 'valuable', as they 'could see the logic behind them'. As one first-year noted: 'Personally, I found it a terrifying experience, but extremely worthwhile and rewarding after the event'.

By identifying the conditional relations ('ifs', 'buts', 'howevers' and all other qualifiers) within such statements, it is possible to employ a verifiable procedure for drawing up terms of analysis that are rooted in the textual evidence, rather than primarily in the researcher's beliefs and theories. A different kind of 'dilemma analysis' to that proposed by Winter (1982) can then be conducted, in which the gaps or dissonances between the 'dilemmas' of the sources/discourses and the pre-recorded theoretical or personal expectations of the researchers can be examined; independently, if need be. When elaborated, such a data-handling method serves to keep 'learning' rather than 'proving' at the centre of attention, and it has been used below to illustrate some of the dilemmas of seminar assessment.

Although it is not surprising to find that over 80% of students are concerned with matters of assessment, analysis of the judgements and conditional relations contained in their responses produces highly complex and divergent patterns of opinion. So, for example, a small group of students rejects any form of seminar assessment, in principle. For these students, even though presentations are 'good' and 'commendable' in developing 'communication skills', 'self confidence' and 'most abilities', they are 'certainly not to be used as an indication of a good history student'. 'How does being able to present a good seminar make me a good historian?' and 'History has nothing to do with this', are two memorable comments. Another and much larger group is concerned with the role of students as assessors; dividing almost equally between those who believe that students should play a major or increased role in marking, primarily because they are 'fairer' or 'less biassed' than their tutors, and those who believe that tutors alone should determine marks or 'have the final say', because they are less prone to 'petty rivalries' and have 'professional responsibilities'. Even within this group, however, there are notable agreements: assessments would be better if there were clearer and stricter criteria for marking, and if there were more consistency between the assessment practices adopted by different tutors. Such criticisms pose a variety of problems; not least because it should not be assumed that tutors are the most accurate markers (cf. Stefani, 1994), and because these criticisms can be read as evidence of some students' reluctance to fully engage in what one third-year calls 'the very difficult task of assessing peers, particularly one's friends'. Yet in most cases it appears that students are not so much calling for more instruction, as for tutors to pay more attention to ensuring that students are always treated fairly and equitably.

Interpretation of staff opinion

From the transcripts of interviews with tutors, there is considerable evidence both to support the view that the assessment of seminars has stimulated active learning, and to suggest that many of the students' criticisms are well founded. Without exception, tutors believe that the innovation has raised the quality of student discussion and collaboration, to a point at which the active contribution of most students can be regarded as 'a normal habit' or 'part of the culture' of the classroom. For several tutors, this contrasts strongly with their experiences of history seminars in some other institutions. All, however, stress the importance of students presenting and assessing historical arguments and debates in order to develop their understanding of the nature and practices of the discipline. According to one tutor, 'In preparing and presenting papers, students get to think through problems and organise material in a way that is different from an essay'. According to another, 'by observing and assessing they are developing the faculty of being self-critical ... and I think that is probably more effective than my criticisms, which don't seem to have the same force as peer pressure or their own self-critical awareness'. Such comments emphasizing the value of students learning from and teaching one another, can be found throughout the transcripts, and they suggest the need for further efforts to redraw some of the traditional distinctions between 'the teachers' and 'the learners', as may be indicated also by the unexpected tendency of many students to describe themselves and their colleagues as 'researchers'. However, with regard to the traditional role of staff as the assessors and the markers, tutors are by no means united either in their practices or in their opinions.

In describing their conventions for assessing seminars, it is clear that over the three-year period all tutors have experimented with several systems. Some have used the seminar assessment form quite rigorously and enthusiastically, while others have found it too restricting; some have allowed students to submit papers after presentations, while others haven't; some have encouraged group presentations, while others have not permitted them; some have asked presenters to leave the room during marking, while others have involved them in the grading; and some have instituted tutorial feedback at a later date, while others have not done so. It is not surprising, therefore, that what now constitutes agreed departmental practice is by no means always clear to tutors, let alone to students. Nor is it surprising that in some respects tutors' experiences have led them to hold quite contrary opinions. Thus one tutor insists that peer assessment is best suited to third-year classes, and that 'it just doesn't work with first-years, who can't handle it ... because it makes them very uncomfortable, due to inexperience'. But this is plainly contradicted by another, who observes that while 'most first-years enjoy the experience ... it just doesn't follow through to the third year', because students are then much too concerned about their degree results. Interestingly, there is next to no student testimony in support of either view. However, while peer assessment raises problems, it is over who should do the actual marking that staff, like students, are most divided or uncertain.

All tutors have involved students as assessors; in questioning, criticizing, and providing oral and written feedback to presenters. But the extent to which students have been instrumental in awarding marks has varied greatly. Some staff have decided to determine marks in the light of the assessors' comments: 'I take what I think is the response of the meeting' and 'I take cognizance of students' opinion', is how two tutors put it. Some have explicitly 'discussed' or 'negotiated' marks with students (in one case including the presenters), so that 'they can play a real rather than an artificial part' in the whole process of assessment. Others have established ground rules with their groups so that students exercise the main responsibility for awarding marks, and tutors act as 'arbitrators' or 'advisers'. Although in their written statements, students support and oppose each of these approaches almost equally, it is the latter which draws most criticism from those tutors who do not use it, but regard it as 'impractical' or 'unprofessional': 'At the end of the day, I'm responsible for the integrity of the marks to the examination board', is a phrase that one emphatically repeats. Some 'practical' objections, over student numbers and time shortages, do receive some slight support from student comments. But others, such as a new tutor's claim that peer assessment produces 'a strong tradition of students contesting marks', do not appear elsewhere. In reviewing the information collected for evaluation, tutors and students may be able to resolve some of these differences and confusions so as to reach 'a common set of understandings' about the objectives and methods of peer marking, as the facilitator (George Preston) most strongly recommends. However, it should be noted that for all the problems, no tutor wishes to abandon either peer assessment or peer marking, even if the latter is 'an experiment' with which they are not personally engaged. As one 'experimenter' comments: 'I thought that by introducing peer assessment we would just be adding variety to the system. But it has led me to reconsider my whole way of teaching'.

Conclusion

In reflecting upon the innovations reported here, it is clear that while observance of the principles of collaboration and democratic participation in decision-making has facilitated many changes to traditional practices, it has also produced a diversity of approaches to seminar teaching and assessment that many students and some staff find disconcerting or disturbing. It may well be that some resolution or accommodation of these differences can be reached through further action and reflection, but, equally, further discussion may lead to a deeper diversity of teaching and assessment strategies, and to the gradual emergence of a more democratic tradition of educational practices (Carr, 1987). Since the fundamental aim of AR is to improve practices in specific settings, and these are at least in some respects always dependent upon the particular abilities and needs of individual tutors and groups of students in distinctive contexts, it is neither unreasonable nor unethical to build a tradition in which differences are respected and even celebrated. Such a tradition may require greater collaboration and negotiation than ones which only champion theoretical or technical solutions to educational problems, and more recognition that the critical reflections of practitioners on their own and shared experiences can produce many 'practical wisdoms' that both legitimate and undermine all collective judgements and agreements about action. The tendency of some scholars to represent action-researchers as beleaguered teachers who by working together under strict conditions will inevitably improve their practices by moving along a bi-polar scale of rationality does not, in my opinion, help in this respect. Nor does a view that AR methods are most advanced when they 'emancipate' (protect) practitioners from the influences of external agencies and authorities, which are usually represented as irrational and unjust. In order to help articulate and challenge our own claims to be making improvements to student learning, as historians at Bath we need much more exposure to the theories, practices, goals and discourses of 'outsiders', not less. That, perhaps, is the most important lesson of our action-research.

References

Barrow, R. and Milburn, G. (1990) *A Critical Dictionary of Educational Concepts*, 2nd edn. London: Harvester Wheatsheaf.

Biggs, J. B. (1987) *Student Approaches to Learning and Studying*. Melbourne: Australian Council for Educational Research.

Booth, A. (1993) Learning history in university: student views on teaching and assessment. *Studies in Higher Education* 18, 227—35.

Boud, D. (ed.) (1988) *Developing Student Autonomy in Learning*, 2nd edn. London: Kogan Page.

Boud, D. (1990) Assessment and the promotion of academic values. *Studies in Higher Education* 15, 101—11.

Carr, W. (1987) What is an educational practice? *Journal of Philosophy of Education* 22, 163—75.

Cohen, L. and Manion, L. (1994) *Research Methods in Education*, 4th edn. London: Routledge.

Elliott, J. (1988) Educational research and outsider-insider relations. *Qualitative Studies in Education* 1, 155—66.

Elliott, J. (1991) *Action Research for Educational Change*. Buckingham: Open University Press.

Elton, L. (1991) Enterprise in higher education: work in progress. *Education and Training* 33, 5—9.

Gibbs, G. (1992) *Improving the Quality of Student Learning*. Bristol: Technical and Educational Services Ltd.

Gibson, R. (1985) Critical times for action research. *Cambridge Journal of Education* 15, 59—64.

Hammersley, M. (1993) On the teacher as researcher. In M. Hammersley (ed.), *Educational Research: Current Issues*. London, Paul Chapman, 211—31.

Hodgkinson, H. L. (1957) Action research — a critique. *Journal of Education Sociology* 31, 137—53.

Hyland, P. (1995) Measuring and improving the quality of teaching. In A. Booth and P. Hyland (eds), *History in Higher Education: New Directions in Teaching and Learning*. Oxford: Blackwell, 128—52.

Jacques, D. (1984) *Learning in Groups*. London: Croom Helm.

Kemmis, S. (1988) Action research. In J. P. Keeves (ed.), *Educational Research, Methodology, and Measurement: An International Handbook*. Oxford: Pergamon Press, 42—9.

Kemmis, S. and McTaggart, R. (eds) (1988) *The Action Research Planner*, 3rd edn, Victoria, Deakin University Press.

McDowell, L. and Mowl, G. (1995) Innovative assessment: its impact on students. In G. Gibbs (ed.), *Improving Student Learning Through Assessment and Evaluation*. Oxford: Oxford Centre for Staff Development, 131—47.

McKernan, J. (1988) The countenance of curriculum action research: traditional, collaborative, and emancipatory — critical conceptions. *Journal of Curriculum and Supervision* 3, 173—200.

McNiff, J. (1988) *Action Research: Principles and Practice*. London: Macmillan.

McNiff, J. (1992) *Creating a Good Social Order through Action Research*. Poole: Hyde Publications.

Nixon, J. (ed.) (1981) *A Teachers' Guide to Action Research*. London: Grant McIntyre.

Preston, G. (1987) A Review of the Teaching and Learning Strategies used in the Teaching of History at Bath College of Higher Education. University of Bath, M.Ed dissertation.

Ramsden, P. (1992) *Learning to Teach in Higher Education*. London: Routledge.

Rogers, C. (1978) *Freedom to Learn: A View of What Education Might Be*. Columbus: Merrill.

Stefani, L. A. J. (1994) Peer, self and tutor assessment: relative reliabilities. *Studies in Higher Education* 19, 69—75.

Wengraf, T. (1995) Improving student learning by collaborative action research by human sciences undergraduates in evaluative inquiry: evaluating seminar practice. In G. Gibbs (ed.), *Improving Student Learning Through Assessment and Evaluation*. Oxford: Oxford Centre for Staff Development, 180—95.

Whithead, J. and Lomax, P. (1987) Action research and the politics of educational knowledge. *British Educational Research Journal* 13, 175—90.

Whithead, J. (1989) Creating a living educational theory from questions of the kind, 'How do I improve my practice?'. *Cambridge Journal of Education* 19, 41—52.

Winter, R. (1982) 'Dilemma analysis': a contribution to methodology for action research. *Cambridge Journal of Education* 12, 161—74.

Wisdom, J. and Gibbs, G. (1994) *Course Design for Resource Based Learning: Humanities*. Oxford: Oxford Centre for Staff Development.

Wittrock, M. (1986) Students' thought processes. In M. Wittrock (ed.), *Handbook of Research on Teaching*. New York: Macmillan, 297—314.

Zuber-Skerritt, O. (1991) *Action Research in Higher Education: Examples and Reflections*. Brisbane: Griffith University Centre for the Advancement of Learning and Teaching.

22 Using research to improve student learning in small groups

Diane Garland
Plymouth Business School
University of Plymouth

Introduction

The many benefits of working effectively in small groups are well documented in the literature. West (1994), however, points out that effective group working is very difficult to achieve. Research with management groups suggests that to be more effective groups should be structured using certain criteria (Belbin, 1981, 1993). However in higher education little evidence exists as to the effectiveness of student learning in small groups and to ways in which student learning may be improved. This chapter is based upon research conducted at Plymouth Business School, University of Plymouth, with undergraduates and staff with the aims of (1) ascertaining the effectiveness of small group work as a learning method; (2) identifying difficulties experienced with group work; and (3) proposing possible solutions to the difficulties encountered with the intention of improving student learning. The chapter documents the research strategy adopted, analyses the students and staff responses to their group learning experiences, and reports the consequent changes being incorporated into the Human Behaviour in Organizations module of the Business Studies degree.

Research strategy

Questionnaire data (40 items) was obtained from 875 undergraduate students enrolled on 9 Business School degree courses, The students consisted of 468 males and 407 females. The majority of the students (701) were under 23 years of age, with 174 students being older than 23 years. All were full-time students. Questionnaire data (32 items) was obtained from 31 staff teaching on those courses. Twelve members of staff set individual work only on Business School undergraduate programmes. Analysis was therefore conducted using the responses of the students and the 19 members of staff who set small-group work on such courses. Respondents were asked to rate their level of agreement with statements about small-group work using the scale Very Much Agree, Agree, Disagree, Very Much Disagree. This scale was utilized as all the students had participated in small group work in modules taken prior to the research being conducted and the researcher believed all respondents would be able to respond to each item. Reported in this paper are the main findings of the research.

The staff response

Reasons for setting group work: benefits for staff

The majority of respondents agreed:

- group work saves time when marking students work, and
- group work is less expensive to set up, supervise and equip than projects undertaken individually.

Taken together, the above replies suggest respondents believe group work to be less costly both in terms of human and physical resources.

Benefits for students

Respondents were in complete agreement that group work enables students to develop other personal transferable skills, e.g. time management, negotiation, presentation skills, interpersonal sensitivity. The following benefits for students were identified with the perceived most important first:

- group work enables students to be involved in more complex, larger-scale projects than they could attempt as individuals.
- group work increases the amount and quality of discussion between students, encouraging informal peer tutoring and peer feedback.
- group work helps to develop a balance of personal transferable and academic skills.
- the development of group-work skills enhances the prospects of employment.
- group work enhances the depth and breadth of student knowledge.

Difficulties experienced with group work

Almost all (95%) staff respondents believe:

- the 'free rider' is a real problem in group work.

Although many staff (73%) disagreed with the statement that group work produces better quality learning outcomes than individual students could achieve, there was little support for the notion that all assessed work should be individually completed (83% disagreed).

Assessment issues

Analysis of the data with regard to assessment produced more varied results with the level of agreement across all four categories being almost equal in response to the following issues:

- the lecturer should be the sole assessor of student group work, and
- the group mark should be differentiated in line with the individual's contribution.
- only the group product should be assessed. It is unnecessary to assess the group process.
- peer assessment should be a part of the group assessment process.

- the lecturer should monitor group process.

There was more agreement amongst respondents (60—70%) with regard to the following:

- the lecturer is only able to assess the end product or outcome of the group.
- evidence of the individual's contribution to a group project should be submitted for assessment and amendment to marks as deemed necessary by the lecturer.
- student self-assessment helps students increase self- awareness of group-work skills.
- student groups should not receive one overall group mark.

Training and development issues

Staff respondents are in complete agreement that:

- feedback and guidance are important aspects in the development of group-work skills, with the majority (79%) believing:
- group-work skills should be developed within and throughout the academic programme; 68% of respondents would like to see:
- training provided for staff in the principles and theoretical aspects of group work, with 58% of respondents acknowledging that:
- a training workshop designed to help lecturers find ways of coping with difficulties experienced in group work would be useful.

The student response

Some of the results varied between courses and according to age and gender of respondents. In this chapter, the author will highlight only those findings where a significant difference was found in relation to the findings being presented.

Benefits of group work

Student respondents acknowledged the following benefits of group work, with the perceived most important first:

- helps to develop other personal transferable skills;
- fosters discussion between students and encourages informal tutoring and support (which respondents identified as being beneficial);
- helps to develop a balance of personal transferable and academic skills;
- enhances prospects of employment;
- allows more complex work to be tackled than individuals could manage on their own;
- increases breadth and depth of subject knowledge.

Difficulties experienced with group work

Respondents experienced a number of difficulties. 89% agreed:

- the 'free rider' is a real problem in group work with 64% of respondents finding it:
- unusual for all members to fully co-operate in group work.

It seems that a sense of a lack of fairness and equity prevails here. Clearly this is one area that needs to be addressed.

Despite the above difficulties there was limited support (39%) for the notion that:

- assessed work should be individually completed and not group work.

63% of the younger students disagreed while the mature students were equally divided in their view.

Logistical difficulties

Group size

Table 1

What should be the maximum size of a group?	%
10 – 12	0
7 – 9	0
6	28
5	33
3 – 4	39
	100%

Table 1 shows that students prefer to work in smaller rather than larger groups, with a clear preference for groups to have a maximum of six members. Most respondents (91%) believe:

- students should be allowed to choose their own group members and many respondents (75%) believe:
- lecturers underestimate the time needed to complete group work, the latter being particularly cited by students undertaking BTEC and the BA Business Administration programmes where students have considerable experience of group working. Over 90% of respondents agreed:
- the timing of group work and workload often causes difficulty, with 43% mature students particularly citing this as a difficulty.

Assessment issues

Analysis of the data produced a more varied student response with regard to assessment with mixed views across courses with regard to the following:

- peer assessment should be part of the group process.
- self-assessment is helpful in increasing self awareness of group-work skills.

- Student groups should receive one overall group mark.

However, the majority of the student respondents believe that:

- the lecturer should monitor group process, and that
- group work should be differentiated in line with the individual's contribution;
- evidence of the individual's contribution to a group-work project should be submitted for assessment and amendment to marks as deemed necessary by the lecturer;
- the lecturer should not be the sole assessor.

Students were equally divided in their views on whether group members were the only people able to monitor group process.

Student preference for individual work

A small majority of the student respondents (59%) expressed a preference for individual work rather than group work. While younger students and males were almost equally divided in their preference, 69% of the mature students and 65% of female respondents preferred individual work. This raises the question as to why this might be. A number of factors may be significant:

- Culture

In the UK, the educational system often emphasizes individual working almost to the exclusion of group working. The traditional individually assessed examination paper has long been utilized and accepted as a 'fair' method of individual assessment by students. For some mature students group working is a completely new mode of working. Recent research evidence, however, highlights issues of inter-rater reliability and admissions of cheating in one form or another by undergraduates (Franklyn-Stokes and Newstead, 1993). Group work may require a culture change in student (and some staff thinking).

- Gender

There appears to be no clear evidence to suggest why female respondents in this study prefer individual working. Logistical difficulties, together with assessment and training and development issues as outlined in this chapter may contribute to this finding.

Training and development issues

Almost all student respondents (96%) believe:

- feedback and guidance is important in the development of group-work skills

The majority (83%) agree that:

- group-work skills should be developed throughout the academic programme, and
- training in the principles and theoretical aspects of group work should complement practical activities.

Conclusions

There are many benefits of working effectively in small groups for both staff and students. However the research has shown that a number of practical difficulties may emerge, which need to be considered and to be addressed if the full benefits of group working are to be realized.

Overall, the research findings suggest that student learning in small groups is most effective when:

- group work is carefully planned;
- group size is kept to a minimum (the maximum is six);
- aims and objectives are clear and agreed by group members;
- assessment strategies are linked with the learning objectives of the group work;
- close monitoring of group process by staff is included as part of the assessment procedure;
- peer group support is present;
- on-going, reflective, peer and staff feedback and guidance occurs;
- training and development of group-work skills is provided.

Changes being incorporated into the Business Studies degree, foundation year in the light of the research findings

Plymouth Business School already has in place an extended Business Skills Induction programme which includes a co-ordinated set of group-work activities, entitled 'Team Focus'. A major aim of these innovative activities is to introduce students to the skills of working in groups. 'Team Focus' has been developed over a number of years and is a derivation of 'Upshot 1992' (Garland, 1993) and 'Team Spirit' (Garland, 1994).

Human Behaviour in Organizations

The Human Behaviour in Organizations module immediately follows the induction programme and this year is being amended in the light of the research findings above with the aims of developing student group-working skills and improving student learning. This module is currently running with 380 students. The format has been changed to include an integrative business case study based upon topic areas covered in the lecture programme. Group-work theory is included as part of the lecture programme and in addition to recommended reading material, each student receives an individual copy of *Working in Groups*, a student manual (Garland, in press) containing a number of exercises for individual completion and to help students with the development of group-work skills. Students are required to work throughout the module in groups of six, to develop a group learning contract and to solve a number of problems posed by the case study. Information regarding the problems to be solved is given to group leaders via regular briefing sessions as the module progresses, for distribution to their members. The regular briefing sessions also provide an opportunity for group members to bring any issues to the attention of the module leader through the group leader. Monitoring of the group process is on-going with groups being required to meet at least fortnightly. Minutes of group meetings are submitted after each meeting is held. Staff may also visit group meetings to monitor progress. As a safety net, surgery time slots are provided for individual group members to consult module leaders, although in practice this has rarely proved necessary. Through a combination of the above methods feedback and guidance for both staff and students are occurring.

The module is assessed by:

1. an end of module group report which includes solutions to case study problems set throughout the module and which carries a 30% weighting; group members are also required to submit a copy of their group learning contract, together with individually signed statements of each member's contribution to the report; and

2. an individually assessed multiple choice questionnaire (70% weighting) based on lectures and set reading covering the topics areas included in the lecture programme.

References

Belbin, R. M. (1981) *Management Teams, Why They Succeed or Fail*. London: Heinemann.

Belbin, R. M. (1993) *Team Roles at Work*. Oxford: Butterworth-Heinemann.

Franklyn-Stokes, A. and Newstead, S. (1993) Undergraduate cheating: studies across disciplines and institutions. Paper presented at the British Psychological Society Annual Conference (1993) London.

Garland, D. Y. (1994) UPshot 1992. In Thorley, L. and Gregory, R. (eds), *Using Group-based Learning in Higher Education*. London: Kogan Page.

Garland, D. Y. (1995) Preparing undergraduates for teamworking: a developmental approach. *Proceedings of the Occupational Psychology Conference, University of Warwick*.

Garland, D. Y. (in press) *Working in Groups*.

West, M. A. (1994) *Effective Teamwork*. London: British Psychological Society and Routledge.

23 Student teachers' integration of formal and informal knowledge of learning and teaching

G. M. Boulton-Lewis, B. C. Dart and J. M. Brownlee[1]
Queensland University of Technology

The place of psychological knowledge in teacher education

Teaching-related knowledge falls into three main kinds; declarative (knowing that, for example the psychology of student learning), procedural (knowing how, for example knowing how to organize a learning environment and deal with behaviour problems), and conditional (knowing when and why various procedures work most effectively (Berliner, 1986; Borko and Livingston, 1989; Leinhardt, 1990; Marzano, Brandth, Hughes, Jones, Pressersen, Rankin and Suhor, 1988; Shulman, 1986). Each of these kinds of knowledge consists of informally and formally acquired information. As a profession, teaching draws upon formal and theoretical knowledge in educational and developmental psychology, and teacher educators are responsible for ensuring that the essentials of that knowledge base are constructed by their students. An important extra step in the translation and application of that formal knowledge to enlightened practice is to draw on students' informal knowledge gained from perceptions of their own learning experiences and other experiences. That second step is not yet well integrated into teacher education except in practicum, mainly because the relationship between the procedural knowledge gained in such experiences and the required formal, declarative knowledge base of teaching, is not well understood (Evans, 1991). All teachers (and students) have informal theories of learning and teaching, but until those theories are integrated with the formal knowledge base of teaching, teachers will use their informal knowledge and thus behave like amateurs, however gifted, rather than professionals. Effective teacher education should assist students to achieve an integration of formal and informal knowledge of learning. In the course in which our sample was enrolled the formal taught content includes learning (theories of learning, models of learning, and learning strategies), motivation, structuring effective learning environments, learning styles and teacher expectation effects.

Informal knowledge of learning and teaching

Students' informal and formal knowledge of the learning and teaching processes, and of psychological concepts related to classroom teaching and learning may be quantitative or qualitative (Cole, 1990; Marton, Dall'Alba and Beaty, 1993; Prosser, Trigwell and Taylor, 1994; Samuelowicz and Bain, 1992). In the quantitative tradition, learning is conceived of as increasing, memorizing and applying knowledge. From a qualitative perspective learning is seen as leading to understanding, seeing something in a different way and perhaps

[1] The authors wish to thank Professor John Biggs for his involvement in the project.

changing as a person. In this latter tradition learners' comprehension is gradual and cumulative, with qualitative changes taking place in the nature both of what is learned, and how it is structured. The qualitative tradition has emerged from a variety of different research areas, for example cognitive psychology (Shuell, 1986), alternative frameworks research (Driver and Oldham, 1986), phenomenography (Marton, 1981), but all have a common generic view that people actively construct knowledge for themselves. In consequence the teacher's task is to assist students to transform existing knowledge to approximate more closely the frameworks that are currently accepted. Thus student teachers' own ideas about particular concepts related to learning and teaching, formed in and out of school, also belong in the content knowledge of teacher education programs. The central thrust of this research is that it is important what beliefs student teachers hold because such cognitions are very likely to determine practice (Biggs, 1989a). Effective teaching and assessment is based on qualitative conceptions of learning (constructivist) (Driver and Bell, 1986; White, 1988), while quantitative conceptions (reproductive) lead to counter-productive classroom practices (Prosser *et al.*, 1994; Samuelowicz and Bain, 1992). Studies of expert and novice teachers show that expert teachers hold qualitative conceptions of learning and teaching whereas novices simply tell students what to think, and then assess for retention (e.g. Tang, 1993; Tobin and Fraser, 1988). It is therefore crucial that teachers acquire a qualitative conception of learning and teaching and that their naive or commonsense attributions concerning learning and teaching are transformed into ones that are theoretically informed.

Facilitating the development of psychological concepts

Conceptions and beliefs about learning and teaching are likely to develop in much the same way as other beliefs, such as those concerning the physical world. Children have naive conceptions of physical concepts which are in conflict with the Newtonian and post-Newtonian concepts that are taught in the official curriculum (Gunstone and White, 1981; Marton, 1981) and frequently learn the official content sufficiently to pass school assessments. While this problem has long been recognized in science education little work has been done in the area of teaching educational psychology to intending or serving teachers, where the problem is possibly more difficult because we are dealing with adults, often with many years of seemingly successful enactment of these misconceptions. Therefore, in order to facilitate understanding, which may require confronting powerful prior knowledge that could interfere with new learning, students need to engage in what Baird (1991, p. 102) described as 'the constructivist processes of recognition, evaluation and possible reconstruction of personal views'. This requires reflection and metacognition as well as the acceptance of self-responsibility for learning (Biggs and Moore, 1993). From a constructivist viewpoint learners must assume control of their own learning and responsibility for sense-making must reside with individual learners. Dart (1994a) has described successful outcomes from constructivist approaches to teaching and learning.

Aims and objectives

This research therefore was intended to investigate:

1. the informal conceptions of learning and teaching (declarative, procedural and conditional knowledge) held by teacher education students, with a particular focus on

if and how they become modified and integrated with those concepts taught and assessed from a constructivist perspective in educational psychology courses;

2. how such knowledge is used in classroom decision-making (the link between declarative, procedural and conditional knowledge) and

3. the relationship between that knowledge and actual teaching performance.

Method

Sample

The sample consisted of 33 students from two classes who commenced a one year Graduate Diploma in Education at the beginning of 1995. One student held a PhD in science, 7 other students held first degrees in Science, 14 held first degrees in Arts and the remaining 11 students held degrees in a variety of disciplines. Their ages range from 20 to 41 years with a mean of 26 years and a standard deviation of 6.7 years.

Procedure

1. Students were asked to write statements at the beginning of the year, about what they knew about learning and teaching. They will be asked to write such a statement again at the end of the year. This allows the students to describe declarative and procedural knowledge of learning [objective (1)].

2. Students responded in writing at the beginning of the course to a teaching/learning scenario which required interpretations and explanations. The scenario required students to describe and interpret the teaching/learning process involving a secondary school student who demonstrated poor concentration, dependency on others, attributions of success to 'luck', high anxiety, low self-esteem, disruptive behaviour and a poor teacher-student relationship. They will respond to the same scenario at the end of the course. The discussion of the scenario taps procedural and conditional knowledge and their connection with declarative knowledge and hence allows us to compare what they know with what they would do and how they justify that. This addresses objectives (1) and (2).

3. Videotapes will be made of one teaching lesson per student followed by stimulated recall (cf. Meade and McMenimam, 1992) to determine the extent to which formal knowledge determines their behaviour and their conceptions of teaching. The discussion of their own teaching during the stimulated recall sessions assesses procedural and conditional knowledge and their connection with declarative knowledge and hence allows us to compare what they know with what they do and how they justify that [Objectives (1), (2), and (3)].

4. Questionnaires were used to provide information relating to personal and environmental variables predicted to influence motives and strategy use in learning as well as to identify those motives and strategies. Students' preferences for a constructivist learning environment were obtained by using the Measure of Constructivist Learning Environments (MCLE) (Dart, 1994b). There are three sub-scales: Collaboration, Responsibility and Autonomy. Respondents rated each item on a 4-point Likert scale (4 = strongly agree, 1 = strongly disagree). Students were also asked to indicate the extent of their agreement with mastery and performance goal

orientations. This was also measured on a 4-point Likert scale (4 = strongly agree, 1 = strongly disagree).

Students' metacognitive awareness was measured using the Metacognitive Awareness Inventory (Schraw and Dennison, 1994). This includes three sub-scales to measure knowledge of cognition (declarative, procedural and conditional knowledge) and five sub-scales to measure regulation of cognition (planning, information management strategies, comprehension monitoring, debugging strategies and evaluation). Respondents rated each item on a 4-point Likert scale (4 = strongly agree, 1 = strongly disagree).

Finally a modified version of the Study Process Questionnaire (SPQ) (Biggs, 1987) was administered to students. This was modified on the basis of confirmatory factor analysis (T&LiTE, 1994). The SPQ measures surface, deep and achieving motives and strategies. Corresponding motives and strategies scores can be added to give approaches to learning. For example surface approach comprises surface motive and surface strategy scores; deep approach comprises deep motive and deep strategy scores and achieving approach constitutes achieving motive and achieving strategy scores.

They will complete similar questionnaires at the end of the year.

Analysis

This chapter is a description of the analysis of the data from the beginning of the year pre-teaching statements, scenario and questionnaires. The overall plan for analysis of the data for the research is described in terms of already completed data analysis and data to be analysed.

(a) Completed data analysis

First, the open statements were categorized on the basis of the level of structural organization of knowledge of learning and teaching using the SOLO Taxonomy (Biggs and Collis, 1982). This taxonomy has been used for assessing students' general conceptions of coursework (Prosser and Trigwell, 1991; Trigwell and Prosser, 1991a, 1991b), and levels have been proposed for assessing tertiary students' knowledge of learning (Boulton-Lewis, 1992, 1994; Boulton-Lewis and Dart, 1994).

Second, the open statements and scenarios were analysed to determine the formal and informal content of students' knowledge of teaching and learning. This was undertaken using the Q.S.R NUD*IST (Non-numerical Unstructured Data Indexing Searching and Theorizing) (Richards and Richards, 1994) package which facilitated the organization, cross-referencing and synthesizing of the qualitative data that emerged from the statements and scenario reflections.

Third, the questionnaire data were analysed and descriptive statistics (means and standard deviations) calculated for the variables in the four questionnaires.

(b) Data to be analysed

First, the levels of structural organization, and informal and formal knowledge at the beginning and end of the year, will be compared and explained as they relate to the lecturing and teaching strategies adopted in the course.

Second, students' conceptions of teaching as evidenced in the videotapes will be categorized (cf. Samuelowicz and Bain, 1992; Prosser *et al.*, 1994) and the relations between their behaviour, beliefs and knowledge will be examined.

Third, the questionnaire data will be analysed quantitatively to allow for comparison between pre- and post-personal and environmental variables predicted to influence motives and strategies in learning as well as changes in these motives and strategies as they apply to learning in the course.

Qualitative results

SOLO levels

The learning statements were classified according to the five levels of the SOLO taxonomy in the formal mode and frequencies were determined for each level: prestructural ($n = 0$), unistructural ($n = 4$), multistructural ($n = 23$), relational ($n = 6$) and extended abstract ($n = 0$). Hence the informal knowledge of the majority of the students was organized structurally at the multistructural level. This indicates that they can describe relevant aspects of teaching and learning but the informal knowledge is not organized in an integrated way such that it can be applied flexibly in practice (cf. Boulton-Lewis, 1994).

Informal knowledge of psychological concepts: the scenario

Students' knowledge of motivation was the focus of discussion since the scenario required students to consider such issues. See Appendix 1 for a description of the scenario task. Students' knowledge of motivation was judged to be formal if there was evidence of appropriate understanding of concepts in their description, analysis and application to related areas of knowledge. Ramsden (1988) states that formal knowledge is evidenced by the ability to apply principled understandings in the teaching discipline. Hence formal concepts are demonstrated by relational understandings but may be expressed in either theoretical and/or everyday language.

In the scenario reflection, the students attributed Prunella's difficulty to low self-esteem/confidence which manifested itself in a fear of failure, acceptance of failure, disruptive classroom behaviour, dependence on others, and general learning and motivational difficulties. The difficulties described were attributed to physiological changes, a lack of support and negative teacher expectations. All of these responses reflected students' informal declarative knowledge of motivation since they generally described concepts in naive, 'everyday' language with no evidence of principled relational understanding. Strategies were also suggested to develop Prunella's self-confidence. These responses represent informal procedural knowledge because 'knowing how' is described again in terms of commonsense, everyday language with no evidence of principled relational knowledge.

Identification of difficulties

Low self confidence/esteem

The majority of scenario reflections identify Prunella's difficulties in terms of self factors. As a consequence, a number of students ($n = 17$)[2] perceived that Prunella was experiencing a fear of failure which was contributing to her difficulties within the classroom:

> *For Prunella, with her low self-confidence . . . the pressure of performing tasks by herself is frightening . . . Her fear lies in making mistakes and perhaps being ridiculed. (11S)*[3]

---

[2] *(n = 17) refers to the frequency of responses.*
[3] *(11S) refers to the student identification number in relation to the scenario reflection.*

Many students (*n* = 21) also believed that this fear of failure was entrenched and Prunella had learned to accept failure:

> *Prunella now sees herself as an underachiever and in turn has accepted she cannot learn. (12S)*

The students (*n* = 18) also perceived that Prunella is disruptive in class as a result of the problems she is experiencing:

> *She truly believes she will not be able to cope. Her anxiety during individual work is a symptom of this. Prunella's giving up is the result of fear and the hope of help. Her disruption is an attention-seeking device — 'if someone notices perhaps they will help'. (38S)*

As a result of perceived low self-confidence, many students (*n* = 18) believed that Prunella had come to be dependent on others, including the teacher and her peers:

> *I believe self-esteem to be the root of her problem. No self-esteem means no confidence, which would account for dependence on others, the constant questioning of the teacher and her failure to attempt difficult tasks. (30S)*

Some responses also focussed on general learning difficulties (*n* = 11) and motivational concerns (*n* = 13).

Physiological changes, lack of support and teacher expectations

Some students commented (*n* = 5) on how they perceived Prunella's difficulties were associated with the onset of puberty while other students perceived that Prunella was experiencing a loss of self-confidence/esteem due to either a lack of family (*n* = 9), peer (*n* = 7) or teacher support (*n* = 3). Teacher expectations (*n* = 12) were also attributed to Prunella's poor self-esteem/confidence by some students.

Strategies

In response to Prunella's perceived difficulties, students described a number of strategies to improve Prunella's self confidence. These included setting achievable goals, providing individual support, encouraging independent learning skills and offering encouragement/positive reinforcement.

Setting achievable goals

Many students (*n* = 22) believed that in order to develop confidence Prunella would need to be gradually introduced to tasks appropriate for her needs:

> *You would have to encourage her by [giving] her simple tasks, gradually building up her confidence thus [increasing the difficulty] of the problems or questions asked of her. (29S)*

Individual support

It was also considered important that Prunella experience a degree of individualized support in order to improve her self-confidence/esteem (*n* = 19):

> *Prunella needs attention on a one-to-one basis, so I think I would try to arrange help outside the classroom as well as in. Arrange meetings after class or after school and start from scratch in the areas she has problems with. (17S)*

Additionally, some students (*n* = 7) commented on the need for clear and precise instructions.

Encouraging independent learning skills, positive reinforcement/encouragement

Encouragement of independent learning skills and risk-taking were viewed as strategies for building Prunella's confidence (*n* = 11). Many students (*n* = 23) believed that they would offer Prunella positive reinforcement and/or encouragement to foster self-confidence/esteem. Some students (*n* = 2) noted that this praise would have to be realistic and not administered artificially.

To summarize, students perceived that Prunella's difficulty in the classroom context was related to a lack of self-confidence/esteem which is manifested in a fear of failure, an acceptance of failure, dependence on others, disruptive behaviour and general learning and motivational difficulties. This constitutes these students' informal declarative knowledge of motivation.

The students described strategies which include setting achievable goals, encouraging independent learning skills, offering individualised support and encouragement/positive reinforcement in order to facilitate Prunella's self-confidence. These strategies demonstrate the connection between their informal declarative knowledge and informal procedural and conditional knowledge.

Informal knowledge of psychological concepts: the learning statements

The learning statement required the students to describe their beliefs about learning which resulted in comments relating to learning and teaching. All of these responses reflect students' informal declarative knowledge of learning since they also describe concepts in naive, 'everyday' language with no evidence of relational understanding.

Learning

Of the total number of learning statements (*n* = 33), 25 students indicated qualitative conceptions or beliefs about learning in general. That is, they believed learning to be a process of making meaning as opposed to a view of learning as acquisition of information without linking to prior knowledge. In order to determine the nature of the conception of learning, responses were considered holistically:

Understanding basic content in order to develop your own ideas and opinions with the aid of others so as to increase knowledge and retain it . . . Once you have that understanding you can formulate and develop your own way of elaborating facts into opinions/ideas. Learning must involve development of oneself and one's knowledge in a particular area. (17)[4]

Of the statements that described qualitative conceptions of learning, many (*n* = 19) reported using deep approaches to learning. Typically these responses referred to actively developing individual meaning, ideas or opinions:

For the student to take in this information, to reflect critically on the information and to ultimately develop his/her own perceptions on the subject. (3)

In terms of learning outcomes, there were four responses. Three students' responses described learning outcomes that were congruent with their qualitative perspective of learning. These included feeling confident, being able to explain what you are doing and being able to interpret and understand fully. The other response described learning

---

[4] *(17) refers to the students' identification number used for the written statements.*

outcomes in terms of high grades which was congruent with that students' overall quantitative conception of learning.

The statements that were judged to be quantitative in their conceptions of teaching and learning ($n = 8$),[5] described learning as simply a process of knowledge acquisition without any construction of meaning.

Regardless of whether the response was considered qualitative or quantitative in its perspective of learning, some students ($n = 9$) considered that valuing a task was necessary for learning. There were also comments made regarding individual learning styles ($n = 3$); the range of complexities in learning task difficulty ($n = 4$); the impact of learning on other areas apart from cognition ($n = 5$) and the variety of learning environments available apart from classrooms ($n = 7$).

Teaching

Of the 12 students who responded specifically in terms of some aspect of teaching, 8 were considered to be qualitative and 4 quantitative in their overall perspective of learning. Mostly their beliefs about teaching aligned with beliefs about learning. Students with qualitative perspectives of learning described teaching in terms of an interactive process ($n = 2$); encouraging children to explore and think for themselves ($n = 4$); and some teacher guidance ($n = 3$). Students who were perceived to have a quantitative perspective of learning described teaching in terms of a variety of issues ($n = 2$) all of which are congruent with their perceptions of learning (reward for effort; people 'taught' information). One student however does not describe learning in enough detail to make a decision regarding the match between teaching and learning conceptions.

In one response a transmissive one-way view of teaching seemed to be at odds with their reported qualitative perspective of learning:

> *For the teacher to impart his knowledge and expertise on a given subject to the students. Apart from factual material, the teacher can give his/her own personal views on the subject. (3)*

In summary, the statements about learning mostly reflect qualitative conceptions of learning ($n = 25$) with corresponding deep learning strategies ($n = 19$). The quantitative results from the questionnaires presented in the next section also suggest that most students have a qualitative perspective of learning.

---

[5] *One student's response is not detailed enough to make a decision regarding their conception of learning.*

Quantitative results

Table 1 Means and standard deviations for learning variables

Variable	Mean	Standard Deviation
Collaboration	3.51	.36
Responsibility	2.18	.62
Autonomy	2.86	.63
Master goal orientation	3.52	.39
Performance goal orientation	2.84	.52
Declarative knowledge	2.89	.38
Procedural knowledge	2.66	.45
Conditional knowledge	2.79	.38
Planning	2.75	.44
Information management strategies	2.86	.38
Comprehension monitoring	2.80	.43
Debugging strategies	3.83	.60
Evaluation	2.61	.52
Surface motive	3.33	1.23
Deep motive	3.55	.71
Achieving motive	3.74	.92
Surface strategy	2.29	.80
Deep strategy	3.17	.45
Achieving strategies	3.20	.73
Surface approach	2.81	.81
Deep approach	3.69	.53
Achieving approach	3.47	.68

Mean and standard deviations for the variables measured in the four questionnaires administered are presented in Table 23.1. Inspection of the results in Table 23.1 indicate that:

1. students wanted to collaborate with their peers as well as have some freedom in their learning, however, they were reluctant to accept responsibility for their own learning;

2. students strongly preferred a mastery goal orientation in their learning rather than a performance goal orientation;

3. students generally tended to agree that they were metacognitively aware; and

4. students preferred to use deep and achieving approaches to learning as opposed to surface approaches.

To summarize, students indicated in the questionnaires that they had a preference for deep approaches to learning, generally had knowledge of and used a range of metacognitive strategies and wanted to collaborate with peers and experience freedom in their learning.

Conclusion

Formal, qualitative conceptions of learning and teaching are necessary for effective, professional teaching practice. In the scenario reflections and learning statements students described, in informal terms, qualitative conceptions of learning and a beginning knowledge of motivation. However for informal concepts to be transformed into theoretically informed, principled conceptions students need to confront powerful prior knowledge by taking responsibility for sense-making through reflection and metacognition (Biggs and Moore, 1993). Students in this study preferred deep approaches to learning, intended to master and understand the course material, generally had knowledge of and used a range of metacognitive strategies, wanted to experience freedom in their learning, and were reluctant to take responsibility for their own learning. These initial findings suggest that through the use of appropriate learning activities derived from constructivist principles, students may succeed in integrating formal and informal knowledge of learning and teaching. However, their reluctance to accept responsibility might lead to difficulties in students' developing their own perspectives.

References

Baird, J. (1991) Individual and group reflection as a basis for teacher development. In P. Hughes (ed.), *Teacher's Professional Development*. Hawthorn, Victoria: Australian Council for Educational Research.

Berliner, D. C. (1986) In pursuit of the expert pedagogue. *Educational Researcher* **15**, 5—13.

Biggs, J. B. (1989) Approaches to the enhancement of tertiary teaching. *Higher Education Research and Development* **8**, 7—25.

Biggs, J. B. (1987) *Student Approaches to Learning and Studying*. Hawthorn, Victoria: Australian Council for Educational Research.

Biggs, J. B. and Collis, K. F. (1982) *Evaluating the Quality of Learning: The SOLO Taxonomy (Structure of the Observed Learning Outcomes)*. New York: Academic Press.

Biggs, J. B. and Moore, P. J. (1993) *Processes of Learning*. Melbourne: Prentice Hall.

Borko, H. and Livingston, C. (1989) Cognition and improvisation: differences in mathematics instruction by expert and novice teachers. *American Educational Research Journal* **26**, 473—98.

Boulton-Lewis, G. M. (1994) Tertiary students' knowledge of their own learning and a SOLO taxonomy. *Higher Education* **28**, 387—402.

Boulton-Lewis, G. M. (1992). The SOLO Taxonomy and levels of knowledge of learning. Research and Development in Higher Education, 15, 482-489.

Boulton-Lewis, G. M. and Dart, B. C. (1994) Students' understanding about learning. In G. Gibbs (ed.), *Improving Student Learning*, pp. 263—77. Oxford: Oxford Centre for Staff Development.

Cole, N. S. (1990) Conceptions of educational achievement. *Educational Researcher* **19**, 2—7.

Dart, B. C. (1994a) Teaching for improved learning in small classes in higher education. Published electronically in the *Proceedings of the Australian Association for Research in Education, University of Newcastle, 27 November—1 December*.

Dart, B. C. (1994b) Measuring constructivist learning environments in tertiary education. Paper presented at the *Annual Conference of the Australian Association for Research in Education, University of Newcastle*.

Driver, R. and Bell, B. (1986) Students' thinking and learning of science. *School Science Review*, 443—56.

Driver, R. and Oldham, V. (1986) A constructivist approach to curriculum development in science. *Studies in Science Education* **13**, 105—22.

Evans, G. T. (1991) Judging approaches to pre-service teacher education by using models of knowledge and skill development. In H. W. Kam (ed.), *International Yearbook of Teacher Education 1990. Improving the Quality of the Teaching Profession*. Singapore: Institute of Education.

Gunstone, R. and White, R. (1981) Understanding of gravity. *Science Education* **65**, 291—9.

Leinhardt, G. (1990) Capturing craft knowledge in teaching. *Educational Researcher* **19**, 18—25.

Marton, F. (1981) Phenomenography — describing conceptions of the world around us. *Instructional Science* **10**, 177—200.

Marton, F., Dall'Alba, G. and Beaty, E. (1993) Conceptions of learning. *International Journal of Educational Research* **46**, 4—11.

Marzano, R. J., Brandth, R. S., Hughes, C. S., Jones, B. F., Pressersen, B. Z., Rankin, S. C. and Suhor, C. (1988) *Dimensions of Thinking*. Alexandria, Virginia: Association for Supervision and Curriculum Development.

Meade, P. and McMeniman, M. (1992) Stimulated recall — an effective methodology for examining successful teaching in science. *Australian Educational Researcher* **19**, 1—18.

Prosser, M. and Trigwell, K. (1991) Student evaluations of teaching and courses: Student learning approaches and outcomes as a criterion of validity. *Contemporary Educational Psychology* **16**, 293—301.

Prosser, M., Trigwell, K. and Taylor, P. (1994) A phenomenographic study of academics, conceptions of science learning and teaching. *Learning and Instruction* **4**, 217—31.

Richards, T. and Richards, L. (1994) Q.S.R. NUD*IST. California: Aladdin Systems Inc.

Samuelowicz, K. and Bain, J. (1992) Conceptions of teaching held by academic teachers. *Higher Education* **24**, 93—111.

Schraw, G. and Dennison, R. (1994) Assessing metacognitive awareness. *Contemporary Educational Psychology* **19**, 460—75.

Shuell, T. J. (1986) Cognitive conceptions of learning. *Review of Educational Research* **56**, 411—36.

Shulman, L. (1986) Those who understand: knowledge growth in teaching. *Educational Researcher* **15**, 4—21.

T&LiTE (1994) The Teaching and Learning in Tertiary Education (T&LiTE) Project. A report prepared for the Teaching and Learning Committee, Queensland University of Technology by the Research Concentration in Cognition in Learning and Development, School of Learning and Development, Queensland University of Technology.

Tang, T. K. W. (1993) Do teachers' beliefs influence students' learning? In J. B. Biggs and D. A. Watkins (eds), *Teaching and Learning in Hong Kong: What Is and What Might Be*. Education Papers No. 17. Hong Kong: University of Hong Kong.

Tobin, K. and Fraser, B. J. (1988) Investigations of exemplary practice in high school science and mathematics. *Australian Journal of Education* **32**, 75—94.

Trigwell, K. and Prosser, M. (1991a) Relating approaches to study and the quality of learning otcomes at the course level. *British Journal of Educational Psychology* **61**, 265—75.

Trigwell, K. and Prosser, M. (1991b) Relating learning approaches, perceptions of context, and learning outcomes. *Higher Education* **22**, 251—66.

White, R. (1988) *Learning Science*. Oxford: Basil Blackwall.

Appendix 1: Scenario for investigation

Consider the following situation:

Prunella Needshelp is a student in your Year 9 (*insert your main teaching area here*) class. She seems to be having trouble with her work, insofar as, even though her primary school and Year 8 results indicate that she is of average ability, she is achieving at a D level (*limited achievement*).

When given exercises to work, she selects the very easy ones and gives up quickly when she encounters any problems. She lacks confidence in herself and appears to be dependent on others as she continually asks other students what to do and how to do it. Prunella asks many questions of the teacher that attempt to clarify the teacher's expectations and the way she should be proceeding with the given task. She appears threatened on the occasion when a discovery or inductive learning approach is used that requires students to use initiative and independence in finding things out for themselves. When asked questions by the teacher, delivering reports to the class or working on the chalkboard, Prunella appears anxious. On receiving assignments and exam papers back, she is heard to say she was lucky when receiving a passing mark and that she was dumb on receiving a failing mark. At this stage, she has given up on her work and is becoming slightly disruptive. Other students are tiring of her interruptions.

As a result of what the teacher believes is Prunella's apathetic attitude towards her work and her limited achievement, the teacher has now given up on Prunella, she is sometimes impatient when she asks questions and the only demand that she makes on Prunella is that she is not disruptive in class.

From the information above (i) analyse the teaching/learning process as it relates to Prunella, (ii) try to identify Prunella's problems, and (iii) describe and discuss what you would do, if you were the teacher, to help Prunella's learning.

24 Learning outcomes in higher education: the impact of outcome-led design on students' conceptions of learning

Joanna Allan
University of Wolverhampton

Introduction

Gibbs (1992, p. 149—50) has commented on the 'coherent, rich and illuminating picture' provided by research into how students learn in higher education, how students develop and change and into what influences their approaches to learning, yet, as he points out, 'it has led to few changes in course design'. A fundamental change in the design of a group of modules at the University of Wolverhampton has led to the introduction of an outcome-led design which represents an attempt to harness this extensive body of research into student learning to a coherent practical model which will improve the quality of teaching and learning within higher education.

Curriculum design is concerned with defining and manipulating the principal components over which the teacher *has control* in order to maximize learning in a given context (save when curriculum is negotiated). Laurillard (1979) has suggested that the variables identified in curriculum theory — assessment, teaching and course structure — are critical in determining student learning. It has also been argued by Entwistle and Ramsden (1983, p. 111) on theoretical grounds that

> curriculum (what is to be taught and learnt), pedagogy, (how what is to be learnt is transmitted) and assessment (what counts as valid realisation of knowledge on the part of the learner) are those components of the academic environment which are most intimately related to learning.

This is not to suggest that learning is not affected by other factors, some of which obtain prior to learning, but rather that the scope of curriculum design is confined to the variables which are within the control and remit of the teacher.

The outcome-led model

The learning outcome-led model is underpinned by the principle advocated by Mager (1962) that students will learn more, and learn more quickly, if they know where they are going. More recently Ramsden's research on 4,500 students in 50 higher education institutions has led him to assert that 'it is indisputable that, from the students' perspective, clear standards and goals are a vitally important element of an effective educational experience' (1992, p. 127) and he goes on to suggest that 'clear goals and intellectual challenge' are the six key principles of effective teaching in higher education.

Figure 1 Learning outcome-led design

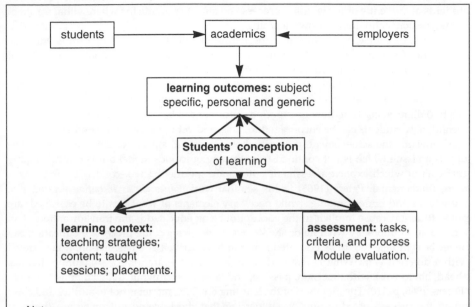

Notes:

i.   Only outcomes which are assessed are stated. Module evaluation feeds back into the outcomes – hence the two-way arrows;

ii.   The outcomes and the assessment tasks and criteria determine the nature of the learning context – hence the one-way arrows;

iii.   The outcomes, assessment and learning context are congruent, together they determine a student's conception of learning. The student's conception of learning determines the approach they adopt and ultimately the assessment tasks and criteria which are fulfilled and the outcomes they achieve. The student's conception of learning (and teaching) influence their evaluation of the module. Hence the one-way arrow from the learning experience to the students conception of learning and the two-way arrows between the student's conception of learning and the outcomes and assessment.

The essence of the model (see Figure 1), is that the anticipated outcomes, the assessment criteria and tasks are lucidly expressed, not in the jargon which is used in validation events, but in language which is intelligible to the learner.

For each individual module the outcomes are expressed in terms of subject-specific outcomes, generic academic and personal transferable outcomes. The generic academic and personal transferable outcomes which students are advised to develop during their undergraduate study are made available to students (see Appendix 1 and Appendix 2) and the outcomes of this type included in each module relate to these frameworks. Each outcomes is accompanied by an explicit statement of the assessment task and criteria designated for the assessment of that outcome (see Appendix 3). The weekly sessions are clearly stated in the module guide and relate specifically to facilitating the outcomes which have been stated. While providing a rigorous scaffold for learning the model places the students at the centre of the learning process and aims to provide the wherewithal for them to take responsibility for their own learning.

It might, of course, be argued that the nature of intellectual challenge transcends the fulfilment of specific learning outcomes, however complex and interrelated, and that it involves a journey into the unknown. Herein lies a fundamental paradox for the intention is that, while the aim is for all students to meet the same outcomes, this is not to be at the expense of independent thought, and the exclusion of serendipity learning. This dilemma has two dimensions: first, how unexpected outcomes can be recognized and rewarded and second, how students can be encouraged to meet, and yet transcend the stated outcomes, to work towards the achievement of specified outcomes and still make them their own. The first is an issue which is not confined to a learning outcomes model but is implicit in any curricula in which explicit assessment criteria are specified. The second issue is perhaps more fundamental. Peters (1965) in his seminal work *Education as Initiation* argued that knowledge and understanding, while necessary elements of what it is to be educated, are not sufficient because implicit in the concept of being educated is the transformation of an individual's outlook by what he or she knows. In this respect the process of education can never be complete for, 'to be educated is not to have arrived at a destination; it is to travel with a different view. What is required is not feverish preparation for something that lies ahead, but to work with precision, passion, and taste at worthwhile things that lie to hand.' (Peters, 1965, p. 110) The intention of the learning outcome model is not to stultify and close down the process of education by suggesting that the learning outcomes are the final destination, but rather to make use of the sharply focused outcomes and assessment tasks and criteria to influence the student's conception of learning and to thereby encourage him/her to foster deep approaches to learning.

While the context of learning is significant, the critical variable in determining the approach the student adopts, and thereby the quality of the learning outcomes which are subsequently achieved, remains the students' conception of what constitutes learning in a given context or module. Ramsden (1990, p. 29) summarizes the extensive theoretical and empirical work in student learning by stating that 'indisputable connections have been established between students' perceptions of assessment, teaching and the effectiveness of their learning'. Gibbs (1995, p. 23) confirms this relationship by asserting that the 'the connection between these underlying conceptions of learning and the approach students take to specific learning tasks is so strong that it is possible to predict the quality of learning outcomes directly from students' conceptions of learning'. Students respond to the situation and the signals which they *perceive* as tantamount to what constitutes learning in a given module. But students' interpretation is not necessarily congruent with what has been intended by the lecturer — it is this very gap between intention and actuality which curriculum design seeks to close.

Conceptions of learning

Research undertaken by Van Rossum and Schenk (1984) with first-year undergraduate psychology students based on the study of a text, confirmed the assertion by Marton and Säljö (1976) that there is a relationship between study strategy and learning outcome with new study material, and of Säljö's (1979) assertion that there is a relationship between learning conception and the study strategy adopted by students, 'the strategy followed by a subject is connected with his/her learning conception and with the quality of the learning outcome' (Van Rossum and Schenk, 1984, p. 82). They also found that 'a large number of students begin their study with a fundamentally reproductive learning conception', and that female students have 'significantly more often a reproductive learning conception' (1984, p. 79).

The categorization of students' conception of learning by Van Rossum and Schenk was based on early research in student learning undertaken by Säljö (1979) in which five distinctly different conceptions of learning were identified. Further work by Van Rossum and Schenk, (1984) Giorgi (1986), and Martin and Ramsden (1987) was isomorphic with Säljö's findings and has accordingly established five discrete conceptions of learning (A—E listed in Table 1). A sixth conception — Changing as a person — was posited by Van Rossum and Taylor (1987) and replicated by Marton *et al.* (1992) and has been added to the original five categories.

Table 1 Categories describing conceptions of learning

> *quantitative*
> A Increasing ones knowledge;
> B Memorizing and reproducing
> C Applying;
> *qualitative*
> D Understanding;
> E Seeing something in a different way;
> F Changing as a person

These conceptions are seen as hierarchical with each conception subsuming those that precede it. The conceptions differ qualitatively. As Entwistle (1991, p. 2) has pointed out, 'it appears that there is a major distinction between whether learning is seen as requiring the *reproduction* of information presented, or the *transformation* of that information in the process of coming to understand it for oneself'. The conceptions are thus defined within a quantitative qualitative dichotomy in which conceptions A, B and C are perceived as being quantitative and D, E and F as qualitative (see Table 1).

Taylor (1993) working at Queensland University of Technology in Australia used these categories to analyse students' statements on learning and to classify their responses in terms of the conceptions he and his colleagues found. Table 2 shows that, 'the majority of undergraduate respondents saw learning as less complex than understanding' Taylor (1994, p. 72) and that the majority of undergraduate students held an essentially quantitative view of learning which is consistent with the findings of Biggs and Moore (1992, p. 20).

Table 2 Proportion of undergraduates expressing each conception

	Conceptions of learning						
	A	B	C	D	E	F	Total
Number of responses	160	156	137	321	47	20	841
% for each response	19.0	18.5	16.3	38.1	5.6	2.4	

Source: Taylor, 1994, p. 72.

While the largest category saw learning as about understanding, the proportion who saw learning as being associated with seeing something in a different way or changing as a person was quite small. A comparison between undergraduates' and their teachers' conceptions of learning in the study confirmed Morgan's (1993) suggestion that students are not likely to hold as qualitative a conception of learning as their lecturers. Since students' approach to learning, and ultimately the level of outcome which is achieved in a certain learning context will be determined by his/her conception of learning, then this mismatch suggests that students will be unlikely to meet their teachers' expectations. This has serious consequences in a learning context in which the expected outcomes are consistent with the lecturers' conception of learning. The categorization of students' conception of learning and the extent to which the learning outcome-led model has resulted in a closer relationship between lecturers' and students' conceptions of learning in traditional and outcome-led modules are thus the key research issues which are addressed in this paper.

Method

The research approach was from a phenomenographical perspective which involves an enquiry into how the world is construed by students and their interpretations of their learning contexts. As such, it is what Marton (1981) refers to as a second order activity for which the underlying rationale 'is that people act on their interpretation of the situations they find themselves in rather than on the objective, matter-of-fact characteristics of situations' (Säljö, 1988, p. 36).

The study involved a number of interrelated data collection instruments:

- focus group interviews with 73 students in 6 groups, studying traditional and learning outcome designed modules;
- a written response to the following statement by 84 students each studying one of three learning outcome-led modules and 33 students each studying one of two traditional modules:

*I want you to focus on this module and write about a page on your ideas about learning in **this** module. Please consider:*

i what you actually mean by learning, what you think learning is in this module;

ii what you know about your own learning **in this module;**

iii how you actually go about learning **in this module;**

iv how you know you have learned something **in this module.**

There are no right answers, I am interested in your perceptions related to learning **in this module.**

- a questionnaire to the students to ascertain respondents age, sex and level of awareness of the design of the module;

- recorded interviews of academic staff who were teaching the modules on which the written statements regarding conceptions of learning were made.

The categorization of the written statements on students' conceptions of learning was based on the 'Categories describing conceptions of learning' (Table 1). Detailed insight into the discrete nature of each category was gleaned from Marton *et al.* (1992). However a number of students used a construct which did not readily apply to any of the given categories, and consequently it was ascribed, by the researcher, to an appropriate category and added to the detailed descriptions used to decode the data. The students expressed the construct as 'raising awareness/gaining a broader view of . . .'. This was deemed to be consistent with Marton *et al.*'s (1992) 'pole' of acquiring knowledge, gaining more pieces of knowledge without the learner's seeking to use what has been learned and was thus assigned to category A — Increasing one's knowledge.

The responses in respect of conceptions of learning from the focus groups, the written statements of the students and the interviews of academic staff were all analysed using the taxonomy posited in Table 1.

The modules are classified according to level. Level 1 represents first-year undergraduate work, level 2 represents second-year undergraduate work and level 3 final-year undergraduate work. There was no level 1 traditional module available in the subject portfolio of modules analysed.

Results and discussion

Conceptions of learning in learning outcome-led modules

The students' level of awareness of the outcome-led modules was very high at each of the undergraduate levels. 100% of all of the respondents were aware that they were studying outcome-led modules, 71.4% from the first session of the module and 28.6% by the time they were working on their first assignment. 100% at each level were conscious that the outcomes were defined in terms of subject specific and transferable skills and 89.2% were aware of the inclusion of 'generic academic outcomes'. Out of the 9 respondents who were not aware of the generic academic outcomes 5 were at level 1, 1 at level 2 and 2 at level 3 (see Table 3).

Table 3   *Relationship between the lack of awareness of 'generic academic outcomes' and students' conception of learning*

Level of module	Age	Conception of learning
level 1	36 – 40	D
level 1	18 – 21	B
level 1	18 – 21	B
level 1	18 – 21	B
level 1	18 – 21	B
level 2	22 – 30	C
level 3	18 – 21	B
level 3	22 – 30	B
level 3	31 – 35	B

While the level 1 respondent, a mature student, had a conception of learning assigned to category D — understanding — the remaining four students at level 1 were classified in the quantitative category B of memorizing and reproducing. At level 3, three out of the four students who were in the B category were also unaware of the academic outcomes. These data are taken from a small sample (84 respondents), but it does suggest the need for further research to ascertain whether there is a causal link between a lack of full appreciation of the anticipated outcomes and the conception of learning which students have acquired.

Table 4 Conceptions of learning in learning outcome-led modules

	Conceptions of learning						
	A	B	C	D	E	F	Total
responses level 1	0	18	4	21	1	0	44
% of responses level 1	0	41	9	48	2	0	
responses level 2	0	3	15	1	1	0	20
% of responses level 2	0	15	75	5	5	0	
responses level 3	0	4	4	12	0	0	20
% of responses level 3	0	20	20	60	0	0	
Total responses	0	25	23	34	2	0	84
% of responses	0	30	27	40	2	0	

As Table 4 shows there is a clustering of conceptions at level 1 in the quantitative category B (40.9%) and in the qualitative category D (47.7%). There is no apparent explanation for this dichotomy which requires further study. None of the 44 level 1 respondents was categorized in conception A in which increasing one's knowledge is seen as the sole purpose of learning. This data is at variance with that of Taylor (1994) who found that 19% of undergraduate students saw learning as a process of gaining more knowledge and Van Rossum and Schenk (1984, p. 82) who found that 'a large number of students begin their study with a fundamentally reproductive learning conception'. It is perhaps even more notable given that Taylor's sample was taken across all years of undergraduate study, while this data refers to first-year undergraduate (level 1) students where a less qualitative conception of learning might well be expected. An analysis of the responses from all three years of undergraduate study on the learning outcome-led modules also shows that none of the 84 respondents was classified in conception A. While this might be attributable to the nature of the subject from which the modules were taken, this explanation does not account for the disparity between the number of students classified as conception A in the learning outcome and traditional modules, both types of which were taken from the Education Studies portfolio.

Table 5 Conceptions of learning in Traditional modules

| | Conceptions of learning | | | | | | |
	A	B	C	D	E	F	Total
responses level 2	3	9	5	1	1	0	19
% of responses level 2	16	47	26	5	5	0	
responses level 3	1	4	8	1	0	0	14
% of responses level 3	7	29	57	7	0	0	
responses	4	13	13	2	1	0	33
% of responses	12	39	39	6	3	0	

As Table 5 shows 15.8% of respondents at level 2 and 7.1% at level 3 (12.1% overall) studying traditional modules were assigned to conception A compared with no respondents on the learning outcome-led modules. The lower figure of 7.1% of respondents for level 3, as opposed to 15.8% at level 2 is consistent with expectations that students will acquire an increasingly qualitative conception of learning as undergraduate study progresses. The percentage is lower than that found by Taylor (1994), but the traditional module sample in this study did not include level 1 students where a higher proportion of respondents in category A might reasonable be expected to be placed. These results suggest tentatively that students studying learning outcome-led modules have acquired a more qualitative conception of learning than might be expected of undergraduate students.

These data reflect the comments made by students in the focus groups where none of the respondents studying learning outcome-led modules saw learning as solely the acquisition of knowledge. Analysis of the level 1 focus group was consistent with the dichotomy between the perception of learning as memorizing and reproducing material for assessment purposes (conception B) and as understanding, grasping new ideas and gaining insight into relationships between ideas principles and concepts (conception D) which was found in the written statements.

The following verbatim comments from students' statements at level 1 were classified as conception B:

> *I think learning is having lectures, taking in facts, also showing that you have learned information through doing assignments. (R (Respondent) 006)*

> *I try to use memory skills in order to retain information and use it for assignments, but whether my understanding is correct or not I do not know. (R011)*

> *Learning is about learning information in order to write the assignment essay and to give a presentation. (R017)*

> *Learning is about finding out information and being able to regurgitate it. (R030)*

and the following as conception D:

> *Learning in this module involves considering all different points of view, of being aware of the dilemmas in post-16 education and understanding the future implications. (R001)*

> *I realise that I have learnt something if I am able to talk about topics and ideas related to the module quite confidently and discuss and argue different points coherently. (RO12)*

> *In this module I need to learn a lot about issues related to post 16 education and challenge them . . . this is the point when I can start to critically examine the issues. (R016)*

Analysis of the level 2 learning outcome-led module reveals a quite different distribution, 75.0% of respondents being classified as having conception C (see Table 4). Verbatim comments classified in this category include the following:

> *Learning in this module is about using information learnt in the lectures to do research. (R058)*

> *Learning is about how you go about doing research and about actually doing it. (R060)*

> *It's about learning new theories of conducting research and using them. (R068)*

> *Learning is about forming a basis for successfully completing a research project, rather than factual learning. (R073)*

The high number of respondents who saw learning as applying knowledge and procedures is wholly consistent with the outcomes of the module (see Appendix 3) which state unequivocally that this module on educational research methodology requires students *to apply* principles and procedures to a piece of small-scale research. The practical perspective of the level 2 module and the consequent high proportion of students placed in category C explain the low incidence (1 respondent out of 20 respondents) of conception D at level 2 in relation to both the level 1 (21 out of 44 respondents) and level 3 modules (12 out of 20 respondents) (see Table 4). These data are out of kilter with Taylor's (1994) findings in respect of the extent of the clustering around a single category, the high proportion of students whose perception of learning is in category C and the very low incidence of conception D.

The data for the level 2 learning outcome module differ considerably from the level 3 module. As might be expected the incidence of conception D — understanding — is higher at this level than at both levels 1 and 2. Verbatim comments include the following:

> *It's about the various factors affecting appraisal and its contentiousness as an issue — we need to discuss the issues involved and relate them to other areas. (R089)*

> *Learning is about the complexities of appraisal and how it affects my work as a trainer. It's about holding a meaningful debate about appraisal. (R091)*

> *Learning in this module is about the context, history and mechanics of appraisal as well as understanding the issues in its use. (R093)*

60% (12 out of 20 respondents) were classified in category D — understanding — (see Table 4). This figure is much higher than Taylor's (1994) data which gave a percentage of 38.1% but Taylor's findings were across all undergraduate levels and gives no indication of the percentage of students at level 3 who were placed in category D. However when all three learning outcome modules are taken together 40.4% of respondents were classified in conception D which corresponds closely to Taylor's (1994) figure of 38.1% of students in this category. This contrasts with the data from the traditional modules (see Table 5) which places only 6.0% (2 out of 33) of students in category D overall and where the highest proportion of students fall equally between categories B and C.

As can be appreciated from Table 4 20% (4 out of 20) of respondents on the level 3 learning outcome-led module were classified in each of categories B and C and no students were deemed to have conceptions A, E or F. The absence of any respondents from categories A and F across the three learning outcome-led modules also suggests that students share a perception of what learning is not about in the given modules. This consensus is shared by respondents from the traditional modules (see Table 5) in respect of category F no students seeing changing as a person being related to what learning is about in a specific module, but not, as discussed, in respect of conception A.

The data from the level 3 module represent a distinct clustering around a single conception of learning as in the level 2 learning outcome module. At level 1 clustering was also apparent but at this level in respect of two categories B and D. This suggests that students share a conception of what constitutes learning in the learning outcome-led modules. This is also apparent to a lesser extent in the traditional modules (see Table 5) where 47.4% (9 out of 19) of respondents in the level 2 module were placed in category B and 57.1% (8 out of 14) in the level 3 module were placed in category C. However the crucial difference lies in the relationship between how students and lecturers conceive learning in these modules and whether the clusters represent mismatch or congruence between their conceptions.

Congruence between students' and lecturers' conceptions of learning

Table 6 shows how the module lecturers conceive learning in the learning outcome and traditional modules. In the level 1 learning outcome-led a module team of lecturers was involved in the delivery and all three lecturers were interviewed. There was congruence between the conceptions held by each member of the module team.

Table 6   *Lecturers' conceptions of learning in the learning outcome and traditional modules*

	Conceptions of learning				
	A	B	C	D	E
outcome-led modules					
level 1				√	
level 2			√		
level 3				√	
Traditional modules					
level 2				√	
level 3				√	

Analysis of the interviews with level 1 lecturers showed that all three emphasized both the acquisition of basic knowledge and concepts and the understanding and analysis of different perspectives and consequently their conception was categorized as D. Critical comments in determining the category of conception are highlighted in the Verbatim extracts from the interviews below:

*I think it's really about, it's about getting hold of an enormous amount of information and **analysing** that information, **selecting** that information. **Looking critically** at that information. And all that information has a particular set of concepts and vocabulary about it, which is to do with education training . . . I sort of start off at the beginning of the module, I say we are going to have loads of debates about education, but we could, we could have debates that aren't a million miles away from this about other aspects of kind of British society and British life. So you need to think about **the underlying issues** here. You know, the social issues, the political issues and the economic issues. Then, maybe we can get some interest out of transferring them into education. (Lecturer 1)*

*Oh, there must pick up an awful lot about the education system post 16 . . . We are giving them tools, we are giving them knowledge. We're asking them to learn, you know, we, we are providing them with the opportunity to pick up knowledge. But we are also giving them , hopefully, trying to get them to **understand, analyse** and to be critical but at a less sophisticated level than at level 2 — that's how I see it. (Lecturer 2)*

*There's a certain amount of content they'd expect to know, which is one level. There's an understanding, and **an articulation of different views on that content,** if you like — **perspectives**. There's an understanding that many things to do with people, involving people, are relative, and **the complex nature of the issues**. That's what I'd expect them to understand at the end of it, to varying degrees. I suppose that there's a factual element and there's also the point that **things are never quite as straight forward as made out, there's different ways of seeing the same thing, the same facts**. (Lecturer 3)*

The interview with the level 2 lecturer revealed a different conception in which the emphasis on the module is unequivocally about the application of research principles to a practical project (conception C). The extract from the interview with the lecturer below illustrates this point:

*So what do I think learning is about? Well I think very quickly they have to **learn something about the paradigms and therefore about the theoretical underpinning of education and social studies research**. So there is an element of that which is theoretical and based upon clear academic argument. However, they also then have to learn to interpret that **and apply** it in a practical sense. So I think in this, within this module, there is the, that application of **theory to practice**, . . . They're learning how to develop a train of thought in argument, and also I think, they're learning a **process of writing a project**. Yes a process, and we give them quite a structured process, and they learn each part of that process. So they learn what we mean by the theoretical underpinning, they learn about the methods of data collection and analysis and they learn about presenting that information . . . I think they need to have a knowledge of processes, a knowledge of how everything works and **then apply it to a particular situation**.*

Marton *et al*. (1992) describe this category as emphasizing application within what they call the 'external horizon' which is 'in the learner's life world' (p. 287); this is consistent with the application to a student project which is referred to by the lecturer in the extract above. Marton *et al*. (1992) also suggest that while the distinguishing feature of the conception remains application, reference to the acquisition phase may well be made. This aspect is also reflected in the lecturer's inclusion of the acquisition of underpinning theory and knowledge of data collection instruments in his statement and firmly places his conception within the C category.

Discussion with the module tutor for the level 3 module resulted in a categorization of that module in conception D (see below).

*I **expect a formal sophisticated understanding of the fact that there are different perspectives**. If you look at how a level one student articulates it, often it is not as clear in their articulation as some of the level 3. It's not as well referenced, it's not as well argued, the points aren't made so clearly, **it's shallower, effectively**. . . . They need to understand the fact that you can **have four arguments and you must not consider any of them wrong, they are different stand points of the same thing**. Now in this module student need to articulates that, to know it, presents it very well to give a good level of intellectual argument.*

The lecturer for this module was the same person as 'lecturer 3' on level 1 learning outcome-led module. He saw a progression from the 'shallower' perspectives which might be expected at level 1 to greater sophistication at level 3. This, however, is reflected in the criteria which are used to assess the students' work rather than in the categorization of the conception *per se*. While the development of different perspectives is a feature of conception E as well as D, the former strongly emphasizes what Marton *et al*. (1992) call the 'external horizon' as being 'located in the world beyond the study situation' (1992, p. 291), such that the student has a different view of the world and changes his or her conception of something and interpretation of reality. As these aspects were not articulated by the respondent the conception was assigned to category D — understanding.

An analysis of the interviews of the lecturers on the traditional modules resulted in their conceptions of what learning was about in their modules being categorized as E at level 2 and D at level 3. The comments below are from the level 2 lecturer on the traditional module:

*Well I suppose, fundamentally, it's about **getting their head round issues** surrounding the content of the module across the age range, across the life span. So that the outcome is an awareness, **an ability to develop thinking skills**, then they can **critically analyse** what is actually happening, . . . in society and in schools and in further education. . . . if you like, an ability to **really use*** *information really in a very sophisticated fashion. . . . to develop thinking skills and apply that thinking to whatever the context.*

The extract illustrates that the lecturer sees the external horizon as being in 'society, schools and further education' which is consistent with Marton *et al.* (1992) definition of conception E as located within 'the world beyond the study situation' rather than D which is confined to the students life-world. The lecturer also emphasizes the development of critical thinking skills which can be related to 'what is actually happening'. Marton *et al.* (1992, p. 291) suggest that 'conceptions D and E form a pair in which the former relates to the acquisition phase and the latter to the application phase, as with conceptions A and C'. The emphasis on application of critical skills together with the wider horizon suggested by the level 2 lecturer resulted in her conception of learning for this module being categorized as E.

The level 3 traditional module lacked the wider external horizon apparent in the level 2 module being confined to the study situation. The module is concerned with the application of knowledge and skills as the comments below indicate:

> *Right. I think learning in this module is partly about, it's learning . . . some of the views some of the concepts about learning and training, about how people learn. Ideas about good practice in training, . . . It's about practising, planning and preparing to train or teach people. It's about **learning how to look critically at that**, I think . . . Students need to spin off from, kind of practical **concrete things to do with learning or training, to some of the kind of debates** to do with conceptual, you know criticising, synthesising, conceptually engaging in debates about those things in a sense more conventionally academic that those things generate.*

But this application is related to the students life-world, rather than being contextualized in a wider context and thus places the conception firmly within category C. This is the category in which 57.1% (8 out of 14) of the respondents were placed. However the lecturer also conceives the module as being about critically examining the issues surrounding training which represents the 'qualitative' aspect of the conception which suggests category D in which the module was placed.

Table 7   *Congruence between students' and lecturers' conceptions of learning defined by level*

	Conceptions of learning					
	A	B	C	D	E	F
outcome-led modules						
level 1	0	41	9	48	2	0
level 2	0	25	70	0	5	0
level 3	0	20	20	60	0	0
Traditional modules						
level 2	16	47	26	5	5	0
level 3	7	29	57	7	0	0

Table 7 gives the percentage of students whose conceptions of learning were assigned to each category and in bold indicates the conception held by each lecturer or team of lecturers based on the analysis discussed in this section. The degree of congruence in the learning outcome-led module is high being 47.7% (21 students), 70.0% (15 students) and 60.0% (12 students) respectively at levels 1, 2 and 3. This contrasts with the single respondent at level 2 and at level 3 on the traditional modules who held conceptions of learning congruent with those of their lecturers. 94.7% of students on the level 2 traditional module and 92.9% of students on the level 3 traditional module held conceptions of learning which were in a lower category than their lecturers. These findings confirm Morgan's (1993) assertion that lecturers are likely to hold a more sophisticated conception of learning than their students. The data also contrasts markedly with the learning outcome-led module where 50%, 25% and 40% of respondents at levels 1, 2 and 3 respectively held a less sophisticated conception.

Conclusion

The aim of this study was to undertake research into the effect of learning outcome-led design on students' conceptions of learning and to investigate how students and lecturers conceive of learning in given modules. The findings for the traditional modules are consistent with those of previous research into students' conceptions of learning undertaken by Taylor (1994) and Morgan (1993), whereas the results from the learning outcome-led modules suggest that the redesign has led to changes in how students perceive learning.

First, there is a greater clustering of conceptions in learning outcome-led modules than in traditional modules. Second, as Table 7 suggests, the learning outcome-led design has resulted in a much greater degree of congruence between how lecturers and students regard learning. This contrasts with the mismatch between the conceptions of learning held by lecturers and students studying the traditional modules. Third, the conceptions held by students on learning outcome-led modules span fewer categories. Tables 4 and 5 show that no students on either type of module holds a conception categorized as F, and that no students on learning outcome-led modules hold a view consistent with conception A.

A relational view of learning as expressed by Ramsden (1988) suggests that improving learning is about changing students' conception of learning. An impressive body of research (Entwistle and Ramsden, 1983; Watkins, 1983; Marton and Säljö, 1976, 1984; Van Rossum and Schenk, 1984; Biggs, 1987; and Whelan, 1988) has justified unequivocally Säljö's assertion that students' conception of learning profoundly affect their approach to learning and that, in turn, there is congruence between the approach adopted and the quality and quantity of the learning outcomes. The module design adopted in this study sought to articulate clearly how the lecturer conceived learning in each module and to raise the students' consciousness in respect of what learning is about. While the findings of this study are based on a relatively small sample of respondents, they suggest that the outcome-led design can contribute to changing students' conceptions of learning and thereby to improving the quality of teaching and learning within modular courses.

References

Allan, J., Bottley, J., Green, P., Jennings, S., Penfold, B., Somervell, H. and Wanklyn, M. (1994) *Record of Achievement Project*. University of Wolverhampton.

Biggs, J. (1987) Process and outcome in essay writing. *Research and Development in Higher Education* 9114—25.

Biggs, J. and Moore, P. (1992) *The Process of Learning*, 3rd edn. Sydney: Prentice-Hall.

Entwistle, N. (1984) Contrasting perspectives on learning. In Marton, F., Hounsell, D. and Entwistle, N. (eds), *The Experience of Learning*. Edinburgh: Scottish Educational Press.

Entwistle, N. (1988) Motivational factors in students' approaches to learning. In Schmeck, R. (ed.), *Learning Strategies and Learning Styles*. New York: Plenum.

Entwistle, N. and Entwistle, A. (1991) *Developing, Revising and Examining Conceptual Understanding in Degree Courses: The Student Experience and its Implications*. University of Edinburgh.

Entwistle, N. and Ramsden, P. (1983) *Understanding Student Learning*. London: Croom Helm.

Entwistle, N., Hanley, M. and Hounsell, D. (1979) Identifying distinctive approaches to studying. *Higher Education* 8, 365—80.

Entwistle, N. and Tait, H. (1990) Approaches to learning, evaluations of teaching, and preferences for contrasting academic environments. *Higher Education* 19, 169—94.

Fransson, A. (1977) On qualitative differences in learning. iv: effects of motivation and test anxiety on process and outcome. *British Journal of Educational Psychology* 47, 244—57.

Gaff, J., Crombag, H. and Chang, T. (1976) Environments for learning in a Dutch University. *Higher Education* 8, 285—99.

Gibbs, G. (1992) Improving the quality of student learning through course design. In Barnett, R. (1992) *Learning to Effect*, Buckingham: SRHE.

Gibbs, G. (1995) Changing lecturers' conceptions of learning through action research. In A. Brew (ed.), *Directions in Staff Development*. Buckingham: SRHE and Open University Press.

Giorgi, A. (1986) A phenomenological analysis of descriptions pf conceptions of learning obtained from a phenomenological perspective. In Marton, F. Dall'Alba, G. and Beaty, E. (1992) Conceptions of learning. *International Journal of Educational Research* 19, 277—300.

Laurillard, D. (1979) The processes of student learning. *Higher Education* 8, 395—409.

Mager, R. (1962) *Preparing Instructional Objectives*, rev. 2nd edn. California: David Lake Publisher.

Martin, E. and Ramsden, P. (1987) Learning skills or skill in learning? In Richardson, J., Eysenck, M. and Wareen Piper, D. (eds), *Student Learning Research in Education and Cognitive Psychology*. Milton Keynes: Open University Press.

Marton, F. (1981) Phenomenography — describing conceptions of the world around us. *Instructional Science* **10**, 177—200.

Marton, F. and Säljö, R. (1976) On qualitative differences in learning: 1 — outcome and process. *British Journal of Educational Psychology* **46**, 4—11.

Marton, F. Dall'Alba, G. and Beaty, E. (1992) Conceptions of learning. *International Journal of Educational Research* **19**, 277—300.

Marton, F. and Säljö, R. (1984) Approaches to learning. In Marton, F., Hounsell, D. and Entwistle, N. (eds), *The Experience of Learning*. Edinburgh: Scottish Educational Press.

Morgan, A. (1993) *Improving Your Students' Learning: Reflections on the Experience of Study*. London: Kogan Page.

O'Neil, M. (1995) Towards a model of the learner in higher education: some implications for teachers. In Smith, B. and Brown, S., *Research Teaching and Learning in HE*. London: Kogan Page.

Peters, R. (1965) Education as initiation. In Archambault, R. (ed.), *Philosophical Analysis and Education*. New York: Humanities Press.

Ramsden, P. (1979) Student learning and perceptions of the academic environment. *Higher Education* **8**, 411—28.

Ramsden, P. (ed.) (1988) *Improving Learning: New Perspectives*. London: Kogan Page.

Ramsden, P. (1990) *Evaluating Teaching: Supporting Learning*. Brisbane: Annual Conference of the Higher Education Research and Development Society of Australasia.

Ramsden, P. (1991) A performance indicator of teaching quality in higher education: the course experience questionnaire. *Studies in Higher Education* **16**(2), 129—50.

Ramsden, P. (1992) *Learning to Teach in Higher Education*. London: Routledge.

Ramsden, P. and Entwistle, N. (1981) Effects of academic departments on students' approaches to studying. *British Journal of Educational Psychology* **51**, 368—83.

Säljö, R. (1979) *Learning in the Learner's Perspective. 1: Some Common Sense Conceptions*. Reports from the Institute of Education, University of Göteborg, No. 76.

Säljö, R. (1988) Learning in educational settings: methods of inquiry. In Ramsden, P. (ed.), *Improving Learning: New Perspectives*. London: Kogan Page.

Svensson, L. (1984) Skill in learning. In Marton *et al.* (1984) *The Experience of Learning*. Edinburgh: Scottish Educational Press.

Taylor, P. (1993) *Focusing Tertiary Teaching on Learning*. Paper delivered at the 5th European Conference of EARLI. Aix en Provence, 31 August to 5 September 1993.

Taylor, P. (1994) Learning about learning: teachers' and students' conceptions. In Nightingale, P. and O'Neil, M., *Achieving Quality in Learning in Higher Education*. London: Kogan Page.

Van Rossum, E. and Schenk, S. (1984) The relationship between learning conception, study strategy and learning outcome. *British Journal of Educational Psychology* **54**, 73—83.

Van Rossum, E. and Taylor, I. (1987) *The relationship between conceptions of learning and good teaching: a scheme of cognitive development*. San Francisco: paper presented at the Annual Meeting of the American Educational Research Association.

Watkins, D. (1983) Depth of processing and the quality of learning outcomes. *Instructional Science* **12**, 49—58.

Whelan, G. (1988) Improving medical students' clinical problem-solving. In Ramsden, P., *Improving Learning: New Perspectives*. London: Kogan Page.

Appendix 1: Generic academic outcomes

1. Make use of information

Criteria:
- supplement notes with appropriate reading;
- reference correctly;
- select and use relevant references and quotation to support the points you are making;
- use specialist texts and journals to substantiate your arguments;
- draw together material from a variety of sources into a coherent argument.

2. Analyse

Criteria:
- identify ideas, concepts and principles that underpin theories in your subjects;
- explain the relationship between different elements of a theory;
- distinguish between evidence and argument and hypothesis;
- evaluate ideas and concepts;
- recognize the difference between assertion and argument;
- recognize and acknowledge inconsistencies in arguments.

3. Think critically

Criteria:
- examine problems from a number of perspectives;
- question and challenge viewpoints, ideas and concepts;
- make judgments about the value of evidence, concepts and ideas;
- develop and be able to justify your own opinions on significant ideas and concepts in your own subject.

4. Synthesise ideas and information

Criteria:
- relate new ideas and concepts to previous ones;
- relate theoretical ideas to practical tasks;
- integrate learning from different modules you have studied;
- organize and structure ideas, concepts and theories into a coherent whole.

Allan *et al.* (1994) Record of Achievement project. University of Wolverhampton.

PERSONAL TRANSFERABLE SKILLS

The ability to:

1. Communicate effectively:

i. Writing skills:- write accurately and effectively in a variety of structured formats (e.g. essay, reports, instructions), and demonstrate the appropriate conventions in each. Recognise different audiences and demonstrate use of appropriate writing styles, and relate these to appropriate audiences.

ii Oral presentation skills:- give present material in a variety of structured formats (e.g. formal presentations, formal and informal explanations, instructions). Recognise different audiences and make use appropriate styles, including interactive responses.

2. Organise

Identify and use existing resources effectively; develop flexibility in approaches to the management of work in hand. Recognise task demands and manage time effectively. Monitor, review and reflect upon self-management.

3. Gather Information

Gather information (archival and library material, data, statistics) and develop effective storage and retrieval systems. Interpret, analyse and synthesise material in a variety of forms (statistical or textual data, in an appropriate context)

4. Use Information Technology

Create, store, send and retrieve data in a variety of forms (word-processing, E mail, databases, spreadsheets, graphics). Make effective use of information from a variety of sources e.g. CD-ROM, JANET, Internet.

5. Act Independently

Develop autonomy, initiative, self-motivation and resourcefulness; demonstrate decision-making and problem-solving skills. Assess progress, and monitor, review and reflect upon own performance and achievements.

6. Work in Teams

Work co-operatively in groups, share decision-making and negotiate with others. Awareness and ability to adopt a variety of roles. Listen to relevant opinions before reaching decisions and relate the ideas of others to the task in hand. Evaluate the strengths and weaknesses of group effectiveness and of own performance within it.

7. Numeracy

Process numerical information related to real-life problems and interpret the outcomes. Develop sufficient symbolic and vocabulary skills to express and interpret a variety of coded statements.

It is important to remember that self-assessment should be incorporated into all of the above, in order that students can: identify learning processes and gains made; develop self-knowledge and the ability to reflect upon effectiveness; record, monitor and review progress; make decisions about further development of skills.

Allan et al (1994) Record of Achievement project. University of Wolverhampton.

Appendix iii LEARNING OUTCOMES OF THE LEVEL 2 MODULE

Subject specific outcomes
1. Make a clear statement of a research issue and appropriate research questions.
Range
Small-scale case study research.
Assessment
Written assignment, self- assessment

2. Select and justify a research approach, appropriate for a specific research issue.
Range
Scientific, Interpretive and Action Research paradigms. Eclectic approach.
Assessment
Written assignment, self- assessment

3. Select and justify an appropriate methodology and data collection instruments, for a specific research issue.
Range
Interviews, questionnaires observation.
Assessment
Written assignment, self- assessment

4. Identify the major sources of literature relevant to a given research issue.
Range
Publications from Britain and USA, 1985 onwards.
Assessment
Written assignment self- assessment

5. Apply knowledge of validity, triangulation & research ethics to a given research issue.
Range
Small-scale case study
Assessment
Written assignment, self- assessment

6.Write, pilot, use and evaluate data collection instruments.
Range
Interviews, questionnaires, observation
Assessment
Presentation
Personal Transferable Outcomes
Communicate Effectively - oral presentation skills
Range
whole group involvement
Assessment
Presentation

Gather Information - Analyse and present data.
Range
Small-scale, data from interviews, questionnaires and observation
Assessment
Presentation

Work in Teams
Range
Seminar work & group presentation
assessment
written assignment, self-assessment, log-book

Presentation
Organise - Self-assessment
Range
Directed time, in seminars, group work
Assessment
Log-book

Academic outcomes
Make use of information
Range
small-scale research
Assessment
Written assignment, presentation

Analyse
Range
small-scale research
Assessment
Written assignment, presentation

Think critically
Range
small-scale research
Assessment
Written assignment, presentation

25 The wretched document: an analysis of the talk and perceptions of academic staff on the process and procedure of validation and review, course planning and teaching preparation

David Woodman
Roehampton Institute London

and Marcus Redley
University of Surrey

Background

This piece of research arose out of an apparent widespread antipathy, on the part of academic staff, towards the formalization and regulation of scrutiny and validation procedures in higher education. There was anecdotal evidence of a growing hypocrisy in the preparation of validation documents. These documents were treated by some staff as cut off from the activities of teaching and learning; the very activities they were meant both to describe and validate. Complying with the recommended institutional guidelines was frequently met with exasperation expressed in terms like 'I can't see what difference it will make but if that is what you want then ...'

There are differences between institutions that can account for the specific development of their validation and scrutiny procedures. The unique and peculiar history of Roehampton Institute London, the institution in which this research was carried out, created the conditions which justified its heavy-handed approach to academic scrutiny. It had been through a series of tests of its procedures in order to gain accreditation from its validating university and to be awarded the power to confer its own degrees by the Higher Education Quality Council. Consequently, there was a tendency to leave nothing to chance which resulted in a strong, centrally organized, defence replete with double-checking sweepers. Hence the scrutiny system had been designed with control and regulation in mind and this had inevitable consequences for the autonomy and independence of academic staff, leading to expressions of dissatisfaction and disaffection.

As chair of the Institute's Teaching and Learning Committee one of the authors was interested in the impact, if any, that this formalization of procedure was having on the activities of teaching and learning. It seemed to many staff that we were moving away from a system that supported and relied upon professional competence and expertise to one in which these values were undermined.

The purpose of the research, therefore, was to investigate the connections between validation procedures and documents on the one hand and teaching and learning on the other. The space between the validation process and teaching and learning is occupied by the planning and preparing of courses and programmes of study, including the preparation of individual teaching sessions. It was decided that this should be the focus of the research. How do staff talk about the preparation of their teaching and what are their frames of reference?

Methodology

To gather the data the Institute employed a researcher/interviewer (Marcus Redley) to conduct qualitative interviews with 24 members of staff selected from a range of departments.[1] The interviews, which lasted half-an-hour, were tape-recorded and transcribed. The interview questions ranged between: how classes, modules and degree programmes were planned; the use and writing of module booklets for students; and the use and writing of validation documents. The analysis of the transcribed interviews has taken two forms.

1. the interviewer's analysis of the interview data as the talk-of-academics with its displays of professional competence; this is the form adopted in the researcher's/interviewer's analysis;

2. an analysis of the interviewer's analysis and the transcribed documents that makes inferences about the conditions and circumstances described by the respondents to understand the politics of regulation implicit in the validation process.

Our analysis, in fact, mirrors some of the conceptual and intellectual dilemmas articulated by many of the respondents. For many staff their perception of their teaching preparation and planning is couched in terms of the subject and its applications ie. between intrinsic value and extrinsic worth. Similarly, the first analysis works on the rhetorics of academics' talk while the second attempts to contextualize that talk within politics and structures of higher education. The repertoires and rhetorics used by staff in describing their planning and preparation are related to a micro-politics within the institution and an academic macro-politics beyond it. It is our hope that we have achieved a rapprochement, if not a reconciliation between these two research orientations.

Academic talk

At this stage of our analysis it is assumed that the respondents' interview accounts are neither true or false but real.[2] The interviews were interactional encounters[3] in which the respondents were held morally accountable as lecturers; an identity that the respondents accomplish and manage in their talk. Consequently the analysis focuses on how the respondents rhetorically managed and presented themselves as culturally competent[4] lecturers in response to the interviewer's questions and how this moral order is constitutive of the academy in general.

The data collected was neither particularly novel or striking. It was the commonplace talk of the staffroom and the committee meeting — indeed many of the respondents claimed to have been or were about to discuss the very topics that were raised in the interviews. The interviews were routine and 'factual' accounts of how classes, courses and degree programmes were planned together with the respondents reported concerns about local and

1. Art (3), Business Studies (3), QTS (5), Educational Studies (2), Environmental Studies (2), History (3), French (2), Sociology and Social Policy (5)

2. Silverman, D. (1985) Qualitative Methodology and Sociology. Aldershot, Gower, p. 176.

3. Redley, M. (1995) Face-to-Face Interaction in Research Interviews. Unpublished PhD thesis, University of Surrey.

4. Baruch, G. (1981) Moral tales: parents' stories of encounters with the health professions. Sociology of Health and Illness. 3, 275—95.

national changes in higher education.

The respondents accounts of planning and preparation — no matter how pedestrian — relied upon the use of various distinctions and qualifications which became the key for our entry into the data. For example, one tutor, Brenda R, from a subject that might be considered vocationally relevant, stated that the programme required the,

> *academic but also the practical (Brenda R)*

and she goes on to say,

> *let's face it, we're trying to get, um, students who are employable you know and it, um, so they don't need just to have essay writing skills, they need to be able to write reports. (Brenda R)*

The respondents accounts of planning and preparation were organised in terms of such dichotomies: the academic and the practical, essay and report writing skills (as in the extract above). These apparent oppositions can be seen analytically as interpretative repertoires, 'broadly discernable clusters of terms, descriptions and figures of speech often assembled around metaphors or vivid images'.[5]

The first repertoire we call the real world. This is evidently the world beyond the academy, the world of the job-market, the practical and the applied. The second, the academic, is the world within the academy, the world of the theoretical and the pure. Thus the 'real world' repertoire is used to make reference to a worldly realism of needs and practices while the 'academic' repertoire distinguishes the intrinsic value of education. These repertoires cannot be discretely constituted, except in certain rhetorical instances, and no respondent claimed an adherence to only one repertoire. The two repertoires are the building blocks of a culturally competent account describing academic work in these research interviews. Moreover, they are the terms in which debates about education in general and higher education in particular are conducted and organised.

At another higher level the two repertoires, the 'real world' and the 'academic', can be typified using Weber's theory of rational action.[6] Thus the 'real world' encompasses the idea of *zweckrational* action in which the means to a given end are rationally calculated. Education as a *zweckrational* activity has its formal expression in statements of aims, objectives and learning outcomes and the idea that education is a means of equipping students with skills, which are particularly relevant to the work place. The 'academic' repertoire encompasses the idea of *wertrational* action in which actions are performed for their intrinsic value. *Wertrational* action is an action in which the ends and the means are identifiable as being one and the same: education for its own sake. The respondents' accounts of educational practice make an implicit distinction between education as either a *zweckrational* or *wertrational* activity.

These repertoires, and this analytical distinction, are not merely features documented by our research but are also constitutive of it, and this reflects the contrasting imperatives of the research. Our empirical analysis in the next section highlights and illustrates this tension. In this section we present a detailed 'intrinsic' analysis of respondents talk showing how the repertoires operate on the descriptions of educational discourse. The subsequent section uses the accounts of respondents talk 'extrinsically' to discuss some features of the micropolitics of higher education.

---

5. *Weatherall, M. and J. Potter (1992)* Mapping the Language of Racism: Discourse and the Legitimation of Exploitation. *London: Harvester/Wheatsheaf, p. 90.*

6. *Weber, M. (1978)* Economy and Society. *Berkeley: University of California.*

Descriptions of the teaching process

Three extracts have been selected for a detailed and illustrative analysis. In the first of these extracts the respondent describes how the competing demands of a worldly and practical education conflict with demands of an academic one. The second extract, taken from an interview with a different respondent, illustrates the extent to which a reconciliation of these demands might be possible. The final extract describes the respondent's interpretation of the possible consequences that a skills model might have on academic standards.

In this extract a lecturer in education is discussing the validation process and how it can lead to the re-definition of a programme's content.

Jean S: [...] So if you have the same staff and the same, you know, validating the same programme, you can sort of inherit, um, something that perpetuates itself that does not necessarily(indistinct). What you need to have is um a sort of steady sort of inflow of stimulating new, new material, but that means that every now and then got to question quite clearly and its quite painful to jettison something because it can actually mean you're rejecting colleagues. So that's quite a, quite a sensitive area. Somebody, if somebody has a reputation and the whole raison d'être is about one particular area, um they'd be gutted if you sat on them. Or if there's an internal dispute, like say there was one between [name] who used to do the transition er the transition from work er from school to work and that was um the problem for somebody who was interested in business education and who had quite a kind of um practical business orientation, and this was challenged by somebody who was philosophically unable to stomach any of that because he had a belief that education was to do with flowering individuals and them reaching their full potential which cut across the sort of training and pragmatic stuff. Now that was a very serious conflict and they both couldn't be accommodated.

I: Right.

In describing how it is possible to have a 'sort of steady sort of inflow of stimulating new, [new] material' Jean says that 'something' — a particular subject — might have to be 'jettison[ed]' and that can be 'painful' because you are 'rejecting colleagues'. This is, in Jean's account a 'sensitive area'. The reason for this sensitivity is further elaborated in terms of someone's 'whole raison d'être' being in a particular area and they would be 'gutted' if you 'sat on them' — jettisoned their particular subject area.

Jean then provides an instance of an 'internal dispute', explaining that [NAME] who 'used to do' (teach a module presumably) on the transition from school to work and was interested in this 'problem', because of an interest in 'business education' and what Jean calls a 'practical business orientation'. Jean then reports that 'this was challenged' by 'somebody who was philosophically unable to stomach any of that because he had a belief that education was to do with, you know, the flowering [of] individuals'. Her account constructs a contrast that is loosely defined, which is signalled rather than explained: 'a practical business orientation' as opposed to 'philosophically unable to stomach any of that'.

The philosophy of the person with the queasy stomach is not specifically stated beyond the reported belief that education is to do with the 'flowering [of] individuals' and the 'practical business orientation' is suggestive rather than a precise description. These are intelligible in the context of an interview about teaching in higher education, because they have been construed as opposing views — (the reported challenge) and because of the interviewer's (and the reader's) ability to gloss the terms as indicating positions in a debate;

i.e. education as a means to an end (*zweckrationality*), the 'practical business orientation'; and education as an end in its own right (*wertrationality*), a philosophical stomach and the 'flowering [of] individuals'.

Thus rather than make explicit the details of these opposing views - and possibly risk replaying the debate with the interviewer - Jean's account, with a few suggestive details, leaves the interpretative work to the interviewer and as a consequence trades upon the interviewer's common sense knowledge of education to render these suggestive expressions intelligible. It is our common sense knowledge of this debate in education and the ability of participants in the debate to signal rather than make explicit their cases that is a recurrent feature of the data.

The next extract is taken from an interview with a member of staff in the history department and it follows on from a response where she has listed a number of alternatives to examinations.

Susan W: 'we're playing with the idea of um, of, of assessing differently, bringing in different sorts of assessment like, obviously those I've mentioned, the viva, group project work, having things like, perhaps, assessing their seminar presentations or assessing um, a short piece of work on a document or something like this.' *(Susan W)*

The interviewer hears this list as relating to transferable skills, a fact that amuses both the interviewer and interviewee. The interview then continues:

Susan W: (Laughter) Good — nothing like the interviewer interviewing the interviewee. Um, no I mean I mean I rather, you know in some ways I rather mean I rather, you know in some ways I rather hate the jargon and a lot of this thing about transferable skills and, I mean you know there is a pressure, you know, we are being encouraged, things like the group projects I suppose, you know, should be the kind of thing that's wanted in the workplace for their curriculum vitae, that they have worked in groups and you know that they've co-ordinated their, and blah, blah, blah you know and all that sort of stuff. I mean I don't like any rationale, um, outside, a sort of, an academic rationale really. I mean I don't want a kind of functional, commercial thing impinging and you know, but I mean I think, you know, it, if the group project works well it is a sort of interesting different exercise and has its own value I think. Um, I'm not sure what to think about um, all these different bits that are currently being discussed in the department, you know should we be assessing different sorts of things. I mean I think that, um, on one hand I firmly believe in the essay as a filler,and you know many people say why should we always just do essays, but I mean I think the essay where you, you know you have to introduce, present a case, argue it, conclude, you know I think that's excellent, I think there's, and there's no substitute for, for writing down ones ideas in terms of sort of clearing, you know, clear intellectual or whatever exercise and I mean I absolutely hold to that and I think that should remain [edited] but, um, coming back to the other ideas um, seminar process is incredibly difficult to assess these things and I mean all these things have an obviously large subjective element but you could say that, you know, compared to the Continent, we have actually three German members of staff, um, you know we do very little oral uh examining in this country and that there is a place for it, um, so sort of oral work, oral presentations have rather been neglected here. So that's one, and whether one in fact then, the other aspect I mentioned was taking perhaps a document or a piece of text and giving some sort of presentation that, which could be written, it could be a short piece of written work or it could be an oral, or whatever, um, you know how one weaves these things in I'm not sure but then again that's a subject of discussion and its um, overall one doesn't want to complicate the picture too much [edited] you know, there are all sorts of pulls and tugs in the discussions but as I say we are just in the early stages of this so I can't give you any conclusions. *(Susan W)*

Susan says of herself 'I rather hate the jargon and a lot of this stuff about transferable skills.' She then accounts for a 'pressure' and says 'we are being encouraged' to see group work as something that is wanted in the 'workplace' and on students' curriculum vitae. As she accounts for it this 'pressure' means that the students will have 'worked in groups and you know that they've co-ordinated their, and blah, blah, blah you know and all that sort of stuff'. She thus describes group work as something that is relevant to the students' future employment and can be put on their curriculum vitae as a means to secure employment. The jargon that Susan hates is a 'pressure' towards making education more relevant to the students' future employment, i.e. an ends/means *zweckrationality*. It is however a feature of her account that the nature of this relevance (of education to work) is cryptic 'blah, blah, blah you know and all that sort of stuff'. It is up to the interviewer to make sense of this utterance in the light of what she has already said. In making sense of this utterance the interviewer renders intelligible and thus colludes with Susan's claim that the accounted for pressure — to do group work because it is 'the kind of thing that is wanted in the work place' — is real and actually exists.

Susan accounts for herself as not liking any rationale outside of the academic. A point she re-states 'I mean I don't want a kind of functional, commercial thing impinging'. However she goes on to say; 'if the group project works well it is a sort of interesting different exercise and has its own value I think'. By saying that group work has 'its own value' she is disassociating it from 'functional, commercial' interests and locates group work within an 'academic rationale', a *wertrational* frame of reference.

Describing herself as 'not sure what to think about um, all these different bits that are currently being discussed in the department' she makes the case for the importance of the essay as a form of assessment. 'On the one hand' signals the existence of an alternative argument although she does not specify it. But her argument is in opposition to those — unspecified people who say 'why should we always just do essays'. Susan 'firmly believes in the essay as a filler'; the essay is an exercise in which 'you have to introduce, present a case, argue it conclude' and it is in her account 'excellent', 'there is no substitute for writing down one's ideas in terms of sort of clearing, you know clear intellectual or whatever exercise and I mean I absolutely hold to that and I think that should remain'. When she says there is 'no substitute' for the essay as a clear intellectual or 'what ever exercise' she seems to be making a contrast between the intellectual and some other sphere of life, to which essay writing skills are transferable — presumably the work place.

After a discussion of essay length Susan returns to the topic of assessment. 'The'seminar process' is accounted for as 'incredibly difficult to access' because of a 'large subjective element' (assessment being ideally objective). This stands as a potential critique of assessing seminar presentations but she then makes a comparison with the Continent, 'we do very little oral uh examining in this country'. When Susan says 'we actually have three German members of staff' she alludes to their experience of oral examining, and her own 'second hand' experience. Thus when she says there is a place for oral assessment and that it has been neglected in this country she has established the academic credentials of the method and that the department has staff with the experience to overcome the 'largely subjective element'.

Susan then turns to the use of documents for assessment as in: a 'presentation', a 'short piece of written work' an 'oral' or 'whatever'. She describes herself as 'not sure how one weaves these things in', it is a 'subject of discussion' but 'overall one doesn't want to complicate the picture too much'. Thus the use of documents as a method of assessment is potentially a legitimate form of academic assessment, provided it is 'woven in' and not too 'complicated'.

'There are all sorts of pulls and tugs in the discussion' she claims. 'Pulls and tugs' — contradictory forces that relate to her commitment to an academic rationale (*wertrationality*) and the 'encourage[ment]' to teach 'the kind of thing that's wanted in the work place' (*zweckrationality*). In addition there is Susan's commitment to the essay and 'people saying why should we always do essays'; the assessment of oral presentations as 'largely subjective' and their use on the Continent and the weaving in of assessments using documents. Of these 'pulls and tugs', she says 'we are just in the early stages of this so I can't give you any conclusions' — the issue is left unresolved.

In this extract, Susan 'hate[s] the jargon' she associates with a 'functional commercial thing, education as a means to an end in the 'workplace'. Further she allies herself with the academic as an end in itself, 'I don't like any rationale um outside a sort of an academic rationale really'. The various forms of assessment, group work, oral and the use of documents — that the interviewer identified as associated with transferable skills and thus with an ends/means educational rationality, are presented as having both an academic and a workplace rationale. Thus group work assessment which is associated with the jargon of transferable skills and education as a means to an end — can if 'done well' have 'its own value'. Oral presentations are also part of the jargon of transferable skills, which while neglected in England can be a legitimate academic exercise as is the case on the Continent. The use of document-based assessment could be 'woven in' to an academic rationale as well. Thus Susan's account locates forms of assessment, associated with the 'functional commercial' jargon that she hates, into an academic rationale, thus hinting at some rapprochement between the two positions.

In the final extract Vera is describing why one of the modules for which she is a convenor had its method of assessment changed the previous year. The students used to do a three hour exam that was based on a case study now the students do a one and half hour case study exam and a written project that is assessed both as a written text and as a presentation. Vera associates the change with a means/ends rationality and a'dilution' of academic standards.

Vera Y: [...] um last year was 50% so 50% exam, 50% project.

Q: And what was the rationale behind that change?

Vera Y: Um, its, its sort of said, well in the real world, its like um in management doing project team work and presentation those are equally important [pause] and that academic quality[pause] so its 100% academic is not perhaps realistic enough and so, so [NAME] sort of proposed this new structure and so we all agreed to give it a try and prove to them, and now we have this for a semester and its proved quite alright because um students like varieties and also um, the whole course based on one final exam is quite scary to some of them so its, its helpful to have the marks spread a little bit and the only things perhaps um is the academic content academic side a bit diluted. But then this all depends what really, what objective you want to achieve.

Q: And in what sense is the academic side a bit diluted?

Vera Y: Um because when you have, used a three hour exam, and it used to be a very big case.

She says that the assessment last year was '50 % exam 50 % project', and is then asked 'what was the rationale behind that change?' She answers this by reference to what she describes as the 'real world' of 'management' which requires 'project team work and presentation[s]' which are 'equally important'. 'Equally important' to what Vera does not specify and the utterance 'and that academic quality' is left hanging until she says'100 % academic is not perhaps realistic enough'. Thus she contrasts the real world of 'management', and the 'academic'. The difference between the two is not defined in terms of absolutes, but in terms of relative percentages. Thus the change that the account describes in the method of assessment can be understood in terms of a percentage, a matter of degree, rather than an absolute change between the requirements of the 'real world' and the 'academic'.

Vera reports that [NAME] proposed this 'new structure' and it was 'agreed to give it a try and prove to them'. Who the 'them' refers to is not clear. She continues, 'and now we have this [new structure of assessment] for a semester and its proved quite alright'. To say the new form of assessment has proved 'quite alright' is not, we would suggest, outright praise. She describes how the new form of assessment has proved 'quite alright'; the students 'like varieties' (a case study exam and project work as opposed to just a case study exam). Furthermore, 'one final exam is quite scary to some of them [the students] so its helpful to have the marks spread quite a bit'. This account of the change of assessment proving 'quite alright' is not constructed in similar terms to 'real world' management skills that was initially used to describe the rationale for the change. She then qualifies her account of the change in assessment and this might well be more in line with her less than out-right praise of the change: 'the only thing is perhaps um is the academic content the academic side is a bit diluted'. It is interesting to note her reformulation, 'academic content' for 'academic side'. It is possible that to say the academic content is a bit diluted is a much stronger formulation than to say the academic side is a bit diluted. In its stronger form this might cast doubt upon the academic value of the module and by association upon Vera as the lecturer responsible for it. She explicitly addresses the dilution of the academic side when she says, 'this all depends what really, what objective you want to achieve'. The available objectives are, in her account not made explicit, but presumably refer to the outcomes of pursuing either a 'real world' of management *zweckrational* or 'academic' *wertrationality*. Thus what initially was accounted for as a percentage difference between the concerns of 'real world' of management and the 'academic' has finally become a choice between two different objectives.

Vera described at length how the three hour case study exam was based upon contemporary journal articles describing a company's market position and its current dealings, which the students had to analyse in terms of potential outcome. She also describes her own experience of the form of assessment during her postgraduate studies, and says of it:

Vera Y: [...] You see that's the best way of learning something, its a real challenge you put in front of the students and also you really, I believe you really draw out the best of quality of the students and really you see their ability of treating a real issue, I mean that's all you need for a good manager really.

Q: But that's what you're saying they don't do now.

Vera Y: But now its like a its impossible because 1/2 hours you can't do a very through solid big major case [...] *(Vera Y)*

In this account the case study is the 'best way of learning something', 'a real challenge you put in front of the students....you really draw out the best of quality of the students...you see their ability of treating a real issue....that's all you need for a good manager really'. In praising the three hour case study exam, in a markedly different manner from the new form of assessment ('quite alright') and in different terms 'that's all you need for a good manager really' (from 'varieties' and being less 'scary') Vera establishes the credentials of the three hour case study exam and in doing so her account transcends the distinction between 'real world' management and the 'academic' because the 'best way of learning something' (the 'academic') is also 'all you need for a good manager really' (the 'real world').

In these three extracts the respondents have made use of the two repertoires. The accounts draw attention to the competing demands of these rationalities and the difficulties that are to be had in seeking to reconcile them. The practice of education is contested using these two repertoires, the 'Academic' and the 'Real World'. The repertoires are used to describe and justify particular educational practices. Thus the opposition between *zweckrationality* or *wertrationality* is embodied in how forms of education are described and legitimated. Finally the terms of the debate are not always consistently applied in the evaluation of outcomes. The debate as to whether education should or should not be a *zweckrational* or a *wertrational* activity is only limited by the rhetorical skills of the respondents.

Descriptions of preparation and validation

Validation, course planning and teaching preparation and the work of the academy more generally is 'accomplished' by the respondents artful use of the two repertoires in formulating a rationale for their educational practices. These discursively produced educational rationales are part of the process of defining the nature of institutional boundaries, departments and disciplines. Some departments are perceived and perceive themselves as celebrating one or other repertoire. These perceptions may not be shared by all staff within a department but they do help to create specific cultures. Such cultures, however loosely defined, do help us to account for why staff seem to respond differently in terms of their relative attachment to the institutional processes of validation and review .

The view among the staff interviewed was that the validation and scrutiny process has changed, for better and for worse. This change can be understood as a shift between two contrasting models (or views) of the validation document. Under the old system the validation document was a like a licence the department received to teach a subject discipline. It accredited the department without stipulating its organisation and delivery. If this approach emphasised the assurance of quality rather than control then the new system was the obverse. The model of the licence gave way to that of the manual. The driving licence legitimates, the driving manual regulates. Where the licence entrusts, the manual distrusts. Figure 1 represents this historical shift in emphasis.

Figure 1

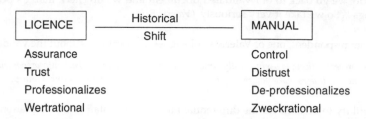

The justification provided by the Institute's management for this change was that a more rigorous and systematic scheme of validation with its manual-type document would:
- generate greater accountability;
- improve teaching and student learning;
- symbolize the Institute's commitment to academic standards.

Underlying the desire to research this field was an assumption by us that staff resistance to the increased formality of the scrutiny and validation procedure had produced a situation in which their teaching and their management of student learning was structured independently of any validation procedure. Jim expresses this hostility clearly,

Jim S: And uh I think there's a widespread feeling that um, that the requirements in the process of validation are perhaps excessive in the sheer amount of documentation that's required and there's a sort of huge contradiction in sort of um, in, in, you know, spreading your time, specifying the learning outcomes of the students and the things that they are supposed to be getting out of it when the process of re-validation you know, consumed a whole month of my time and the students got no learning outcome at all because there was no bloody time to give them, you know ...

I mean I found something very curious in the whole process as well that, that they specify the criteria for each of these different sections of the validation process so sort of narrowly in order to get everything into such a sort of uniform pattern that there's actually not any obvious place in the validation document when you talk about the content of what you're doing. *(Jim S)*

Was it the case that staff treated validation as a test that had to be carefully prepared for like an examination and once passed they could engage in acts of selective amnesia? As Lenny states,

Lenny D: Well I am sure that the purpose of producing the validation document is for validation, as far as I'm concerned. It's out of date by the time its been validated and its even more out of date as each year progresses. *(Lenny D)*

There turned out to be considerable variation in the extent to which staff embraced or rejected the 'manual' model of the validation process as the key to curriculum development and improvements in student learning. It is certainly not the case that staff as a whole are antipathetic to it. For example, a member of the team of staff responsible for initial teacher training, Valerie, speaks for her colleagues when she observes,

Valerie B: I think there is a very genuine desire to make the validated document the definitive ... document and certainly with the programme that I'm now associated with we do, we go back to our validated document and we do check that it's possible to do things ... So we take it very seriously. *(Valerie B)*

> *the process, I think is useful, really, and it, it in turn actually feeds back into preparation really because it, it does make you re-look at what you've been doing and re-think. (Jean S)*

Another respondent, one of Valerie's colleagues, also enthuses about the validation process,

We will try to account for the differential attachment of staff to the validation process later in the chapter. Meanwhile we want to concentrate on how staff frame their responses to questions about how they typically set about planning and preparing their teaching. In asking these questions and its supplementaries we were trying to elicit the extent to which validation procedure and documents were relevant to the process of course planning and teaching preparation.

There was no single conceptual point of origin that staff identify as the basis of their preparation, but the most common reference points were course booklets, course content and pedagogy. Although not exclusively, the programme or course booklet is cited as the point of departure for those staff who teach on programmes that are highly structured and are linked to the requirements of external agencies, e.g. the Teacher Training Agency. There is relatively little room for discretion but this appears to be accepted as inevitable. There is a difference between those course booklets that are simply the outcome of individual staff initiative and those which by virtue of having been produced by a team of staff have a quality which transcends the individual. These latter booklets incorporate the formal and systematic requirements of the programme and in turn reflect the conditions laid down by external agencies.

> *The validation document is discussed, that we've approved that we will teach, um, because mine is a professional course and about teacher training we have to consider um, what the regulations are about teacher training courses, so we have both the validation document and what's called um, a CATE regulation. (Jean S)*

For most staff the requirements of the validation document remain implicit. For example, a member of staff in the History Department when asked if she referred to the validation document in planning and preparing classes said,

> *No, I'd say I don't ... I mean I know in my head what, when it comes to, to, um, what I seek to do in my courses ... (Susan W)*

However, others appear to treat the validation document as obligatory reading:

> *First of all I look at the validation document to see and what we've actually put on there, what were our aims, objectives, learning outcomes, indicative tests, etc., etc. (Valerie B)*

In those disciplines in which staff identify themselves, through their teaching and research, as the protectors and transmitters of a corpus of knowledge their accounts of planning and preparation are constructed in a manner that celebrates developments in the discipline and within that the autonomy of staff decision-making. A senior member of staff in one such department states,

> *I think there's a constant re-invention of the programme, which has been very healthy um, adapting to new curriculum developments in [subject named], the subject's changed enormously um since I did*

my first degree and so they went through constant re-cycling of yourself and sort of professional development aspect involved in the teaching and in re-designing courses ... (Jim S)

Preparing classes is also frequently framed in terms of pedagogy. The approach to preparation is described in terms of whether a member of staff will be primarily lecturing, managing a seminar or organising small group work. In a department that would be considered as more 'academic' than 'real world' in orientation colleagues account for their preparation as follows:

Well for a lecture I would obviously read and think and write a lecture ... (Susan W)

Well obviously if it's a lecture you re-read your lecture notes before you give the lecture, um or you update from time to time ... (Jason B)

Conclusion

How is it possible to account for the variation between staff in terms of their attachment to or disaffection with validation procedures at Roehampton Institute. First, we do not believe that psychological explanations have much to commend them. Differences between individuals within the same department or subject can usually be explained in terms of their position and length of service within the Institute. A convener of a programme is likely to be less critical of validation process and procedure than a more junior member of staff because they have a greater personal stake in and understanding of those processes and procedures. In addition, the interviews suggest that the similarities within departments are far greater than differences between individuals. It would seem to us that the culture and structural position of departments are the most salient factors. Staff in the Faculty of Education and particularly those involved in initial teacher training show a much greater attachment to and acceptance of the scrutiny and validation process as some of the extracts above would indicate. These staff compare markedly with staff in History and Modern Languages. Other departments fall between the two extremes.

A departmental culture in this context refers to the nature of the academic and professional values shared by staff which give a sense of identity to a department or other academic unit. The nature, strength and consistency of the culture depends upon an array of conditions, including:

- the perceived academic status of the department ie. the extent to which staff are committed to ideas of a liberal education, education for its own sake;
- the relative autonomy of a department's work, i.e. is its work regulated by external agencies?;
- the strength of the department's research record. The stronger the record the greater the chance that the department will perceive itself and be perceived by others as having high academic status;
- the vocational relevance of the department's work ie. how closely is its education tied to vocational and/or professional requirements?

- the relative attachment of the department to institutional versus wider academic values: professional versus institutional values;
- the unit of resource of the department. The perception of underfunding by staff, compared with other departments, is conducive to resistance to central policies and procedures like those of academic validation and scrutiny.

These conditions resonate with each other as a set of reference points that produce cultures of either resistance or acceptance in relation to validation procedures. The validation document symbolising the process as a whole is either **ours** or **theirs**, i.e. 'the wretched document' (Jim S). Resistance is likely to be greater from amongst the least vocational of departments, with higher academic status, greater autonomy, stronger research records, a commitment to wider academic values and a weaker resource base. With the exception of their research record, which is strong, the Faculty of Education broadly represents the other end of the continuum, hence its relative acceptance of validation procedures.

What are the implications for the development and management of teaching and learning in institutions of higher education? First, those staff in Educational Development Units, and those that manage them, must look beyond accounts of resistance that are constructed in terms of either the 'bolshie individual' or the inherent conservatism of academics. We must seek to understand the nature of academic and departmental cultures, how they operate, how they are sustained and the conditions of their existence. Many of these conditions are beyond the control of individual staff, departments and institutions but an awareness of how they influence decision-making is the first and most important step towards a 'softening up' of resistance.

Lastly, the purposes of validation and review require greater clarification. At present there is some considerable confusion about the process in so far as it aims at both **quality control** and **curriculum and pedagogical development**. The procedures designed to achieve the former aim must not imperil the latter.

26 'Watching the detectives': developing students' analytical and evaluative research skills

Charley Hardwick
Information Team Manager
The Nottingham Trent University

and Jan Hooper
Tutor Librarian
Brooksby College

Introduction

The research described in this chapter derives from the relationship between a particular course and a specific service offered by a library. The course is the honours degree in Environmental Health, which is housed within the Department of Building and Environmental Health at The Nottingham Trent University (NTU); and the service is the Information Skills Programme (ISP), an award-winning[1] approach launched by NTU's Library and Information Service (LIS) in 1991.

In focusing on this relationship, the authors acknowledge that the usefulness of the findings in relation to other courses and other skills programmes, both at NTU and elsewhere, may be reduced. At the same time, the concerns which prompted the research are not peculiar either to the course or to the ISP. Similar programmes at other university's share many of the characteristics of the ISP, and issues relating to delivery methods and the 'contextualizing' of skills input will be widely recognized. However, there is a danger that by moving between general concerns and specific solutions, the work and views of others may be overlooked. It should, therefore, be borne in mind that the general descriptions of the ISP, which are given below, are just that — general overviews that necessarily exclude details of other innovative work being done at NTU, and which is recorded in the annual reports for the ISP, available from LIS (Hardwick et al., 1991/92 onwards).

Background

Environmental Health and the ISP

The introduction of the BSc (Hons) in Environmental Health in 1990 predated the launching of the ISP by a year. However, the new degree included an information skills element, scheduled to be delivered in the early weeks of the first year, and designed to underpin

---

1. *1993 Partnership Awards — Digital Equipment Prize for* The Future of Libraries with Resource-based Learning.

some immediate project work. In those pre-modular days, the skills input was located within the Resource and Communication Skills element of year one, and was allocated about eight hours of class contact time.

Notwithstanding the absence of an official LIS programme for teaching information skills, the 35 students were instructed by the appropriate LIS information specialists, who operated a 'team teaching' approach. In this way, specialists in law and statistical information were able to supplement the main input from their LIS environmental health colleague. Wherever possible, the team designed the sessions in order to allow students to handle and use the sources that would eventually provide the information for their projects. The basic aims of the sessions were, therefore, twofold: firstly, to make students aware of the existence of a range of abstracts, CD-ROMs, current awareness services, etc.; and, secondly, to provide guidance on the use of these sources.

The experience gained with the Environmental Health students contributed to the decision to launch the official Information Skills Programme in 1991. A declared aim of the ISP was to enable students to 'use information sources intelligently' (Naylor and Hardwick, 1990).

Student feedback from the course – 1989 – 92

Since the first-year Environmental Health projects were essay-based, with no marks being awarded for proficiency in the underlying information-gathering processes, there were no opportunities to assess skills input against measurable outcomes. A small percentage of marks may have been available for accuracy in bibliography compilation, but information specialists were neither involved in this assessment nor were they informed of the marks. They could only note that immediate feedback, taken from students at the final session each year, generally indicated a positive response to the information skills element of the first term programme; including the tuition on citing references!

Other sources of information about the students' abilities and attitudes were, however, extremely interesting, and they appeared to lend weight to some of the general concerns about the ISP that were emerging in 1993. Firstly, a significant number of Environmental Health students continued to approach the LIS Subject Information Desk for help in the weeks following the skills sessions. By this time the projects had been set, and it became obvious that, in general, the students had not retained quite basic information. Secondly, the course reports for the period record low student opinion of the Resource and Communication Studies (RandCS) programme. It was frequently rated lowest for 'interest and perceived importance', and was the aspect of the course on which students expended the least amount of independent study time!

The ISP in its third year

A review at this time showed that the ISP was contributing to over 60 award bearing programmes, from HND to post-graduate level. In 1993/94 alone, 2,637 students received tuition via a wide variety of delivery methods ranging across formal lectures, worksheet based activities, and drop-in 'clinics' or 'surgeries'. A staff development project had resulted in the creation of a prototype computer-based, self-teaching package for undergraduates researching for final year 'dissertations'. In many areas, close linkages with appropriate coursework had been achieved; occasionally to the extent that ISP input and assessed outcomes were also closely tied.

Despite these achievements, and their national recognition, there was an awareness that the programme needed to develop further in the areas of assessment, integration with coursework, and delivery of higher level skills. Assessment and integration were seen as key issues in relation to student motivation and skills retention. The question of higher level skills emerged from two inter-related developments: the first was the fact that the ISP input to undergraduates was predominantly taking place in the first years of courses, and was, as we have seen, tending to concentrate on transmitting 'knowledge' and 'comprehension' of information sources; the second was the ISP tutors' exposure to ideas about levels of learning. This latter development raised questions about the possibility of designing and delivering different levels of skills tuition, capable of supporting students' changing approaches to libraries and information sources as they progressed through their courses.

Environmental Health, with its sympathetic approach to the issues of core and transferable skills, was being re-designed at this time, and the course lecturers were keen to experiment with a new approach to ISP input.

New demands from the course

Following modularization, the integrative project work in the Environmental Health degree was transferred to the new Trent Health Department modules (THD). A stated aim of THD was to 'develop professional skills through all years of the course'; and the first module (THD/1), as well as having a substantive teaching function, was therefore designed to prepare students for the higher level skills demanded by project work in the second year of the course (in THD/2). Since THD/2 would call for students to adopt an evaluative stance in respect of an individually selected information source, there was a need for information skills input in THD/1 to go beyond introducing sources and teaching students how to use each one.

This new approach to developing 'professional skills' also resulted in the closer integration of ISP input with THD teaching. In 1993/94, this was achieved by the simple expedient of having all THD/1 sessions jointly presented by the appropriate course lecturer and the LIS information specialist for environmental health. This practice was continued in 1994/95, but by then integration was further reinforced by allocating a significant percentage of assessment marks to the skills element of the project exercise. However, in 1993/94, despite modularization, the project still retained the RandCS three essay format, with the emphasis continuing to be placed on the assessment of the product. As we shall see from the research findings, this delayed move towards assessing issues of process had significant consequences.

Research: phase one

Literature survey

A key article has stated that if library user education programmes are to develop successfully it is vital that 'planners and teachers of these programmes firstly became thoroughly cognisant of the various educational and learning theories' (Fleming, 1986). While the authors cannot claim thoroughness in these areas, they did become aware that by requiring students to adopt a reflective approach to information gathering activities, the chances of skills retention would be improved. Furthermore, a reflective approach to information sources would underpin the critical stance required for the evaluative elements in THD/2.

In the USA, theories of reflective practice and critical thinking are accepted as key components in the design of library instruction courses (Schon, 1983 and 1987; Dewey, 1988). Not surprisingly, there is therefore a comprehensive literature outlining the practical methods by which the theories might be applied. Among the examples discovered during this phase of our research was an approach using small group discussions for assessing the usefulness and reliability of sources (Totten, 1989/90). Another writer described skills instruction that incorporated the requirement for students to compile annotated bibliographies (Engeldinger, 1988).

For the UK, our review of the professional librarianship literature for the period prior to 1992 unearthed no accounts comparable to those from the USA (Hooper, 1994). Indeed, the first description of a programme designed to engender in students critical and evaluative approaches to secondary sources appears in 1992, and details work undertaken at the University of Northumbria (Walton and Nettleton, 1992). The account outlined the first use of research diaries as a vehicle for library user education. Previous work by Burgess (1981) had stressed the importance of the diary as a valuable tool in empirical research, and in 1994 another writer was to describe a different approach from that adopted at the University of Northumbria (Goodall, 1994). However, it was Walton and Nettleton's methods and ideas in particular that seemed to offer greater potential than the techniques employed in the USA.

In the first instance, the methods used at Northumbria appeared to provide an appropriate way of channelling focused pastoral care to a particular group of distance learning students who were undertaking research for final-year projects. Although this initiative, within the Department of Surveying, met with a mixed response, it proved to be a valuable learning experience. It also suggested to the authors that, as Walton and Nettleton had recommended, a diary approach might be more successful if used with full-time students at an early stage in a course.

Research records

Since the distance learning students had tended to interpret the word 'diary' literally, it was decided to substitute the term 'record' instead. This did not alter the basic working definition that informed our approach: the research record was intended to be a personal record of a student's activities, thoughts and progress in relation to the information gathering process. A variety of different formats could be used including loose-leaf file, notebook, index cards — even a diary!

The advantages of the research record were felt to be as follows: it would serve to formalize the process of research and establish good study habits early in a student's academic career; it would provide a framework within which to work; and, finally, it would form a focal point for recording any items of information acquired during the research process, so forming a central source of data collection.

Research records in use, 1993/94

The idea of research records was introduced to the Environmental Health students at a session jointly presented by the course lecturer and the information specialist. The session was in three sections, with inter-relationships between the three continually being emphasized by the presenters. The first section involved the lecturer in describing the *THD/1* projects exercise; the second allowed the information specialist to convey some basic information skills (formulation of search terms, use of boolean operators, etc.); and the third section involved both presenters in advising on the use of research records, and outlining the mandatory submission of a research report with the completed essays (on pro-formas provided). The report, which required students to list sources used (CD-ROM, current-awareness services, etc.), and to describe aspects of their engagement with the research process (problems encountered and solutions devised), was not to be assessed.

During the ten-week duration of the project exercise, two drop-in 'clinics' were timetabled at which both lecturer and information specialist could review students' progress, and offer advice and guidance. Finally, the students attended seminar group review sessions at the end of *THD/1*, at which the lecturer gave feedback on the essays, and the information specialist covered issues arising from the research reports. It was during this session that both verbal and questionnaire feedback was taken on student reaction to employing research records.

Research: phase two

Student feedback, 1993/94

Seventy-five per cent of the students completed and submitted the research report pro-formas; a task which, in itself, required a degree of reflection. However, the free comment section produced a number of observations, frequently reinforced during the seminar group review discussions, that cast doubts on the success of the exercise from the skills point of view.

It was clear that students did not see the *process* elements of the project exercise as a learning experience of the same order of importance as the substantive subject, or *product* aspects. They tried to circumvent these parts of the project exercise by, for instance, using 'information sources I felt would give me what I wanted the quickest'. Others commented that research activity in the Library was a 'waste of time', and indicated that they were focusing on the need to obtain the key article, rather than seeing the research as a learning process that would have future benefits. There was also heavy reliance on peer group discussion which, though a legitimate research method in itself, may have aided many in by-passing the very experience it was intended they should gain (see Valentine, 1993).

From the questionnaires, completed by 60% of the students, the following emerged:

- 51% kept a research record.
- 45% found record-keeping 'useful', 'beneficial' or 'worth the effort', and 15% thought it 'burdensome' or a 'waste of time'. However, in their research reports these individuals commented that the long-term usefulness of the technique was recognized, but that *this particular project had not required them to undertake extensive recording.*
- The questionnaire asked students to assess the keeping of research records in the light of a number of intended outcomes. Some of these involved 'mechanistic' skills (bibliography compilation) and some covered evaluative and reflective elements. The 'Yes' results (ranked) were as follows:

  - To complete a bibliography? 54%
  - To become more aware of how to find information? 54%
  - To become aware of your study habits? 51%
  - To consider different methods of gathering information and their usefulness? 36%
  - To reflect upon your practice? 30%

- To keep track of your project and maintain direction? 27%
- To be more critical of your practice? 24%
- The development of your ideas? 21%

- Students were asked if assessment marks should be awarded for research skills, and their response was ambivalent. However, during the seminar group discussions it emerged that skills assessment would generally be welcomed, if appropriately designed.

Finally, 63% of those replying to a separate questionnaire, issued by the course tutor, rated the *THD* module as 'unsatisfactory'. The results of the questionnaire were incorporated in the annual course report, which recorded a 'poor confidence in and handling of the material'.

Conclusions drawn from 1993/94

In general, the indicators pointed to a limited realization of the aims of the ISP input for this first year of *THD/1*. Although some students claimed to have become 'more aware of their study habits', there was still a readier acknowledgement of the enhancement of 'mechanistic' skills than of those relating to critical and evaluative approaches to information sources. Moreover, the nature of the essays had allowed students to avoid having to consult some sources directly, with the consequence that there was often little for them to record or evaluate!

Planning for 1994/95

It was decided to abandon the three essay format, and instead to base THD/1 on a single project. At the same time, successful elements from the previous year were retained, and some were reinforced. For instance, students had identified the joint involvement of course and library staff in *THD/1* as very beneficial, but had criticised the timing of the drop-in 'clinics'. The latter were, therefore, re-scheduled for strategic points in the research process, in an attempt to correspond with Ruggiero's stages of 'investigation' and 'idea production'; and, later, 'evaluation' and 'refinement' (Ruggiero, 1988).

To complement these modifications, two aspects of the new, project based exercise were specifically designed in order to focus students' attention on the information gathering process. Firstly, the award of assessment marks was re-structured, with 35% being divided between the research proposal (20%), the research report (10%) and the bibliography (5%). Secondly, and in order to facilitate the corresponding part of the marking scheme, the research report pro-formas were re-designed in order to accommodate the requirement that students should write a brief critique of four of the sources used (e.g. CD-ROM, current-awareness service, abstract, etc.).

Finally, an additional set of pro-formas was designed for the actual recording exercise. These were based on the individual sources students might use. Each form provided space for bibliographical recording and note-taking, and included a simple evaluation matrix. Although the use of these pro-formas was not obligatory, it was hoped they would provide the students with models for the compilation of their own personal research records.

Student feedback, 1994/95

Feedback was again taken via questionnaires, verbally at *THD/1* seminar group reviews, and from the completed research reports (which were submitted by 84% of the students, compared with 75% in 1993/94). The questionnaire responses revealed the following (with 1993/94 figures given in brackets, wherever possible):

The response rate was 88% (60%).

- 78% (51%) had compiled a research record, but only 9% made use of the pro-formas.
- Only one student described the process elements as a 'waste of time'. Furthermore, 85% (45%) of those who had kept a research record found the activity either 'useful' (40%), 'beneficial' (26%) or 'worth the effort' (19%).
- Skills learned — as in 1993/94, the responses revealed that students saw the value of research records primarily in connection with 'mechanistic' elements of information gathering. However, the higher percentages for 1994/95 in all areas may well reflect the general increased importance given to *process* during the year. The ranked 'Yes' results were as follows:
  - To complete a bibliography? 73% (54%)
  - To become more aware of how to find information? 69% (54%)
  - Become aware of your study habits? 57% (51%)
  - To consider different methods of gathering information and their usefulness? 54% (36%)
  - To keep track of your project and maintain direction? 42% (27%)
  - Be more critical of your practice? 40% (24%)
  - To reflect upon your practice? 35% (30%)
  - The development of your ideas? 23% (21%)
- 88% of respondents thought the skills learned through the *THD/1* project would be useful, both on the course and in their future careers.
- The above was reinforced by 74% of the students supporting the allocation of marks for *process*. One commented: 'Writing the report is the easy bit. The research is the real hard work.' Another noted: 'Yes, because if marks are allocated for research skills, it helps to highlight the importance for later projects.'

Conclusions and comparisons

Although they reflect important changes, the statistics themselves do not do justice to the more positive attitude the students adopted to *THD/1* in 1994/95. The revised project, with its adjusted assessment schedule, clearly reinforced the students' appreciation of the importance of the *process* element of the exercise, and their understanding of its inter-relationship with the final *product*. However, the particular contribution made to these developments by research records is difficult to discern. Indeed, several students commented that they would probably have kept some sort of record, even without the stimulus of either the pro-formas or the assessed research report. Therefore, the fact that a greater number were able to claim enhanced reflective and critical skills in some areas in 1994/95, may well derive from factors other than the research records themselves.

The future

Research records

If the use of research records is still unproven as a distinct method for encouraging a higher level engagement with secondary information sources, this could be attributed to a number of factors; the authors' research methodology, the design of the record pro-formas, or even the decision to maintain the confidential nature of the research records. However, they are part of a package that works well in terms of drop-in 'clinics', more effective student use of LIS guides and handouts, and at the research report and feedback stages. With these and other positive points in mind, the authors have recommended two key changes for the coming year. Neither directly affects the research records element of *THD/1*, but the fact that they sandwich the research activity suggests that they could influence students' approaches to record keeping.

Planning for 1995/96
THD/1: two recommendations
The stages in the research process that Ruggiero defines as 'exploration' and 'expression' are allocated 20% of the marks within the 'research proposal' phase of *THD/1*. Previously, the information specialist has not participated in the research proposal seminars. However, in 1994/95 several students again selected topics for which published sources were either scarce or difficult to acquire. The fact that this undermined some key aims of the exercise was discussed with the students, who supported the idea of scheduling research proposal 'clinics' to which the information specialist would contribute. This move could help in steering students' ideas towards projects that more closely fit with the *process* aims of *THD/1*.

At the outcome stage, the research report pro-formas should be re-designed to give clearer guidance on source evaluation techniques. This could well involve the use of sentence stems in order to stimulate the student to comment on, for instance, the currency of a CD-ROM, its coverage, and the suitability and availability of the sources it lists. If both this approach and the new research proposal 'clinics' are successful, students may be encouraged to look more carefully at the advantages of maintaining accurate research records.

THD/2
Present proposals for *THD/2* will involve students in submitting a critique of a selected primary source (a journal article, textbook, sets of statistical data, etc.). Although the details for ISP input have not been finalized, there are likely to be opportunities for harnessing information skills to the task of analysing and evaluating primary sources. Instead of evaluating CD-ROMs, the task will now be to use such databases to help place a single text within a wider body of work. Whilst this presents opportunities for some skills revision, the requirements of THD/2 may also provide a vehicle for introducing new research tools that were omitted in the first year. The obvious importance of citation searching to the business of contextualising a single source suggests that the BIDS/ISI databases will be extremely relevant to *THD/2* work, and the potential of the Internet will also be investigated.

Conclusion

The use of research records within the ISP has come full circle. Initially, the concept influenced the new approach to project work within the Environmental Health degree. Subsequently, the project exercises incorporated an assessment schedule that allocated marks to research proposals and research reports. Now, the authors' own researches suggest that it is these elements that, if planned with care, can invigorate the students' approach to keeping records. Deprived of this context, the research records on their own would appear to be a less potent vehicle for encouraging the higher level skills of analysis and evaluation.

In the absence of some form of assessment, students would probably still keep various personal records, but it is unlikely that these would contain any formal reflections on the relative values of the secondary information sources used.

Despite this fact, the authors agree with Walton and Nettleton that research records should be personal, in order not to discourage students from recording those potentially productive three-o-clock-in-the-morning thoughts. Taken together with the other findings described in this paper, this suggests that research reports are the aspect of *THD/1* that could well yield the most promising immediate developments, rather than research records.

Thanks to Ann McCarthy for her friendship and support.

Bibliography

Bodi, S. (1992) Collaborating with faculty in teaching critical thinking: the role of librarians. *Research Strategies* **10**(2), Spring, 70.

Burgess, R. (1981) Keeping a research diary. *Cambridge Journal of Education* **11**(1), 75—83.

Dewey, J. (1988) *How We Think: A Restatement of the Relation of Reflective Thinking to the Educative Process*. Chicago: D.C. Heath. Quoted in Grimmett, P. and Gaalen, L. E. (eds), *Reflection in Teacher Education*. New York and London: Teachers College Press, Columbia University, p. 6.

Engeldinger, E. A. (1988) Bibliographic instruction and critical thinking: the contribution of the annotated bibliography. *RQ* **28**(1), Fall, 195—202.

Fleming, H. (1986) User education in academic libraries in the UK. *British Journal of Academic Librarianship* **1**(1), Spring, 35.

Goodall, D. (1994) Use of diaries in library and information research. *Library and Information Research News* **18**(59), Spring, 17—21.

Hardwick, C. W. *et al.* (1991/92 onwards) *Information Skills Programme: annual reports*. The Nottingham Trent University: Library and Information Service.

Hooper, J. M. (1994) Developing library research skills in academic libraries: the effectiveness of the research record. An unpublished MA thesis, Loughborough University of Technology.

Naylor, A. and Hardwick, C. W. (1990) *Information Retrieval Skills: Project Report*. Nottingham Polytechnic.

Ruggiero, V. R. (1988) *Teaching Thinking across the Curriculum*. New York: Harper & Row, p. 2. As quoted in Bodi (1992), ibid.

Schon, D. A. (1983) *The Reflective Practitioner*. London: Temple Smith.

Schon, D. A. (1987) *Educating the Reflective Practitioner*. Jossey-Bass.

Totten, N. T. (1989—90) Teaching students to evaluate information: a justification. *RQ* **29**(3), 348—54.

Valentine, B. (1993) Undergraduate research behaviour: using focus groups to generate theory. *Journal of Academic Librarianship* **19**(5), 302.

Walton, G. and Nettleton, S. (1992) Reflective and critical thinking in user education programmes: two case studies. *British Journal of Academic Librarianship* **7**(1), 31—43.

Flexibility and responsibility: facing the challenge of student-centred learning

Karen Hinett
University of Central Lancashire

Introduction

Higher education institutions in Britain are being made increasingly accountable for their scholarly activity. Government initiatives such as Enterprise in Higher Education (EHE) promote the acquisition of 'transferable skills' for students in an attempt to produce graduates suitable for employment in the 1990s. In addition, research exercises and quality audits threaten funding and force staff and management to question current practice. Higher education is being asked to offer evidence of its 'productivity' and 'cost-effectiveness' in much the same way as private industry. The talent and ability of 'consumers' (students) are being offered, as quantifiable output (degree classification) and evidence of success.

As a result of government reform, a huge increase in student numbers, an increasingly disparate student body which comprises part-time, mature, open access, women returners etc. higher education institutions are having to re-consider their teaching and assessment methods and be receptive to the needs of students. The 1992 University of Central England (UCE) student satisfaction survey asked four groups of 'stakeholders', staff and students, employers, quality assurers and the government and quality assessors to identify criteria which were of priority importance to them. Five of the top ten criteria identified by all four stakeholders related to assessment, the acquisition of transferable skills and encouraging students to become responsible learners.

Conflicting interests of quality and accountability often means that assessment tries to serve several purposes. Universities either adopt the resource and reputation view of assessment which focuses on the grades of students entering university or the 'talent development view' (Astin, 1993) which focuses on the progress a student has made since entering the university — in other words how much a student has learnt and developed during their time at university.

This chapter will question whether assessment can serve both accountability and quality of assessment by considering the perceptions and expectations students have of higher education and assessment. Interviews with students on the 'Personal and Academic Development Program' (PDP) at the University of Central Lancashire (UCLP) and Alverno College, Milwaukee will be used in addition to the relevant literature on student learning. Finally, conclusions will be drawn about moves forward in assessment and a case will be made for criterion referenced assessment as a way of promoting student centred learning.

The PDP and research

The PDP is a five-credit, one semester elective available to all first-year students and has been in operation at UCLP since 1993. The elective offers training in information technology, presentation and communication and learning to learn. The programme aims to combine the acquisition of transferable skills with an emphasis on individual development. Research has suggested that these two aims are distinct (Assiter and Shaw, 1993); however the research design aimed to encourage meaningful learning by using a variety of assessment, self, peer, group, practical work, and presentations with points built in for reflection and discussion about the learning that took place. The students were also required to complete 'learning logs' which encouraged them to think about what and how they had learnt and how this related to them personally. This formalized the reflective process (Boud, 1988) by making the students write down their thoughts and critically analyse how and why their learning developed.

Students on the PDP were asked to volunteer to be interviewed about their expectations of higher education and their perceptions of learning. It was anticipated that these students would be open-minded about assessment techniques and approaches to learning since they had all experienced a range of styles on the PDP. The students opt to take PDP as an elective therefore most subject disciplines were represented with the exception of the natural sciences. Students who had taken the course in 1993/4 and who were originally interviewed in 1994 were re-interviewed in 1995 as second-years. In all 15 students were interviewed from each year with a representive ratio of males and females and mature and younger students.

Student perceptions: year one

As first-years the students explained their general surprise at being expected to work independently. Many themes emerged from the interviews however the most predominant theme was assessment although the students did not articulate it by name.

With the exception of one, all the students said that their assessment had been 100% written coursework and examinations. Not surprisingly they were unhappy about examinations and felt that these were 'unfair' and that certain students were disadvantaged, since successful revision was dependent on memory and not comprehension of subject matter. None of them objected to the written coursework as they expected this to be the norm.

Grading and comparison to peers

A typical reaction to grades from the first-years was, 'you only need 40% to pass'. This appeared as a general cliché adopted by the younger students as an excuse for enjoying their social life and not taking their studies seriously. They immediately translated the percentage required to progress to second year as an indication of the amount of work they should be doing. Since they realized that any grade above this would not help them in instrumental terms they put in minimal effort. Other students placed more importance on the grade as an indication of their ability and talked about them as a motivating factor:

> When you get a good mark it gives you confidence, it probably gives you a bit of an incentive to work. You have a honeymoon period when you feel more positive about your work.

Students use the grades as an incentive to perform better and deliberately place themselves in situations of competition between themselves and peers. The majority of students admitted comparing their grade with peers, 'If they get a better mark I can see that they did the assignment in a different way and then I can learn to improve my own.' In this way the students use the competition constructively and as an aid to personal improvement; however, others admitted, comparing yourself to others gives you instant satisfaction. 'If they beat you it motivates you and if you beat them then the motivation isn't as high.' Playing grades off against each other often means that the student is so engrossed in his or her personal battle with another student that the subject matter is reduced in status and the grade becomes the only meaningful symbol of success.

Self-assessment and learning logs

The students had mixed reaction to self-assessment but on the whole were wary of it. Most of them considered the tutor to be the 'expert' and trusted their judgement. 'I think the whole point of assessment is someone else looking at you.' Self-assessment was new to most students and they were apprehensive about the validity and reliability of their own evaluation. 'How can you trust what you feel about it? You might not look at it critically enough.' Many of them talked of bias and did not think that they would adequately evaluate their own performance. One student described her apprehension;

> I think it's harder to assess yourself than be assessed, it's quite hard to know yourself. In terms of the teacher you can try and interpret what they want and the kind of essay they want you to write, you can think of who's marking it.

She unwittingly attributes the problem of self-assessment to a lack of criteria. Students 'cue seek' (Miller and Parlett, 1974) and endeavour to find out what the tutor wants. If the criteria is not made explicit they guess. This concern about lack of information is articulated by many students, they feel they cannot assess themselves since they do not know what is expected of them.

Considering the students apprehension about self-assessment their reaction to learning logs was surprisingly good. The majority of students were very enthusiastic, 'this was actually worth something, you're getting assessed on thinking about something rather than remembering it. It made me think about what I'd learnt.' Students claimed that the learning logs forced them to think about their learning, that they 'helped you clarify things'; others talked of them in a counselling form claiming they 'made you feel better, they help you. I know more about myself than I think I've ever done.' However, those students who favoured the logs emphasized that they were not easy to complete, 'criticizing yourself and analysing yourself is quite a hard thing to do'.

Generally students seemed to appreciate being given the opportunity to make sense of the learning for themselves. However, one student could not see the point in the logs and admitted, 'I lied on most of them. I'm not very honest when I write about myself, I just write what the teacher wants to hear.' Another student admitted that 'I felt I had to detach myself in some way from my emotions to write learning logs because I felt they had to be more informative, more academic.' These are fairly common reactions to self- assessment from first-years since they are reluctant to move away from the security of tutor assessment and find the responsibility of self-evaluation difficult.

Feedback

As a whole students were pleased to get feedback on assignments and the majority said they used it to help them plan for the next piece of work. Students were unhappy about assessment which offered no feedback, in particular examinations, 'all you get is a grade at the end and that doesn't help you in the future, it doesn't tell you where you've gone wrong'. Other students were pessimistic about feedback and the assessment process, 'They do write comments but not to a real personal extent, they don't seem to show that they've really read it and bothered about it.' Several students complained about timing, 'I know there's a lot of us but I think they could get the work back by the time the next essay has to be done.'

The first-years as a group seemed confused about the assessment system, many blamed themselves for poor work, others simply accepted the feedback that was offered to them as standard since they had nothing to compare to. Several students commented that the assessment offered to them on the PDP was different to that on their main course of study. They made reference to the variety of assessment open to them and appreciated being able to complete the assignments as they progressed through the course. Many students referred to assessment which 'all comes at the end of semester' and several complained that when they did get feedback it was given too late to be of any use. Self-assessment was seen very much as a novelty and students seemed genuinely surprised that anyone should be interested in their opinions: 'This had to come from within, it was about us and yet you had to relate it to the external, things we'd learnt, it's strange.'

Student perceptions: year two

By contrast to the first-years, year-two students were increasingly disillusioned by the assessment process. Without exception students complained about assessment being predominantly written and examination-based; hardly any of them had been asked to give a presentation since finishing the PDP in first year and only one had been engaged in self-assessment. The main concern, however, was with feedback and criteria of assessment.

When asked about what was expected of them the majority of the students said they did not know: 'they haven't said what they're looking for', 'you don't know what is expected of you, you haven't got a clue', 'you don't know what they want, you just hope that you've done the right thing'. The students talked about 'guessing' and 'trying to work out what they want'. All students commented that when they were given a criterion it was only to highlight the difference between a degree classification and did not know what was expected of them in terms of ability or research. Several students referred to tutors in terms of 'us and them' as if assessment were a battle between student and tutor. One student referred to the assessment process as a 'conspiracy'. 'Sometimes I think they make things up as they go along. I think there is a general standard to be met, I don't know what it is but I'm sure the tutors know.'

Combined honours students complained about a lack of consistency between departments, while single honours students complained of a discrepancy between tutors' marks in the same department. The student comments would suggest that there is a lack of a clear and explicit rationale and criteria for assessing their work. Many were resentful of a system which seemed to challenge and negate their efforts.

The students all welcomed feedback and spoke strongly about the value it had in helping them to plan for future assignments and in developing their talent and ability: 'You can build on the feedback and learn from it, you don't make the same mistakes twice.' All agreed that feedback was necessary for improvement and this was the root of the problem. Many students complained of a lack of feedback and many were dissatisfied with the quality of the information they received:

> *I get very little feedback. There's more feedback if something is wrong. I want more explicit comments, for me that would clarify exactly where they got the marks from.*

Students suggested that feedback was often too general and concentrated only on the negative aspects leaving the student confused about what was good about the work and providing little foundation upon which to build. In addition the students reiterated the first year's sentiments about timing and complained that even when feedback was given and was constructive it was often too late to be applicable.

The group as a whole appeared to have been denied the opportunity to assess themselves, which, considering the varied subject background of the students, was distressing. Some of the students admitted to assessing their work for themselves and a couple of students claimed they had continued with their learning logs even though they were no longer assessed. The majority of students argued that they would welcome the opportunity to assess themselves. These students had been equally receptive to learning logs and on reflection still considered them to be useful, 'They were good because they made you stop and think. It was good, there ought to be more of that.'

The second-years expressed similar sentiments to the first-years about grades: some felt they were motivated to achieve good grades, others felt threatened by the system, 'if you get a bad mark it really puts you off'. All students placed great importance on grades and several admitted to being obsessed by them, 'grades are vital, I'd die if I got a bad mark'. The majority admitted to being more concerned about grades than they were in first year. When asked, most of the students valued the PDP and said that it had helped them and several suggested that it should be made a compulsory course.

The UCLP experience of assessment

There are several themes which emerge as a result of the students' perceptions of assessment. Grades are considered by the first-years as a means to an end, enabling progression into second year. However by the second year, grades are elevated in status and are seen as the end product to be achieved. There are several possible reasons for this. Firstly, the students are denied a variety of assessment styles and have to accept the written form as the norm; this prevents creativity and denies the student responsibility for their own work. Secondly, they are denied an explicit assessment criteria which forces students into 'guessing games' and attempts to 'play the system' which both reduces the student's power to achieve and wastes energy that could be spent in critical analysis and deeper levels of cognition. Thirdly, this particular group of students, having been given a formalized criteria for self- assessment in the form of 'learning logs' had not been given the opportunity to develop their skills of analysis and evaluation in other courses. Many of the students had not given another presentation, or been given the opportunity for oral assessment; however, they claimed that 'transferable skills' had been promoted as important. As a consequence the students have been stripped of any confidence and self-esteem that might have been built up in the first year.

The UCLP 1994 student satisfaction survey reveals that 71% of students are 'moderately satisfied' with information about the assessment procedures. However, this figure is misleading since only 47% are satisfied with the clarity of the marking procedure and just 55% are satisfied with the helpfulness of comments on assessed work. The problems lie in the assessment design. Assessment is summative, a final mark or comment is given at the end of a learning period (usually a semester) which denies the student the opportunity to learn from mistakes and to reflect on earlier learning experiences. Great emphasis is placed on the output — the written essay, the examination paper, the completed dissertation — whereas the input and environmental factors that affect the learning process are ignored (Astin, 1993). Assessment is thus predominantly incentive driven, students are spurred on by competition with peers and the promise of good grades.

Norm-referenced assessment of this kind does not allow the student the opportunity to assess and evaluate her own work, to consider her own development and the learning that takes place; in short it denies reflection and encourages instrumentalism. Astin (1993) argues:

> *assessment and feedback should be an ongoing, iterative proceeding that is integral to the learning process rather than a one-time activity carried out only at the end of the learning process.*

Lack of meaningful feedback means that the student becomes fearful and resentful of the assessment system which does not seem to favour them. Students respect tutors not because of their expertise but because of the power they have as assessors; instead of viewing themselves as equal partners on a journey of development, students sees the tutor as someone to impress or manipulate in order to gain good marks (Astin, 1993). Achieving good grades becomes the main aim; however, students are denied bargaining power since without a clear criteria within which to work they become victims of a system which denies them the currency with which to trade.

The system described of incentive driven, summative, norm-referenced assessment is one currently in operation at many UK institutions. Such a system serves the resource and reputation view of education. The use of output (grades and degree certificates) allows evidence to be offered of accountability to stakeholders such as government and employers. However, while incentive-driven assessment is useful as a political tool it does little for the talent-development view of assessment. The educational experience of other stakeholders, the staff and students is compromised and, arguably, quality and excellence are forfeited for cost-effectiveness. It is difficult to imagine how these two seemingly conflicting styles of assessment might be reconciled. Alverno College, Milwaukee has pioneered with their assessment-as-learning programme and have attempted to produce both talent development and provide evidence of accountability.

The Alverno model

Alverno is a 'small, urban Catholic liberal arts college for women' (Schmitz, 1994). The concept of assessment employed at the college stems from the premise 'that what learners achieve — not what teachers provide — is at the centre of the educational universe'. They define their assessment-as-learning' as:

> *a multidimensional process, integral to learning, that involves observation and judgement of each student's performance on the basis of explicit criteria, with resulting feedback to the student.*

Assessment at Alverno is performance-based and centres around the achievement of eight 'abilities':

- communication;
- analysis;
- problem-solving;
- valuing in decision-making;
- social interaction;
- global perspectives;
- effective citizenship;
- aesthetic response.

Each 'ability' has its own specific criterion of achievement measured on a six-point sequence scale. Students must demonstrate competence at each level of the sequence. Levels are considered in terms of 'concepts and terms that are informed by a context, wither disciplinary or interdisciplinary, that comes as close as possible to a professional or other life situation' (Schmitz, 1994). Each ability must be demonstrated as integrated within the discipline, for example problem-solving might be shown as an ability of engineering. Abilities must also be developmental and 'can be defined in pedagogical, cumulative levels that describe increasingly complex elements or processes for learning and assessing performance' (Schmitz, 1994). Finally, abilities must be transferable to other contexts and must prepare the student for a variety of academic and life experiences.

All abilities, whether they be content-specific or generic are defined by tight criteria at each sequence level. Assessment sheets at all levels are available to students throughout their college career allowing them to plan their work in advance, to know what is expected of them at each level and to monitor their own progress. Group interviews with eight students in total took place during November 1994. Students were asked about their experience and perceptions of learning with particular attention paid to assessment.

Students were very enthusiastic about their educational experience at Alverno:

> *Performance-based learning is exactly that, every day I'm in class, the participation, the discussion, you're always on your toes, it's not three times a semester you take a test it's every day.*

Students have to relate each ability to the wider context of the discipline and show critical understanding of how each ability integrates with subject matter. They are able to do this because of the explicit criteria. Since all assessment is performance-based and criterion-referenced students are not in competition with each other but focus exclusively on their own personal development. Some students admitted to staff that they felt 'threatened' by the assessment; however, the majority feel safe in the knowledge that they can make mistakes and know where they have gone wrong since they can check their performance against the criteria. Astin advocates criterion-referenced assessment over norm-referencing because:

> *it tells us something about the student's absolute level of performance, and it in no way limits the number or proportion of students who can achieve excellent performance. Excellence, under a criterion-referenced approach to assessment is not artificially rationed.*

At Alverno all students have equal access to achievement since they can monitor their progress via the criteria, and be aware of areas of development through the lengthy feedback that is given on each transcript. Students are not graded as such, they receive a 'satisfactory' or 'unsatisfactory' grade therefore all peer competition is eliminated. In addition, students are given training in self and peer assessment and consider themselves to be on a developmental journey which requires help from staff and peers. In this way a strong team spirit is fostered.

> *Not only is the feedback itself extremely informative and useful to the student, but since the process itself requires the professor to get to know the individual student's work personally, narrative feedback strengthens and enhances the relationship between student and faculty member. (Astin, 1993)*

Degree classification and grade point average (GPA) is not given at Alverno; instead student's receive a lengthy transcript of their ability. This qualitative, formative judgement gives much more detail about what the student can do and how she has developed; it focuses on changes and improvements that have taken place and as such embraces the talent development view of assessment. Arguably, the transcripts do not offer quantifiable output which can be used as evidence of accountability by stakeholders; however, resource and reputation are secured at Alverno since the institution now has an international reputation for fostering talent and producing competent graduates. Staff will agree (albeit reluctantly) to translate the final transcript into a GPA if graduate schools insist.

Self-assessment is one of the key features of the Alverno assessment process and students are introduced to the concept at orientation days and induction sessions. Reactions range from 'It's painful, but it works and I learn more' to 'I like the self-assessment because I can reflect back and know I should study more in this area.' The students are encouraged to trust their own judgement and to consider themselves as capable learners. As a result the majority of students are full of confidence and enthusiastic about their time at university. In addition, the students see their learning as an organic, holistic experience. The students have difficulty separating their social lives from college and many are devoted to their studies. This appears to be because of the generic and content specific abilities teamed with a sense of ownership of learning. The students become reflective and are responsible for their learning since they are fully involved in the planning, exposition and evaluation of their work (Boud, 1988).

The Alverno model of assessment-as-learning is offered as an example of good practice and as a way of fulfilling both the talent development and resource and reputation view of assessment. It facilitates independent learning which results in flexible responsible students by using criterion-referenced, performance-based assessment with formative feedback. However, Alverno is a small, private, all-female liberal arts college with few students. The assessment system cannot be directly translated to a British system of mass higher education which incorporates modularization, semesterization and credit accumulation and transfer (CATS). However, lessons can be learnt from the approach.

Flexibility and responsibility

Changes in higher educational over the past decade mean that students (consumers) are now demanding more of their university experience. Institutions need to respond to the diversity of the student body by offering multidimensional assessment which allows students to plan their learning, to make sense of modularization and to gain from university both the subject specific and generic skills needed to contribute to the workforce. Flexible learning strategies such as open and distant learning, teamed with group, peer assessment and self-assessment allow the student more ownership and control over their learning and create a relationship of equality between staff and student.

> *If institutions wish to revise their assessment practices to focus more on the talent development mission, they must view assessment much more as a form of feedback that can be used to enlighten both teacher an student about the student's progress and the effectiveness of teaching. (Astin, 1993)*

Students need to be given useful, formative feedback on their work which requires a deconstruction of existing assessment paradigms which concentrate on incentive led, summative, written assignments as the basis for awarding grades. The student voice from UCLP suggest that students would welcome more feedback, particularly verbal feedback and this needs to be given at times which are useful to them. This does not necessarily have to make huge demands on tutor's time but requires a shift in emphasis from heavy teacher-led, content-driven seminars to more student-led, interactive workshops. With training for both staff and students, such seminars can be facilitated by the students themselves.

The status of self-assessment needs raising. Students on the PDP were generally very positive about learning logs and saw the benefit they could have on personal development. However, many of these students did not acknowledge the learning logs as a form of self-assessment and were apprehensive about grading themselves because they were lacking in confidence and considered the tutor to be the expert. Students need to be given the opportunity to assess themselves and their peers in order that they feel responsible for their work. Where assessment comprises a written assignment without criteria, which is graded by a tutor and given back to the student without adequate feedback, the student cannot take responsibility or ownership of her work since it is apparently out of her control.

Conclusions

The PDP programme can be considered a successful innovation in terms of the students' appreciation. Many of them enjoyed the variety of assessment, found the learning logs to be helpful, if daunting at first, and considered the skills being offered important to their education and development. However, the research implies that by the second year students become disillusioned by the assessment process and adopt an instrumental approach to their work. The students 'learn' the culture of the institution (Becker *et al.*, 1968) by year two and rather than being receptive and open to new forms of teaching and learning become focused on their goal of achieving grades since they rationalize that grades equal success. Arguably, a lack of institutional consistency can lead to student discontent and surface learning.

Responsibility cannot be created by introducing group discussions, or self-assessment alone. Commitment to talent development must be institution-wide and reflected in the mission statement (or ethos) of the university. Astin (1993) argues;

> *Assessment is a potentially powerful — but greatly misused, misunderstood and under-used tool for improving higher education policies and practice.*

If we are to develop responsible, flexible learners the student perception of assessment must be acknowledged and decisions have to be made about whether we choose incentive-driven, accountable assessment or whether we embrace academic freedom and transform assessment into a qualitative, meaningful experience for students.

References

Assiter, A. and Shaw, E. (1993) *Using Records of Achievement in Higher Education*. HEC, Kogan Page Ltd.

Astin, A. (1993) *Assessment for Excellence — The Philosophy and Practice of Assessment and Evaluation in Higher Education*. Phoenix: American Council on Education Series and the Oryx Press.

Becker, H. (1968) *Making the Grade: The Academic Side of Life*. New York: Wiley.

Boud, D. (1988) *Developing Student Learning and Autonomy*, 2nd edn. Kogan Page.

Harvey, L., Burrows, A. and Green, D. (1992) *Criteria of Quality — Summary Quality in Higher Education Project*. Birmingham: University of Central England.

Miller, C. and Parlett, M. (1974) *Up to the Mark: A Study of the Examinations Game*. SRHE Monograph No. 21.

Schmitz, J. (ed.) (1994) *Student Assessment-as-Learning at Alverno College*. Milwaukee: Alverno College Institute.

University of Central Lancashire (1994) *Student Satisfaction Survey*. UCLP.

28 Problem-solving approaches of some first-year Chemical Engineering students

G. F. Walker
School of Science and Technology, University of Teesside

Introduction

This work is based on a dissertation submitted to the Open University as part of an MA in Education and grew out of an earlier investigation into problems with mathematics experienced by first- year science and engineering students conducted as part of the same MA.

One of the outcomes of the earlier investigation was to highlight a perception by the teaching staff that many students have an underlying weakness in basic mathematics which is seen as a major contributory factor in the problems they experience in their courses. These findings were confirmed in a study by the Engineering Council (Sutherland and Pozzi, 1995) which came to similar conclusions based on a wider sample than my own. In addition, this weakness is often compounded by a poor understanding of the basic scientific laws and principles on which much first- year work is based. Furthermore, discussion with colleagues suggests that the students often seem to possess poor problem-solving skills. It is essential that engineering students develop effective problem-solving skills during their university careers as the essence of engineering is being able to use one's skills and knowledge to solve practical problems. The lack of skills in solving practical engineering problems was implicit in many of the criticisms of engineering education in the Finniston Report (Finniston, 1980). Accordingly, it was felt worth while to study the way that first-year students approach problems to see if it was possible to identify some of the factors which lead to success.

Problem-solving

Problem-solving is a major feature of human activity. We are constantly being confronted with and successfully solving problems of all kinds. In spite of this, the explicit development of problem-solving skills in undergraduates has traditionally been given very little attention. Nevertheless, there have been a group of workers, particularly in North America, who have been concerned with teaching students the basics of problem-solving skills. Much of their work is based on that of Polya (1945) whose particular interest was in solving mathematical problems. More recently, in the UK there has been some increase in interest in developing problem-solving skills under the general heading of 'Personal transferable skills' or 'Common Skills'. The Business and Technology Education Council (BTEC) include 'Problem Tackling and Solving' in their programme of common skills (BTEC, 1992).

If the solving skills of students are to be improved, it is important first to define and characterize what is meant by a problem and then to identify the key features of a solution and the processes by which one may solve a problem. DeBono (1970) defines a problem simply as 'The difference between what one has and what one wants' and this seems as good a working definition as any. Wicklegren (1974) suggests that a problem statement should contain three elements:

1. a set of *givens*, i.e. conditions and information available initially; the givens may be explicit or implicit;

2. *operations*, i.e. actions that may be taken to move the problem towards

3. the *goal*, i.e. the desired end state of the problem. Like the givens the goal may be explicit or implicit and may not be clearly stated initially.

The process of solving a problem then involves moving from the givens to the goal by means of appropriate operations.

Problems may be classified into a number of categories. DeBono (1970) identifies three basic categories:

1. problems that require more information or better ways of handling information;

2. problems that require a rearrangement of information already available and

3. the problem of 'no problem', i.e. the adequacy of the present arrangement prevents a better one being seen or 'one is not even aware a problem exists'

The first two categories may be seen as being two ends of a spectrum of problems. At one end of the spectrum are open-ended problems where the problem is often very loosely stated and multiple solutions are possible. In such cases, much of the effort in solving the problem involves defining the problem and negotiating an agreed goal. Engineering design problems, for example, are of this nature. At the other end of the spectrum are fully defined problems with the goal clearly stated and all the information required to achieve a solution supplied. Such problems are often known as 'exercises' and are typical of the problems found at the end of chapters in basic mathematics, science and engineering textbooks. The range of problems is summarized in Table 1.

Table 1 Categories of problem

Category	Open ended	Fully defined
Features	Many givens implicit Goal initially unclear Multiple solutions possible	Givens explicit Goal clearly stated All information for solution provided

Solving a problem is a process, and a number of models have been proposed to represent the problem-solving process. Most of the extant models are based on Polya's original four stage model. This comprises:
1. understand the problem;
2. devise a plan;

3. carry out the plan;
4. look back, review. (Polya, 1957)

Koen (1984) criticized Polya's basic model on the grounds that it implies a linear process which does not accurately represent the way people actually solve problems. He states that

People actually circulate within the proposed plan — iterating, backtracking and skipping stages.

Koen also proposes a simpler model which effectively merges the second and third of Polya's stages, *viz.*

1. analyse the problem;

2. synthesize a solution;

3. evaluate the results.

By combining this with the iterative approach described above, you have a model which is both simpler and more sophisticated.

Schoenfeld (1985), on the other hand, proposes a more detailed, multi-stage model:

1. read;

2. analyse;

3. explore;

4. plan;

5. implement;

6. verify.

A successful attempt to solve a problem will proceed through all of these stages. Schoenfeld also identifies a set of factors which are additionally held to be important for successful problem-solving. These are:

Resources:	Knowledge and access to knowledge
Heuristics:	Useful mental operations or procedures; inventory of available techniques. These may or may not be discipline specific
Control:	Selecting and pursuing 'right approaches'; recovering from inappropriate choices; overseeing the whole process
Belief:	About the nature of problems in the domain.

An experienced and successful problem-solver will score strongly and/or positively in each of the four factors.

Both Polya and Koen also advocate the use of heuristics in the solving of problems. Koen identifies the following characteristics of a heuristic:

1. It does not guarantee a solution.

2. It may contradict other heuristics.

3. It reduces the time for solving a problem.

4. Its acceptance depends on immediate context rather than absolute standards, i.e. it works!

Lester (1985) also criticizes Polya's basic model. He feels that Polya's model concentrates purely on the cognitive aspect of problem solving and neglects the metacognitive. He redefines each of Polya's stages to include a metacognitive component:

1. *Orientation* — strategic behaviours to assess and understand a problem

2. *Organization* — planning of behaviour to conform to plans

3. *Execution* — regulation of behaviour to conform to plans

4. *Verification* — evaluation of decisions made and of outcomes of executed plans

He then defines the metacognitive component in terms of three sets of variables:

1. *Person variables: one's belief system, affective characteristics that affect performance, one's assessment of one's own capabilities.*

2. Task variables: *Awareness of features of a task that influence performance. These involve content, context, structure, syntax and process.*

3. *Strategy variables*: Awareness of strategies that aid in comprehending, organizing, planning and executing.

Larkin *et al.* (1980) compared problem-solving strategies among novice and expert problem-solvers when solving some basic physics problems. The differences may be categorized under three main headings: Knowledge of domain, Problem definition and solution strategies. Their findings are summarized in Table 2.

Table 2 Comparison of expert and novice problem solvers

Factor	Expert	Novice
Knowledge of domain	Greater quantity of knowledge. 'Chunking' of related knowledge	Less knowledge. Knowledge relatively unstructured
Problem definition	Defines problem (qualitatively) in terms of system. Works from fundamentals.	Moves quickly into writing and solving equations. Works in terms of symbol manipulation
Solution strategies	Works forward from givens to desired outcomes. Solves problem by accumulating information about unknowns	Works backwards from unknowns. Requires goals and sub-goals to direct search
Others	Solves problem relatively quickly. Makes relatively few errors	Takes more time. Makes more errors

Source: Bases on Larkin *et al*, 1980.

The student sample

The study was based on a group of six HNC Chemical Engineering students who attend the university for one day per week. They were chosen because they were a small, self-contained group. For most of their day in the university they are taught together with the full-time HND course but they have a tutorial on their own in the evening. Their qualifications and employment are summarized in Table 3.

Table 3 Qualifications and employment of student sample

Student	Qualifications	Employment
Andy	BTEC NC in Science	Research Technician in Pharmaceutical company
David	City & Guilds Process Plant Operation part III	Chemical Plant Operator in UK subsidiary of US chemical company
John	BTEC NC in Mechanical Engineering	Technical Assistant in a minerals processing company
Len	OU – Maths Foundation Fundamentals of Computing Maths in Computing	Research Technician in Pharmaceutical company
Martin	GCE A-level Maths C Chemistry C Physics E BSc (Hons) Chemistry	Research Technician in major UK chemical company
Stewart	BTEC HNC Industrial Measurement and Control	Safety Technician in major UK chemical company

The problem the students worked on was from a module called 'Mass and Energy Balance'. This module was selected because it is both fundamental to Chemical Engineering and almost invariably causes considerable difficulties among first-year students at both degree and HND/HNC level. Mass and energy balance is concerned with the flows of materials and energy through processes and represents the first stage in analysing or designing a process. The scientific laws and principles on which it depends are basically those of conservation of mass and energy and of chemical combination. In addition, a good grasp of basic algebra is required. The essence of the subject is not in learning new concepts, but in applying existing ones to practical situations.

The actual problem involved producing a flow diagram of an industrial steam-boiler system and calculating the quantity of steam raised for a given quantity of fuel burnt. It was not a completely straightforward problem but should not be beyond the students at this stage of their course.

Data collection and analysis

The teaching in this module is based on students working on problems during class time, sometimes in informal groups at others in formal groups. An audio recording was made of the students working on a class exercise as a group. Consideration was given to the use of video rather than audio but problems of availability of the equipment at the required times prevented this. It was believed that recording students working in a group would enables the strategies and tactics employed by the students to be made explicit.

A full transcript was made of the recording and was analysed in a two-stage process. The first stage involved providing a commentary on the dialogue to illuminate the activities that were occurring. This was based on an approach developed by Barnes and Todd (1977) who suggest that every time a participant in a dialogue makes an utterance, they offer two frames to the other participants. The interaction frame identifies the relationships and the processes occurring between group members. The content frame infers the developing understandings of the group as they progress towards a solution. An example of a portion of the annotated transcript is given in Table 4.

Table 4 Section of transcript annotated using Barnes and Todd's (1977) model

	Utterance	**Interaction frame**	**Content frame**
46 D	That should be . . .		Sequencing equipment
		Both see sequence	Both sharing
47 S	should be . . .	together and follow through	understanding
48 D/S	The the . . er . . air preheater		
49 S	Then you can do it in sequence can't you?	S unsure	
			The relationship of the
50 S	[To T] (. . .) boiler's actually part of your furnace isn't it?	so seeks confirmation	various equipment is still not clear

The annotated version of the transcript was used for a second stage analysis. This involved both taking an overview of the data and looking at specific sections in some detail and made use of Koen's iterative model of problem solving.

Overview of the solution process

The students effectively solved the problem in the time available although they needed help to do so. Achieving a solution required the completion of three major tasks:

1. producing a flow diagram of the process;

2. completing a mass balance, i.e. calculating the quantities of fuel, air, flue gases and water/steam passing through each stage of the process;

3. completing an energy balance, i.e. calculating the quantity of heat involved at each stage of the process.

An outline of how the solution was achieved is described in Figure 1.

Figure 1 Summary of Solution to Problem

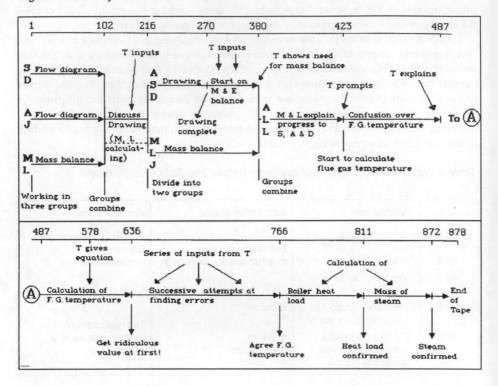

Figure 1 indicates how the group worked and what were, for them, the major problem areas. Initially, they divided into three pairs, with two pairs working mainly on the flow diagram and the third on the mass balance calculations. At 216, the flow diagram was essentially complete and the group reorganized itself. Len and Martin, now with John, continued the mass balance calculations while Andy, Stewart and David produced a 'definitive' version of the flow diagram. Once this task was completed, the latter group then proceeded to start on some energy balance calculations but ran into a series of difficulties. At 380 the two sub-groups combined and worked as a single group for the remainder of the time. From 423 to 766, they were tackling what proved to be the major difficulty, that is calculating the temperature of the flue gases (i.e. the products of combustion) leaving the furnace. This temperature was the key to the energy balance and once it had been calculated, the remainder of the problem was relatively straightforward.

Having described the solution process, it is now possible to take a look at some of the features of that process.

The first thing to be noted is that the talk is almost entirely concerned with the task in hand. There is almost no digression from this and what little there is tends to take the form of banter which is used to relieve tension periodically. This can be illustrated effectively with an excerpt from the very beginning of the tape which shows how quickly the group settle down to work on the task in hand with very little in the way of preliminaries.

General noise of question being read, books and papers being moved and group settling down.

They organize themselves into three pairs:

Dave and Stu	*Start work on a flow diagram*
Martin and Len	*Start on calculations*
Andy and John	*Also start work on a flow diagram*

1	M	We've got recycle here
2	?	... (Indistinct)...
3	M	(...) practice on these!
4	?	You should crack this one between you
5	?	... (Indistinct)...
6	A	You gonna do t'diagram then?
7	D	We're doing it over here
8	A	Uh! [*Cough obscures reply*]
9	?	... (Indistinct)...
10	A	(Indistinct query)
11	L	... (Indistinct)... two percent ... two point four percent
12	M	Just put S1 and S2 ...
13	A	That comes out ...
14	S	Fuel composition ... degrees C twenty percent excess air
15	S	That'll be in that line won't it? (...)T

As can be seen from the transcript, the group organized themselves into sub-groups and settled down the task with very little fuss. The overall effect is a very businesslike one. This businesslike approach tended to be a feature of this group of students compared to the full-time HND students who tended not to work in such a concentrated fashion when put in a similar situation. It may well be a function of the relative maturity of the group members and the fact that these students only have the one day per week at the university and need to make the most of their time.

On the other hand, the excerpt above suggests that very little preliminary analysis of the problem was undertaken before getting into the detail. This is behaviour typical of novice problem-solvers (Larkin *et al.*, 1980) and is reinforced by the fact that Len and Martin were performing calculations at a very early stage.

Another aspect of the solution process was the uneven level of contribution by the various members of the group. A count was made of the number of utterances made by each participant (including the tutor) and the results are summarized in Table 5.

Table 5 Statistics of utterances

Utterances	Speaker						
	A	D	J	L	M	S	T
1–150	16%	29%	2%	3%	4%	44%	2%
151–310	31%	12%	1%	17%	13%	19%	8%
311–462	16%	4%	2%	18%	27%	4%	30%
463–612	10%	1%	3%	11%	40%	9%	26%
613–762	9%	2%	2%	20%	35%	5%	26%
763–878	1%	0%	1%	27%	37%	5%	29%
Overall	**14%**	**8%**	**2%**	**16%**	**26%**	**14%**	**20%**

Unknown attributions have been excluded

Table 5 shows that Stewart, Andy and David are predominant early on but that Martin and Len come to dominate later on. It also shows John saying very little throughout. It also shows the tutor participating very little in the early stages but becoming more prominent later. The largest single contributor was Martin, and, had the tape picked up their conversation in the early stages, his and Len's contribution would have been proportionately larger still. If one were to assume that equal contribution would lead to approximately equal numbers of utterances, then a Chi-squared test shows the variability in the numbers of utterances is statisticaly significant ($p < 0.01$ throughout). A possible explanation could lie in the background of the students. Andy, David and Stewart are prominent at the stage of drawing the flow diagram and all three have a significant plant background and will be familiar with using flow diagrams. Martin and Len on the other hand had spent their careers to date in the Laboratory. This suggests that the group were in fact playing to their strengths though John's apparent minimal contribution is still hard to explain — he was certainly not a lazy student and seemed to relate well to the others. The only clue lies in the nature of many of his utterances which seemed to involve queries. Some examples are given below.

405 J?   What's going on (. . .)

416 J   What's that heat at the end there? . . . Where do you get that from?

417 A   You put that in there (. . .) your temperature . . .

756 J   What have you added twenty five for?

By no means all his utterances were like these but he did seem to produce a higher proportion of this type of query than any of the others. This suggests that he may have had difficulty following the drift of things at times and may account for his minor contribution.

Another aspect highlighted by Table 4 is the contribution made by the tutor. Initially, the tutor's contribution was minimal and tended to be confined to replies to questions directly to him, for example.

50	S	[To T] (. . .) boiler's actually part of your furnace isn't it?
51	T	[*suddenly realizing he is being spoken to*] Yeah . . er I mean Yeah
52	S	You have your tubes don't you with your . . . your water in
53	T	Yeah . . . Yeah
54	S	Then it flashes off in steam (. . .)
55	T	Yeah . . . assuming it's . . . it depends whether it's fire tube . . . but Yeah you will have your furnace heating your tubes . . .
56	S	Yeah . . . Yeah

In this case, T is not giving away any more than he has to!

This continued until about the time that the two sub-groups of three combined into a single group when the tutor began to take a more active role.

360	T	Let's prod you along a little bit because if you think about it . . .
361	S?	Yeah?
362	T	There's your air preheat coming (. . .) . . . There's your air preheat . . . Yeah? . . . You know your . . . You know how much you're going to raise your air temperature?
363	S	Uh
364	T	. . .

In contrast to the previous excerpt, the tutor here is actively offering help. The explanation begun at 362 ended at 380 with the tutor pointing out the need for a mass balance. Over the next phase, the tutor becomes very actively involved in helping the group overcome their difficulties in calculating the temperature of the flue gas leaving the furnace. By the time they had calculated this all important temperature, time was getting on and some the tutor's contributions show another change and take the form of moving the students along so that they can complete the task on time.

766	M	Ok that's . . . So that's before the air preheater . . . So now we've three two three there
767	T	So now you can do your heat balance over your . . . boiler
812	M	OK so that's (. . .)
813	T	So now you need to work out how much steam you're gonna raise from that, then scale it to six kilogrammes per second
814	M	OK, so we've got that and that and (. . .)
815	T	and the last bit is just a matter of P V equals N R T at various places
843	T	What you need to do is scale everything to . . . six kilogrammes per second
844	M	We've got that many . . .?
845	T	You've got that many kilogrammes from one hundred kilomoles of fuel
846	M	Yeah

847 T   So you need to scale it ... Then you can get your volume just by P V equals N R T

848 M   So hundred kilomoles gets us thirty-five thousand kilogrammes

Overall, the tutor's role appears to be that of providing 'instructional scaffolding' (Applebee, 1989), i.e. giving assistance in solving a problem which is just beyond the students' ability to solve unaided — even when working in a group.

Producing a flow diagram

Producing the flow diagram is worth a closer look because it is a significant task in its own right as well as being an important stage on the route to solving the overall problem. In fact text books almost invariably advocate drawing a diagram as an early stage in solving the problem. Nevertheless producing all but the simplest of flow diagrams is a non-trivial task and this one was no exception.

In looking at the production of the flow diagram, the transcript was interpreted to recreate what might have been produced at each stage. Figure 2 represents a summary of progress in producing the flow diagram.

Figure 2 Production of flow diagram

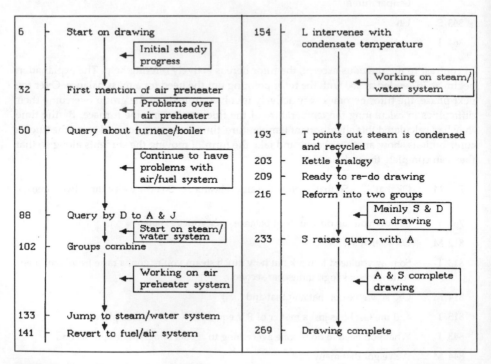

On the basis of Fig 2 and the transcript, it is possible to recreate the stages in producing the diagram.

For example, following the exerpt below, something like Figure 3 might have been expected.

6	A	You gonna do t'diagram then?
7	D	We're doing it over here
8	A	Uh! [*Cough obscures reply*]
9	?	. . . (Indistinct). . .
10	A	(Indistinct query)
11	L	. . . (Indistinct). . . two percent . . . two point four percent
12	M	Just put S1 and S2 . . .
13	A	That comes out . . .
14	S	Fuel composition . . . degrees C twenty percent excess air
15	S	That'll be in that line won't it? (. . .)
16	J	Atmospheric pressure . . .
17	?	. . . (Indistinct) . . .
18	A	(. . .) got a furnace . . . (. . .), fuel going in
19	?	. . . (Indistinct). . .
20	S	(. . .) going in the tubes in't . . . give you your furnace . . . your water in the tubes . . .
21	M	ten degrees C
22	S	flashes off and gives you steam doesn't it?
23	S	So we can draw it actually differently can't we? . . . actually draw it as a furnace . . . with . . . fuel going in like a . . . like a reformer isn't it?
24	?	You what?
25	S	like a . . . [General *noise drowns out*] . . . isn't it, with the tubes going down?

Figure 3

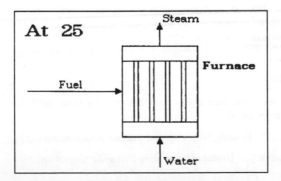

The discussion continues, sometimes haltingly, sometimes with confidence and involving a considerable amount of jumping about, backtracking, and going over ground that has already been covered until the diagram looks something like that in Figure 4.

Figure 4

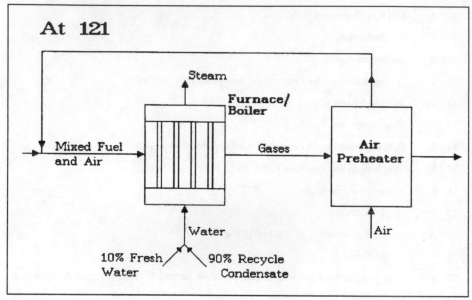

The final resolution involves some prompting from the tutor.

193 T   It gets condensed back down to a hundred and . . . you got . . . You need a condenser in there . . . On your block diagram . . . 'Cos it goes in at three hundred and ninety eight point three . . . the condensed steam.

194 A   Yeah?

195 T   and ten percent of the condensate is lost

196 A   So ten percent goes out there?

197 T   Ah No . . . No, No . . . it goes out of your cond . . . out . . . not out as steam . . . that . . . that shows it going out as steam. It would have to go out of the bottom . . . the bottom side of the condenser 'cos it's . . .

198 T   condensate

General noise of working

199 A   That's at three hundred at this point before it goes through there . . . then the condensate comes down here?

200 ?   Heating it . . . Heating water up and putting it back again (. . .)

201 ?   . . . (Indistinct). . . [*sound of paper being torn and crumpled up*]

202 ?   ... (Indistinct)...

203 ?   It's a kettle is that!

204 T   You what?

205 ?   [*several voices*] It's a kettle isn't it?

206 T   It's a kettle ... yeah

207 ?   ... (Indistinct)...

208 M   You should be laughing on this problem Stu! [*Laughter*]

At this point, the flow diagram is effectively solved and all that remains to be done is to redraw it tidily. The result will similar to Figure 28.5.

Figure 5 Completed flow diagram

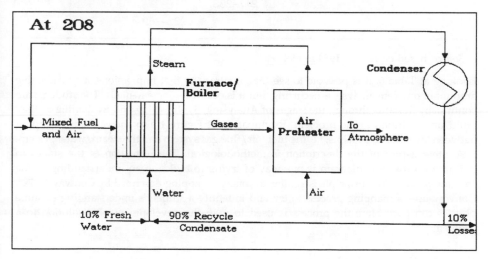

If we look more closely at the process described here, it provides an interesting example of Koen's (1984) model of problem-solving, i.e.

a   Analyse the problem

b   Synthesise s solution

c   Evaluate the results

It is possible to identify the three stages of Analysis, Synthesis and Evaluation in the transcript. Table 6 provides a summary of utterances that can be ascribed to each of the stages. Utterances positioned between two categories have been ascribed to both categories.

Table 6 Analysis of process of drawing flow diagram

Analysis	Synthesis	Evaluation
18		
20–23		
32–41	42–48	
60–81	83–85	86
90–102		
		103–121
		122–138
139–153		
154–192	203–208	
	217–233	
		233–269

Source: Based on Koen's 1984 model

Looking at Table 6, it is possible to see that, contrary to first impressions, a considerable amount of problem analysis is occurring, but it is occurring incrementally. The students are continually iterating through the stages of Analysing, Synthesizing and Evaluating as they build up a solution to the problem. Examination of Figure 1 also shows them swapping between the two sub-systems, i.e. the fuel/air/flue gas system and the steam/water system.

Another aspect of the description is methodological. The recreation of the stages in building up the flow diagram is one way of trying to build up an understanding of the solution process. The principle is similar to concept mapping described by Conway (1979). Conway uses a mapping process to try and indentify a student's understanding of some physics concepts. Here the process is used to map the development of a solution to a problem.

Concluding remarks

Looking back over the outcomes described in the previous section, it is clear that the process of solving a problem is an iterative one and problem-solving models need to reflect this. Koen's (1984) model, although in some ways a simple model, seems be a fair representation of the process identified in this chapter. The present group also displayed some of the characteristics of novice problem-solvers. In particular, they did little initial planning or analysis of the problems and their attempts to search for suspected errors tended to the unsystematic. On the other hand, I feel that sub-goals are necessary, even for experienced problem-solvers, for all but the simplest of problems. The problem set here was more complex than most that are described in the literature, but was not, in itself, a particularly complex one. Nevertheless, when solving this problem myself, I divided it into three major tasks, each of which was a significant problem in its own right. It is not surprising, therefore, that this group floundered at times even though they were a group of mature and competent students. This highlights, for me, the importance of assisting students through the solution of problems of varying complexity if they are going to develop effective problem solving strategies.

The study suggests the value of co-operative problem-solving in assisting the students to develop effective strategies. This may come through interaction with the student's tutors or peers and both have effective roles to play. As a consequence of this study, I have introduced small-group exercises into the module from which this study was drawn. Although the exercises proved valuable, further development is needed if their value is to be fully realized.

References

Applebee, A. (1989) The enterprise we are part of: learning to teach. In P. Murphy and R. Moon, *Developments in Learning and Assessment*. London, Hodder and Stoughton.

Barnes, D. and Todd, F. (1977) *Communication and Learning in Small Groups*. London: Routledge & Kegan Paul.

BTEC (1992) *Common Skills and Core Themes: General Guideline*. London: Business and Technology Education Council.

DeBono, E. (1970) *Lateral Thinking*. London: Ward Lock.

Finniston, M. (1980) *Engineering our Future: Report of the Committee of Inquiry into the Engineering Profession*. London: HMSO.

Koen, B. V. (1984) Toward a definition of engineering method. *Engineering Education* **75**, 150—5.

Larkin, J. *et al.* (1980) Expert and novice performance in solving physics problems. *Science* **208** (20 June), 1335—42.

Lester, F. K. (1985) Methodological considerations in research on problem-solving instruction. In A. E. Silver, *Teaching and Learning Mathematical Problems Solving*.

Polya, G. (1957) *How to Solve It*, 2nd edn. New York, Doubleday.

Schoenfield, A. H. (1985) *Mathematical Problem Solving*. Orlando, Academic Press.

Sutherland, R. and Pozzi, S. (1995) *The Changing Mathematical Background of Undergraduate Engineers*. London: The Engineering Council.

Walker, G. (1994) Problem solving approaches of some first year engineering students. Unpublished MA dissertation, Open University.

Wicklegren, W. A. (1974) *How to Solve Problems*. San Francisco, W. H. Freeman.

29 A coordinated programme to test numeracy skills for undergraduates

Richard Thomas, Carl Adams, Lesley Kimber and Malcolm Robertson
Southampton Institute of Higher Education, Southampton

Introduction

This chapter examines the processes involved in setting up a coordinated programme to test, monitor and develop numeracy skills for business-related undergraduates. The chapter covers the practical problems encountered on a substantial project involving four members of staff over two semesters. The project included the production of specially designed multi-choice numeracy tests, work book and teaching material and, incorporating the new numeracy skills component into existing undergraduate programmes.

Background context

Over the last five years the Southampton Institute has seen a dramatic increase in the number of students and a corresponding increase in the number of degree courses offered. In 1992 a core unit, the Skills Unit was introduced on our business-related degrees in the Business School Undergraduate Programme (BSUP). The Skills Unit addressed a range of business-related skills, including numeracy, a large proportion of which dealt with basic business statistics. The aim of the numeracy component was to develop the numeracy and basic statistical skills required for other units on the BSUP and in the wider business context.

The original numeracy component of the Skills Unit attracted a range of criticism including:

- Feedback from students indicated that some found the unit too difficult. Many of the business students had not done any mathematics or statistics for at least two years (i.e. when they took their GCSEs) and so were fairly rusty. Several of the mature students, though seemingly good with numbers, were even more uncertain on maths topics, such as algebra and equations. Conversely, other students, who studied mathematics or statistics at advanced level, found the unit too easy.

- Feedback from staff on the Skills Unit indicated that there were several problems in teaching the unit. The students were of such a wide range of abilities (including those with A level maths down to mature students with no maths qualifications), invariably the teaching material was not at the right level for most students. Further, the students with maths problems would either hold back the rest of the class with remedial work or the students would 'hide' their maths problem by not turning up to tutorials or not participating in the tutorials. In some cases the only time that students with numeracy problems were identified was after the exams. By this time it was too late to take any corrective action (i.e. point the students towards the Study Assistance group or give the students extra work).

- Feedback from staff on other units indicated that the students were deficient in basic numeracy skills. It seemed that our expected numeracy skill level of average students with GCSE mathematics was different to the actual skill level. This was perhaps due to changes in the GCSE syllabuses or mathematical emphasis at schools. Alternatively, it could reflect an unrealistic expectation on behalf of the teaching staff. Whatever the reason, there was a problem in that the numeracy component of the Skills Unit did not develop the relevant skills for other units on the BSUP.

The Institute's Study Assistance group who offer students remedial support in mathematics reported that there seemed to be several students needing mathematics help. The Study Assistance group also run a numeracy test in freshers week, the general results of which are fed back to the students. The numeracy test was aimed at a variety of students including engineering students and many students and tutors felt it was not that relevant for the business students.

The skills team was also concerned that there may be problems with different student groups, such as age groups, gender groups, ethnic groups, and diverse entry groups who may require varied support (e.g. see Fraser, 1994; Hubbard, 1994). At this stage we did not have readily available information to make any comparisons between these groups. This and the overriding dissatisfaction with the Skills Unit was the main driving force behind the research project.

Research aims

The Skills Unit had been running for a few years so it seemed an ideal opportunity to completely reassess its content, the teaching methods and delivery mechanisms. The team decide to tackle these problems as a research project and started out with the following aims:

1. increase quality of learning for the students on the Skills Unit;

2. target teaching resources efficiently;

3. monitor skill levels for students from different entry routes and different student groups.

From these aims we generated a Research Plan consisting of the following main points:

1. identify primary numeracy topics required;

2. decide on type of delivery and testing strategy;

3. develop teaching and learning material and testing material;

4. validate teaching and testing material: pilot testing;

5. monitor student performance and requirements.

Each of these points is described in greater detail in the following sections.

1. Identify primary numeracy topics required

This was started by producing an initial list of topics generated by the team members. This list was based on our own experiences of running the unit and previous feedback from students and other unit leaders. This list was then used as a basis to interview all first- year unit leaders to identify the numeracy topics they expected students to have skills in. They were ask to consider two categories:

(a) skills essential to do unit and

(b) skills beneficial to do unit.

The end result was a detailed list of numeracy topics which the students were expected to have some degree of skill in. The main topics included: Fractions, Decimals, Percentages, Ratios, Index Nos, Approximation, Basic Arithmetic, Powers(2 & $sqroot$), Averages, Maths Graphs, Stats Graphs, Substitution, Algebra and Linear equations. Having decided on the range and level of topics to be covered we then examined the delivery and assessment of this material.

2. Decide on type of delivery and testing strategy

Our biggest problem was the range of skills in the student population. Some were very competent in all the topics, some were competent in most or at least some of the topics while others were very weak in most topics. We decided early on that any delivery had to be as 'Student centred' as possible, i.e. try to match the teaching to individual student needs.

We were also aware of other schemes dealing specifically with developing basic maths skills for the university sector. Some schemes are based on remedial workbooks such as at Stafford College (e.g. Cook and Rimmer *et al.*). Additionally, we were aware of some of the TLTP schemes which seemed to be developing computer-based diagnostic testing and teaching resources (e.g. Appleby, 1995). Yet others seemed to be advocating more use of technology (e.g. Forcheri and Molfino, 1995). We did not want to re-invent the wheel, however, non of schemes we were aware of seemed to be exactly what we wanted, particularly in the area of monitoring of student groups. We consequently decided to develop our own testing and teaching material.

The method chosen was to base the teaching round self study material in the form of a work book. The aim being that student could work through the sections they had difficulty with. This was to be backed up with flexible lectures and tutorials sessions dealing with any problems students found working through the workbook.

It was becoming clear that we needed to give feedback to students on where they were weak and what level of attainment we expected from them. It was also becoming clear that we needed to give this feedback very early on. We decided the best way to do this was test all the students against our list of numeracy topics. This was to be in the form of a bank of multi-choice questions to be run at the start of the course. The advantage of this was that we could 'APL' (Accreditation for Prior Learning) students who were already at the required numeracy skill level and so target resources to the students who needed further study.

So we had decided to develop an integrated basic business maths booklet to be used alongside the tests.

3.   Develop teaching and learning material and testing material

We started from the testing element first, the rational being that once we knew and defined what level of attainment we required of the students then we could teach to that level. Consequently we developed the test specification and many of the test questions before we started developing the work book. The tests were going to be computer-marked using our EDPAC automatic reader. This also entailed designing our own form which would contain student information such as entry route, gender etc.

Given a free hand to design and develop a test for measuring numeracy skills brings out several potential problems and so we consulted reference material on good practice (Ward, 1981). From this reference material it was clear we had to consider the following:

- test specification;
- strategy for structuring questions on question paper;
- strategy for marking questions;
- strategy for handling guessing element/errors.

(a)   Test specification

This entailed determining the topics covered, number of question in each topic and number of questions overall, level of difficulty required in each topic and the type of questions to be included. Fifty questions were decided upon after we had a trial run on third-year students, as described later on. The test specification decide on is shown in Table 1.

Table 1

TOPIC	Mechanical			Interpretation			Analysis			Total
	E	I	D	E	I	D	E	I	D	
Fractions	1	1	0	-	-	-	-	-	-	2
Decimals	1	1	1	-	-	-	-	-	-	3
Percentages	1	1	1	1	1	0	1	1	0	7
Ratios	1	0	0	1	0	0	1	0	0	3
Index nos	0	0	0	1	1	0	1	0	0	3
Approximation	1	1	1	-	-	-	-	-	-	3
Basic arithmetic	1	1	1	-	-	-	-	-	-	3
Powers (^{2} & $\sqrt{}$)	1	1	0	1	0	0	1	0	0	4
Averages	1	1	1	1	1	0	1	1	0	7
Maths graphs	1	1	0	1	0	0	0	0	0	3
Stats graphs	1	1	0	1	1	0	1	0	0	5
Substitution	1	1	1	-	-	-	-	-	-	3
Algebra	1	1	0	0	0	0	-	-	-	2
Linear equations	1	1	0	0	0	0	0	0	0	2
TOTAL	13	12	6	7	4	0	6	2	0	50

Notes: These cells give the number of questions to be used in each category.
Where 0 = No questions in this category – = Inapplicable

The rational for grading the questions into three levels of difficulty was that skills in some of the topics were highlighted by the unit leader as crucial for their units, whereas skills in other topics was viewed as less important.

Table 2 shows a breakdown of these questions into the various categories.

Table 2

Category	Easy	Intermediate	Difficult	Total
Mechanical	13	12	6	**31**
Interpretation	7	4	0	**11**
Analysis	6	2	0	**8**
Total	**26**	**18**	**6**	**50**

Level definitions

We had problems of getting a consensus of what constitutes Easy, Intermediate or Difficult. We ended up with the following definitions.

Easy level: expect the students to be able to complete in all subjects

Intermediate level: expect the students to complete in some of the subjects

Difficult level: above what we would expect from the students in a subject.

Skill definitions

Mechanic: clear rules; automatic process given those rules

Interpretation: using rules in context; show understanding of results (and process)

Analysis: choose appropriate rules and use in context; show reasoning ability; show understanding of process required and understanding of results.

The next stage in developing testing material was to design the multi-choice questions. We approached this by at least two of the team producing questions for each topic, then for the whole team to vet each question. The questions were graded in order of difficulty and addressing different skills such as Mechanical, Interpretation and Analysis. Some of the questions were based on existing GCSE- type questions and material so that we could judge the level to be approximate to GCSE level. Again we had some lively discussions: what one tutor thought was an easy level in a particular topic was considered intermediate by other tutors.

(b)   Strategy for structuring questions on question paper

Next we were faced with how to structure the question paper. After some discussion we investigated four options:

(i) Random

- Questions randomly sorted on the question paper.
- Arguably harder for the students to complete since there is limited indication on the degree of difficulty for each question and lack of continuity in the paper.
- Some students may not reach the end part of the paper as the students' attention may be taken up with harder questions on the earlier part of the paper. This may result in an unrepresentative result for some students (i.e. students not attempting all the easy questions).

(ii) Topic order, graded easy to difficult

- Questions presented in topic order and within the topic questions are ordered by difficulty (i.e. easy first).
- As questions get progressively harder the students can be considered as having training in the topic so may be able to answer some harder questions they would not answer straight off.
- Since the questions are in topic order the students may not reach the final topics on the paper as the students' attention may be taken up with harder questions on the earlier part of the paper. This may result in an unrepresentative result for some students (i.e. student not attempting all the topic areas).

(iii) Topic order, mixed

- Questions presented in topic order but within the topic questions are ordered randomly.

(iv) Grade order

- Here all the questions will be ordered on level of difficulty. So all easy questions together, all intermediate questions together and all difficult questions together.
- The advantage of this would be that students would not get stuck on difficult questions early and may not have time to answer easy questions later on. The disadvantage would be that students might get confused with what topic was being tested. This may result in students having to spend time assimilating the topic in question and also may lose the 'training' element discussed in option B.

We eventually decided on option B, but to give students instructions on exam technique, i.e. if get stuck on a question then continue on to next question. It was felt this would give the best representation of students abilities.

(c) Strategy for marking questions

There are several way of marking the answered questions on the test paper. The ones we considered were:

(i) Credit correct answers, disregard incorrect

This may encourage a stronger guessing element.

(ii) Credit correct answers, penalize incorrect

We decided there were two doing this:

- Have a 'don't know' option which would not attract penalties. This may influence students answering questions in that they may just take the easy route.
- Do not have a 'don't know' option, i.e. force the students to choose an option. This may stifle students answering question that they are not 100% happy with, which again may not result in a true reflection of the students' abilities.

(iii) Award same mark for easy, intermediate and difficult questions.

(iv) Award higher mark for more difficult questions.

We decided on option (i); however, we also decided that it would be beneficial to run the test then mark the tests using different marking criteria, then compare the student grades for the different marking criteria. This we will do at a later stage.

(d) Strategy for handling guessing element/errors

When marking multi-choice questions it is difficult to allocate an exact mark to truly represent the student's abilities since there is an element of guessing by the student. There are some strategies to take account of this 'guessing' element, some of these strategies are as follows.

(i) Ignore any guessing element.

(ii) Give a 'score range' for each students based on probability. For border cases further testing or interviewing can be carried out.

(iii) Correct students' final score by using a correcting algorithm based on a number of correct and incorrect answers. For example:

$$S = R - \frac{W}{N-1}$$

where

S = the corrected score
R = the number of questions answered correctly
W = the number of questions answered incorrectly
N = the number of possible answers each question

(e.g. Ward, 1981)

(iv) Correct students final score by using topic and difficulty related rules, as in Table 2, for example.

Student	Easy Question Topic X	Difficult Question Topic X
A	Pass	Pass
B	Fail	Pass

Table 2 describes the situation in which both student A and B passed the difficult question in topic X. However, one would normally expect students who pass difficult questions to be able to pass easy questions in the same topic. So in this situation the mark for the difficult question will have a higher weighting for student A than student B (e.g. one rule could award 1 point for student A and 0.5 for student B for answering the difficult question correctly).

The same sort of reasoning can be applied to similar or prerequisite topics.

(v) Interview students to ascertain what proportion was guesswork and what proportion was a valid attempt at answering the questions. This could be time-consuming but might give some indication of the level of guess work for each question.

(vi) Leave a 'Don't Know' option for each question. This may have to be used in conjunction with an appropriate Marking Strategy such as *'Credit correct answers, penalize incorrect'* publicized to the students to deter guessing.

Again, it might be beneficial to run using different strategies then compare the student grades for the different strategies.

Develop self-study workbook

There were a variety of existing workbooks available, many covered all the required topics and well as many other topics. There were a few which seemed at the right level. None of the books was exactly what we wanted, i.e. did not give our emphasis for different topics covered, but could accommodate a few changes. However, we were also reluctant to insist that students buy an extra book as most students have harsh financial constraints which meant that the poorer students or those less inclined to buy books would be at a disadvantage. It was decided to produce our own work book and include it in a skill work pack which the students already have to purchase; that way we could ensure each student had access to the material.

(d)   Validate teaching and testing material: pilot testing

Validating teaching material

The work book was based on existing 'good practice' and liaising with unit team and our support services, which offer a range of basic maths books and teaching material.

The process is considered as ongoing and we shall be taking note of student performance and feedback.

Validating the tests

We decided to validate the tests by two methods. The first was to critically review the test specification and each test question by the team. The second method was to conduct two trial runs.

For the first trial run we used third-year students and started with the aims of investigating whether students should use calculators and investigate timing and number of questions. For this trial run we used mostly mechanical questions and it was anonymous testing (i.e. to encourage student participation). The results were surprising. It seemed calculators made little difference to actual mark, though there was some difference in the time students took to complete the test. From this we were able to firm up the number of questions and the amount of time to give students to complete the test, which was 50 questions in one hour. The second trial run was viewed as the final dummy-run test before the new entrants in September. The aim was to check the test specification and the questions. For this trial we used two tutorial classes of level 1 students. We used a full set of questions and made it optionally anonymous testing, though we did offer prizes for participating students who did put their name on the answer sheets (this was so we could do comparisons with grade and performance on other units).

There were some interesting results from this test run. First, in some topic the teams perception of 'Difficult' and 'Easy' was different to students — possibly some indication of the level of guessing. Another difficulty arising from this test run was getting participation from students. We had to have two attempts at this test run; the first attempt was poorly attended, and arguably only attended by 'good' students which would affect the results. We had to stage another test run offering prize incentives and even then had to 'press-gang' a group of students. Again, arguably the students may not be representative, especially the press-ganged students who may not have participated to their fullest. The results for the test was a lower attainment level than was expected, though the students who took the test first time round performed considerably better.

There was also some discussion on what pass mark to set for test (i.e. should it be 40%, 50% or some other level?), eventually we decided on a pass mark of 40% to be reviewed after the first major batch of students had been tested. There were also some changes to a few of the questions.

(e) Monitor student performance and requirements

We were now in a state where we could start collecting relevant information for different student groups. This is considered an ongoing task and we are likely to review the teaching and learning material after the first full cohort has been examined.

Conclusion: overall improvements in teaching and learning

By the end of the project we felt we had achieved a better numeracy component of the skills unit and were able to identify specific improvements including:

- numeracy content of skill more relevant to students needs;
- exemptions handled automatically by 'APLing' whoever pasts the test;
- numeracy problems identified earlier on;
- improved student feedback: identify student weaknesses so remedial action can be taken;
- student centred — self-study, flexible tutorials;
- more efficient use of staff *and* student resources.

There are likely to be problems in running the tests and teaching the full cohort of students; however, we feel more confident in that we are providing better service to our students in the key area of numeracy skills.

Bibliography

Appleby, J. (1995) A diagnostic testing facility for basic mathematics. *Teaching and Learning Technology Programme newsletter* **3**, Spring, 6.

Cook, M. and Rimmer, H. *et al. Maths Xtra*, series of maths work books developed at Stafford College.

Forcheri, P. and Molfino, M. (1995) Knowledge based systems for teaching and learning maths. *British Journal of Educational Technology* **26**(1), 42—54.

Fraser, E. (1994) Problems of gender in university mathematics. *British Educational Research Journal* **20**(2), 147—54.

Hubbard, R. (1994) Addressing the language and culture problems of overseas students in the context of mathematics classes. *Higher Education Research and Development* **13**(2), 133—42.

Ward, C. (1981) *Preparing and Using Objective Questions*. Stanley Thornes.

30   Mind maps: using research to improve the student learning experience

Roger Catchpole and Nigel Garland
University of Plymouth

Introduction

In recent years the value of taking notes in lectures has been questioned and Howe (19??) concludes that 'educational research in this area is surprisingly sparse'. Bloom (1956) and Gagne (1970) state, though, that learning is facilitated if the learner's activity involves the active processing of information. Therefore, if while note-taking, the learner is 'cognitively involved' through actively constructing their own notes and transforming the information being received, note-taking should be potentially of value in terms of improved learning outcomes.

If students are to process information actively either during or after a lecture they will need well developed note-taking skills and techniques. A study of note-taking carried out at the University of Plymouth brings into question whether students coming into higher education have these skills. In the study the great majority of the 80 second-year students not only had a 'get it all down in concise prose' approach to note-taking in lectures, but also stated that they did not process or transform their notes in any way after lectures.

Any learning from such note-taking practice is in all probability going to be of a surface nature. This raises the question: how can students be helped to develop the skills which will facilitate a deeper approach, leading to more effective understanding? In the present investigation a series of experiments were carried out by the authors to try to address this question.

Howe (19??) concludes that there is a need for more research studies into student note-taking which 'examine different types of note-taking strategies' and 'concern themselves with the use made by the students of the notes they have made'. The authors' investigation involved the introduction of a new strategy: the introduction of a new method, mind-mapping (sometimes known as spider diagrams or pattern notes). It also concentrated on the use of mind-mapping to process lecture notes after the lecture.

Mind-mapping was chosen by the authors as the note-taking method for this investigation because, as Buzan (1991) states, 'it incorporates the traditional mental tools of words, numbers, lines, initials and sequence with an additional set of mental tools that are especially powerful for improving memory and creative thinking: image, colour, dimension, space and association or linking'. Hence, it is an ideal method of enabling students, through using the above tools creatively, to make their own 'maps' of information received. The process of mapping that they engage in will involve them in complex cognitive activities which should facilitate improved learning. Also, the product, the mind-map itself, will represent information in a way in which the student has understood it. Mind-mapping will offer the student the opportunity to pull together concepts, create a holistic picture and enhance and consolidate conceptualization.

Background to the investigation

The subjects for the present study were the first-year BA Business Studies students at the University of Plymouth Business School. As a central part of their two-week initial induction these students have a programme of skills workshops which introduce a range of generic learning and transferable skills. One of the authors, Nigel Garland (NG) is responsible for this programme and for teaching the Business Environment Module in the first semester. The other author, Roger Catchpole (RC), a member of the University's Education Development Services Team, has helped in the development of this programme and has run the learning skills workshops. For each skill covered during the initial induction workshops the students are sent 'Guidelines' — re-course booklets. The Effective Note Taking booklet acts as the reference material for the Effective Note-Taking and Note-Making workshop and sets out the basic techniques for mind-mapping.

A key aspect of this skills provision for the Business School students is that the application of the skills is built into the programme of study. The authors worked as an action research team with the aim of getting the students to develop and apply the mind-mapping method as an integral part of the Business Environment module.

The investigation

The authors had three questions in mind.

1. Would making mind-maps, as a means of actively processing their lecture notes after a lecture, aid the students in their understanding of a topic?

2. Would using mind-maps as a revision tool for a particular exam topic question make an impact on their end-of-year examination performance in that question?

3. Would the students take up the use of mind-mapping as a tool for their learning in the long term as a result of their involvement in the exercises built into their programme of study?

Investigation to answer question 1

Method

NG introduced the idea of the exercise to 200 students during the first 15 minutes of one of NG's Business Environment lectures eight weeks into their first semester. RC briefly reminded them of the basic mind-mapping techniques which they had covered during their initial induction skills workshop and reminded them that they had their skills booklet to refer to. Only 94 out of the 210 students present had had any experience of using mind-maps before.

NG then asked the students to:

- take notes on the lecture about to be given on 'Oligopoly', using their normal note-taking method;

- make a mind-map during the following week to summarize and transform their lecture notes, building in information from other sources, if possible;

- bring their mind-maps to the lecture the next week where they would be given time at the beginning of the lecture to explain their mind-maps to a student sitting next to them.

Results

At the lecture the following week 150 of the 190 students attending produced a mind-map of the topic 'Oligopoly' and the great majority actively explained their mind-map with a neighbour.

By a show of hands:

- 110 of these 150 students who had produced a mind-map indicated that they thought the exercise had been helpful in improving their understanding of the topic 'Oligopoly';

- 37 indicated that they felt it had not made a significant impact on their understanding of the topic;

- three indicated they thought the exercise had been a waste of time.

The mind-maps were collected in and studied by NG and RC. They observed that:
- over 50% of the mind-maps demonstrated good use of mind-mapping techniques and represented to NG and RC a fairly comprehensive overview of the topic;

- there was a wide range of use of mind-mapping techniques, e.g. some used colour very effectively, whereas some didn't use it at all. There was a wide variety in the effectiveness of the use of space on an A4 sheet. Some students gave themselves more space by sticking several sheets together. On the whole the mind-maps were accurate but some were incomplete as topic summaries.

Investigation to answer question 2

Method

As he does each year NG told the students at the start of a lecture five weeks before their end of year examinations that, for their Business Environment paper, they would have a choice of two questions from each of the topic areas covered.

NG introduced to the students the idea of using mind-mapping as a means of bringing together concepts, facts and ideas for revision purposes.

RC revised mind-mapping techniques with them again, reminding them of the exercise they carried out in the first semester.

Each student was given a skeleton mindmap on one of the four exam topics (Industrial Policy). This provided a basic structure, but left out the detail. NG chose this topic as it was the most complex of the four and because in past years, few students had chosen the question relating to it. Those that did had demonstrated poor understanding.

NG explained the structure of the handout mind-map and asked the students to build detail onto the skeleton to produce a complete revision overview of the topic. He asked them to be ready to compare their mind-maps with other students at the lecture the next week.

Results

- 30% of the 200 students present had worked on the skeleton mind-map and had brought it to the lecture;
- 60% brought their skeleton mindmap, but had not worked on it;
- 10% had not brought it to the lecture;
- during the time allowed at the start of the lecture 80% were observed working actively on the skeletons mind-maps: some were building on detail, others were comparing mind-maps and discussing them;
- 20% remained off task chatting.

NG then handed out his version of the skeleton with detail added and gave ten minutes for the students to compare theirs with his. As a result many of the 20% now came on task and became involved.

- all but four of the 200 students indicated by a show of hands that they felt the exercise had been of some benefit;
- when given a choice of reasons why they hadn't worked on the skeleton mind-map during the week the majority indicated that it had been 'because of apathy', not because they felt that the mind-mapping was of no value for revision;
- a number of students gave individual feedback to NG after the lecture saying that it had been a mistake to give out the skeleton with the detail added. As one student put it: 'Give us the answer and we will regurgitate it without having to think for ourselves.'

Results: the exams

- *In 1993* only 20 students (10% of the cohort) answered the question on Industrial Policy. The marks of those that did averaged 45% for that question.
- In the year of the study (1994) 116 students (61% of the cohort) answered the question on Industrial Policy with an average mark of 62%.
- The marker noted that most of the answers had 'elaborated on the major policies', had 'shown a good understanding of the complex issues' and 'were, on the whole, factually correct'. They were, though, 'rather clone like'.

Investigation to answer question 3

Method

At the start of the session in the second semester NG asked the students about their use of mind-mapping since the session in the first semester.

Results

- Of the 180 students present, six said they had used mind-mapping for note-taking over that period.
- Only one of these said that this had been because of the exercise they had been set.

Discussion

The majority of the cohort, most of whom were new to mind-mapping, had after a brief introduction to the techniques involved and with the aid of the reference booklet, demonstrated that they were able to create a mind-map. It was interesting, though, that most of the students were only prepared to use mind-mapping as part of a set task. Also, this particular group reacted much more positively to the task of creating their own mind-maps rather than building on skeleton handouts. It would seem that the former task is more stimulating and creative and that this may have encouraged their involvement. It is clear that practice has to be given through set tasks and more opportunities need to be provided for the students to evaluate the impact of mind-mapping on their learning outcomes if they are to build this method into their learning practice.

Knowledge of the improvement in the answers of the Industrial Policy question in 1994 compared with 1993, would probably have given that necessary reinforcement. Although there will always be students who do not find mind-maps useful, as some do not have a tendency to holistic thinking and to thinking in images, mind-mapping is a method which for many could be transferable throughout their programmes of study and post university life.

Not only were the students stimulated by the challenge of creating their own mind-maps but the great majority indicated that they felt that the process had aided their understanding of the topic 'Oligopoly'. It is probable that several aspects of the mind-mapping exercise aided improvement to understanding, although the methodology used provided no direct evidence. As stated in the introduction to this paper, by creating a mind-map these students had to be cognitively involved. This active processing of the information received was then further developed through the comparison and discussion of their mind-maps with each other. But not only the process is held to be of value. Their mind-maps provided the students with an overview of key points and of the relationships between them. As Buzan states, a mind-map organizes information in ways which mirrors its storage in the right side of the brain, reinforcing understanding and particularly facilitating recall of that understood.

The authors are unable to conclude as a result of their revision experiment that the mind-maps made the positive impact on the quantity and quality of the answers of the Industrial Policy question. There were no doubt other factors which may have influenced this improvement, one being that this topic had the attention focused on it by the lecturer, whereas the other three topics did not and the authors action research methodology did not isolate the mind-mapping factor. There was, however, a considerable improvement in the results in understanding and in recall, both outcomes which can be expected from the use of mind-maps. In this case it is likely that any effects that the mind-maps did have was as a result of the students' revision using the product, a 'map' of the topic, laid out in a fashion which suits recall. It would have been interesting to carry out an experiment in which one half of the students revised from mind-maps that they had created, the other using one built on a given skeleton. An expected difference would be less clone-like answers from the former group.

Future work

The authors consider that the results so far indicate that it will be worthwhile to continue to introduce students to mind-mapping and to encourage the development of its effective use through integration of provision into a programme of lectures.

It is clear from this study, though, that students will need much more exposure to the use of mind-mapping if many students are to build its use into their independent study. Future work will have to focus more on helping the students become aware of any benefits the method has on their learning outcomes and on helping to develop a culture which encourages positive attitudes to the use of alternative learning methods and techniques.

The authors realize that the full potential of learning skills such as mind-mapping will not be developed just through inputs as part of lectures, induction workshops and the use of paper-based resources. Students will need access to other resources. To this end the University of Plymouth has produced a computer-based learning skills package 'Skills Shop', which has been networked for this September. Also, purchase of a Windows based mind-mapping package, which will also be networked, is planned.

References

Bloom, B. S. (ed.) (1956) *Taxonomy of Educational Objectives. Handbook 1: Cognitive Domain.* New York: David McKay.

Buzan, T. (1991) *Mind-mapping Executive Excellence.* Institute for Principle Centered Leadership.

Gagne, R. (1970) *The Conditions of Learning*, 2nd edn. New York: Holt, Rinehart & Winston.

Howe, M. J. A. Howe What is the value of taking notes? *Improving College and University Teaching.*

31 Tackling the problem of skills development in a modular degree programme: the Skillswise Project

Jennifer Blumhof, Andrew Honeybone, Debbie Pearlman
and Keith Pinn
Division of Environmental Sciences
University of Hertfordshire

Introduction

In July 1994 the Environmental Education Action Research Group (EEARG) at the University of Hertfordshire was asked to address the problem of the coordinated provision of personal transferable skills (PTS) development within the Combined Modular Degree Programme (KST) at the University of Hertfordshire. As a first step, a pilot PTS short course, the Skillswise Project, was designed for final-year KST students studying a wide variety of subjects. As described in this chapter, the project sought to integrate PTS development with academic content through a problem-based approach and to evaluate the course through action research.

Background to the Skillswise Project

As reported elsewhere (Blumhof, Honeybone, Pearlman and Pinn, 1994), EEARG was established in 1993 to undertake action research projects into the participants' own teaching within the Division of Environmental Sciences. Following Zuber-Skerritt (1992) action research was defined as 'collaborative, critical enquiry by the academic themselves (rather than expert educational researchers) into their own teaching practice, into problems of student learning and into curriculum problems. It is professional development through academic course development, group reflection, action, evaluation and improved practice.'

Previous projects had included the Integrated Skills Project (Blumhof, Broom and Stallibrass, 1994) which sought to integrate PTS development with academic content within the BSc Environmental Studies Degree. It was on the basis of this experience that, with help from the last tranche of Enterprise in Higher Education funding, the invitation came from KST staff to help them resolve the long-standing problem of the lack of attention given to PTS within KST. The difficulty arose because KST students, as is common on similar combined studies programmes in other institutions, study two or three subjects in parallel. Individual departments remain responsible for the academic content of their own courses. Thus, with practice on the provision of PTS development varying between departments, there is the danger that, with the many different combinations of subjects, some KST students will get no PTS development whilst others will have some overlap and repetition. It was recognized that the complete solution to the problem required some change in the structure of the KST degree. However, by means of the Skillswise Project, the focus of this chapter, a more immediate and partial solution could be offered which would ensure that at least some opportunity for PTS development was provided to all final-year students who wanted it.

There is now considerable evidence (e.g. Bridges, 1994) to suggest that bolt on or stand-alone skills training is rejected by many students who see it as being irrelevant to their mainstream work. Therefore, drawing on those findings and on our own work in the Division of Environmental Sciences, the approach we adopted in the Skillswise Project was to integrate PTS development with academic content. We selected, in collaboration with KST staff, skills which were relevant to the students' final-year studies, notably research skills and career development skills.

However, given that part of our aim was to foster a critical approach to the use of skills (hence the title Skillswise), integrating skills and academic content in itself would not necessarily lead to this critical perspective and encourage deep learning if a traditional subject based approach was adopted. Therefore we sought to achieve the integration of skills and content through a problem-based approach (Margetson, 1994). Such an approach has been seen as an effective means of promoting active student involvement in the learning process, fostering problem-solving, self-education skills and communication skills and improving students' abilities to access and utilize information resources (Ricchetti, 1995) and (Boud and Felleti, 1991). These qualities are very similar to the course design strategies seen by Gibbs (1992) and others as helping to foster in students a deep approach to their learning.

Scope of the project

Given the limited timescale (two months) and funding (£2000) for the project, a decision was quickly taken that the fundamental issue of how to incorporate PTS across the KST degree as a whole was beyond the scope of the resources immediately available. That issue would be addressed as part of a forthcoming course review. In the meantime, a smaller project could be undertaken to help rectify some of the deficiencies in skills development for final-year students who had little previous experience of explicit PTS provision. For the project to be of maximum benefit to such students, it was agreed that it should be run in the form of a short course at the start of their final year and it would concentrate on two areas of skills development, namely research skills and career development skills. The specific skills aims of the project were to provide students with further guidance and practice in problem-solving, time management, investigative skills, teamwork skills, leadership skills, interview skills, self-evaluation, self and peer assessment and visual presentation. These PTS aims were then related to the academic content aims as described in the next section.

The project started in July and had to be completed in time for the start of the new academic year in late September. However, even though the Skillswise Project in itself was only small, it was hoped that, if successful, it might provide at least some elements of a model that could be applied more widely across the KST degree programme.

Structure of the course

The course was designed to run over the first seven weeks of the autumn term. During that time, apart from in induction week, students would also be studying their regular courses. Therefore, in order to make sure that students were well underway with the Skillswise course before their other work started, there was an intensive three-day programme in induction week. This intensive programme had two main elements. Firstly, there were framework lectures outlining the structure and content of the project and, secondly, there were workshops during which skills were introduced and integrated with the academic content through a variety of tasks such as team-building exercises. Over the following five weeks, group work was scheduled to take place one afternoon per week. A classroom was made available and at the beginning of these weekly sessions a 'surgery' with staff was offered as students refined their problem definition and analysis. The students' group work culminated in the presentation of posters on their selected problems. These posters were marked through staff and peer assessment followed by final course review and evaluation sessions. The detailed programme for the course is shown in Table 1.

Table 1 Programme for the Skillswise short course

Induction Work

Day 1   *Framework lecture:* introduction to the course (structure, skills development self-evaluation process, distribution of briefing packs) (1hr. 5mins.) (SL)

Framework lecture: introduction to the Mediterranean case study and poster presentations (1hr.) (SL)

Group task 1: team selection and review of interview process for next day (30mins.)

(ITW)

Day 2   *Group task 2:* selection of team leader (preparation of job description sheet, video on CV and interview skills, preparation of CV's and interview strategy, interview, selection and response, debriefing) (3hrs.) (ITW)

Workshop: team management: Team leader's responsibilities, organization of meetings, and project/time management (1hr. 15mins.) (ITW)

Group task 3: Team demolition exercise (1hr.30mins.) (SL)

Day 3   *Workshop: skills and poster topics:* review of skills needed for topic research and poster presentation including

Group task 4: completion of skills development sheet and allocation of skills research to group members (1hr.15mins.) (ITW)

Group task 5: Review of Mediterranean Reader and preliminary discussion of poster presentation topics (1hr.30mins.) (ITW)

Workshop on the Mediterranean: (a) 'surgery' with staff – opportunity to raise issues and discuss poster presentation topics (30mins.) (SL)

(b) further team review of Mediterranean Reader and opportunity to view videos on Mediterranean Region (2hrs.30mins.) (ITW)

Weekly Workshop Sessions (Week 2-7)

Week 2   Library skills (1hr.) (SL) followed by team workshop (2hrs.) (ITW)

Weeks 3-5 'Surgery' (1hr.) (SL) followed by team workshop (2hrs.) (ITW)

Week 6   Poster presentation and peer team assessment (3hrs.) (SL)

Week 7   Allocation of individual marks, debriefing, course evaluation (3hrs.) (SL)

(SL)   Staff-Led sessions

(ITW)   Sessions where students are expected to carry out Independent Team Work.

The mechanism used for integrating PTS development with academic content was problem-based learning focused on the Mediterranean Region. Students, working in small groups, were asked to identify a problem within that region for detailed study. The aim, in relation to academic content, was to help students acquire an understanding of issues in the Mediterranean and work towards solutions with the aim being achieved to a greater extent through the use and development of the skills outlined above. Thus their brief asked them to identify, analyse and suggest solutions to their selected problem, drawing on their subject expertise and utilizing a variety of skills.The Mediterranean Region was chosen firstly because we felt it would have broad appeal, being part of the recreational or living experience of many people these days and secondly, because it would have relevant connections with the subject curriculum of many KST courses.

Although one of the skills aims of the course was for students to develop their investigative skills with the onus being on the students to identify their own sources, it was recognized that motivation and initial learning would be undermined if sufficient sources of information were not readily available. Therefore, in addition to the framework lecture that provided an outline of key issues in the Mediterranean Region, a Mediterranean Reader was prepared to provide a starting point for the specific problem-based work by each group. The reader was supported by a selection of videos. Similarly a Skills Reader was provided to aid PTS development. Given the need for students to be quite clear about the aims and structure of the course, the introductory framework lectures were further supported by a student briefing pack (a lecturer briefing pack was also prepared so that other KST lecturers who had not been involved in the formulation of the project would be able to run the course). Thus, with the development of this extensive range of materials, resource-based learning was used to reinforce the problem-based approach. Overall the emphasis was on active and independent learning in small groups with students having the opportunity to negotiate and focus their study by reflecting on their own particular interests and learning requirements. This approach provided the opportunity for learning to be more open in both the logistical and educational senses (Boot and Hodgson, 1987).

One example of this more open approach was the team-building exercise during which groups prepared individual five point contracts to which their group would adhere. One group's contract specified:

- total commitment to completion of a successful project;
- ensure each member is offered appropriate and equal tasks to match their abilities;
- respect for each other's input and contribution;
- accept constructive criticisms and democratic decisions;
- be sensitive to others' needs and personal dispositions.

These contracts were then used again to help guide the allocation of individual marks within the peer and self-assessment process.

Evaluation methodology

In line with the action research approach, we sought to undertake a robust evaluation of the Skillswise Project through the process of 'triangulation'. This process has been described by Robson (1993) as a method of verifying something by getting a 'fix' on it from two or more places, i.e. by using multiple sources, methods, investigators or theories. In the case of the present project this meant that several evaluation methods were used, featuring both quantitative and qualitative research techniques. Since the project was concerned with student learning, students were the central source of information and in order to guarantee maximum student response, the return of completed evaluation sheets was required as an essential element of successful course completion.

Fig 1 Self evaluation sheet

Self evaluation sheet	Name.................................	
The completion of this self evaluation sheet is an essential part of the assessment for the Skillswise short course. In order to derive maximum benefit from this form of assessment you should be as honest as possible. This sheet must be handed in at the end of the poster presentation and peer team assessment session.		
What went well/what are you more confident about?	What didn't go so well/what are you least confident about?	How could you have improved your performance?

Firstly, students were asked to complete a self-evaluation sheet (Figure 1) commenting on what went well, what did not go so well and how their performance could have been improved for each of the course's three elements — induction week, skills work and case study/poster work. This part of the evaluation process was designed to encourage reflection on their own performance and thus turn experience into learning.

Secondly, students were asked to complete a course evaluation sheet (Figure 2) at the end of the debriefing session on the poster presentation and assessment process. The academic and skills aims of the course were listed and students were asked to indicate how well each element was achieved on a scale of 1—5. A further qualitative section seeking the students' views about the organization of the course — what went well, what didn't go so well and possible improvements — was included. This qualitative part of the course evaluation and also the self-evaluation form were based on methods that had been used for other courses in the Environmental Studies Degree which were in turn adaptations of ideas suggested by Gibbs and Haigh (1984).

The third method of evaluation, cross-checking on the first two, involved a class discussion of student views on the course and on what they had learnt. This session provided two opportunities: firstly, students were able to expand on their written comments and secondly, staff were able to seek clarification of points from the evaluation forms. Finally, after collating the responses obtained from the three methods, the course team reflected on the results and discussed possible improvements for the future. This reflection was then supplemented by the presentation at the ISL Symposium and the subsequent discussion.

Fig 2 Course evaluation sheet

Course Evaluation Sheet *To what extent do you think that the aims of the Skillswise short course were achieved?* *(1 = very well achieved, 5 = very poorly achieved)*					
Academic Content Aims					
To help you acquire an understanding of:					
A range of issues in the Mediterranean region	1	2	3	4	5
Problems that might arise	1	2	3	4	5
Policies to solve perceived problems	1	2	3	4	5
Skills Aims					
To provide you with further guidance and practice in:					
problem solving	1	2	3	4	5
time management	1	2	3	4	5
investigative skills	1	2	3	4	5
teamwork skills	1	2	3	4	5
leadership skills	1	2	3	4	5
interview skills	1	2	3	4	5
self evaluation	1	2	3	4	5
self and peer assessment	1	2	3	4	5
visual presentation	1	2	3	4	5
Comments about the organisation of the Skillswise short course					
Things that went well/were good					
Things that didn't go so well/were not so good					
Proposals for improvement					

Results

1. Course evaluation scores

Of the 37 students who took the Skillswise course 30 completed the course evaluation sheet (Figure1) and the scores are shown in Table 2.

These results indicate an encouragingly positive response from students towards the achievement of all the aims. In all cases, a majority of the students considered that the aims were well or very well achieved and in no case did more than three students think that an aim was poorly or very poorly achieved. In the students' eyes the best achieved aim was teamwork skills.

Table 2 Course evaluation scores: responses to the question 'To what extent were the aims of the course achieved?' (1 = very well; 5 = very poorly)

	1	2	3	4	5	Average
Academic content aims						
To help you acquire an understanding of:						
A range of issues in the Mediterranean region	4	18	6	1	0	2.14
Problems that might arise	3	22	4	0	0	2.03
Policies to solve perceived problems	0	19	7	3	0	2.45
Skills aims						
To provide you with further guidance and practice in:						
problem solving	2	22	6	0	0	2.13
time management	4	13	10	2	1	2.43
investigative skills	3	18	8	1	0	2.23
teamwork skills	11	13	5	1	0	1.87
leadership skills	3	15	11	0	1	2.37
interview skills	2	17	9	2	0	2.37
self evaluation	2	15	10	3	0	2.47
self and peer assessment	6	14	10	0	0	2.13
visual presentation	5	14	11	0	0	2.20

Table 3 Summary of comments about the organization of the Skillswise short course

Things that went well were good		
Interview and CV work	19	63.3%
Structure and course/background material	16	63.3%
Teamwork	14	46.7%
Development of research and new skills	4	13.3%
Things that didn't go so well/were not so good		
Information gathering	10	33.3%
Too many other pressures/commitments	7	23.3%
The course was too long	5	16.7%
Not enough guidance	4	13.3%
Proposals for improvement		
More guidance	12	40.0%
Run course in first and/or second year	12	40.0%
More emphasis on CVs, interviews etc	10	30.0%
Shorten length of time allocated for poster	3	10.0%

Table 4 Self-evaluation results

INDUCTION WEEK	Total	% of return
What went well/what are you most confident about?		
1. Groupwork	25	83.3%
2. CV and interview skills	14	46.7%
3. Team demolition and contract exercises	12	40%
4. Information given/the week as a whole	9	30%
What didn't go so well/what are you least confident about?		
1. Teamwork	7	23.3%
2. Time commitment/management	6	20%
3. Interview and CV writing	6	20%
4. Choosing a topic	5	16.7%
How could you have improved your performance?		
1. Better team organization	8	26.7%
2. Being more enthusiastic	8	26.7%
3. Better time management	5	16.7%
4. Work on CVs and interviews	3	10%
SKILLS WORK		
What went well/what are you most confident about?		
1. Teamwork: communication/organization	13	43.3%
2. Interview and CV skills	12	40%
3. Teamwork: delegating responsibilities	8	26.7%
4. Research and problem solving	8	26.7%
What didn't go so well/what are you least confident about?		
1. Finding relevant information	9	30%
2. Interviews and CV work	8	26.6%
3. Time management	7	23.3%
4. Teamwork and leadership	4	13.3%
How could you have improved your performance?		
1. Improve leadership/group skills	13	43.3%
2. Improve time management	5	16.7%
3. More practice on CV and interview work	4	13.3%
4. Better investigation and research skills	4	13.3%
MEDITERRANEAN CASE STUDY AND POSTER WORK		
What went well/what are you most confident about?		
1. Final poster presentation	14	46.7%
2. Team relationship	12	40%
3. Teamwork and management	11	36.7%
4. Research	7	23.3%
What didn't go so well/what are you least confident about?		
1. Finding information/research	13	43.3%
2. Time management	10	33.3%
3. Topic choice	9	30%
4. Teamwork organization	9	30%
How could you have improved your performance?		
1. More communication in the group	10	33.3%
2. Improve presentation of poster	8	26.7%
3. Time management	7	23.3%
4. More research	5	16.7%

In the second part of this evaluation sheet students were asked to comment on the organization of the course (what went well, what did not go so well, proposals for improvements). Some responses were on course content rather than organization and this possibly highlights a weakness in the evaluation form. The original intention was that content issues would be covered on the self-evaluation sheets but, on reflection, it would appear useful to give students the opportunity to comment on the course content more generally, not just in relation to their own performance. Overall, there were approximately twice as many responses in the 'went well' section as in the 'did not go well' section.

Related responses were grouped into the categories shown in Table 3. As might have been expected for final-year students, the work on interview and CV skills was particularly liked with comments such as 'The videos on interviews and CVs were very useful. Actually filling in our own CVs also helped' and 'Interview skills are obviously very important for final year students.' Concerning the overall organization of the course, over half of the students commented on the appropriateness of the course structure and background material. ('well organised ... easy to follow ... well structured ... very flexible with topic choices... lots of information available').

Favourable comments were also made about the teamwork by just under half the students. ('The group worked well and we learnt how to look, criticise and appreciate other people's work.') This is consistent with the very positive responses to the teamwork aim in the first half of the evaluation form. However, as indicated in the self-evaluation Table 31.4, teamwork and groups skills were seen by many students as areas where they could improve their performance still further.

Forty per cent of students indicated that more guidance would improve the course. ('There needs to be more lecturer-student contact. I think the lecturers should be around more to offer advice and help.') This response, which was also made in the class discussion, appears to highlight a key issue in terms of the respective roles of students and staff in the learning process and of student understanding of those roles. The Skillswise course designers came from an area in which the question of what constituted learning in higher education was discussed with students right from the start of their degree programmes (Honeybone, 1994). Students became familiar with key ideas such as deep and surface approaches, experiential learning, student-centred learning and the facilitating role of staff. However, the group of students taking the Skillswise course lacked this introduction and the normal methods of working within their parent subject areas often differed from those adopted in Skillswise. Therefore it may have been the case that staff gave insufficient attention to explaining to students the thinking behind the course (that thinking was included in the lecturers' briefing pack but not in the students').

There may be a further reason for this student concern that merits investigation: the nature of the weekly workshops which included one hour 'surgeries' with staff were significantly different from the type of problem based tutorials described by Margetson (1994) and Engel (1991). There was not the same level of structure and staff input and some of the groups chose not to attend any of the surgeries. Thus, although the product of the Skillswise course, that is the poster, was generally of a high standard, the process leading to the product was largely hidden once the Induction Week workshops had been completed. In other words, direct evidence on whether skills were actually transferred from the initial workshops to the continuing week by week process of poster production was limited. It could only be inferred from the quality of the posters and from student comments after the event.

The timing of the course generated considerable comment. Problems were experienced by about a quarter of the students because of other course pressures and commitments and 40% made the suggestion that the course should run earlier in the degree programme. This lends support to the longer-term intention of providing coordinated PTS development across the KST degree as a whole with PTS development being embedded in the mainstream courses rather than as an addition. Nevertheless, as an interim measure, the positive student responses indicated the value of the Skillswise course.

2.   Self-evaluation results

Of the 37 students who took the Skillswise course 31 completed the self evaluation sheet and related responses were again grouped for the purpose of analysis.

In the first element of the self-evaluation sheet, where comments were invited on induction week, 83.3% indicated that group work exercises had gone very well ('The leadership tasks and demolition tasks were excellent') and nearly half the students made positive comments about the other skills exercises. From the small number of negative responses it is possible to infer that the students felt positive about the induction programme.

In the second element of the self-evaluation sheet, where comments were invited on the skills work section, nearly half (43.3%) of the students were positive about teamwork ('Good organisation re: meetings for poster project'). But the positive and negative responses to other skills work were similar i.e. about 1/3; 43.3% of students also thought they could improve their performance with enhanced group skills.

In the third element of the self-evaluation sheet, where comments were invited on the Mediterranean case study and poster work, nearly half (46.7%) of students felt that the final poster presentation had gone well and 40% of responses were positive about team relationships. It was also clear that nearly half (43.3%) were concerned about finding information ('There wasn't enough information in the library. This sometimes weakened my confidence ...') and time management had not gone well for 33.3% of students; 33.3% of responses indicated that performance could have been improved if group communications had been better.

The results seem to focus positively on teamwork with a very positive response for the exercises in induction week but rather less positive comments in the second element, skills work, which was intended to be an element in which students continued to develop skills. It was apparent that certain comments made about the induction element appeared to be repeated in the skills work element. For example, 46% of students commented that CV and interview skills had gone well in induction week where structured skills work took place and yet 40% of students also felt that this area of skills work had gone well during the second skills work element (where it was unlikely to be located!). Therefore some revision of the self evaluation sheet is needed to clarify its meaning. Also we may be justified in inferring that this second element of the course may have received less attention by students than was intended and that this may be related to issues of guidance as discussed in the last section.

When comparing the results from the course evaluation sheet and the self-evaluation sheet it is significant that in both cases most comments appear in the 'went well' section from which we can infer that the students were in the main positive about Skillswise and this was also corroborated in the class discussion.

3. Class discussion of student views on the course

In the final class discussion in the last week of the course, time was set aside for students to offer further comments about their evaluation of the course. Staff were also provided with the opportunity to seek further clarification of the students' written points. No entirely new comments emerged but some useful colour was added. For example, the strong positive response was confirmed and it became clear that not only did most students feel that they had learnt from participating in the course but they had also had fun while learning. Teamwork again featured strongly. Some clarification was obtained on the question of the level of guidance in the weekly workshops. There were clear divisions of opinion on this. Some students felt quite confident and happy about working independently after the Induction Week whereas others clearly wanted more staff input. The desire for greater staff input appeared to be linked to perceived difficulties in obtaining information and maybe to overall perceptions of staff and student roles. There seemed to be at least an element (for some students) of wanting the teacher to revert to the didactic supplier of the 'right' answer.

Conclusion

The predominantly positive response of the students including the thoroughness of student comments on the evaluation sheets and the widespread and active participation in the class discussion point towards the conclusion that the Skillswise Project was satisfying a previously unmet need. That view is reinforced by the 100% completion rate of this optional extra course in a highly pressured term and by the high quality of the posters.

Regarding future development of the Skillswise Project, the overwhelming student view was that PTS development should be introduced at the beginning of the first year and should encompass a wide range of skills. From a staff point of view, although there is agreement with the student view that the course should be extended, there remain major problems with implementing this in the context of KST because of the structure of the modular programme and the heavy front-loading of this kind of project. In addition there is the issue of how we, as practising teachers (with the tidal wave of the next academic year bearing down on us), can find the time to plan, implement and evaluate projects as intended.

Nevertheless, in undertaking this action research project focussed on problem-based student learning, we came to a more explicit understanding that our action research approach was in fact a staff form of problem-based learning with its emphasis on qualities such as 'openness, self-directed learning, group work, cooperative peer learning, reflective, constructive, critical evaluation and assessment' (Margetson, 1994). We believe that we have developed a clearer (though still provisional) understanding of the 'problem' and that will provide us with the starting-point for our next round of action research as we plan, act, observe and reflect on our educational 'experiment'. In particular, as discussed above, we will want to:

- refine the details of the evaluation forms;
- clarify the role of the weekly workshops in the learning process so as to make the process more transparent and shift the emphasis of the project more firmly from product to process;
- provide a firmer learning context within which the students can better appreciate (and

critically evaluate) the intentions of the course and its problem-based, student-centred approach;

- develop further our awareness, as practising teachers, of the links between theory and practice.

References

Blumhof, J., Honeybone., A. Pearlman, D. and Pinn, K. (1994) Researchers of our own teaching: theory into practice in the evolution of a teaching and learning strategy for an interdisciplinary environmental studies degree. In Gibbs, G. (ed.), *Improving Student Learning Through Assessment and Evaluation*. Oxford: Oxford Centre for Staff Development, 311—22.

Blumhof, J., Broom, C. and Stallibrass, C. (1994) Integrating transferable skills into the subject curriculum: a case history. In Bridges, D. (ed.), *Transferable Skills in Higher Education*. Norwich: University of East Anglia.

Boud, D. and Feletti, G. (eds) (1991) *The Challenge of Problem Based Learning*. London: Kogan Page.

Boot, R. and Hodgson, V. E. (1987) Open learning: meaning and experience. In Hodgson, V. E., Mann, S. J. and Snell, R. (eds), *Beyond Distance Learning — Towards Open Learning*. Milton Keynes: The Society for Research into Higher Education and Open University Press, 5.

Bridges, D. (1994) Transferable skills: a philosophical perspective. In Bridges, D. (ed.), *Transferable Skills in Higher Education*. Norwich: University of East Anglia.

Engel, C. E. (1991) Not just a method but a way of learning. In Boud, D. and Feletti, G. (eds), *The Challenge of Problem Based Learning*. London: Kogan Page.

Gibbs, G. (1992) *Teaching More Students: 1. Problems and Course Design Strategies*. Oxford: Oxford Polytechnic/PCFC.

Gibbs, G. and Haigh, M.(1984) *Designing Course Evaluation Questionnaires*. Oxford: Oxford Polytechnic Educational Methods Unit.

Honeybone, A. (1994) *Understanding Environments. Some Reflections on an Environment for Learning in Learning about the Environment*. Unpublished dissertation for MA Higher and Professional Education, Institute of Education, London.

Margetson, D. (1994) Current educational reform and the significance of problem based learning. In *Studies in Higher Education*. Abingdon Oxfordshire: Carfax Publishing Ltd, **19**(1).

Ricchetti, R. (1995) *What is Problem Based Learning?* College of Veterinary Medicine, Mississippi State University. http://pegasus.cvm.msstate.edu/pbl/pblhome.html.

Robson, C. (1993) *Real World Research*. London: Blackwell, 290.

Zuber-Skerritt, O. (1992) *Action Research in Higher Education* 1(2). London: Kogan Page.

32 Learning with the help of strategies for vocabulary and terminology acquisition

Susanne Mühlhaus and Martin Löschmann
Kingston University, School of Languages

1. Brief description of courses

We teach students of four-year foreign language degree courses and German + Science joint honours degree courses, where students spend their third year abroad. We also offer language modules and language options within the institution-wide language programme, and external business courses which are tailored to the clients' specifications.

Modularization of foreign language provision has been extended with the beginning of the academic year 1995/96 (see Table 1).

Table 1 German language teaching at Kingston University

Already modular	Modular from 1995/96	Staged modularization	Non-modular	KLXC
G + Science	Language modules	Existing language degree courses	Language option	
• Ap. Chem.	• Hu Sci	• AEL	• Business	
• Ap. Phys.	• Sci	• LEP	• Design	
			• Technology	

AEL: Applied European Languages; Ap.: Applied; KLXC: Kingston Language Export Centre; LEP: Languages, Economics and Politics; G: German; Hu: Human; Sci: Science(s)

Modularization requires greater independence of student learning since some language programmes for post-GCSE and post-'A' level are only offered in a workshop mode with 2—4 tutor contact hours per semester, which are used to check the students' progress with their independent learning tasks. The number of independent learning hours which students should spend in order to complete a module are prescribed in the respective syllabuses.

For German, the subjects taught in the workshop mode are Grammar, Contemporary Germany, Aural German and Technical German.

This chapter concentrates on the Year 1 and Year 2 Aural Programmes and the Technical German Programmes, because here we can look at the foundation level and the final level.

Since 1993 special Aural Packages have been used, which have just been completely revised on the basis of experience gained with the previous package, student course evaluation questionnaires, interviews and specific observations. These Independent Learning Packages are aimed at improving students' listening and summary skills using authentic radio and television broadcasts from various sources including commercially produced learning resources. They are directed towards extending students' vocabulary, register and knowledge of contemporary Germany, Spanish or other languages. Students have to keep a 'journal', where they are to record their own observations and reflections on their independent work and learning programme. The keeping of this journal has proved a particular challenge for students. Learning journals are now used across a wide range of disciplines (see other contributions in this volume). In a recent experimental study, McCrindle and Christensen (1995) showed that a group of students who kept learning journals had a superior learning outcome than a control group without journals.

As the authentic video clips are of varying difficulty, help with vocabulary is sometimes given before viewing a clip, as well as advice on the main focus or background information, etc. In simplified terms, students' work then consist in five steps (six steps for the Year 1 groups) for each item:

1. completing preparatory worksheets and vocabulary exercises (Year 1 only);

2. viewing a set number of video/audio tapes twice;

3. after each video/audio clip, writing a (guided) summary;

4. comparing their summary with a model summary and awarding themselves a mark for their work, thus monitoring their own progress;

5. reading the transcript to resolve possible mistakes and deepen the understanding of the clip, looking up any unknown vocabulary and keeping a vocabulary list in their journal;

6. recording comments about the learning progress in the journal.

In-class vocabulary tests and unseen summaries check that the students have progressed sufficiently and learnt vocabulary. Journals are periodically submitted to the tutor for an evaluation of the work carried out and contribute substantially to the overall mark.

2. Educational aims and objectives of vocabulary and terminology acquisition

Foreign language teaching is characterized by wild swings of the pendulum (Schmitt, 1995, p. 32). While an emphasis on vocabulary learning and grammar had fallen out of fashion years ago, because communicative competence was seen to be more important, it is now recognized that a learner cannot be a good communicator without mastering the appropriate lexis and grammar. At beginners' level it instills confidence in the foreign-language learner to be able to recall a fair number of words and not having to ask the tutor all the time. At an advanced level, only those persons are good communicators who understand and use accurately a range of general words and specific terminology with a near-native appreciation of nuances and with matching collocates.

The aim of vocabulary and terminology acquisition can thus be summarized as follows (based on Löschmann, 1993, pp. 29—35):

To acquire/develop a permanent and quickly retrievable vocabulary which can be applied correctly (register) and in line with the speaker's intentions. The quality of this vocabulary is tested when the user transfers acquired units for creative applications in a new context for receptive and productive use.

We do not distinguish here between the learning of general words and more specific terms but see them as a unit or continuation of each other. Although highly specialized terms represent the highest abstraction in the vertical stratification of language, they are used in conjunction with general words (see Kalverkämper, 1987 and Ahmad *et al.* 1993, Löschmann, 1994 Mühlhaus 1995a, 1995b). One of the sources of word formation of highly specialized terminology are general language words which acquire a different meaning in the specialized context.

It is thus not only necessary to learn a multitude of facts and a large number of new words with their concepts but also previously known words with new meanings and exact definitions as well as absolutely new terms.

3.   Learning problems

Analyses of students' work at the German and Spanish sections of the School of Languages at Kingston University have shown that learners apply learning strategies only to a limited extend in their learning processes. When comparing the learning strategies of first-year and fourth-year students, it is interesting to note that there are no significant differences. Many students viewed the video clips without any expectations or anticipation. There was poor exploitation of written and visual clues and little discrimination between lexical items including terminology.

Instead, many students learn by a surface approach, which was described as 'reduc[ing] what is to be learnt to the status of unconnected facts to be memorised. The learning task is to reproduce the subject matter at a later date (e.g. in an exam)' (Gibbs, 1992, p. 2).

Many students have formed a habit of list learning, memorizing individual lexical items in a more or less random sequence. These lists contain lexis taken out of context and without annotations for usage (register). Students still try to memorize 'endless lists of decontextualised one-to-one correspondences' (Clarke, 1993, see also Esser/Harnisch, 1980). Consistent with previous findings (e.g. Löschmann, 1993, 18—20; Schmitt and Schmitt, 1995), we found that these students often fail to apply memorized vocabulary in a new context.

Commercially available audio/video learning materials contribute to barely efficient learning in various ways. In some of the accompanying material for video and audio clips word meanings are only explained by means of direct translation into the mother tongue. This poses a particular problem if these translations are inadequate or even wrong. Thus we found that vegetable was said to be 'spoilt' instead of rotten. Business people in Potsdam, in their desperation at the slow motion of bureaucracy, were expected to resort to violence and supposed to throw 'roof tiles' instead of bricks on the mayor's desk.

Similarly, we could not recognize a clear principle which the editor of the material had presumably adopted for explaining certain words and not others.

And finally, in the previous package, the learners had no choice but to complete all units of the learning package, whether or not they found the topics interesting and relevant.

4. Innovation

The lack of student learning strategies was one focus of innovation. We are now familiarising Year 1 students with learning strategies as part of the induction. At the beginning of each academic year, there is now an update on this issue for students. The decisive teaching strategy is to make students find out their preferred internal strategies, as not all strategies work equally well for everyone.

In order to become more efficient learners, we guide our students to adopt the deep approach by increasing their awareness of learning strategies and integrating these in their work.

In the deep approach, 'the student attempts to make sense of what is to be learnt, which consists of ideas and concepts. This involves thinking, seeking integration between components and between tasks, and "playing" with ideas' (Gibbs, 1992, p. 2).

Following the three-way typology of O'Malley and Chamot (1990) we distinguish between cognitive, metacognitive, and affective/social learning strategies.

> *Strategies are the often conscious steps or behaviors used by language learners to enhance the acquisition, storage, retention, recall and use of new information. (Ehrman and Oxford, 1990, p. 312)*

Accordingly, learning strategies for vocabulary acquisition are more or less internalized action plans/sequences of actions in order to understand, retain, store, remember and use lexical units and terms.

These can include, for example, underlining or highlighting of unknown or important words. When a learner as a listener (or reader) comes across unknown words s/he should ask her/himself the following questions:

- Which type of video clip (text) is this? (Which purposes does it serve, what is the context, the content, the genre, etc.?)
- Is this given word important or not?
- Is it possible to guess it through the context and through the subject-relatedness?
- Is the word or term defined, explained, paraphrased elsewhere in the text?
- To which register does it belong?
- Is it an internationalism?
- Are there any relationships to my mother tongue?
- Do patterns of word formation help here?

Only when all of these strategies of inference have failed is it justified to consult a dictionary, or teacher, or subject specialist.

When developing vocabulary learning material, it should be decided whether a particular word or term should rather be mastered for productive or receptive use, where any particular learning problems lie and how an item can best be embedded into existing or new concepts.

Metacognitive strategies are beginning to enjoy a wider proliferation. Cardelle-Elawar (1995) has given a recent description of this concept:

> *Metacognition is a theoretical construct that refers to an individual's conscious awareness of his or her own thought processes. Metacognition is related to self-knowledge and self-evaluation. It is essential to the development of students' ability to learn cognitive strategies, such as self-questioning,*

widen the application of these strategies and gain conscious control over them. Students with metacognitive knowledge arc aware of their strengths and limitations during the act of learning. Metacognitive awareness predisposes these students to learn how, when, and why to use cognitive strategies. (Cardelle-Elawar, 1995, p. 82)

This suggests that it is a prerequisite for learning cognitive strategies. The extent to which students are aware of their strengths and limitations during the act of learning is perhaps proportional to the control they have over their own learning process. However, this is an area which is difficult to measure.

McCrindle and Christensen (1995) traced the term metacognition back to Flavell (1976), who introduced it referring to knowledge and awareness of one's own cognitive processes and the ability to actively control and manage these processes.

Bialystok (1985) also assumes in her research that 'the processes of learning can come under conscious and intentional control, and that change in control is highly significant. Access to the processes of learning is a crucial aspect of modifying learning' (p. 256).

The most succinct definition was undoubtedly provided by Angelo (1995) to whom metacognition means three things:

1. being aware of one's own thought process;

2. being consciously in control of those thought processes;

3. being aware of being consciously in control of one's thought processes.

While metacognitive strategies aim at self-monitoring, self-motivation and overcoming learning obstacles, social strategies are those behaviours which involve asking someone else for clarification, etc. This can be a native speaker, a peer or the tutor. A crucial factor is teamwork with other learners (e.g. it would be helpful for students to exchange information about their ways of learning vocabulary).

Due to space limitations, we cannot go into more detail here, but refer the reader/audience to an excellent overview of language learning strategies by Rod Ellis (1994, pp. 529—59).

5. Implementation

In an effort to improve student learning, we have created new and modified existing independent language learning packages. Important changes refer to:

- an extended choice of topics to select from,
- the students finding individual strategies for understanding and summarizing the clips,
- encouraging the students to adopt a self-critical attitude towards the product of their work,
- emphasizing the importance of the journal as a record of students' learning.

In this chapter we can only outline in some detail the improvements for vocabulary learning, which are based on a typology of exercises (Löschmann, 1993, pp. 110—39).

Out of the multi-layered acquisition process, we shall single out the issue of constructing networks of word relations, the assumed organizing principles of the mental lexicon (see also Kielhöfer 1994). This incorporates insights into the workings of memory, based on Klix (1984), Hoffmann (1991), Löschmann (1993). According to these findings, the brain stores information in the form of structured representations, and, the more structured relationships exist the easier it is to remember a lexical item. Moreover, the value of a word is dependent on the relationships it has to other words in the target language.

These structures represent both hierarchical (innerconceptual/vertical/paradigmatic) and parallel (interconceptual/horizontal/syntagmatic) relationships. In the past, innerconceptual relationships were at the centre of teaching/learning vocabulary (e.g. generic and subordinate terms: vegetable — peas, carrots, cabbage, etc.; opposites: warm— cold; and synonymy, quantity/set — element, whole, part etc). If interconceptual relationships were shown and depicted in diagrams at all, only the interconceptual or syntagmatic perspective were presented in isolation (e.g. Aitchison, 1994). Ickler (1987, p. 9) suggested that the syntagmatic dimension, that is, the actual text, is the natural habitat of paradigms. It follows that the connection between paradigmatic and syntagmatic relationships calls for learning strategies which incorporate both perspectives. It is a didactically important feature of communicative competence to generate fluent syntagmatic realizations (or applications) of paradigmatic relationships.

Adapting Hoffmann's diagram, we have incorporated both perspectives in our lexical networks (Löschmann, 1994, p. 43; Mühlhaus, 1995c).

If we take for example the term Grundgesetz (Basic law, i.e. the German Constitution), this evokes questions such as: what, where, since when, why, who; or to put it differently, it evokes relationships of subject, locality, time, causality, and agent (see Appendix, Figure 1).

The advantage of this representation of terminology is immediately obvious, in particular for advanced learners. Meanings are usually complex, if not encyclopaedic. Experience and subject knowledge, that is world knowledge, is closely related to the knowledge of words. In our diagrams it is possible to represent more than one layer of meaning, thus reflecting this complexity.

We ask our students to reflect upon meanings and create lexical networks for a variety of terms. This open-ended activity can also be performed at beginners level. Figure 2 (Appendix) shows such an example for Spanish.

These relationships are, of course, not the only ones possible. The diagrams show, that technical terms are likely to relate to encyclopaedic information whilst more general lexis renders vocabulary-building relationships.

The key issue is that the more links one can make the more likely it is that the information can be recalled quickly and applied appropriately. For this reason, certain lexical items are used again in a variety of activities.

There is also a phonetic side to vocabulary acquisition, which must not be neglected. A good example for applying similar principles in this area is illustrated by resolving the common difficulty for learners of Spanish, especially at beginners' level, to remember the rules for the varying pronunciation of the letters 'c' and 'g'.

The rule is: the letter 'c' is pronounced in two different ways: when followed by a, o, u it is a 'k' sound, when followed by e or i it is pronounced like a voiceless 'th' as in 'thumb' or a sharp 's' like in 'scene'.

We first emphasize the link between a, o, u, all of which are dark sounds and thus 'c' preceding these vowels is pronounced 'k' like the first letter of the word 'kick'. Similarly, for producing the light 'e' and 'i' sounds the mouth stays nearly closed, having just produced the 'th' sound. But, instead of a monotonous repetition of ca, co, cu and ce, ci, this is then linked to words, which are easy to remember.

One can easily imagine a little story linking the words *caramba, coche, cucaracha — escena, cine.*

Table 2 Learning pronunciation rules through association

Letter sequence	Sound	Spanish word
ca	[k]	caramba
co	[k]	coche
cu	[k]	cucaracha
ce	[Θ]	escena
ci	[Θ]	cine

6. Conclusions and outlook

Our data from the student course evaluation questionnaires show that students do not particularly like independent learning and the workshop mode. They are used to classroom teaching and prefer weekly tutor contact hours. None the less, the workshop mode has proved to become a necessity and is here to stay.

At least four ways have crystallized to break down students' psychological barriers against workshops and to restore them to what they deserve to be, that is, an important component of their degree course, which is useful for and valued by students:

1. First of all, students have to understand the importance of workshops in their degree course. It is important to convey that workshops are not a makeshift solution but an integral part of their studies. This is only possible if seen in a wider, not subject-specific, context. Since only one assessment per year is permitted per subject, workshops of one subject support material learnt in another subject, in the assessment-free semester of the former.

2. Contact hours have to be used to reduce strategy deficits. The keeping of a journal or learning diary plays an important role. Students are asked to give retrospective reports on what difficulties they have had with lexis. Learners are also required to work in pairs to discuss the strategies they applied. Pair thinking aloud also provides the teacher with insights about student learning.

3. The Independent Learning Package has to be motivating in terms of content and didactics, so that students like working through it. It is frustrating for students, if the Package repeats topics already dealt with in a seminar. This was one of complaints in the Year 4 student course evaluation questionnaire. Out of six video clips, those which promised new information were viewed first by most students. The fact that working with video clips required performing quite a stereotypical or standardized sequence of tasks has certainly had a detrimental effect on student motivation. Therefore we have included in our new Year 4 Package a greater choice for students and facilitate student control over which clips to view as well as a variation of tasks according to individual preferences.

4. Error analyses show that learners' difficulties to understand authentic commercially available video clips are mainly due to peculiarities in the pronunciation of individual presenters and actors. Sometimes they have a fairly strong regional accent or simply speak too fast. Some clips contain many unknown lexical items. Once the students have accepted that it is possible to cope with a fair number of unknown words if appropriate individual learning strategies are applied, then students are quite happy to work on their strategic behaviours. This is none the less a long process, considering that even in Year 4 it took several contact hours to get the students to abandon the habit of ordering new vocabulary only in the very same way the tutor suggested.

It is for these reasons that vocabulary acquisition strategies and the underlying techniques as well as knowledge of their formation and application have to form part of any syllabus for teaching and teacher training as well.

It is not yet clear whether the number of vocabulary learning strategies is finite or infinite. Learners, teachers and researchers are asked to elaborate new efficient learning strategies. Finding an appropriate learning strategy can have an invigorating effect on learning.

It does not have to be emphasized that computer and multimedia software could help with vocabulary learning. But, so far, there is a lack of software in this area. Existing packages concentrate on drills and, often rather test than train vocabulary knowledge and memory (see also Clarke, 1993). There has been some progress with the use of concordances in the classroom. Wichmann (1995) reported that using English key-word-in-context (KWIC) concordances in her foreign language (German) classroom increased students' awareness of shades of meaning in their own language, while the approach described by Tribble and Jones (1990) refers to the use of concordances of the target language (English). An important step forward is working with bilingual (KWIC) concordances (like the work by Wolff and Rüschoff 1995) and, we have no doubt that we shall soon hear more about these and similar developments.

References

Ahmad, K., Davies, A., Fulford, H. and Rogers, M. (1992) What is a term? The semi-automatic extraction of terms from text. In Snell-Hornby (ed.), *Translation Studies — an Interdiscipline. Selected papers from the Translation Studies Congress, Vienna, 9—12 September 1992.*

Aitchison, J. (1990) *Words in the Mind: An Introduction to the Mental Lexicon*, 2nd edn. Blackwell: Oxford.

Angelo, T. (1995) Finding out how well students are learning what we're teaching. Workshop at the 3rd International Symposium for Improving Student Learning, Oxford Brookes University at the University of Exeter, 11—13 September 1995.

Bialystok, E. (1985) The compatibility of teaching and learning strategies. *Applied Linguistics* 6(3), 255—62.

Cardelle-Elawar, M. (1995) Effects of metacognitive instruction on low achievers in mathematics problems. *Teaching and Teacher Education* 11(1), 81—95.

Clarke, M. (1993) Vocabulary learning with and without computers: some thoughts on a way forward. *CALL* 5(3), 139—46.

Ehrman, M. E. and Oxford, R. L. (1990) Adult language styles and strategies in an intensive training setting. *The Modern Language Journal* 74(3), 311—27.

Ellis, R. (1994) *The Study of Second Language Acquisition*. Oxford: Oxford University Press.

Esser, U. and Harnisch, A. (1980) Eine methodische Variante zur Optimierung des Wortschatzerwerbs. Listen- versus Graphenlernen. *Deutsch als Fremdsprache* **17**(3), 161—6.

Flavell, J. H. (1976) Metacognitive aspects of problem solving. In L. B. Resnick (ed.), *The Nature of Intelligence*. Lawrence Erlbaum: Hillsdale, NJ.

Gibbs, G. (1992) *Improving the Quality of Student Learning*. Technical and Educational Services: Bristol.

Hoffmann, L. (1991) Fachsprachenlinguistik zwischen Praxisdruck und Theoriebedarf. *Deutsch als Fremdsprache* **28**(3), 131—40.

Ickler, T. (1987) Paradigmen als Syntagmen. Über das Lernen von Wörtern in Texten. *Fremdsprachen Lehren und Lernen* **16**(1), 9—24.

Kalverkämper, H. (1987) Die Problematik von Fachsprache und Gemeinsprache. *Sprachwissenschaft* **3**, 406—44.

Kielhöfer, B. (1994) Wörter lernen, behalten und erinnern. *Neusprachliche Mitteilungen aus Wissenschaft und Praxis* **47**(4), 211—20.

Klix, F. (ed.) (1984) *Gedächnis — Wissen — Wissensnutzung*. Akademie-Verlag: Berlin.

Löschmann, M. (1993) *Effiziente Wortschatzarbeit*. Peter Lang: Frankfurt a.M., New York.

Löschmann, M. (1994) Invariantes und Variantes im allgemeinen Sprach- und Fremdsprachenunterricht. In Scott, W. and S. Mühlhaus (eds), *Languages for Specific Purposes*. CILT: London.

McCarthy, M. (1990) *Vocabulary*. Oxford: Oxford University Press.

McCrindle, A. R. and Christensen, C. A. (1995) The impact of learning journals on metacognitive and cognitive processes and learning performance. *Learning and Instruction* **5**(2), 167—85.

Mühlhaus, S. (1995a) Describing medical eponyms. *English Today* no. 42, **11**(2), 48—53.

Mühlhaus, S. (1995b) Tense and terminology in abstracts of medical research articles. Paper given at the BAAL/CUP Seminar on Genre Analysis: Perspectives and Contributions. University of Sheffield, 7—9 July 1995.

Mühlhaus, S. (1995c) Metacognitive Strategies for Terminology Learning, Poster presentation at the BAAL 28th Annual Meeting. University of Southampton, 14–16 September 1995.

O'Malley, J. M. and Chamot, A. U. (1990) *Learning Strategies in Second Language Acquisition*. Cambridge: Cambridge University Press.

Schmitt, N. (1995) Second language reading and vocabulary learning. *BAAL Newsletter* **49**, 32—5.

Schmitt, N. and Schmitt, D. (1995) Vocabulary notebooks: theoretical underpinnings and practical suggestions. *ELT Journal* **49** (2), 133—43.

Tribble, C. and Jones, G. (1990) *Concordances in the Classroom*. Longman: London.

Wichmann, A. (1995) Using concordances for the teaching of modern languages in higher education. *Language Learning Journal* **11**), March, 61—3.

Wolff, D. and Rüschoff, B. (1995) New Technologies. Workshop at the 28th Annual Meeting of the British Association for Applied Linguistics (BAAL) at the University of Southampton, 14—16 September 1995.

Appendix

Figure 1 Network of structured relationships for the term 'Grundgesetz'

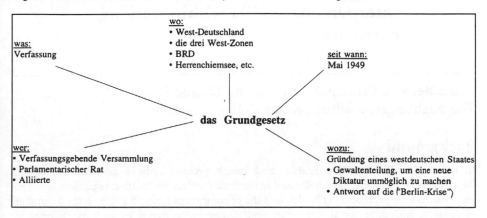

Figure 2 Network of structured relationships for 'estudiar'

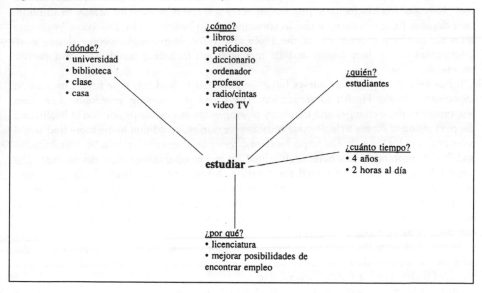

The influence of a research study on the integration of health promotion and interpersonal skills within nursing curriculae

Anne Benson, Principal Lecturer and Dr Sue Latter
The Nightingale Institute, Kings College London

Background

In recent decades, health education and health promotion have assumed increasing importance within society generally and in particular within the health care professions. The emphasis on the promotion of health and the prevention of illness has arisen for a number of reasons, including social, economic and demographic trends as well as changes in patterns of morbidity and mortality. A prevailing political ideology which emphasizes productivity, competitiveness within market systems and attempts to restrain health service costs have also led to a focus on prevention of disease and education for health. In addition, past decades have witnessed a rise in consumerism in health service provision, beginning with the self-help movements of the 1960s and 1970s. Increasingly, people desire more information about their health and its management, including health care and service provision.

It has been proposed that nurses have the potential to lead this new health promotion movement (World Health Organization, 1989) and the nursing profession has been responsive to these changes and trends by placing emphasis on the promotion of health and the prevention of illness as legitimate activities for nurses in addition to the more traditional roles of caring for the sick. The importance of developing the nurse's role in health education and health promotion has been highlighted by recent education policy documents. The United Kingdom Central Council for Nursing, Midwifery and Health Visiting's (1986) proposals for the future of nurse training and education are firmly orientated around the need for nurses to develop their role in health promotion. A major objective of nurse education curriculae is to equip nurses with knowledge and skills to ensure their competency as promoters of health.

However, despite the plethora of recommendations, there has been little attempt in the nursing literature to clarify the meaning of health promotion and the knowledge and skills required within nurse education curriculae.

Findings from a recent research study (Latter 1994) provided some clarity about these issues and led to changes in the way in which the subject was approached within one pre-registration curriculum.

The research study

The focus of the research was to illuminate the way in which nurses perceive and practice health promotion in hospital settings. A review of the health promotion literature was undertaken in order to provide a framework with which to evaluate both nurses' perceptions and their practice. With reference to the individual level at which health promotion operates (as opposed to the broader, structural aspect of health promotion), the literature revealed that there has been a paradigm shift from a 'traditional' approach to a more enlightened 'new paradigm' approach. The former is characterized by authoritarian, prescriptive and generalized information giving from 'expert' to 'ignorant' lay person, whereas current thinking about health promotion emphasizes the need for a holistic, client-centred and collaborative approach. As a consequence, it has been suggested that health promotion is best defined as an approach to any interaction or activity which is characterized by certain key features (Cribb and Dines, 1993; Macleod Clark, 1993). These features include: holism, equity, participation, collaboration, individualization, negotiation, facilitation and support. Empowerment is also seen as central to health promotion and the need to foster self-esteem, self-efficacy and lifeskills within a health promoting interaction has been identified (Tones, 1991). Clearly, nurses will need to utilize certain interpersonal skills (such as active listening, responding to cues, reinforcement and open questioning) in order to achieve this and to ensure that they avoid the more prescriptive 'traditional' approach. This framework provided the background to researching nurses' perceptions and practice and also informs our approach to teaching health promotion and interpersonal skills within the curriculum.

The findings from the study also indicated a need to re-appraise the way in which health promotion is taught. Semi-structured interviews with 132 ward sisters revealed that they had very limited perceptions of the concept of health promotion and that their ideas were akin to the 'traditional' model outlined above. Fifty-three per cent ($n = 70$) of the sample also identified a lack of knowledge and skill as inhibiting their ability to promote health. Many commented on their lack of preparation for health promotion within pre-registration education and the paucity of study days available to update knowledge and skills. This suggests that nurses need a more comprehensive and up- to-date understanding of what health promotion represents and this is incorporated within the curriculum. However, our experience has shown that there is sometimes a difficulty in changing students' initial perceptions of the meaning of health promotion from a traditional to a more enlightened perspective.

The research study also incorporated a case study design in order to illuminate the reality of nurses' health promotion practice. Hospital wards were used as the unit of analysis and multiple methods of data collection were used including: self-administered questionnaires, non-participant observation, tape-recorded nurse-patient interactions and field notes. In view of the lack of previous research in this area, much thought and exploratory work was invested in devising methods which would best capture nurses' health promotion practice. Non-participant observation involved the researcher spending two-hour periods observing nurses' interactions with a small group of 4—5 patients in close geographical proximity to each other. Descriptive notes were made about the nature of these interactions and accounts of what was said. More detailed, verbatim accounts were attempted when an interaction resembled that which could be described as a health promotion encounter. This data enabled an overall picture to emerge of the nature of nurses' encounters with patients. More detailed data on the interpersonal skills characteristics of interactions emerged from the taped interactions. Various formal and informal events were captured on tape, for example, patients' admission histories, advice about medication or diagnosis and discharge advice. These were analysed with a view to establishing the extent to which these exhibited features of a 'traditional' or 'new paradigm' approach to health promotion. It may be interesting to debate the extent to which these methods could be used in evaluative research to examine the impact on practice of the health promotion and interpersonal skills component of our curriculum.

These findings also suggested that there is a need to equip nurses with the knowledge and interpersonal skills required to promote health. Nursing practice on the case study wards was characterized either by an absence or only a minimal development of a health promoting approach incorporating the features described earlier. On some wards nurses' interactions and advice resembled the 'traditional' approach to health promotion, i.e. it was nurse-led and dominated and the advice was prescriptive and generalized. On other wards there were isolated examples of a more participatory and individualized approach, but a comprehensive development of a health-promoting approach using appropriate interpersonal skills to foster, for example, collaboration and self-esteem was lacking. This therefore suggested that nurses need not only to appreciate what health promotion represents, but also to acquire the interpersonal skills necessary to implement this in practice.

To summarize, the research has helped inform our curriculum in the following ways:

- clarity regarding the meaning of health promotion in nursing;
- recognition of the centrality of interpersonal skills in the ability to promote health and therefore the need to integrate these, previously distinct, subject areas;
- influenced the knowledge and skills taught and the nature of the assessment strategy.

Implementing the findings

The findings of Latter's (1994) study presented us with certain educational challenges if we were to equip nurses with the attitudes, knowledge and skills to be competent health promoters.

Until September 1993 interpersonal skills and health promotion lecturers worked as two discrete teams. These were amalgamated into one section. Following this, a process of staff development commenced to ensure that all lecturers were familiar with the shift in philosophical perspective from the 'traditional' to the 'new paradigm' approach to health promotion.

These structural and developmental changes have been crucial in achieving the integration of the two subject areas. Other methods of accomplishing this have been:

1. Team teaching with one lecturer from each specialist area. As well as enabling students to see the connection between the two areas, this has also been beneficial in relation to staff development, with each lecturer learning from the other.

2. Combining theory and practice in the same session. Nurse education is frequently accused of creating a theory/practice gap. If students are able to learn and think about the concept of empowerment and then identify and practice ways of doing it within the same session, both the theory and the practice become more meaningful.

3. Demonstration scenarios by lecturers. Students frequently comment that they have few examples of good practice or role modelling upon which to base their practice. They are unsure exactly what it is they are trying to achieve and have difficulty recognizing

it when it does happen. Lecturers role-play situations in the classroom, these are videoed and then analysed. Although lecturers are by no means perfect role models it does hopefully provide some examples of good practice. It also helps develop skills of analysis and giving feedback. Once again this provides a good learning opportunity for lecturers.

4. Students practising skills in the classroom. Using either invented scenarios or situations from their practice experience students practise the skills. The giving and receiving of feedback is an important part of this process.

5. Integrated assignment. Towards the end of the course students are asked to tape record an interaction between themselves and a client. They analyse this interaction focusing on the extent to which the use of their interpersonal skills facilitated the maintenance or promotion of health. This is submitted as a summative assignment.

Common problems

In trying to achieve integration between the subject areas and accomplish the philosophical shift from the 'traditional' to 'new paradigm' health promotion recurring questions and issues have arisen.

The philosophical shift

It is not surprising that this has proved the most difficult issue. Students frequently hunt for a patient with diabetes to 'do' their tape. This provides a concrete topic around which to give information and advice, i.e. promote health. Taking the perspective that activities such as, enabling the expression of emotion and developing life skills are also health promoting the concept becomes much more slippery and difficult to grasp. In fact as a concept it is in danger of disappearing altogether. Some writers, e.g. Macleod Clark (1993) argue that all therapeutic nursing interventions are health promoting. Thus nursing and health promotion can be seen as synonymous.

Incongruence between espoused theory and theory-in-use

Espoused theory is that to which people claim allegiance and theory-in-use is that which governs practice (Greenwood, 1993). Frequently students will intellectually make the philosophical shift. Indeed it is one to which many claim an easy allegiance. However, implementing this in practice through the appropriate use of interpersonal skills is not so easy. The analysis of tape-recorded interactions has proved an enlightening and useful way for students to examine this incongruence.

The role of the nurse

Students frequently find themselves in a position of conflict and confusion. Having adopted a client-centred approach students sometimes feel unable to do anything other than agree with the client or talk about whatever the client wishes. Although in some circumstances this is entirely appropriate, it can result in unfocused, unstructured interactions which are unsatisfying to both parties.

Another shift is required for students to see that the skills of therapeutic confrontation, structuring and focusing are appropriate interventions and do not mean that they have strayed from a client centred approach. A distinction between a 'client-centred' approach, where both parties have a role, and a 'client-led' approach, where the nurse has no specific role and to some extent neither does the client, has proved useful.

Lack of literature addressing the integration of interpersonal skills and health promotion

This presents an obvious problem for students. Whilst there is plenty of literature concerning both health promotion and interpersonal skills, the conceptual task of achieving the integration falls on the student. This is a sophisticated test of cognitive ability to set for diploma level students. To their credit the majority accomplish this, some producing work of a very high standard.

Conclusion

This account of our experience is an example of how research may be used to improve student learning. The research study provided an opportunity to clarify the philosophy of health promotion which informs our curriculum and highlighted the interpersonal skills that nurses need to acquire in order to enact this in practice. This has led to structural and developmental changes in order to achieve the integration of two previously distinct subject areas. Practical changes in teaching strategies and an integrated assignment have also been developed as a consequence.

In attempting to achieve a philosophical shift and accomplish integration, we have inevitably faced some challenges, not least because this approach to teaching health promotion is innovative. This means that students often lack examples from practice and theoretical literature to draw on to inform their learning.

As we look ahead, it seems that the pertinent questions now facing us concern the need to evaluate the impact of these curricular developments on the quality of nurses' practice.

More specifically we feel that, in order to develop this area further, we need to address the following:

- Should we be assessing competence? Currently we assess the student's ability to analyse their skills and identify strengths and weaknesses. This means that a student can demonstrate very poor interpersonal skills but if she is able to analyse and discuss this she can achieve a high grade for the work.
- If we should be assessing competence how could we do this?
- Does the integration of interpersonal skills and health promotion and its inclusion in the curriculum
  (a) increase students ability to promote health?
  (b) positively influence practice?
- How do we research this?

We hope that a planned research project to assess the impact of these changes on practice will enable us to shed light on the answers to these questions as part of on-going development of our curriculum.

References

Cribb, A. and Dines, A. (1993) What is health promotion? In Dines, A. and Cribb, A. (eds), *Health Promotion: Concepts and Practice*. Oxford: Blackwell Scientific Publications.

Greenwood, J. (1993) Reflective practice: a critique of the work of Argyris and Schon. *Journal of Advanced Nursing* **18**, 1183—7.

Latter, S. (1994) *Health Education and Health Promotion: Perceptions and Practice of Nurses in Acute Care Settings*. Unpublished PhD Thesis, King's College, University of London.

Macleod Clark, J. (1993) From sick nursing to health nursing: evolution or revolution. In Wilson-Barnett, J. and Macleod Clark, J. (eds), *Research in Health Promotion and Nursing Basingstoke*. Basingstoke: Macmillan Press.

Tones, K. (1991) Health promotion, empowerment and the psychology of control. *Journal of the Institute of Health Education* **29**(1), 17—25.

United Kingdom Central Council for Nurses, Midwives and Health Visitors (1986) *Project 2000*. London: UKCC.

World Health Organisation (1989) *Nursing Leadership for Health For All*. Geneva: World Health Organization Division of Health Manpower Development.